SUPERMAN

VOL. 1 THE UNITY SAGA: PHANTOM EARTH

SUPERMAN

VOL. 1 THE UNITY SAGA: PHANTOM EARTH

BRIAN MICHAEL BENDIS
writer

IVAN REIS
penciller

JOE PRADO
OCLAIR ALBERT
inkers

ALEX SINCLAIR
colorist

JOSH REED
letterer

IVAN REIS, JOE PRADO & **ALEX SINCLAIR**
collection cover artists

SUPERMAN created by **JERRY SIEGEL** and **JOE SHUSTER**
SUPERBOY created by **JERRY SIEGEL**
By special arrangement with the Jerry Siegel family

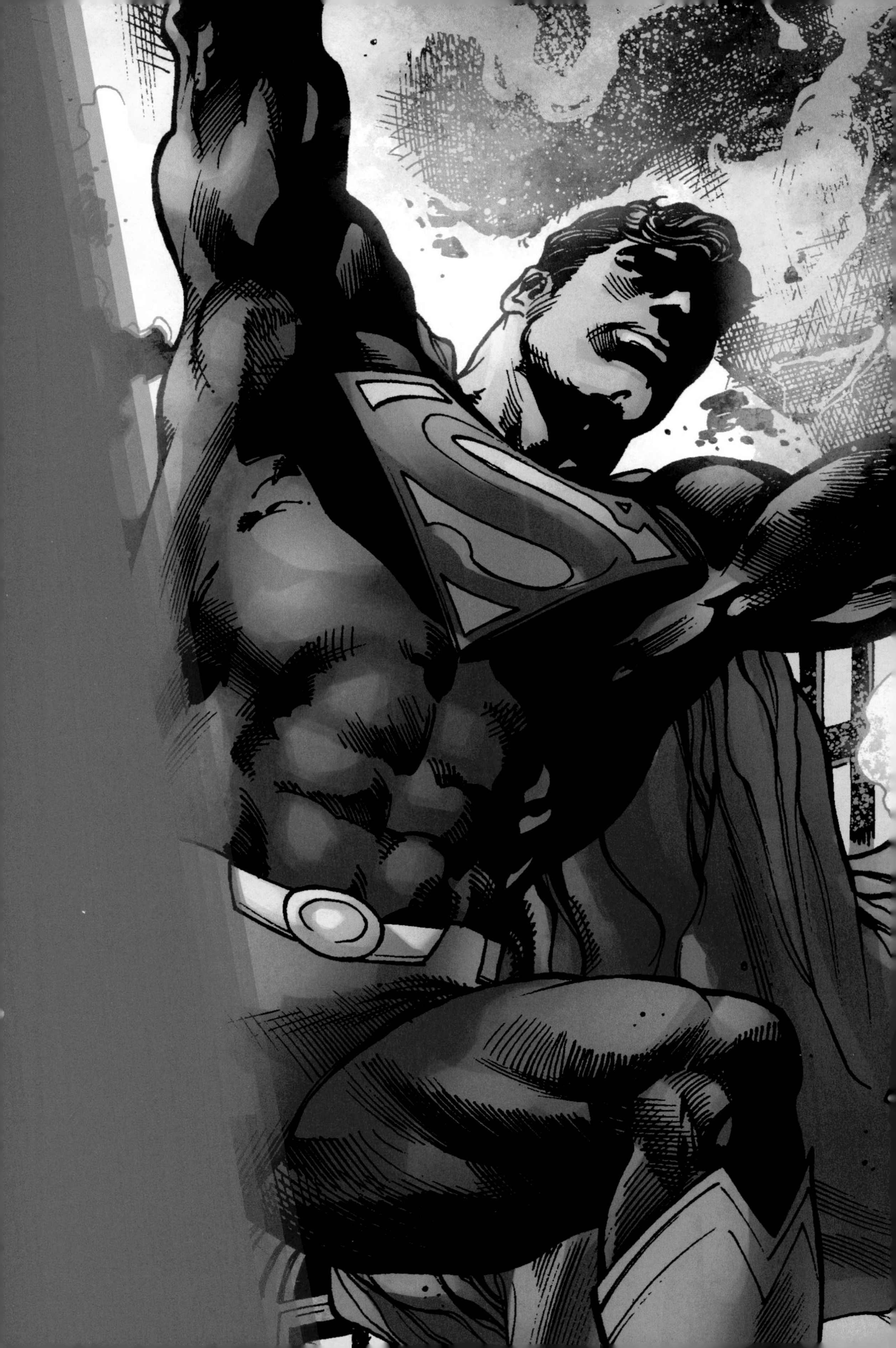

MIKE COTTON Editor – Original Series
JESSICA CHEN Associate Editor – Original Series
JEB WOODARD Group Editor – Collected Editions
ROBIN WILDMAN Editor – Collected Edition
STEVE COOK Design Director – Books
MONIQUE NARBONETA Publication Design

BOB HARRAS Senior VP – Editor-in-Chief, DC Comics
PAT McCALLUM Executive Editor, DC Comics

DAN DiDIO Publisher
JIM LEE Publisher & Chief Creative Officer
AMIT DESAI Executive VP – Business & Marketing Strategy, Direct to Consumer
                            & Global Franchise Management
BOBBIE CHASE VP & Executive Editor, Young Reader & Talent Development
MARK CHIARELLO Senior VP – Art, Design & Collected Editions
JOHN CUNNINGHAM Senior VP – Sales & Trade Marketing
BRIAR DARDEN VP – Business Affairs
ANNE DePIES Senior VP – Business Strategy, Finance & Administration
DON FALLETTI VP – Manufacturing Operations
LAWRENCE GANEM VP – Editorial Administration & Talent Relations
ALISON GILL Senior VP – Manufacturing & Operations
JASON GREENBERG VP – Business Strategy & Finance
HANK KANALZ Senior VP – Editorial Strategy & Administration
JAY KOGAN Senior VP – Legal Affairs
NICK J. NAPOLITANO VP – Manufacturing Administration
LISETTE OSTERLOH VP – Digital Marketing & Events
EDDIE SCANNELL VP – Consumer Marketing
COURTNEY SIMMONS Senior VP – Publicity & Communications
JIM (SKI) SOKOLOWSKI VP – Comic Book Specialty Sales & Trade Marketing
NANCY SPEARS VP – Mass, Book, Digital Sales & Trade Marketing
MICHELE R. WELLS VP – Content Strategy

SUPERMAN VOL. 1: THE UNITY SAGA: PHANTOM EARTH

DC Comics, 2900 West Alameda Ave., Burbank, CA 91505
Printed by LSC Communications, Kendallville, IN, USA. 1/25/19. First Printing.
ISBN: 978-1-4012-8819-8

Library of Congress Cataloging-in-Publication Data is available.

PEFC Certified

This product is from
sustainably managed
forests and controlled
sources

PEFC/29-31-337   www.pefc.org

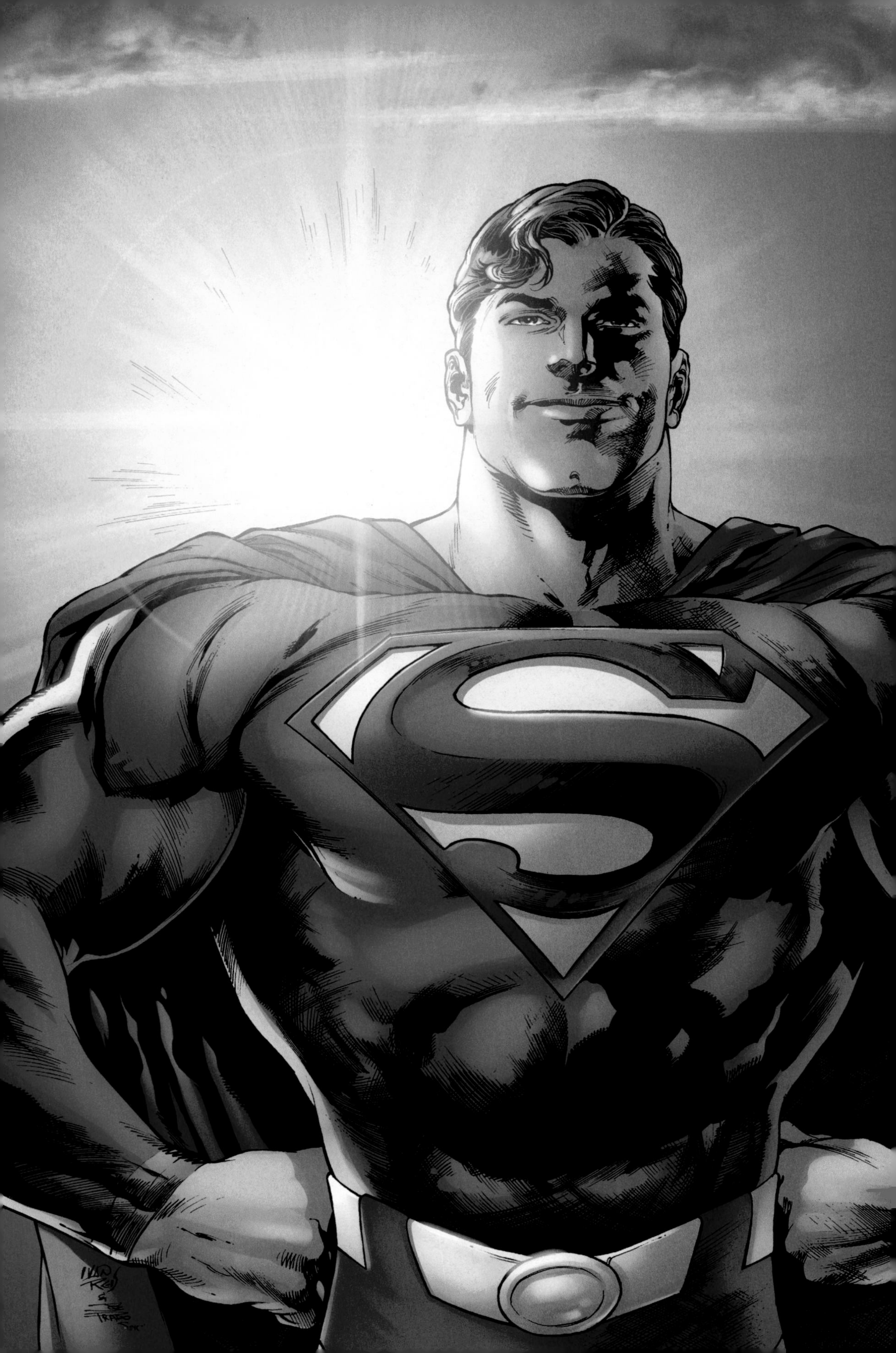

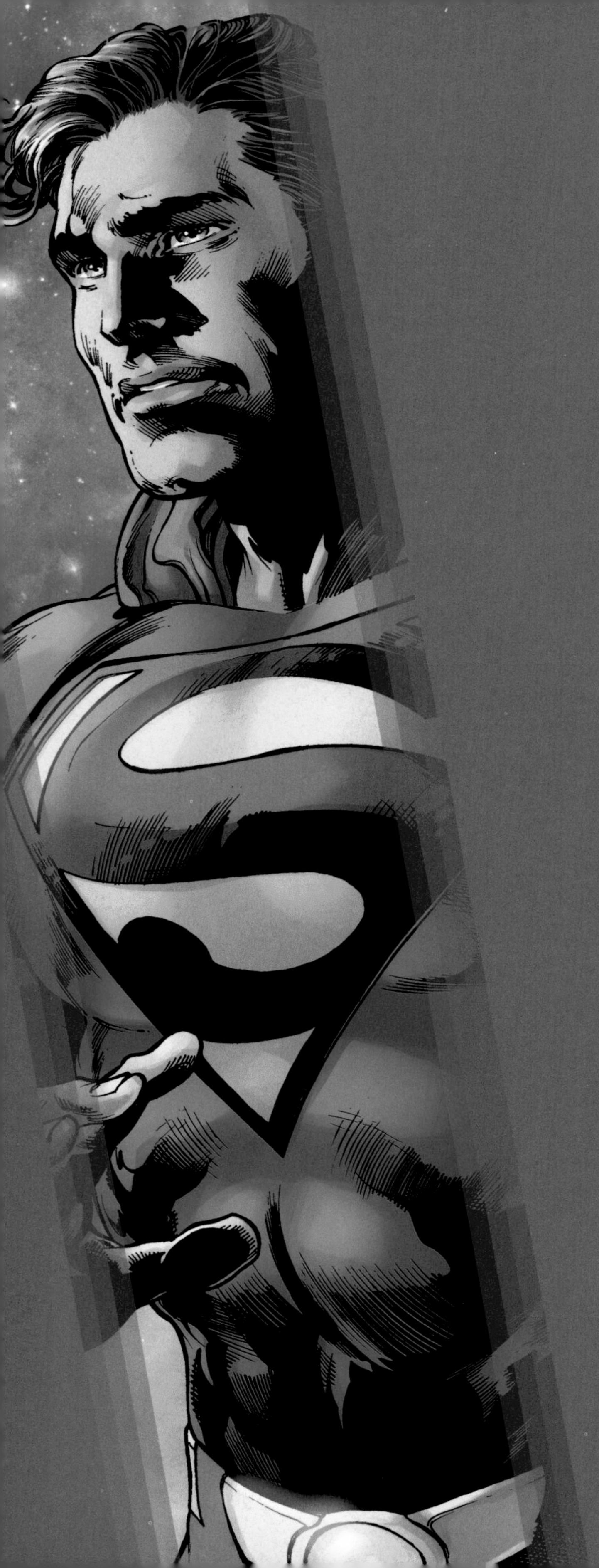

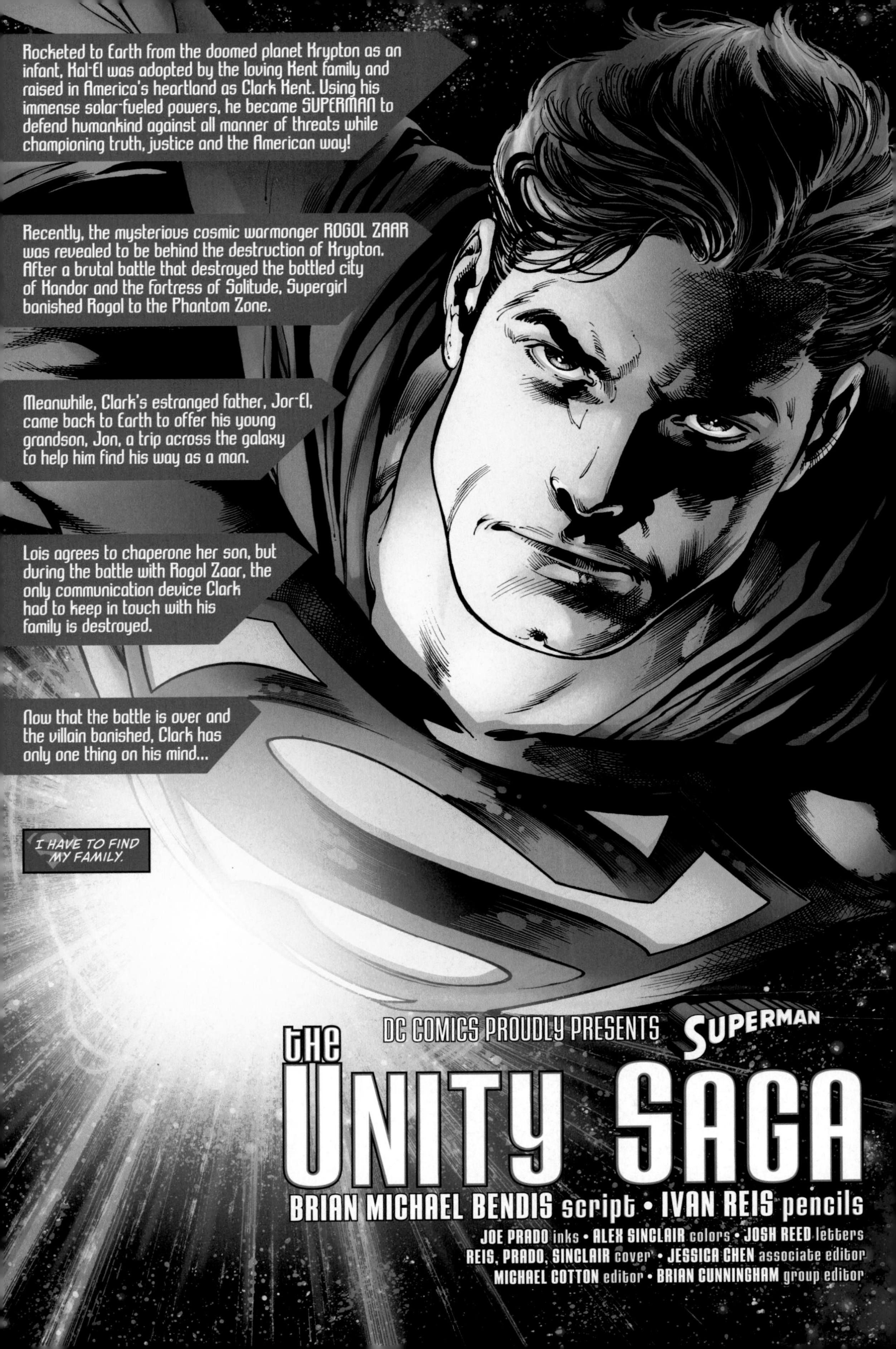
Rocketed to Earth from the doomed planet Krypton as an infant, Kal-El was adopted by the loving Kent family and raised in America's heartland as Clark Kent. Using his immense solar-fueled powers, he became SUPERMAN to defend humankind against all manner of threats while championing truth, justice and the American way!
Recently, the mysterious cosmic warmonger ROGOL ZAAR was revealed to be behind the destruction of Krypton. After a brutal battle that destroyed the bottled city of Kandor and the Fortress of Solitude, Supergirl banished Rogol to the Phantom Zone.
Meanwhile, Clark's estranged father, Jor-El, came back to Earth to offer his young grandson, Jon, a trip across the galaxy to help him find his way as a man.
Lois agrees to chaperone her son, but during the battle with Rogol Zaar, the only communication device Clark had to keep in touch with his family is destroyed.
Now that the battle is over and the villain banished, Clark has only one thing on his mind...
I HAVE TO FIND MY FAMILY.
DC COMICS PROUDLY PRESENTS SUPERMAN
THE UNITY SAGA
BRIAN MICHAEL BENDIS script • IVAN REIS pencils
JOE PRADO inks • ALEX SINCLAIR colors • JOSH REED letters
REIS, PRADO, SINCLAIR cover • JESSICA CHEN associate editor
MICHAEL COTTON editor • BRIAN CUNNINGHAM group editor

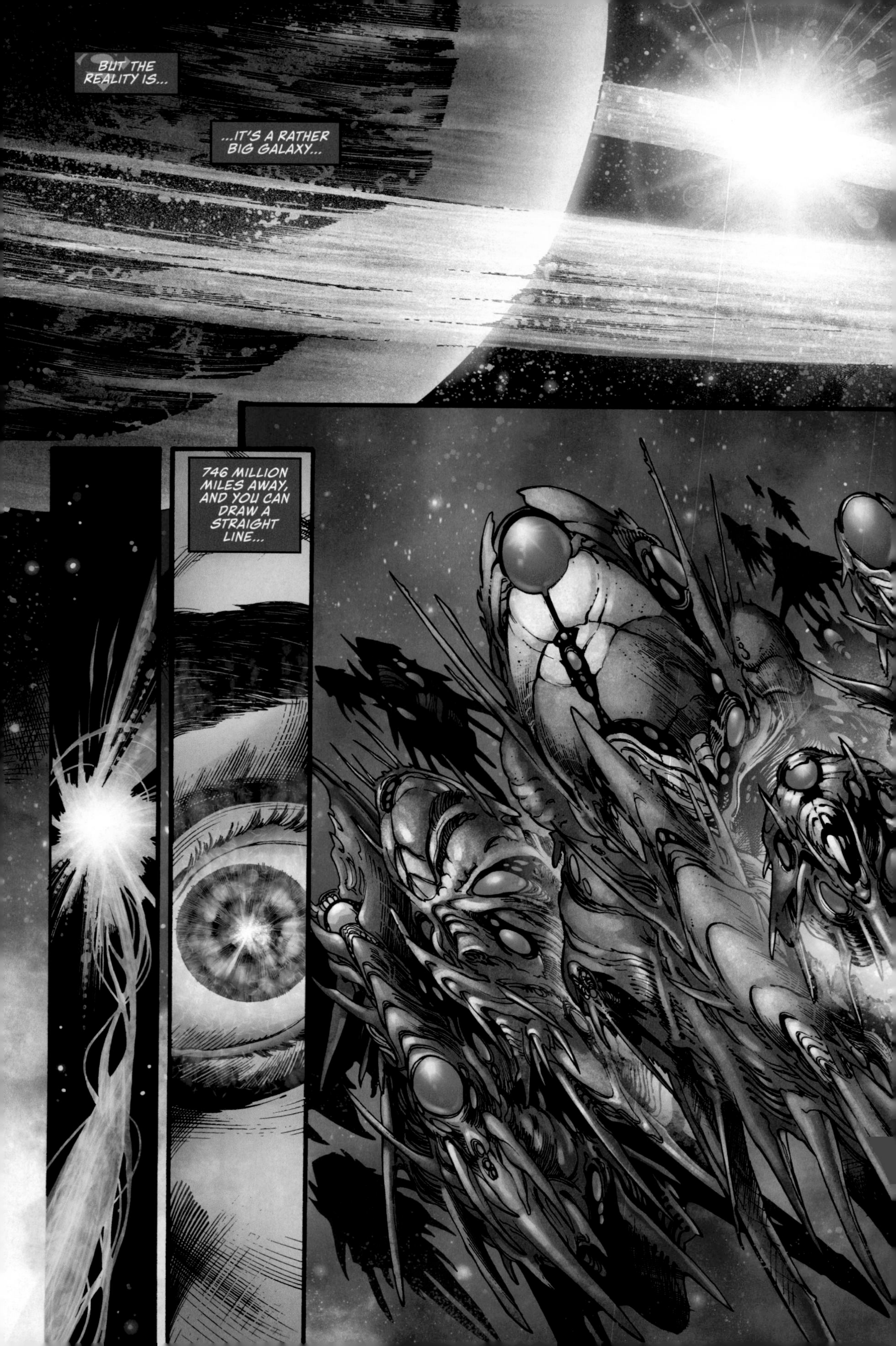
BUT THE REALITY IS...
...IT'S A RATHER BIG GALAXY...
746 MILLION MILES AWAY, AND YOU CAN DRAW A STRAIGHT LINE...

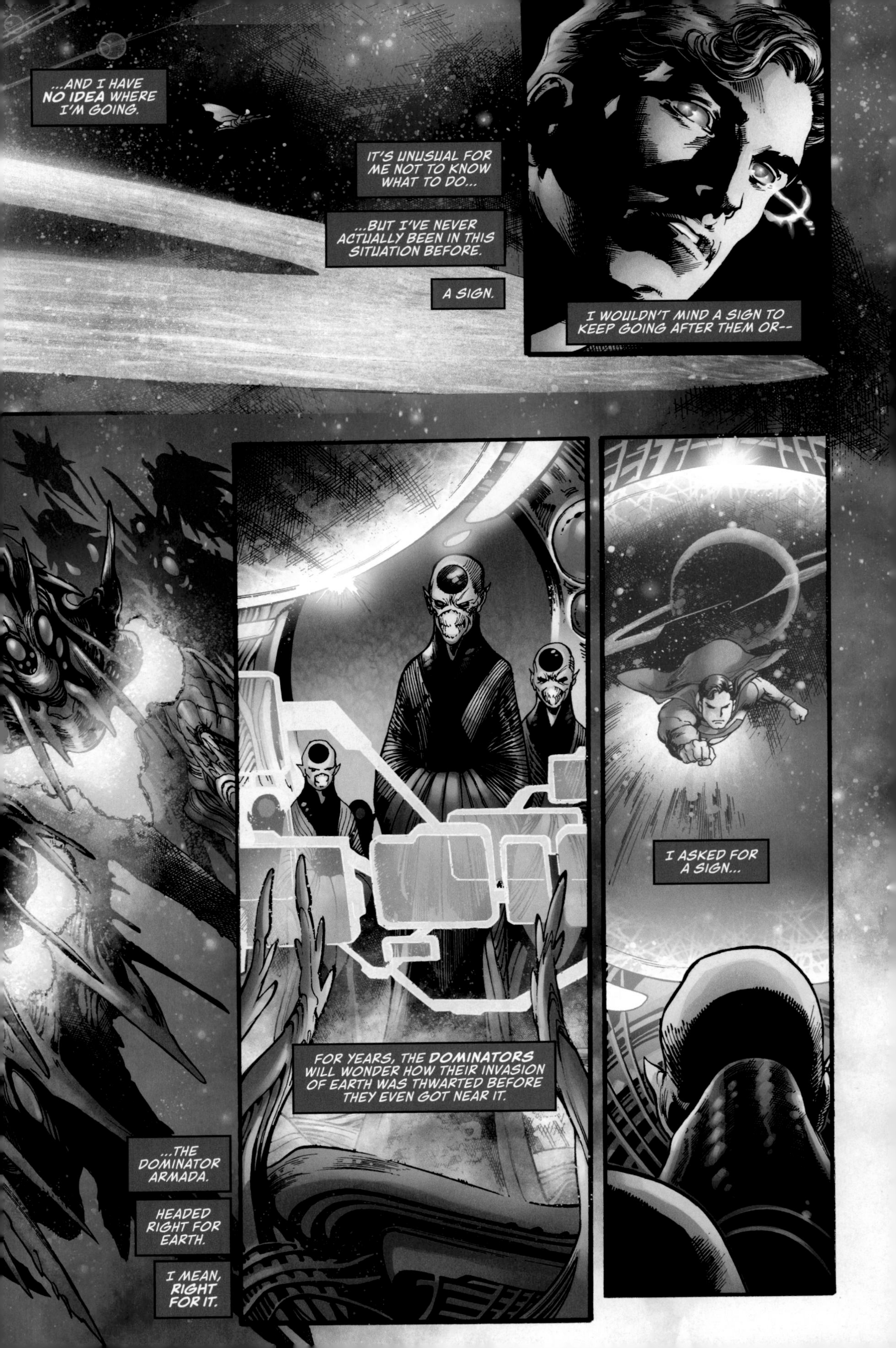

...AND I HAVE NO IDEA WHERE I'M GOING.
IT'S UNUSUAL FOR ME NOT TO KNOW WHAT TO DO...
...BUT I'VE NEVER ACTUALLY BEEN IN THIS SITUATION BEFORE.
A SIGN.
I WOULDN'T MIND A SIGN TO KEEP GOING AFTER THEM OR--
...THE DOMINATOR ARMADA.
HEADED RIGHT FOR EARTH.
I MEAN, RIGHT FOR IT.
FOR YEARS, THE DOMINATORS WILL WONDER HOW THEIR INVASION OF EARTH WAS THWARTED BEFORE THEY EVEN GOT NEAR IT.
I ASKED FOR A SIGN...

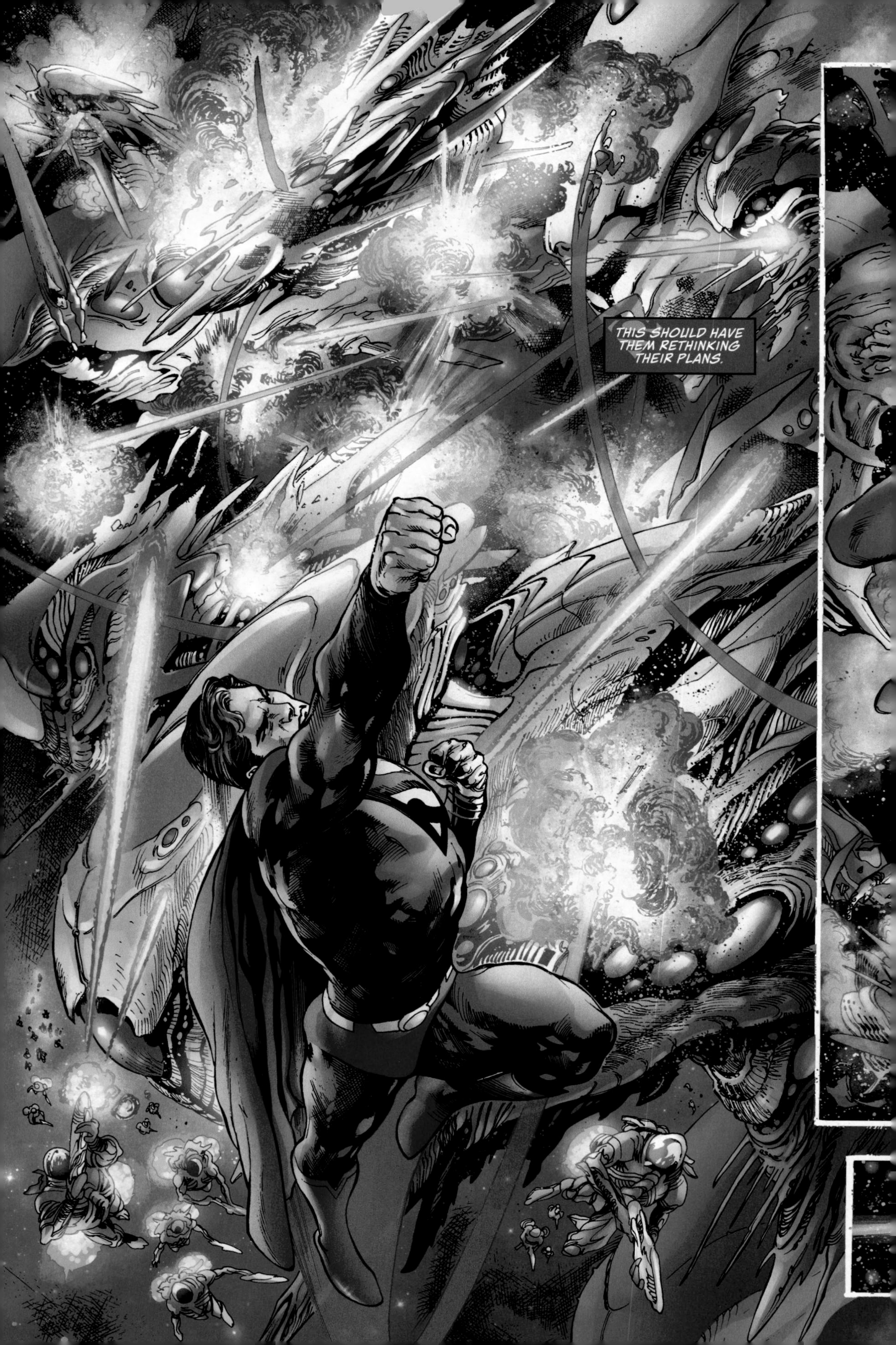
THIS SHOULD HAVE THEM RETHINKING THEIR PLANS.

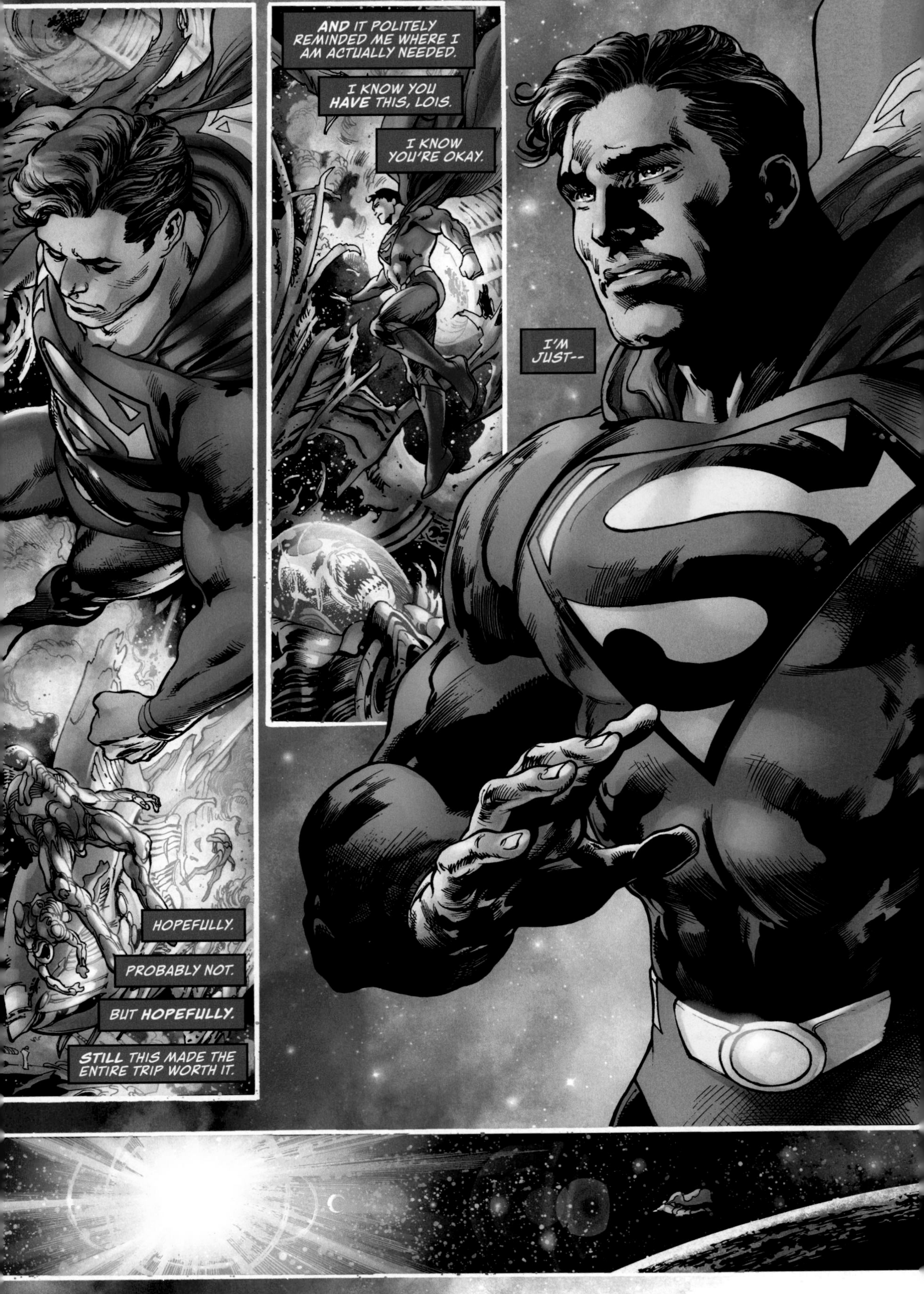
HOPEFULLY.
PROBABLY NOT.
BUT HOPEFULLY.
STILL THIS MADE THE ENTIRE TRIP WORTH IT.
AND IT POLITELY REMINDED ME WHERE I AM ACTUALLY NEEDED.
I KNOW YOU HAVE THIS, LOIS.
I KNOW YOU'RE OKAY.
I'M JUST--

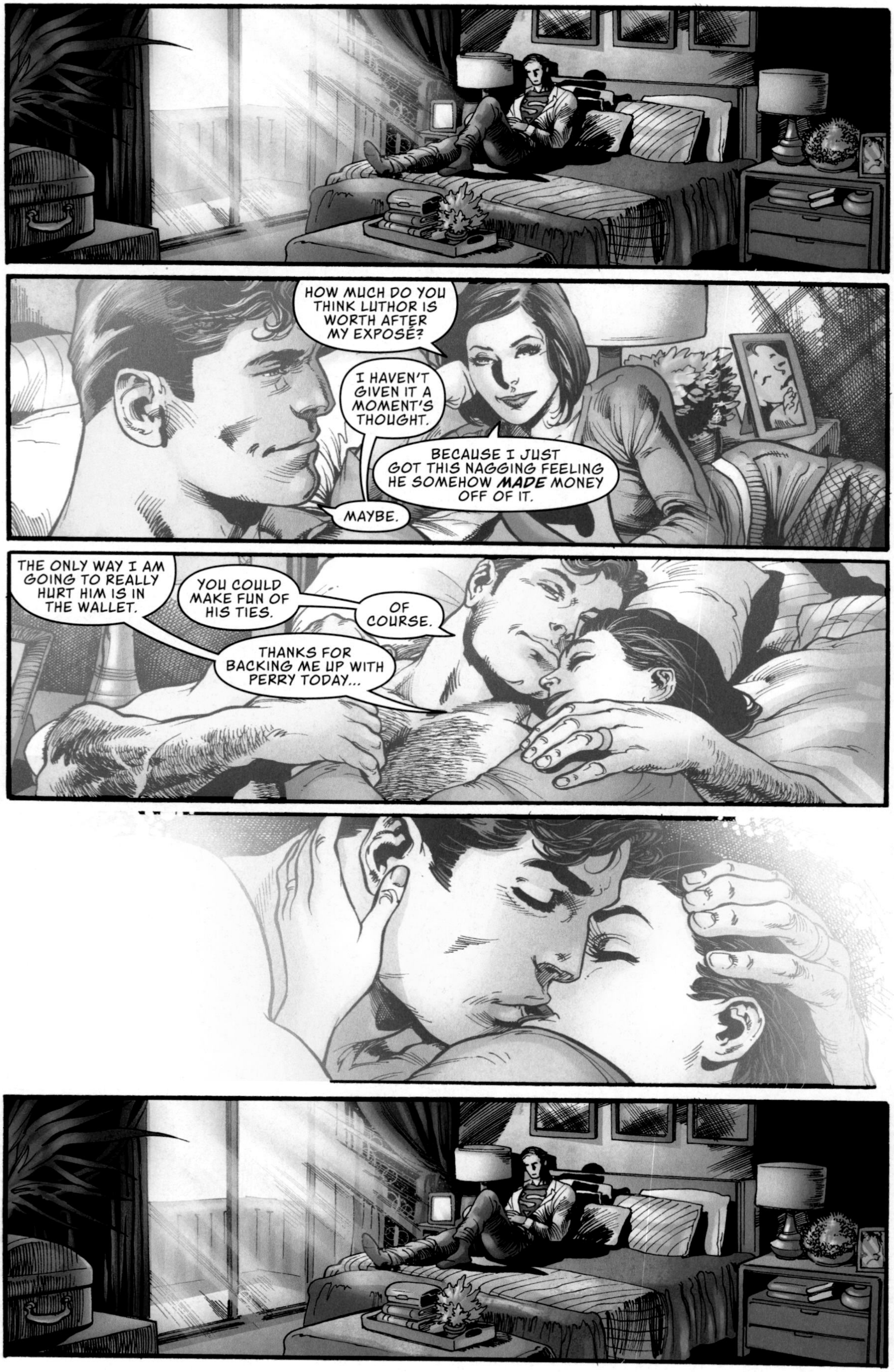
HOW MUCH DO YOU THINK LUTHOR IS WORTH AFTER MY EXPOSÉ?
I HAVEN'T GIVEN IT A MOMENT'S THOUGHT.
BECAUSE I JUST GOT THIS NAGGING FEELING HE SOMEHOW *MADE* MONEY OFF OF IT.
MAYBE.
THE ONLY WAY I AM GOING TO REALLY HURT HIM IS IN THE WALLET.
YOU COULD MAKE FUN OF HIS TIES.
OF COURSE.
THANKS FOR BACKING ME UP WITH PERRY TODAY...

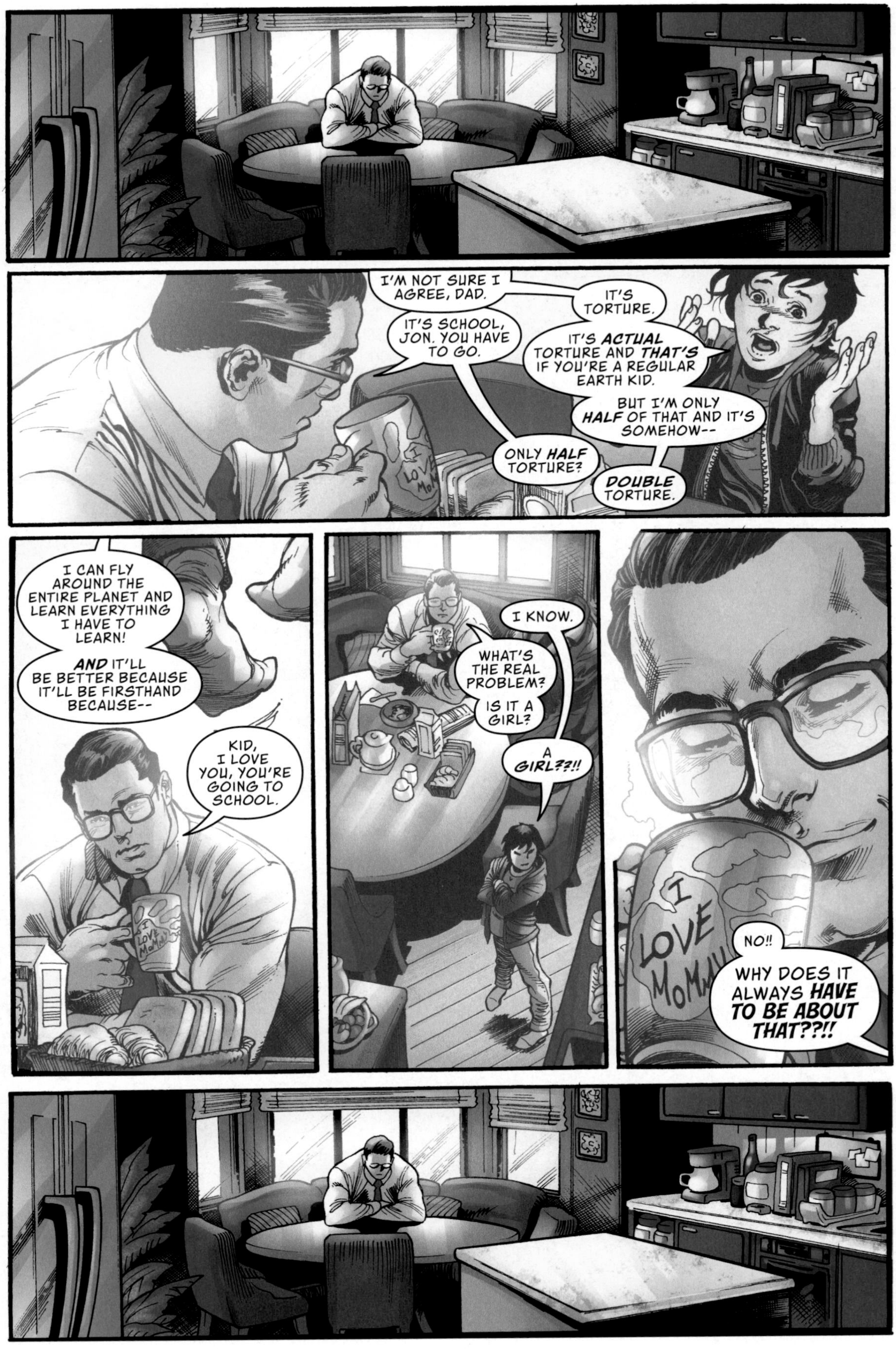

I'M NOT SURE I AGREE, DAD.
IT'S SCHOOL, JON. YOU HAVE TO GO.
IT'S TORTURE.
IT'S **ACTUAL** TORTURE AND **THAT'S** IF YOU'RE A REGULAR EARTH KID.
BUT I'M ONLY **HALF** OF THAT AND IT'S SOMEHOW--
ONLY **HALF** TORTURE?
DOUBLE TORTURE.
I CAN FLY AROUND THE ENTIRE PLANET AND LEARN EVERYTHING I HAVE TO LEARN!
AND IT'LL BE BETTER BECAUSE IT'LL BE FIRSTHAND BECAUSE--
KID, I LOVE YOU, YOU'RE GOING TO SCHOOL.
I KNOW.
WHAT'S THE REAL PROBLEM?
IS IT A GIRL?
A **GIRL??!!**
NO!!
WHY DOES IT ALWAYS **HAVE TO BE ABOUT THAT??!!**

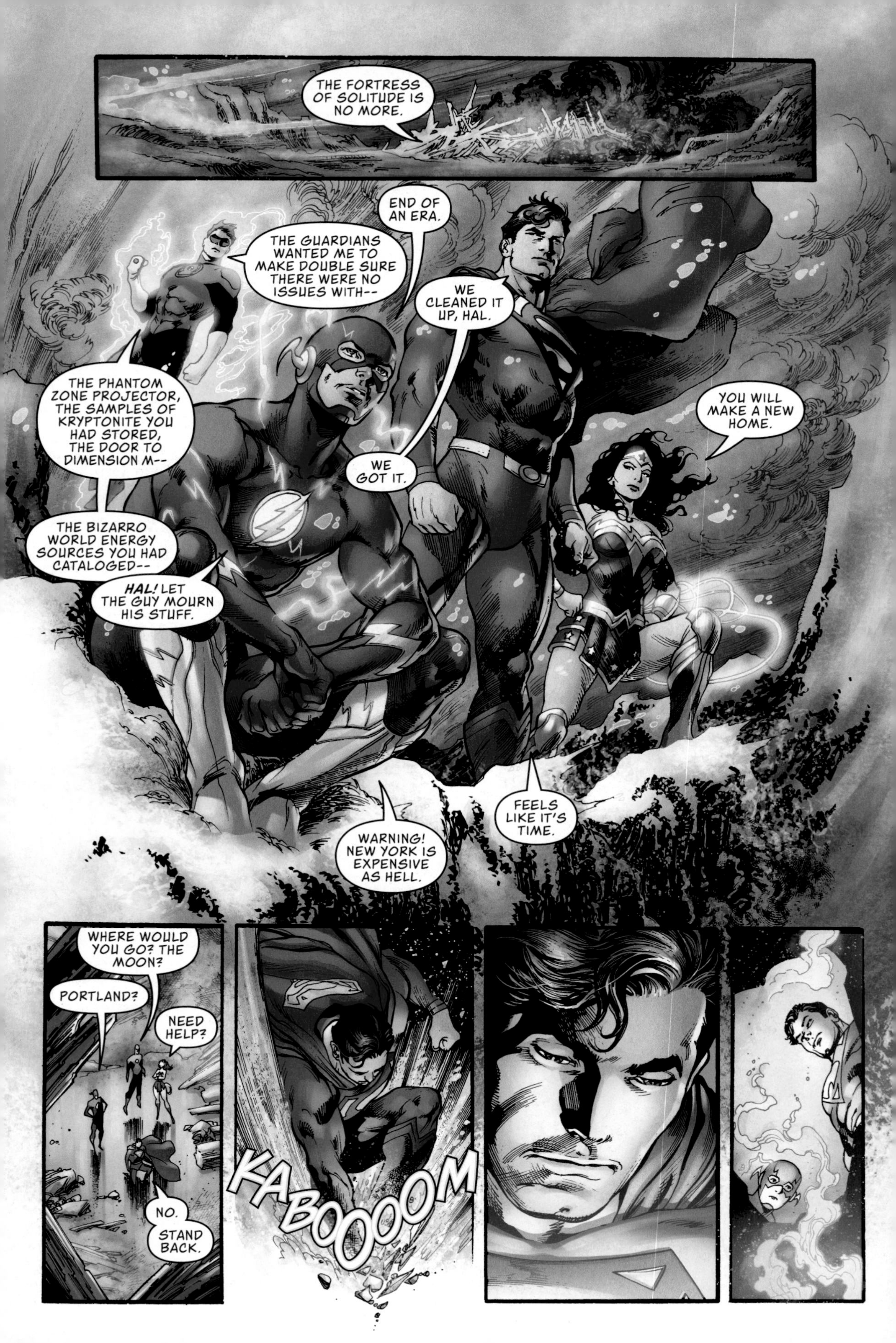
THE FORTRESS OF SOLITUDE IS NO MORE.
THE GUARDIANS WANTED ME TO MAKE DOUBLE SURE THERE WERE NO ISSUES WITH--
END OF AN ERA.
WE CLEANED IT UP, HAL.
THE PHANTOM ZONE PROJECTOR, THE SAMPLES OF KRYPTONITE YOU HAD STORED, THE DOOR TO DIMENSION M--
WE GOT IT.
YOU WILL MAKE A NEW HOME.
THE BIZARRO WORLD ENERGY SOURCES YOU HAD CATALOGED--
HAL! LET THE GUY MOURN HIS STUFF.
FEELS LIKE IT'S TIME.
WARNING! NEW YORK IS EXPENSIVE AS HELL.
WHERE WOULD YOU GO? THE MOON?
PORTLAND?
NEED HELP?
NO.
STAND BACK.
KABOOOOOM

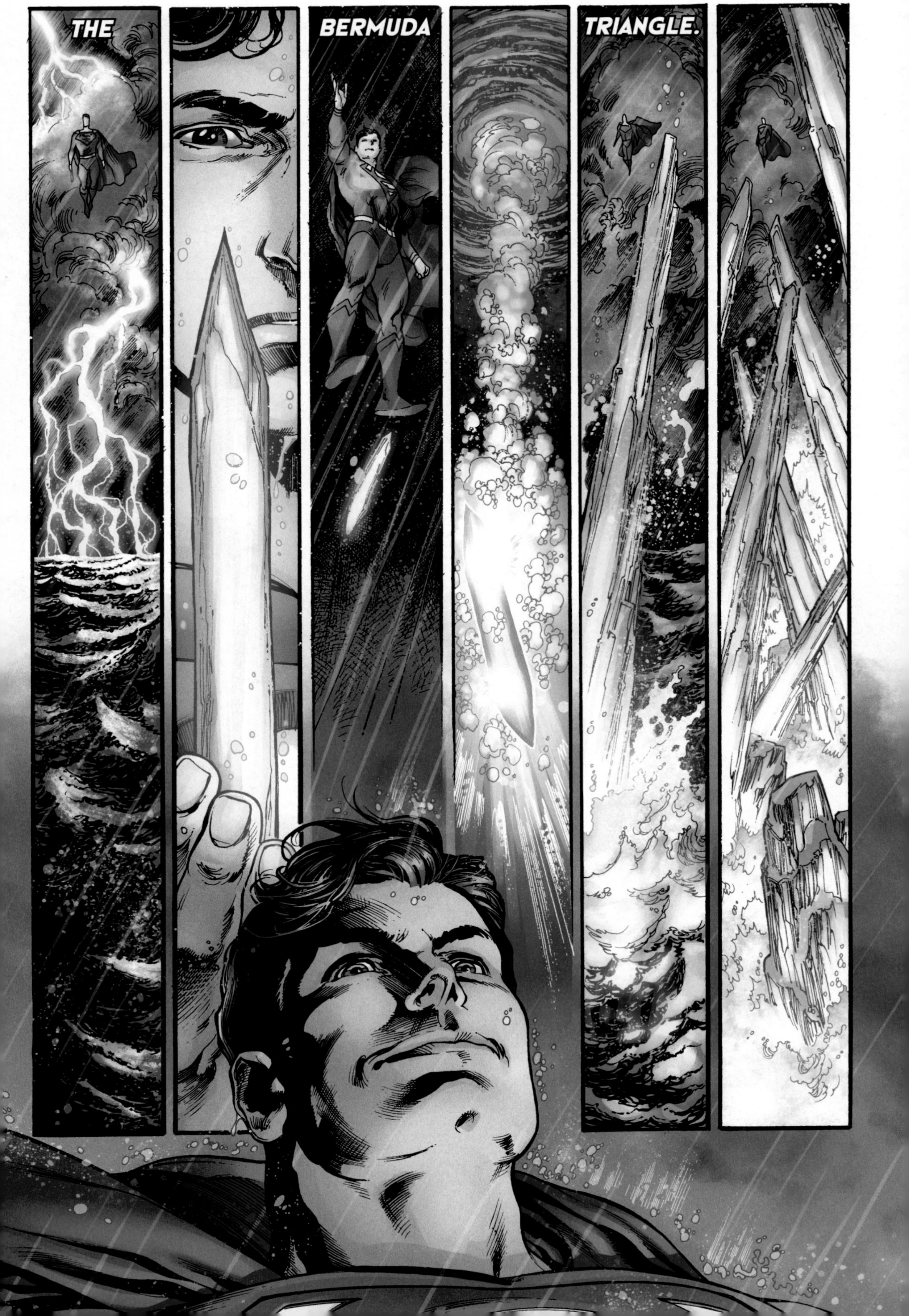
THE
BERMUDA
TRIANGLE.

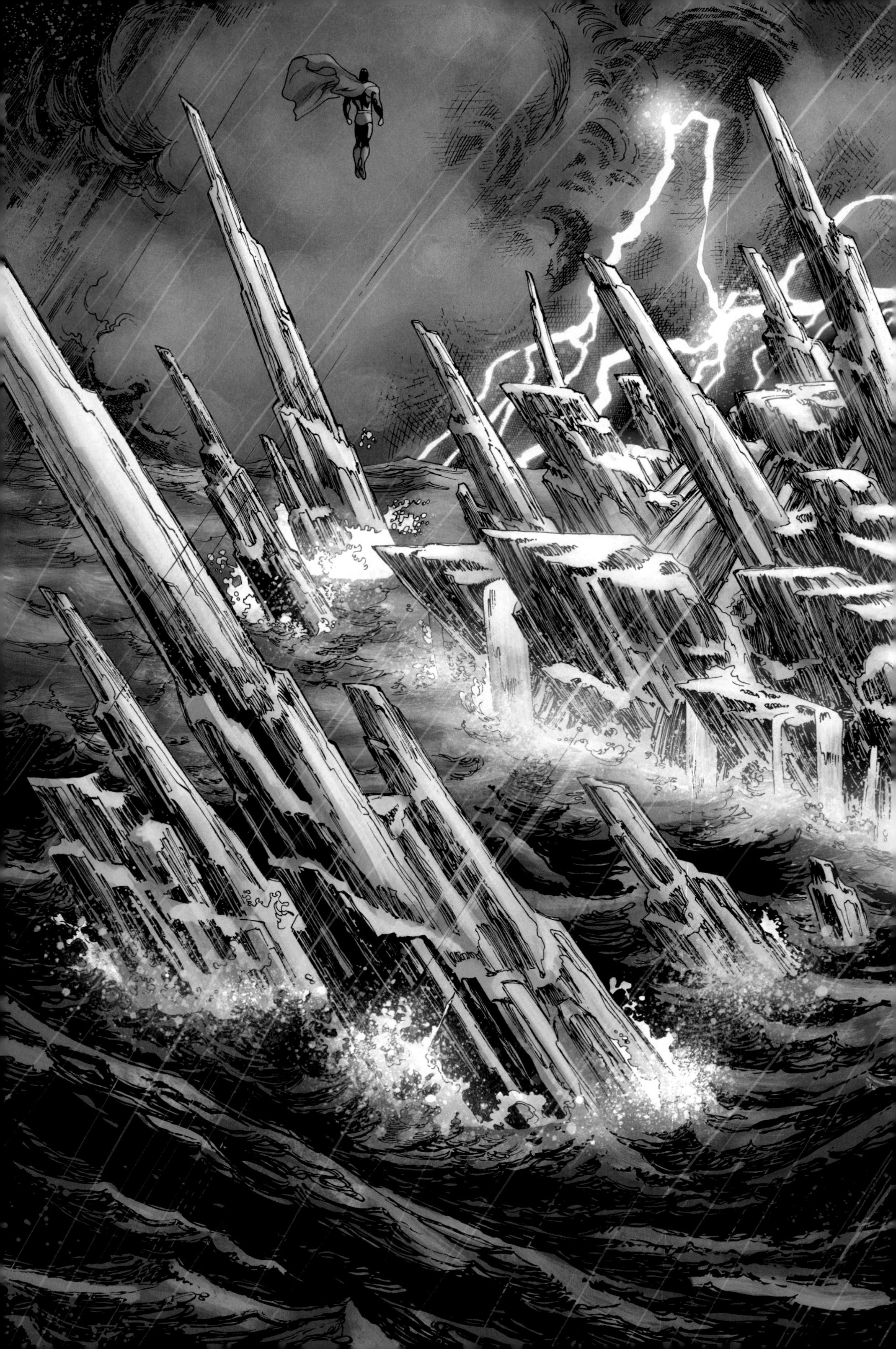

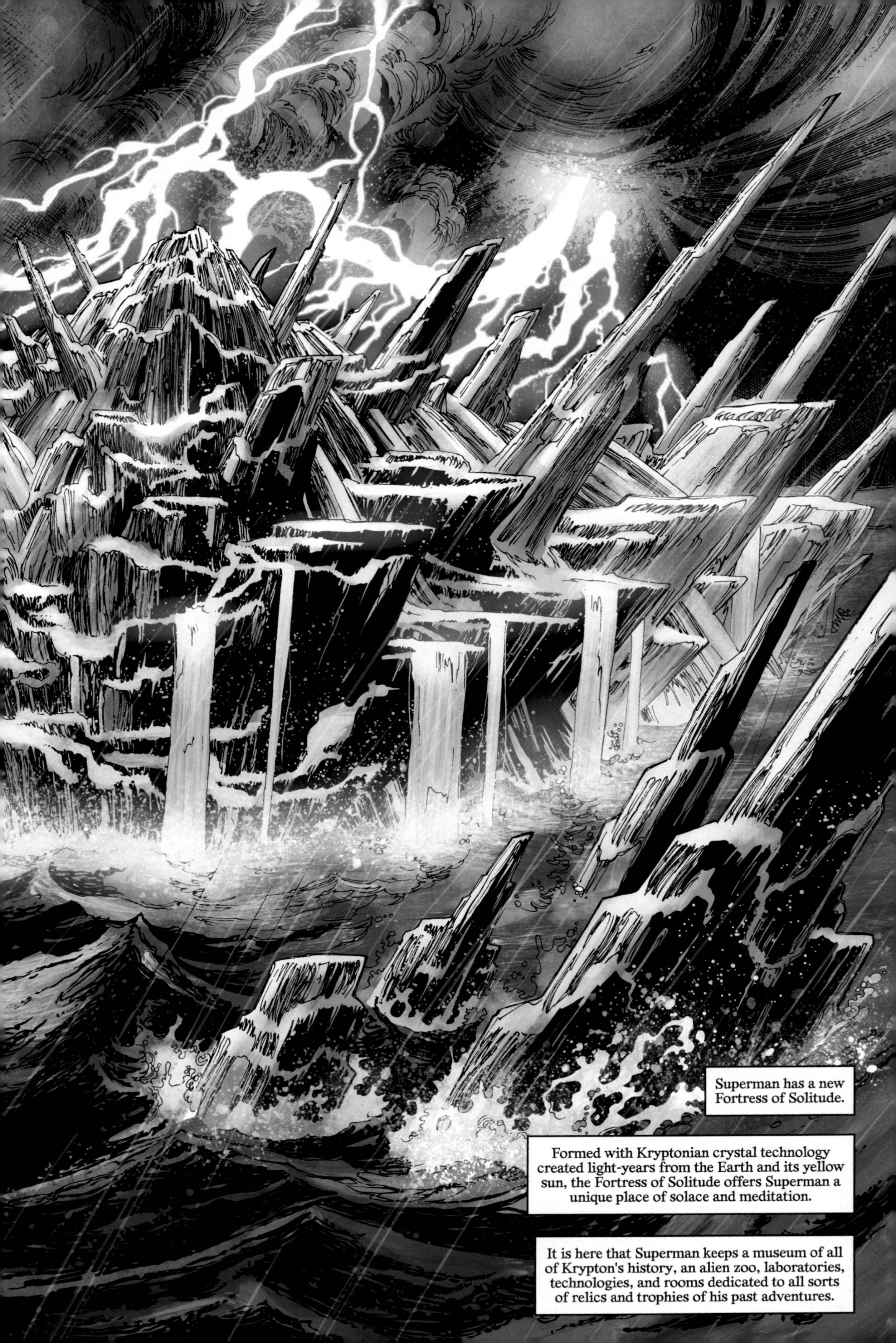
Superman has a new Fortress of Solitude.
Formed with Kryptonian crystal technology created light-years from the Earth and its yellow sun, the Fortress of Solitude offers Superman a unique place of solace and meditation.
It is here that Superman keeps a museum of all of Krypton's history, an alien zoo, laboratories, technologies, and rooms dedicated to all sorts of relics and trophies of his past adventures.

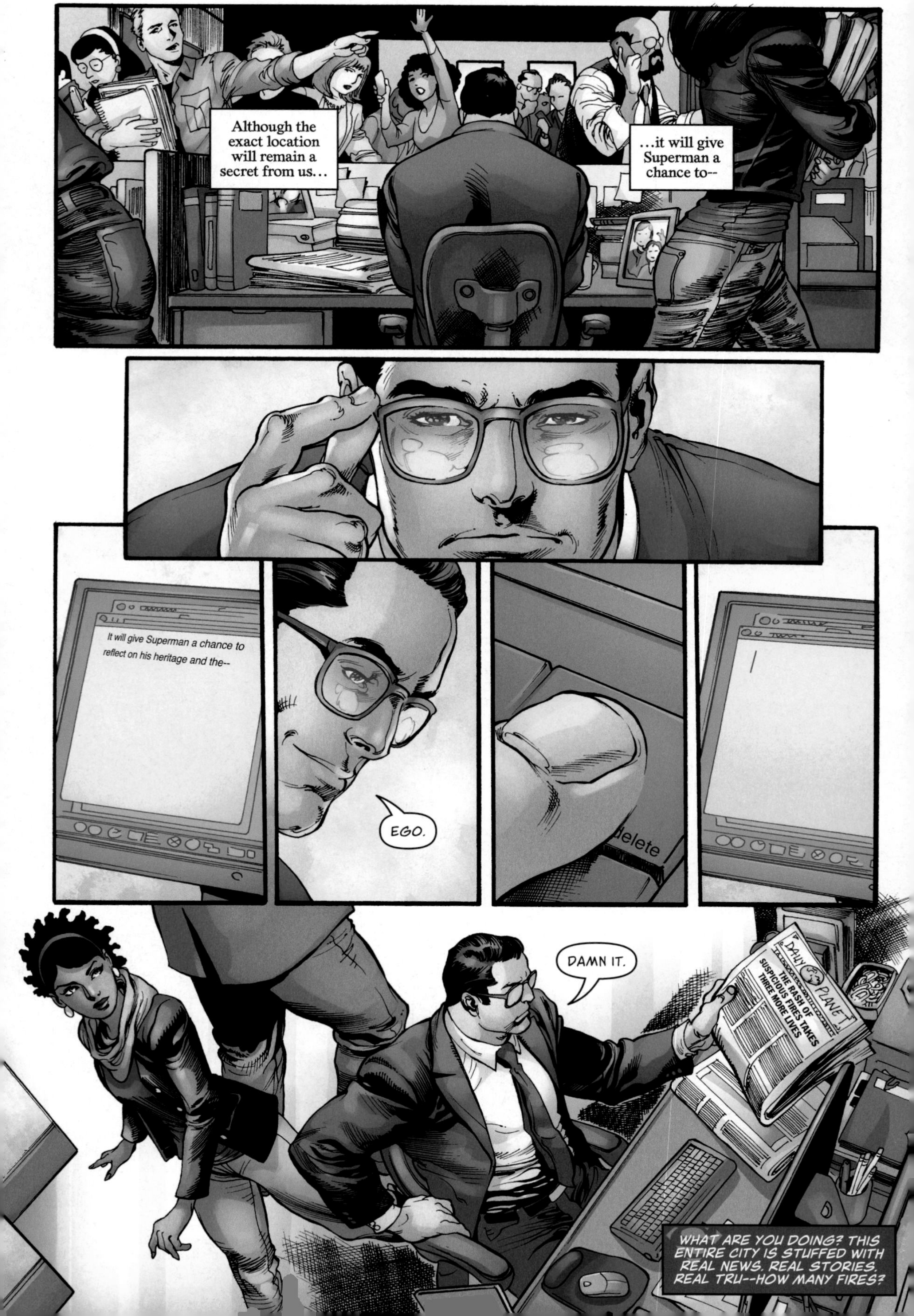
Although the exact location will remain a secret from us...
...it will give Superman a chance to--
It will give Superman a chance to reflect on his heritage and the--
EGO.
delete
DAMN IT.
DAILY PLANET
THE RASH OF SUSPICIOUS FIRES TAKES THREE MORE LIVES
WHAT ARE YOU DOING? THIS ENTIRE CITY IS STUFFED WITH REAL NEWS. REAL STORIES. REAL TRU--HOW MANY FIRES?

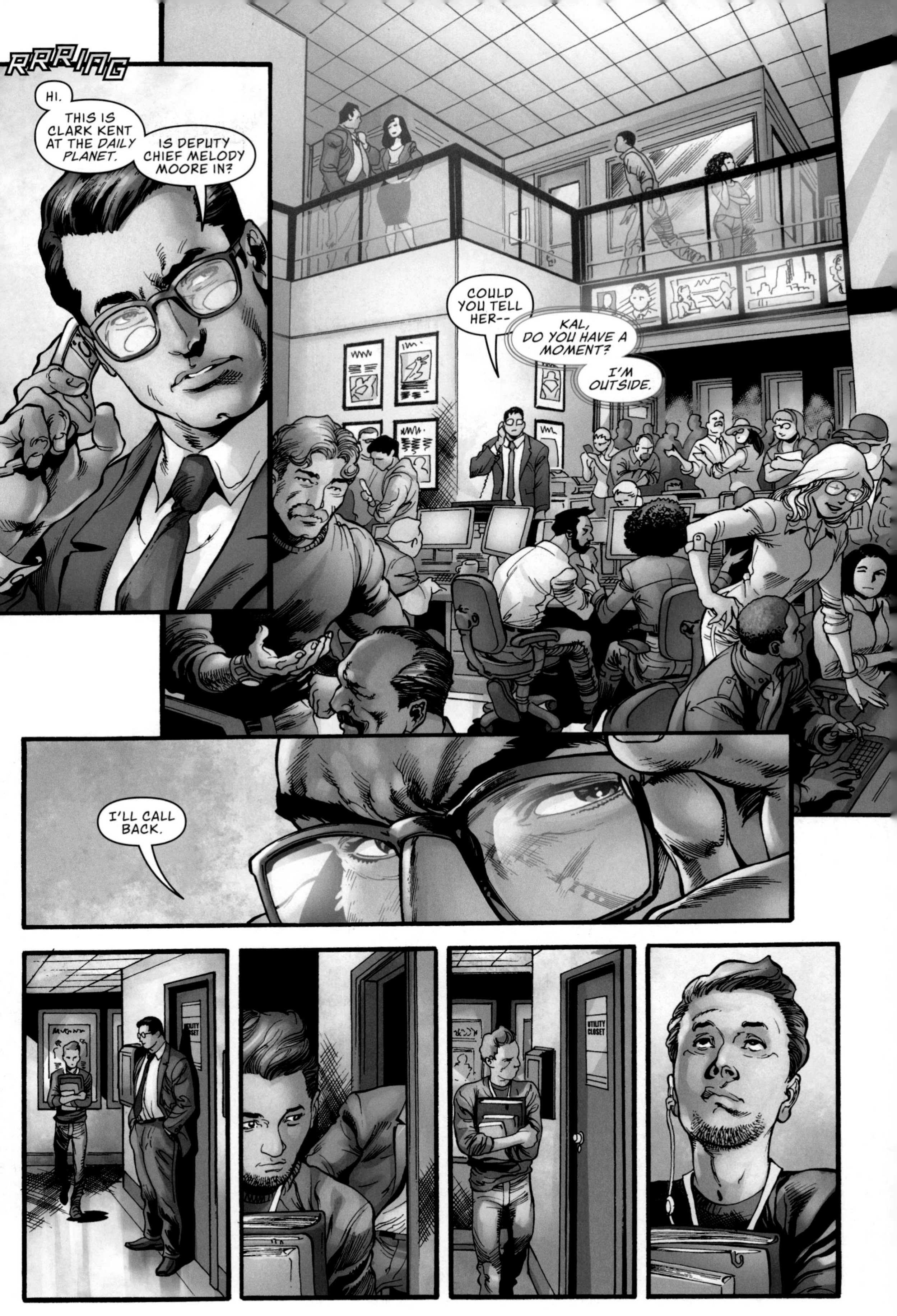
RRRIAG
HI. THIS IS CLARK KENT AT THE *DAILY PLANET.*
IS DEPUTY CHIEF MELODY MOORE IN?
COULD YOU TELL HER--
KAL, DO YOU HAVE A MOMENT?
I'M OUTSIDE.
I'LL CALL BACK.
UTILITY CLOSET
UTILITY CLOSET

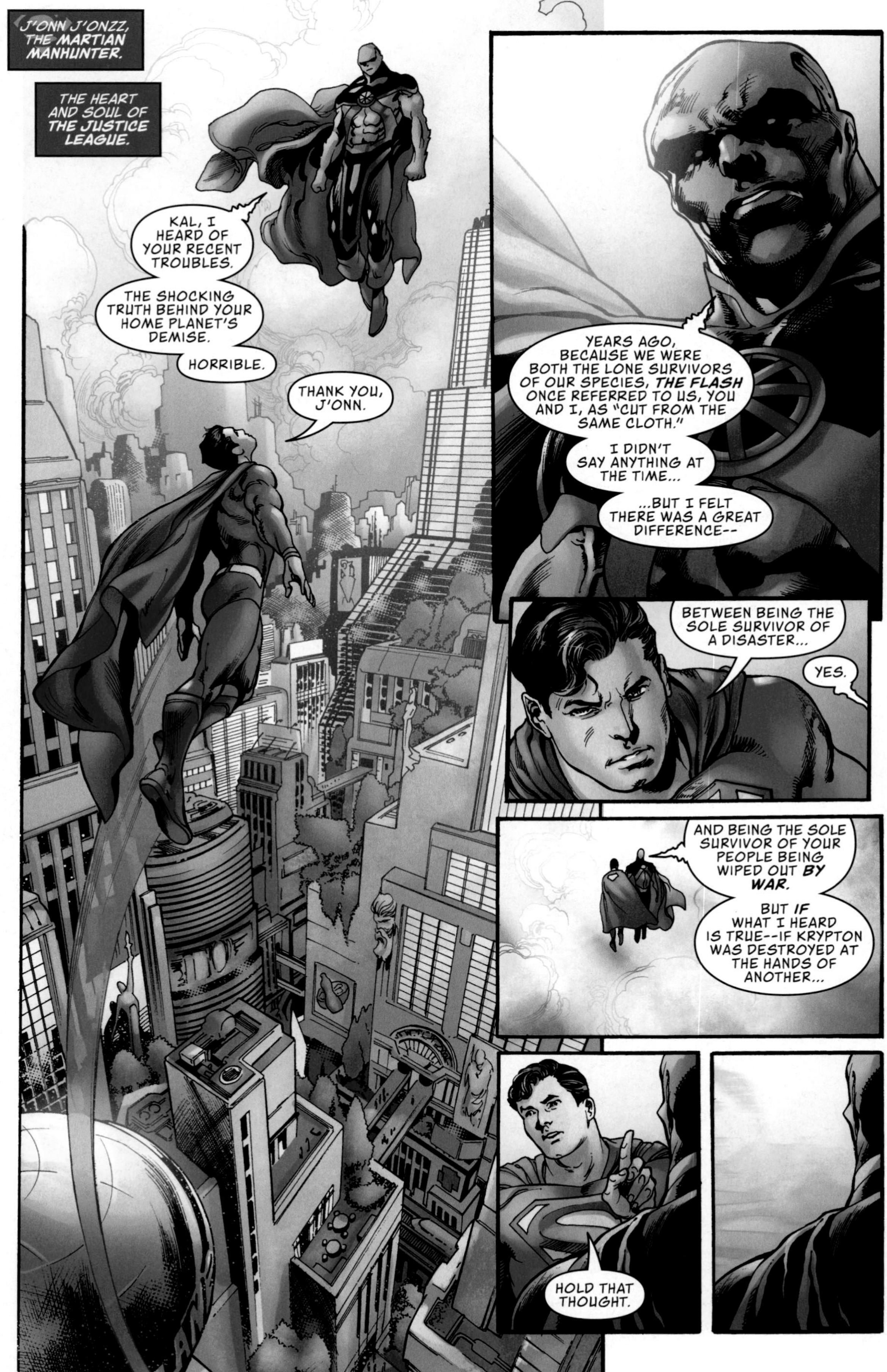
J'ONN J'ONZZ, THE MARTIAN MANHUNTER.
THE HEART AND SOUL OF THE JUSTICE LEAGUE.
KAL, I HEARD OF YOUR RECENT TROUBLES.
THE SHOCKING TRUTH BEHIND YOUR HOME PLANET'S DEMISE.
HORRIBLE.
THANK YOU, J'ONN.
YEARS AGO, BECAUSE WE WERE BOTH THE LONE SURVIVORS OF OUR SPECIES, THE FLASH ONCE REFERRED TO US, YOU AND I, AS "CUT FROM THE SAME CLOTH."
I DIDN'T SAY ANYTHING AT THE TIME...
...BUT I FELT THERE WAS A GREAT DIFFERENCE--
BETWEEN BEING THE SOLE SURVIVOR OF A DISASTER...
YES.
AND BEING THE SOLE SURVIVOR OF YOUR PEOPLE BEING WIPED OUT BY WAR.
BUT IF WHAT I HEARD IS TRUE--IF KRYPTON WAS DESTROYED AT THE HANDS OF ANOTHER...
HOLD THAT THOUGHT.

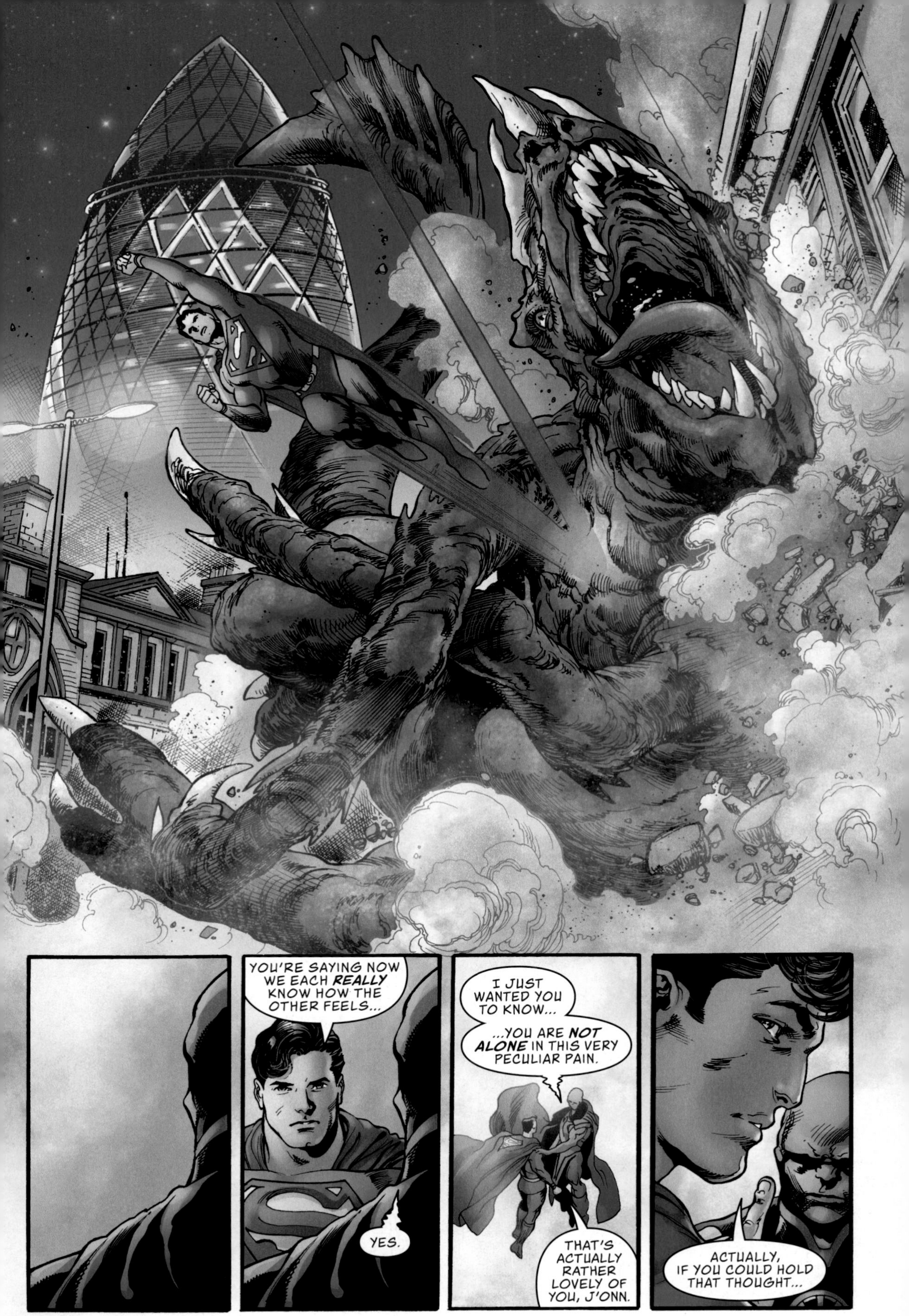
YOU'RE SAYING NOW WE EACH **REALLY** KNOW HOW THE OTHER FEELS...
YES.
I JUST WANTED YOU TO KNOW...
...YOU ARE **NOT ALONE** IN THIS VERY PECULIAR PAIN.
THAT'S ACTUALLY RATHER LOVELY OF YOU, J'ONN.
ACTUALLY, IF YOU COULD HOLD THAT THOUGHT...

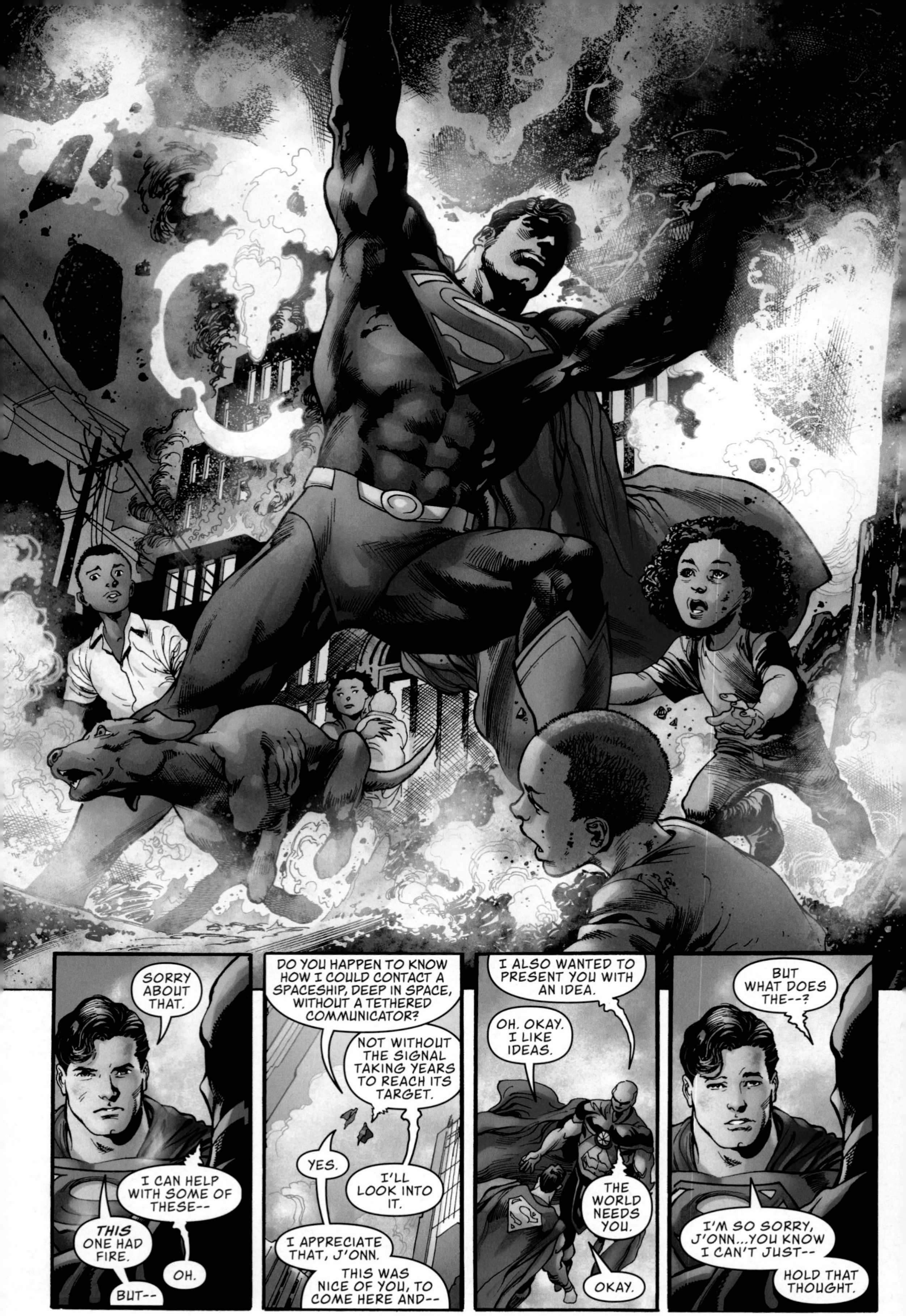
SORRY ABOUT THAT.
I CAN HELP WITH SOME OF THESE--
THIS ONE HAD FIRE.
OH.
BUT--
DO YOU HAPPEN TO KNOW HOW I COULD CONTACT A SPACESHIP, DEEP IN SPACE, WITHOUT A TETHERED COMMUNICATOR?
NOT WITHOUT THE SIGNAL TAKING YEARS TO REACH ITS TARGET.
YES.
I'LL LOOK INTO IT.
I APPRECIATE THAT, J'ONN.
THIS WAS NICE OF YOU, TO COME HERE AND--
I ALSO WANTED TO PRESENT YOU WITH AN IDEA.
OH. OKAY. I LIKE IDEAS.
THE WORLD NEEDS YOU.
OKAY.
BUT WHAT DOES THE--?
I'M SO SORRY, J'ONN...YOU KNOW I CAN'T JUST--
HOLD THAT THOUGHT.

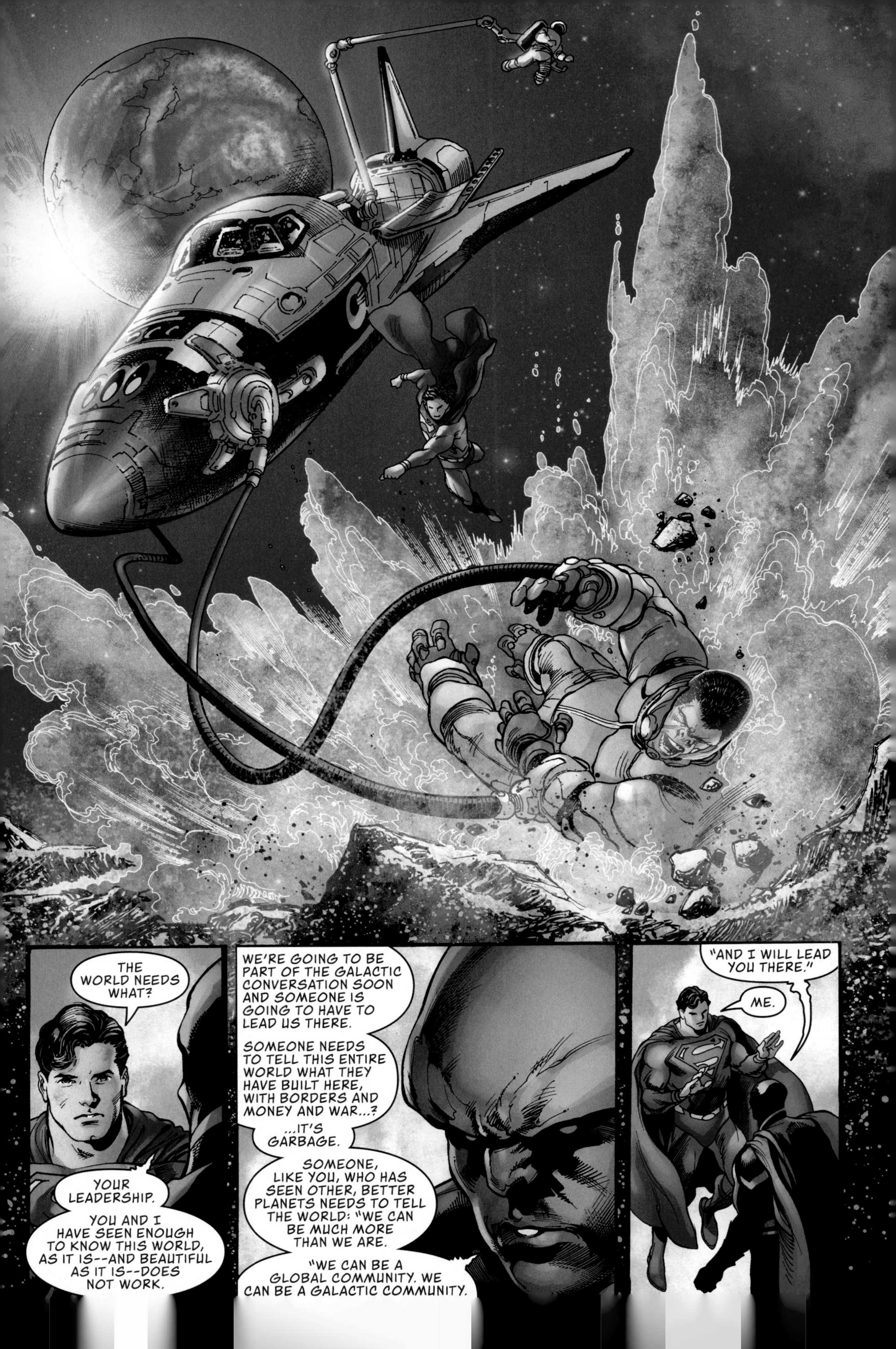
THE WORLD NEEDS WHAT?
YOUR LEADERSHIP.
YOU AND I HAVE SEEN ENOUGH TO KNOW THIS WORLD, AS IT IS--AND BEAUTIFUL AS IT IS--DOES NOT WORK.
WE'RE GOING TO BE PART OF THE GALACTIC CONVERSATION SOON AND SOMEONE IS GOING TO HAVE TO LEAD US THERE.
SOMEONE NEEDS TO TELL THIS ENTIRE WORLD WHAT THEY HAVE BUILT HERE, WITH BORDERS AND MONEY AND WAR...?
...IT'S GARBAGE.
SOMEONE, LIKE YOU, WHO HAS SEEN OTHER, BETTER PLANETS NEEDS TO TELL THE WORLD: "WE CAN BE MUCH MORE THAN WE ARE.
"WE CAN BE A GLOBAL COMMUNITY. WE CAN BE A GALACTIC COMMUNITY.
"AND I WILL LEAD YOU THERE."
ME.

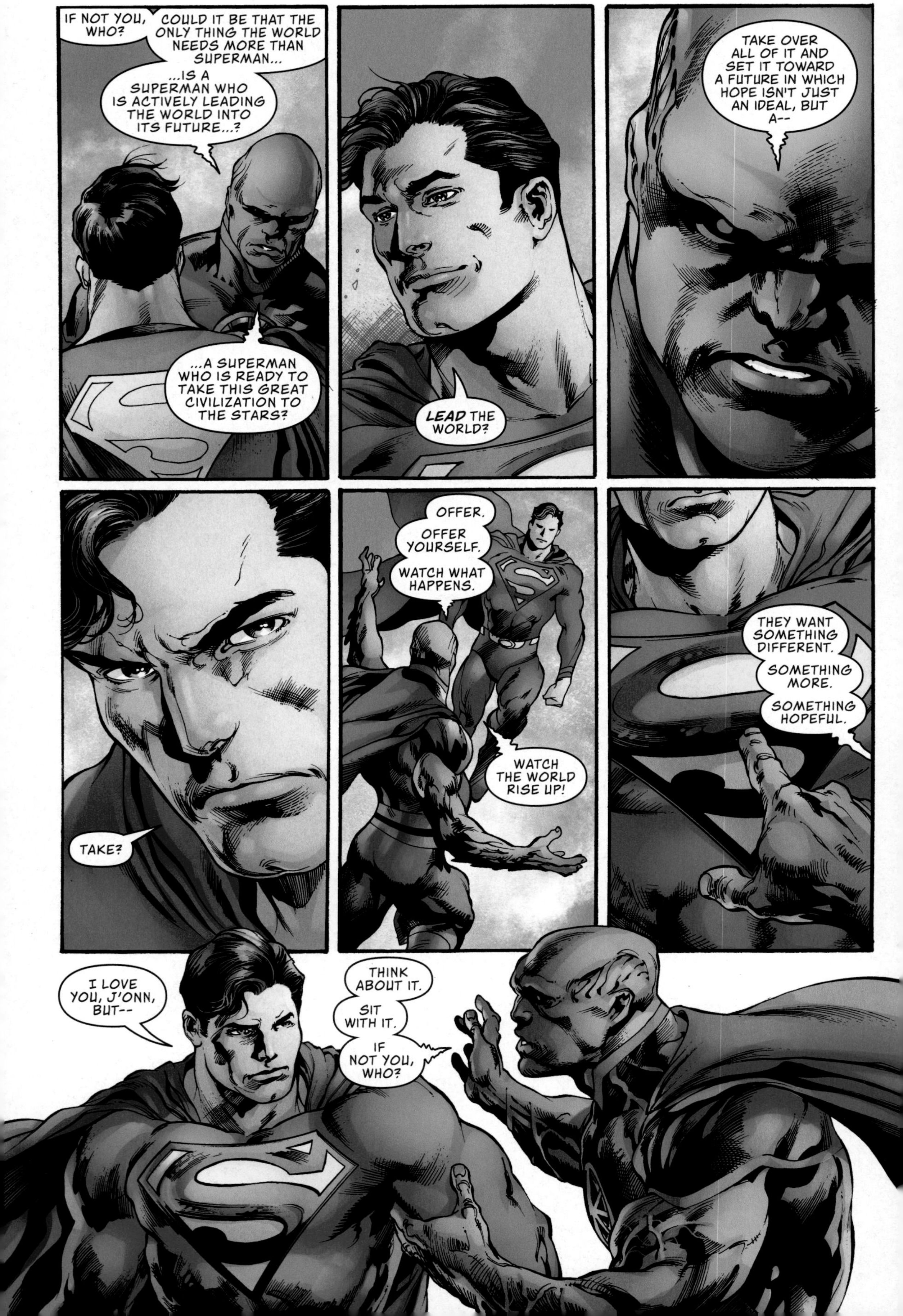
IF NOT YOU, WHO?
COULD IT BE THAT THE ONLY THING THE WORLD NEEDS MORE THAN SUPERMAN...
...IS A SUPERMAN WHO IS ACTIVELY LEADING THE WORLD INTO ITS FUTURE...?
...A SUPERMAN WHO IS READY TO TAKE THIS GREAT CIVILIZATION TO THE STARS?
LEAD THE WORLD?
TAKE OVER ALL OF IT AND SET IT TOWARD A FUTURE IN WHICH HOPE ISN'T JUST AN IDEAL, BUT A--
TAKE?
OFFER.
OFFER YOURSELF.
WATCH WHAT HAPPENS.
WATCH THE WORLD RISE UP!
THEY WANT SOMETHING DIFFERENT.
SOMETHING MORE.
SOMETHING HOPEFUL.
I LOVE YOU, J'ONN, BUT--
THINK ABOUT IT.
SIT WITH IT.
IF NOT YOU, WHO?

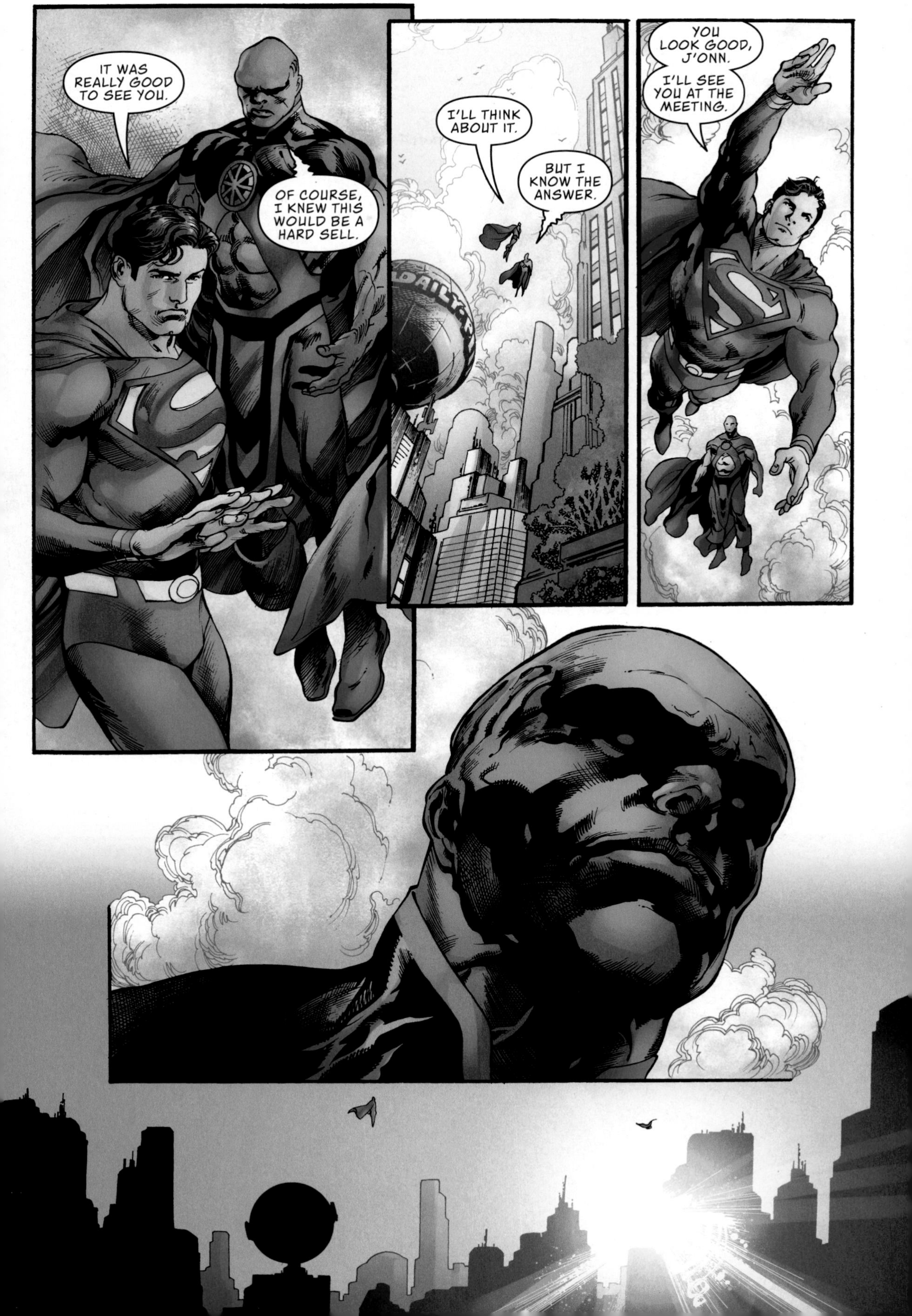
IT WAS REALLY GOOD TO SEE YOU.
OF COURSE, I KNEW THIS WOULD BE A HARD SELL.
I'LL THINK ABOUT IT.
BUT I KNOW THE ANSWER.
YOU LOOK GOOD, J'ONN.
I'LL SEE YOU AT THE MEETING.

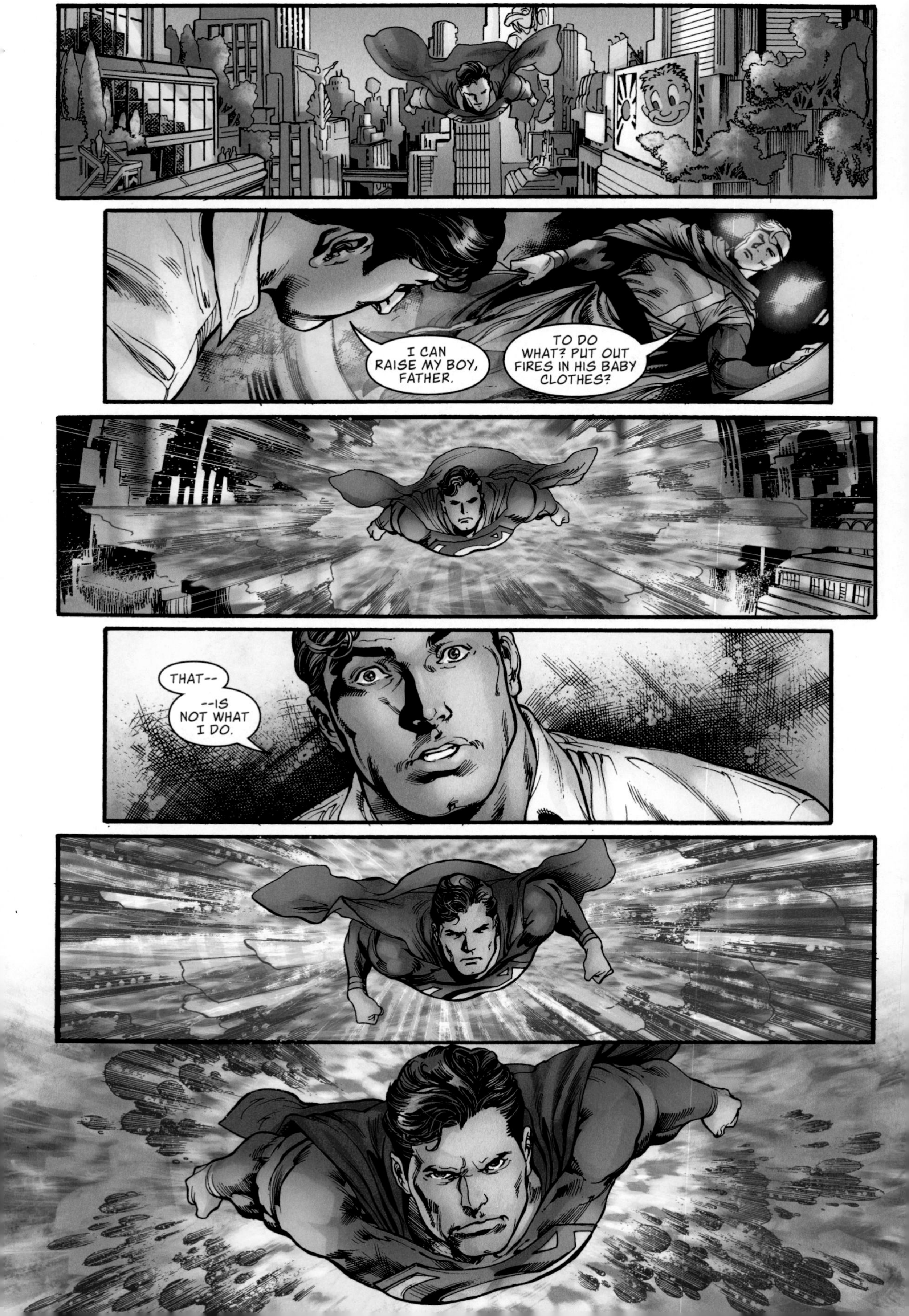
I CAN RAISE MY BOY, FATHER.
TO DO WHAT? PUT OUT FIRES IN HIS BABY CLOTHES?
THAT--
--IS NOT WHAT I DO.

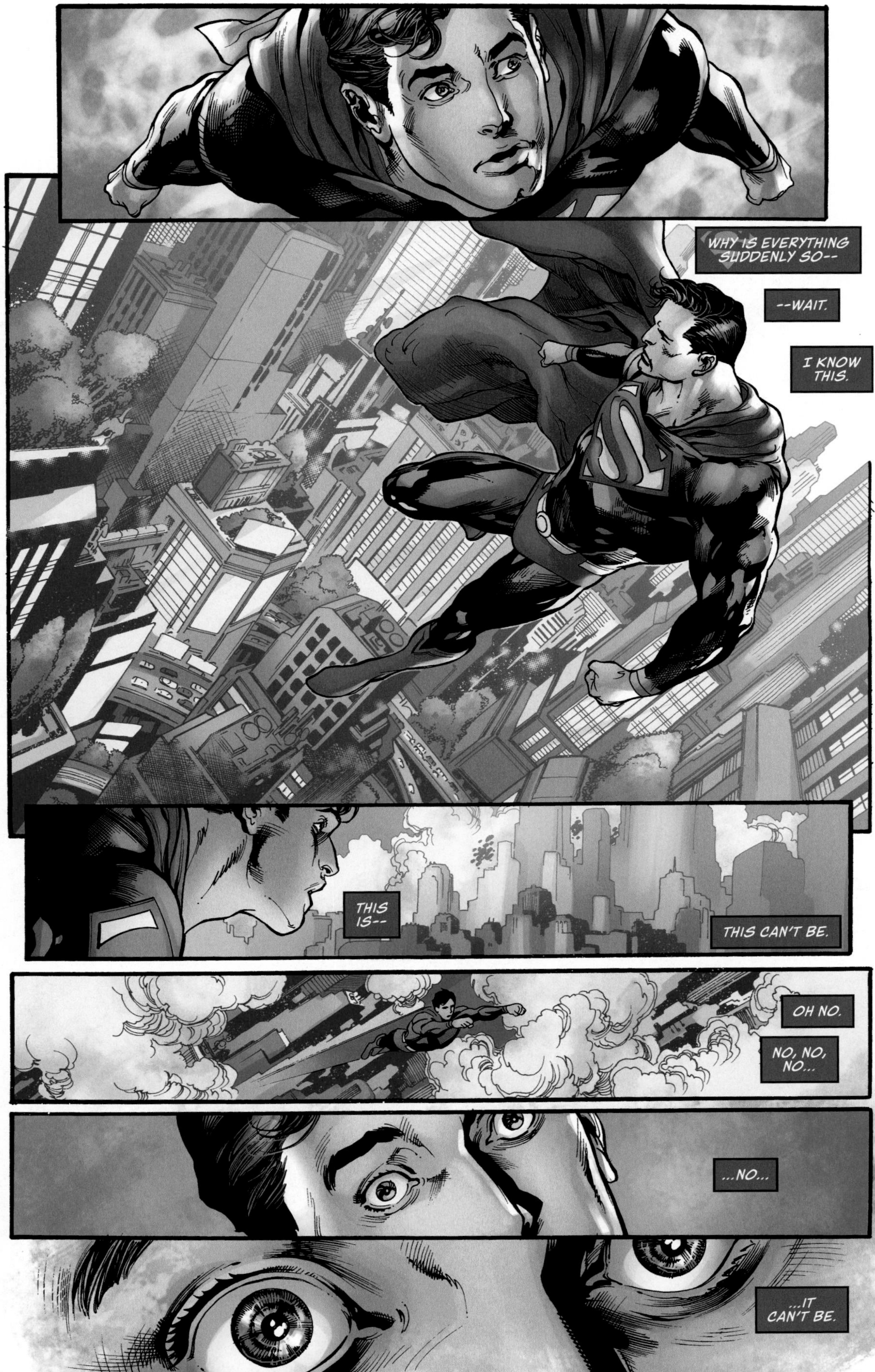
WHY IS EVERYTHING SUDDENLY SO--
--WAIT.
I KNOW THIS.
THIS IS--
THIS CAN'T BE.
OH NO.
NO, NO, NO...
...NO...
...IT CAN'T BE.

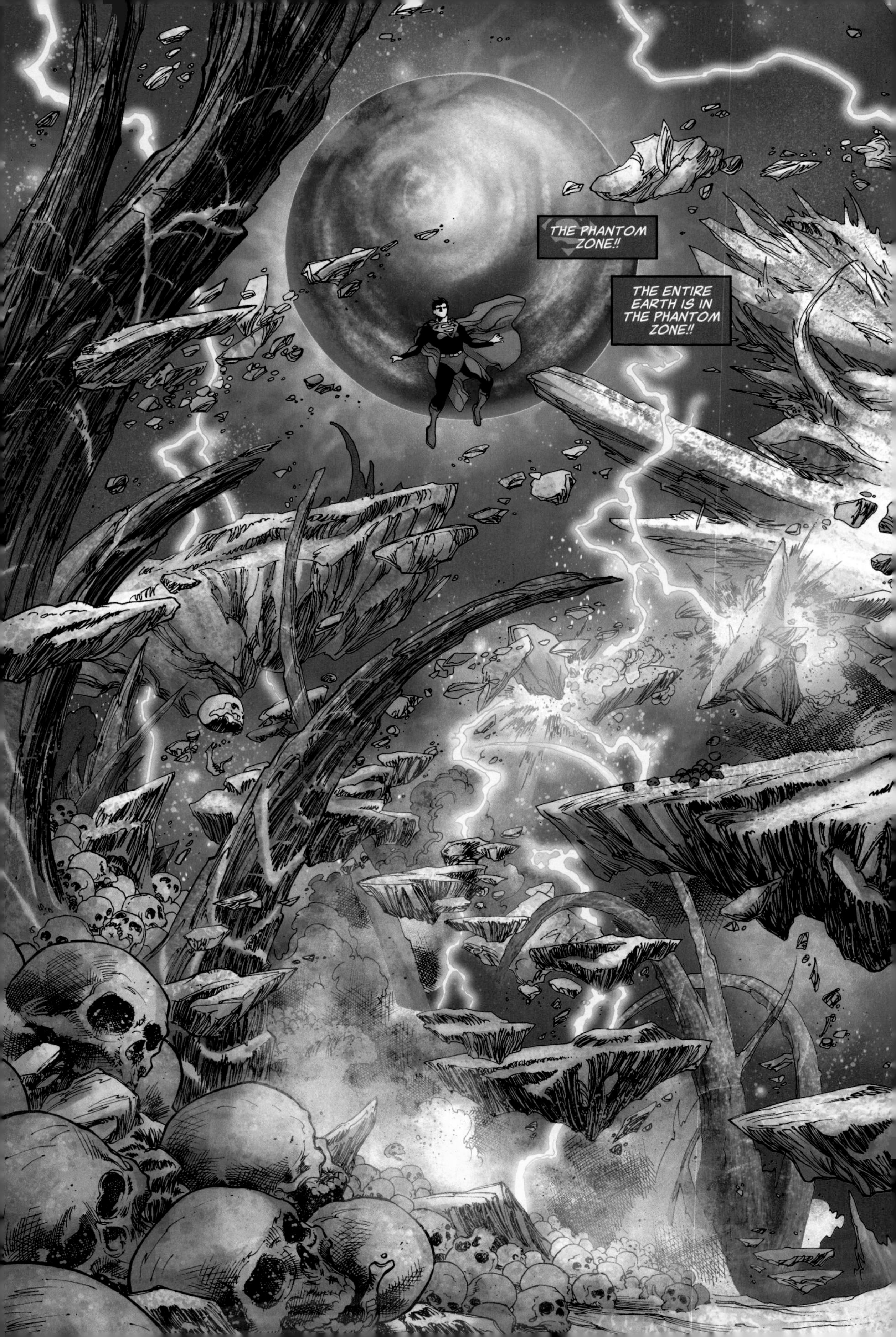
THE PHANTOM ZONE!!
THE ENTIRE EARTH IS IN THE PHANTOM ZONE!!

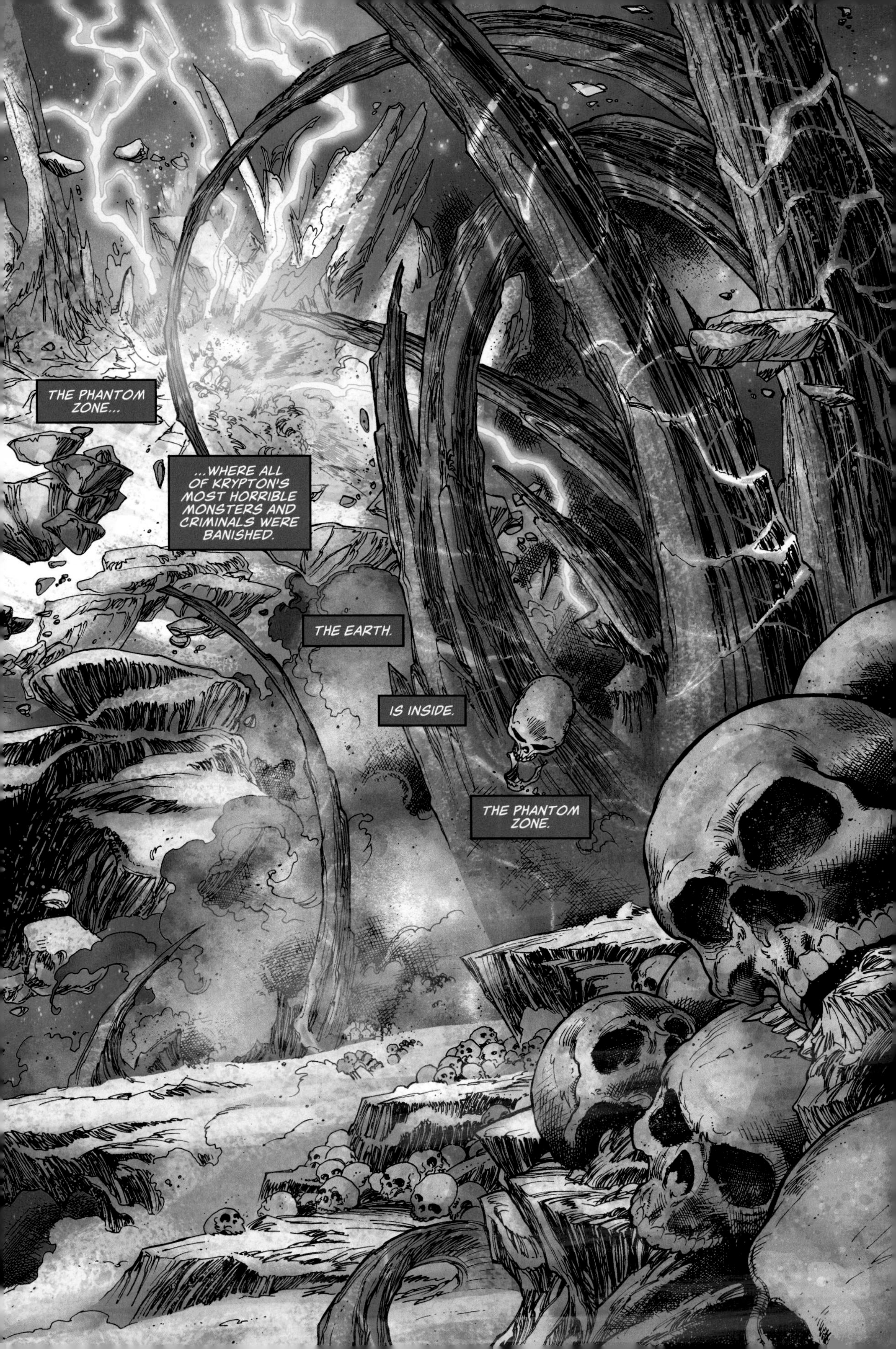
THE PHANTOM ZONE...
...WHERE ALL OF KRYPTON'S MOST HORRIBLE MONSTERS AND CRIMINALS WERE BANISHED.
THE EARTH.
IS INSIDE.
THE PHANTOM ZONE.

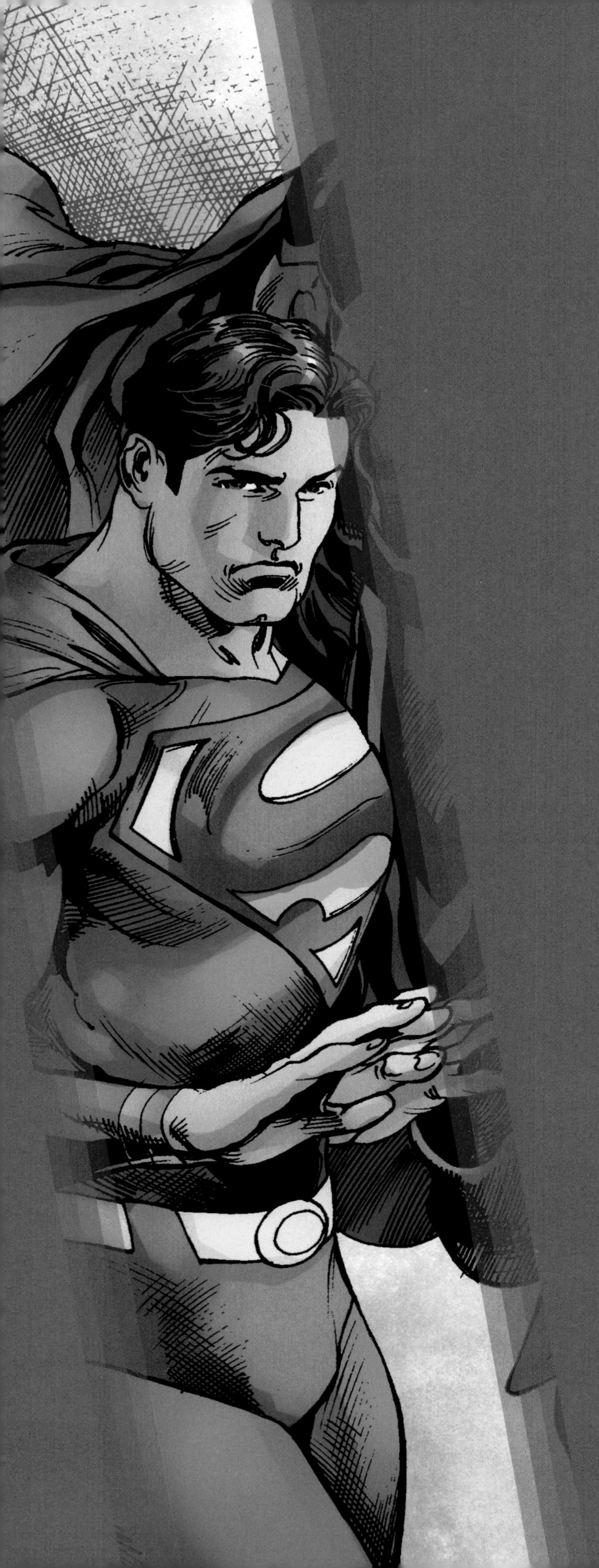

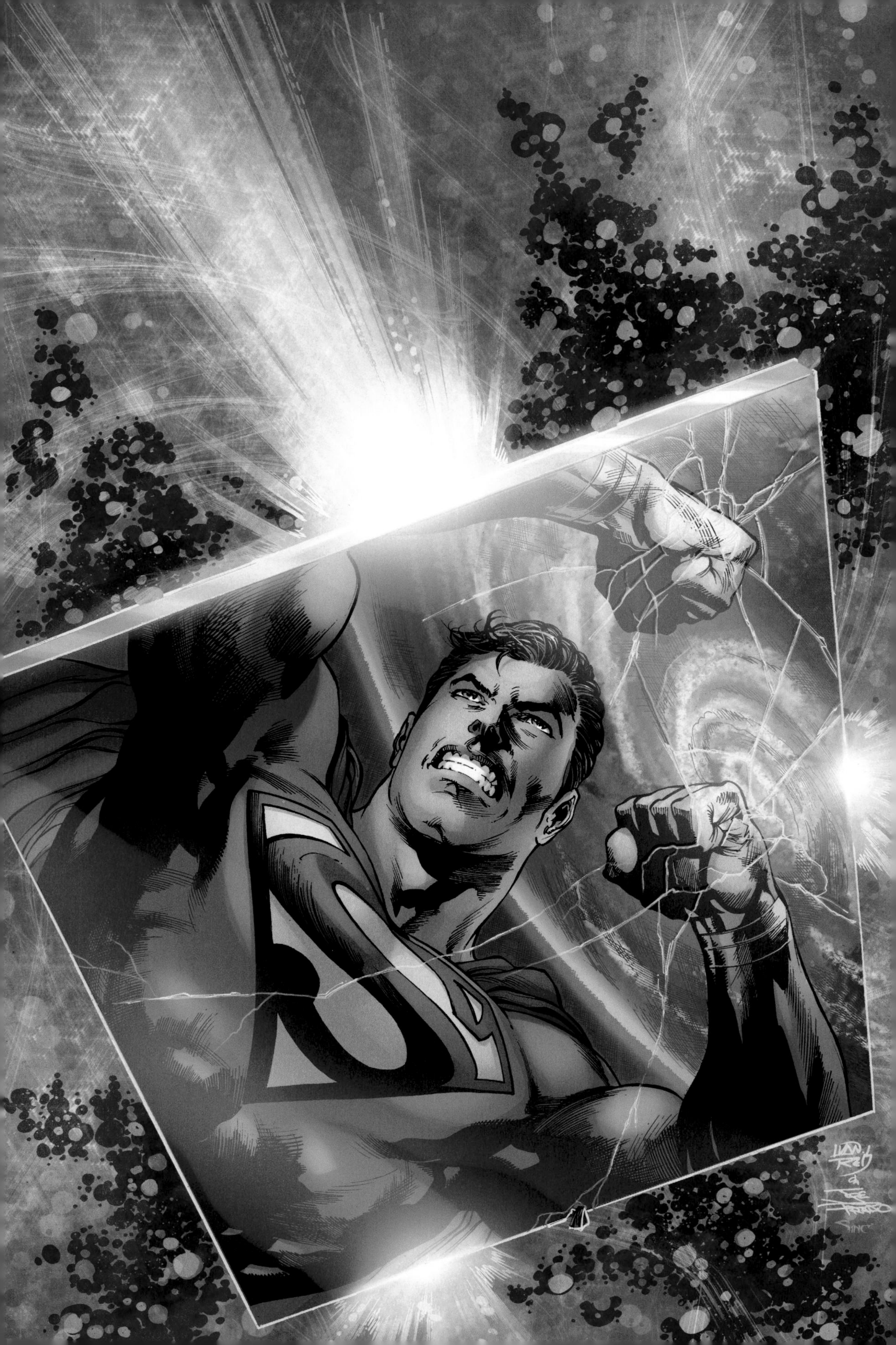

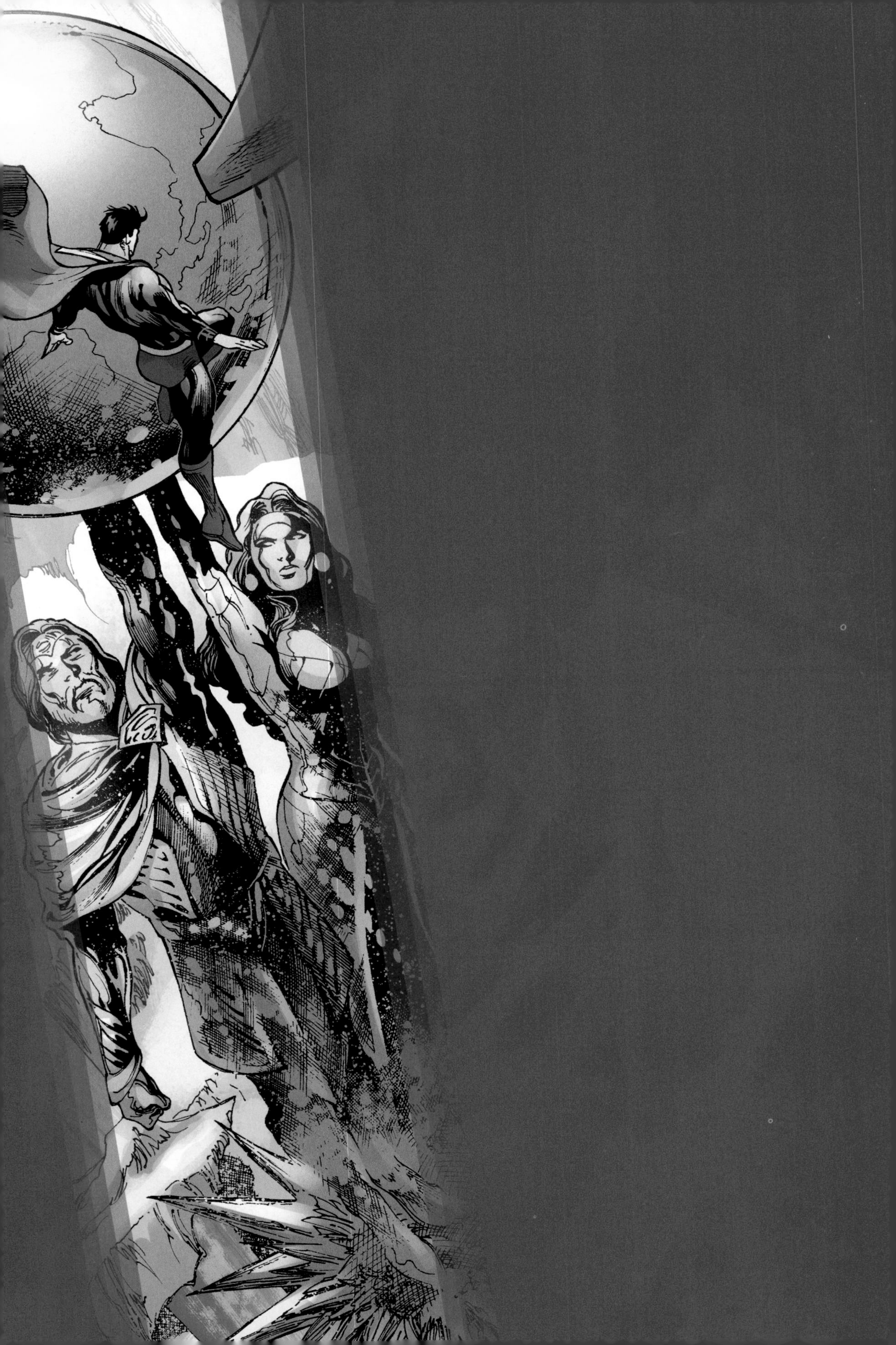

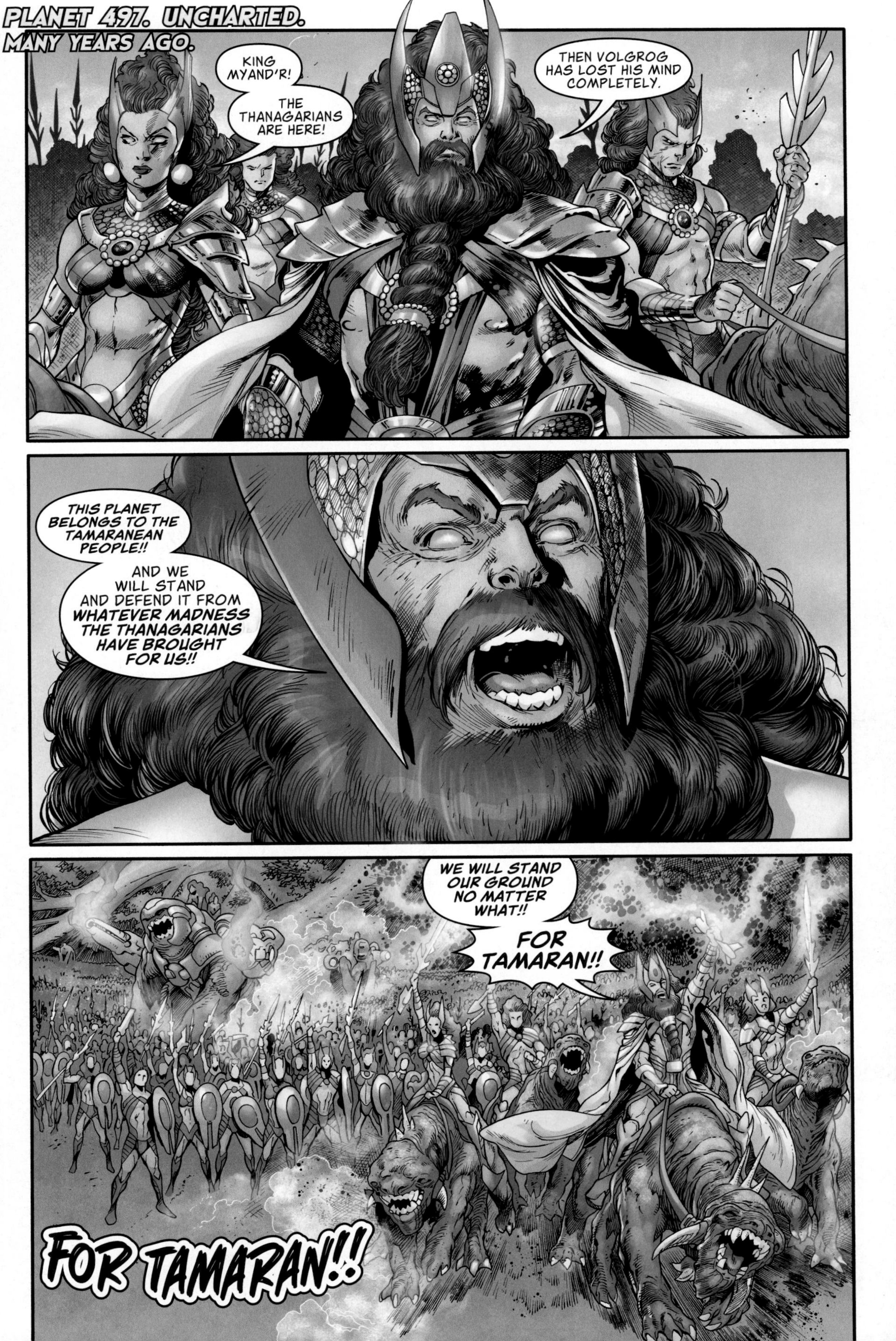
PLANET 497. UNCHARTED.
MANY YEARS AGO.
KING MYAND'R!
THE THANAGARIANS ARE HERE!
THEN VOLGROG HAS LOST HIS MIND COMPLETELY.
THIS PLANET BELONGS TO THE TAMARANEAN PEOPLE!!
AND WE WILL STAND AND DEFEND IT FROM WHATEVER MADNESS THE THANAGARIANS HAVE BROUGHT FOR US!!
WE WILL STAND OUR GROUND NO MATTER WHAT!!
FOR TAMARAN!!
FOR TAMARAN!!

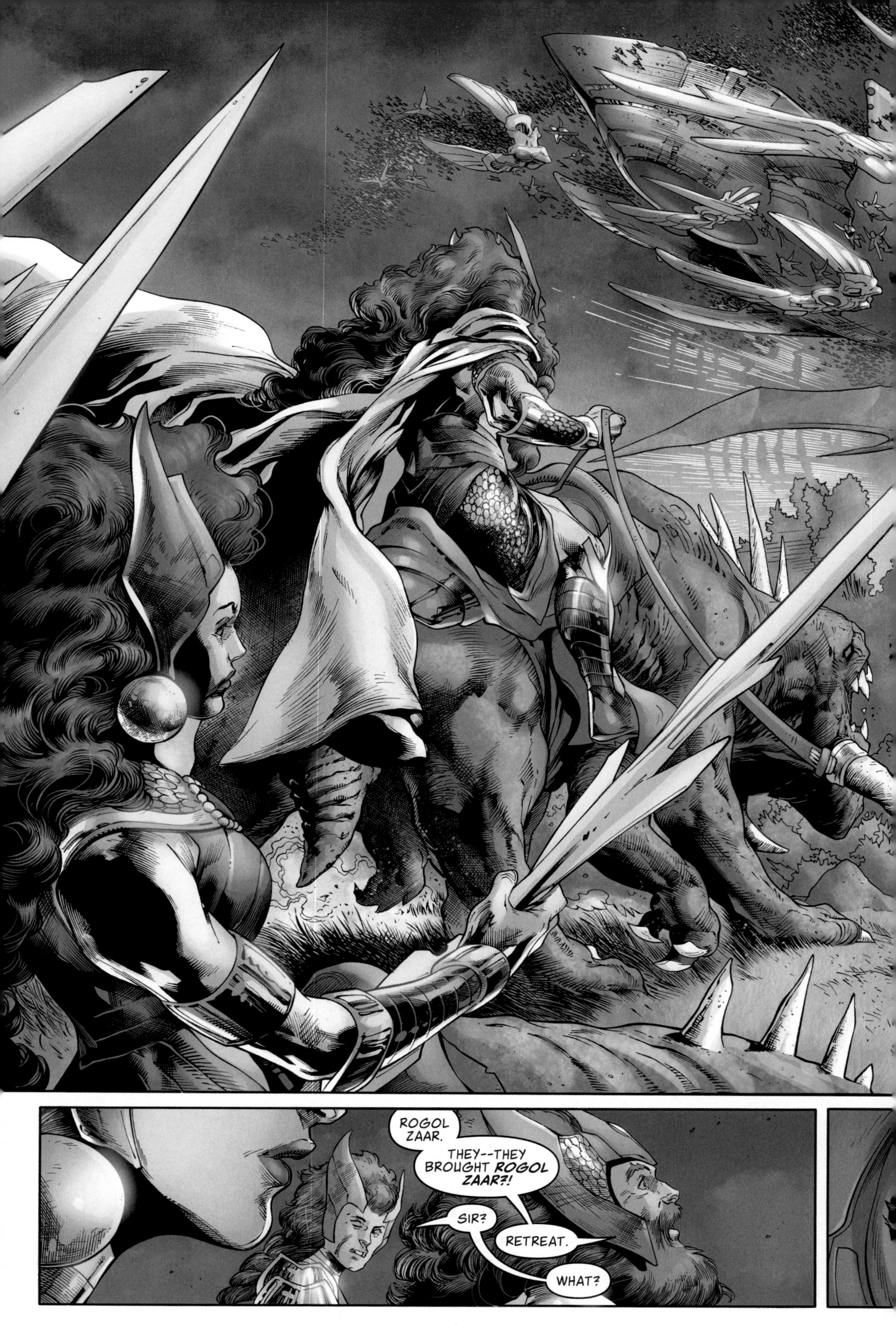
ROGOL ZAAR.
THEY--THEY BROUGHT ROGOL ZAAR?!
SIR?
RETREAT.
WHAT?

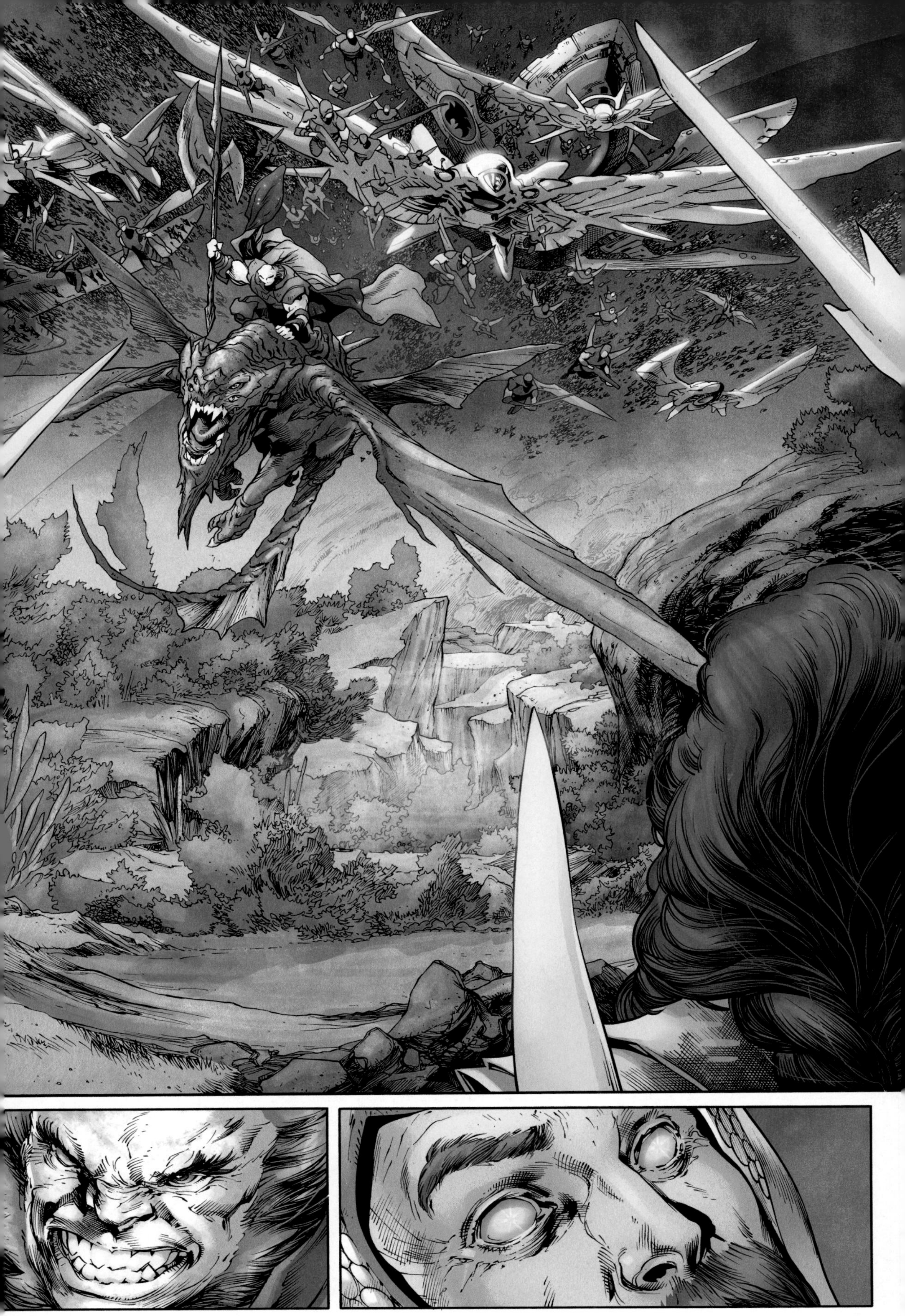

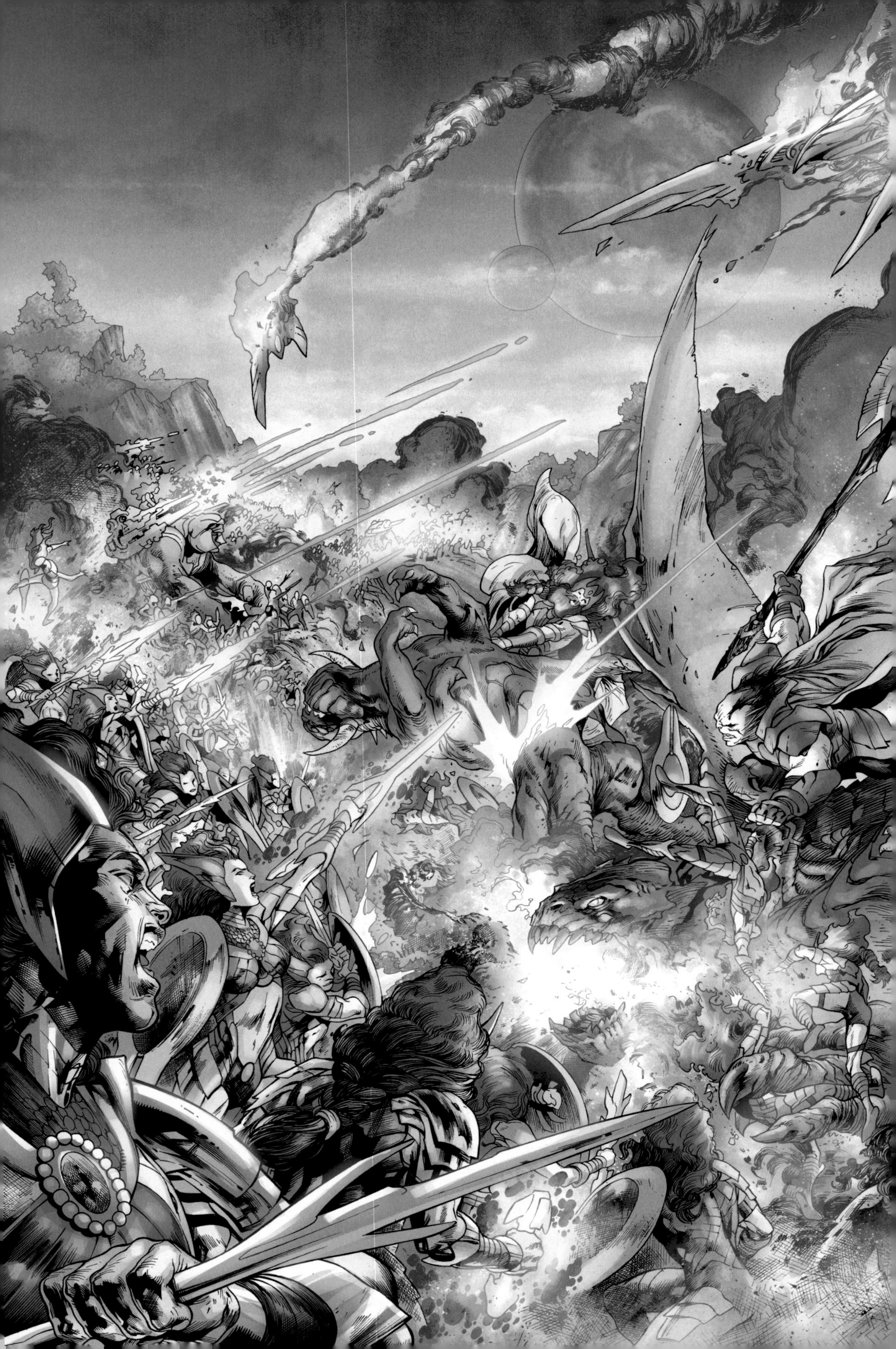

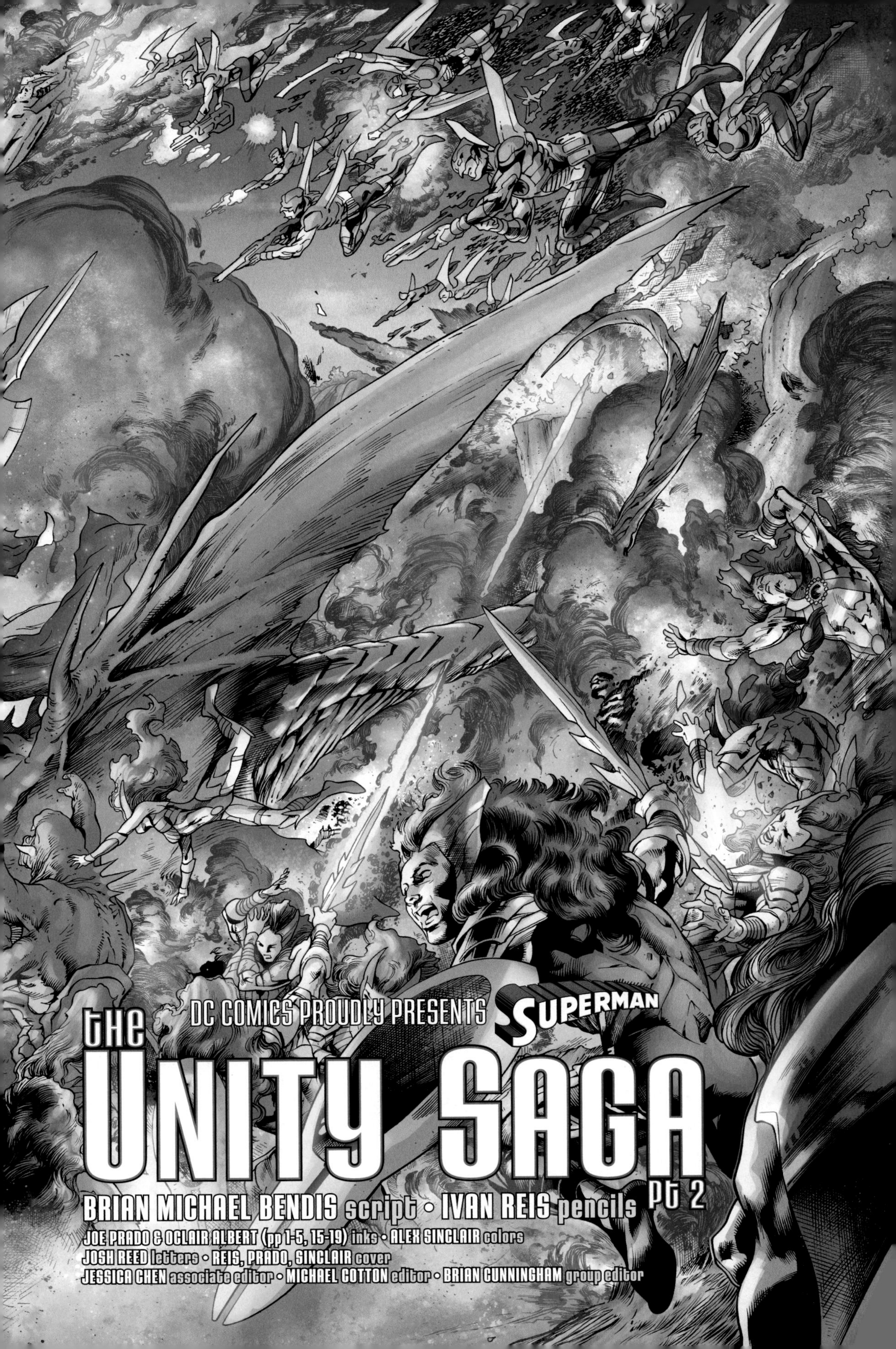
DC COMICS PROUDLY PRESENTS SUPERMAN
THE UNITY SAGA pt 2
BRIAN MICHAEL BENDIS script • IVAN REIS pencils
JOE PRADO & OCLAIR ALBERT (pp 1-5, 15-19) inks • ALEX SINCLAIR colors
JOSH REED letters • REIS, PRADO, SINCLAIR cover
JESSICA CHEN associate editor • MICHAEL COTTON editor • BRIAN CUNNINGHAM group editor

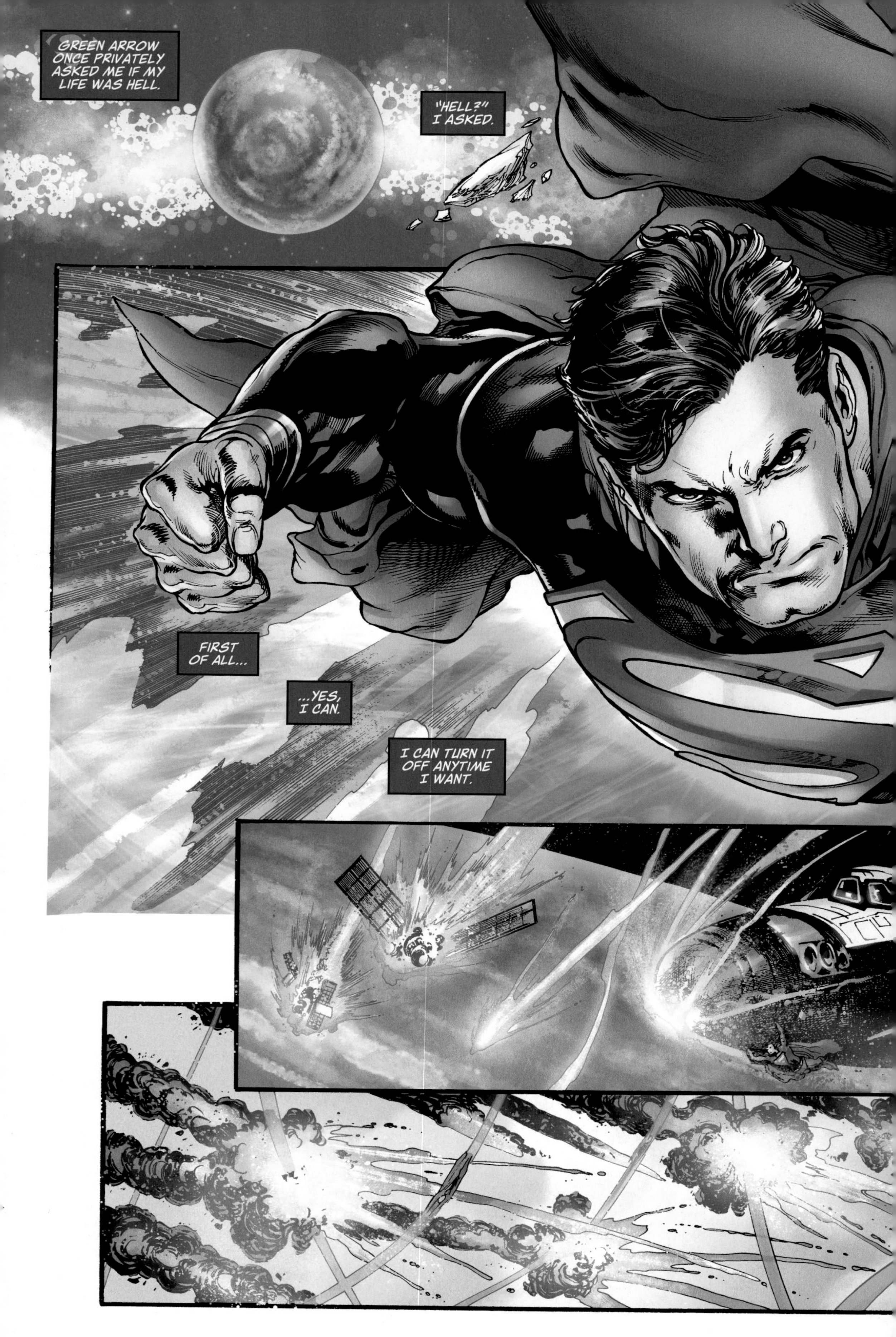
GREEN ARROW ONCE PRIVATELY ASKED ME IF MY LIFE WAS HELL.
"HELL?" I ASKED.
FIRST OF ALL...
...YES, I CAN.
I CAN TURN IT OFF ANYTIME I WANT.

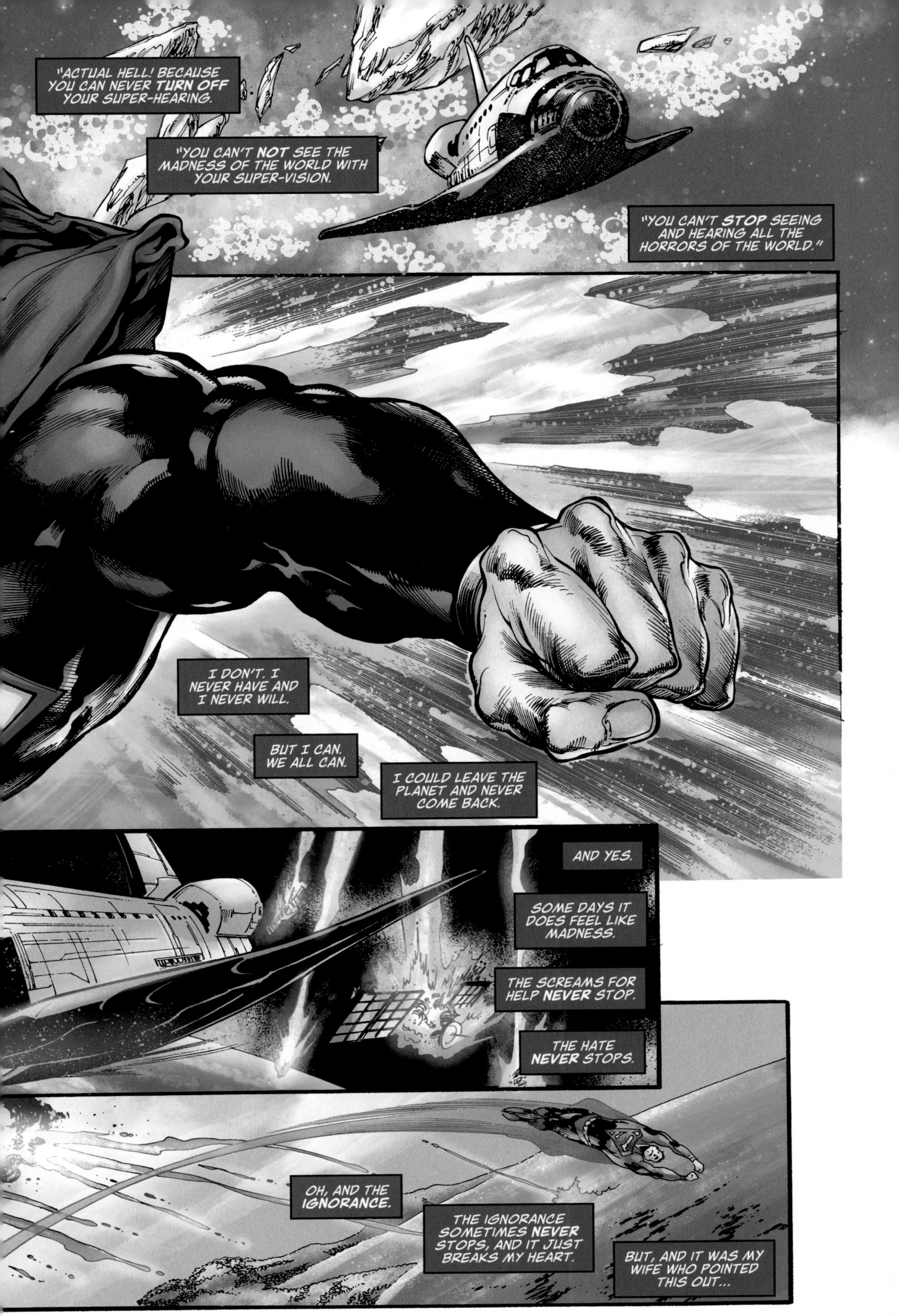
"ACTUAL HELL! BECAUSE YOU CAN NEVER TURN OFF YOUR SUPER-HEARING.
"YOU CAN'T NOT SEE THE MADNESS OF THE WORLD WITH YOUR SUPER-VISION.
"YOU CAN'T STOP SEEING AND HEARING ALL THE HORRORS OF THE WORLD."
I DON'T. I NEVER HAVE AND I NEVER WILL.
BUT I CAN. WE ALL CAN.
I COULD LEAVE THE PLANET AND NEVER COME BACK.
AND YES.
SOME DAYS IT DOES FEEL LIKE MADNESS.
THE SCREAMS FOR HELP NEVER STOP.
THE HATE NEVER STOPS.
OH, AND THE IGNORANCE.
THE IGNORANCE SOMETIMES NEVER STOPS, AND IT JUST BREAKS MY HEART.
BUT, AND IT WAS MY WIFE WHO POINTED THIS OUT...

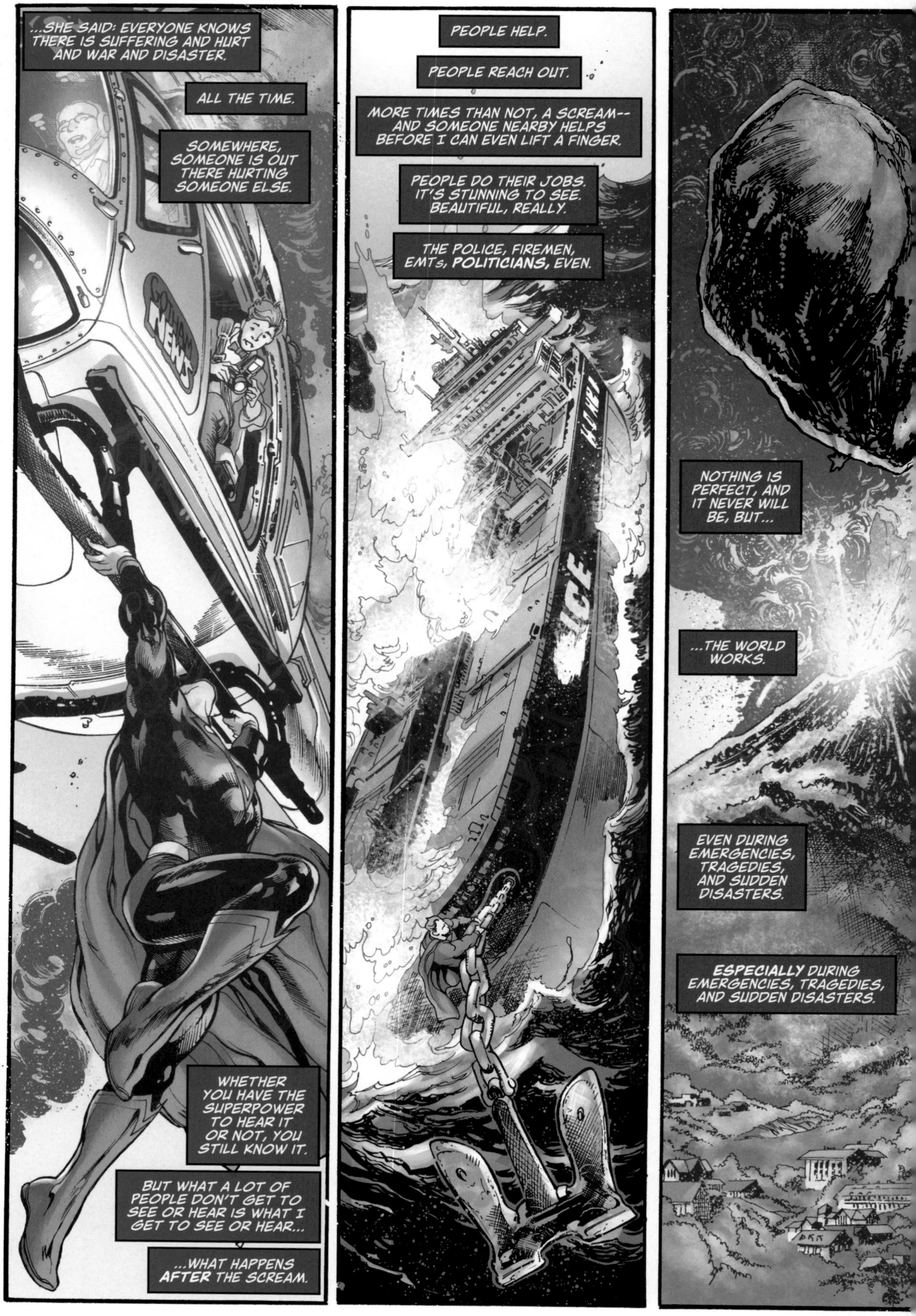
...SHE SAID: EVERYONE KNOWS THERE IS SUFFERING AND HURT AND WAR AND DISASTER.
ALL THE TIME.
SOMEWHERE, SOMEONE IS OUT THERE HURTING SOMEONE ELSE.
WHETHER YOU HAVE THE SUPERPOWER TO HEAR IT OR NOT, YOU STILL KNOW IT.
BUT WHAT A LOT OF PEOPLE DON'T GET TO SEE OR HEAR IS WHAT I GET TO SEE OR HEAR...
...WHAT HAPPENS **AFTER** THE SCREAM.
PEOPLE HELP.
PEOPLE REACH OUT.
MORE TIMES THAN NOT, A SCREAM-- AND SOMEONE NEARBY HELPS BEFORE I CAN EVEN LIFT A FINGER.
PEOPLE DO THEIR JOBS. IT'S STUNNING TO SEE. BEAUTIFUL, REALLY.
THE POLICE, FIREMEN, EMTs, **POLITICIANS,** EVEN.
NOTHING IS PERFECT, AND IT NEVER WILL BE, BUT...
...THE WORLD WORKS.
EVEN DURING EMERGENCIES, TRAGEDIES, AND SUDDEN DISASTERS.
ESPECIALLY DURING EMERGENCIES, TRAGEDIES, AND SUDDEN DISASTERS.

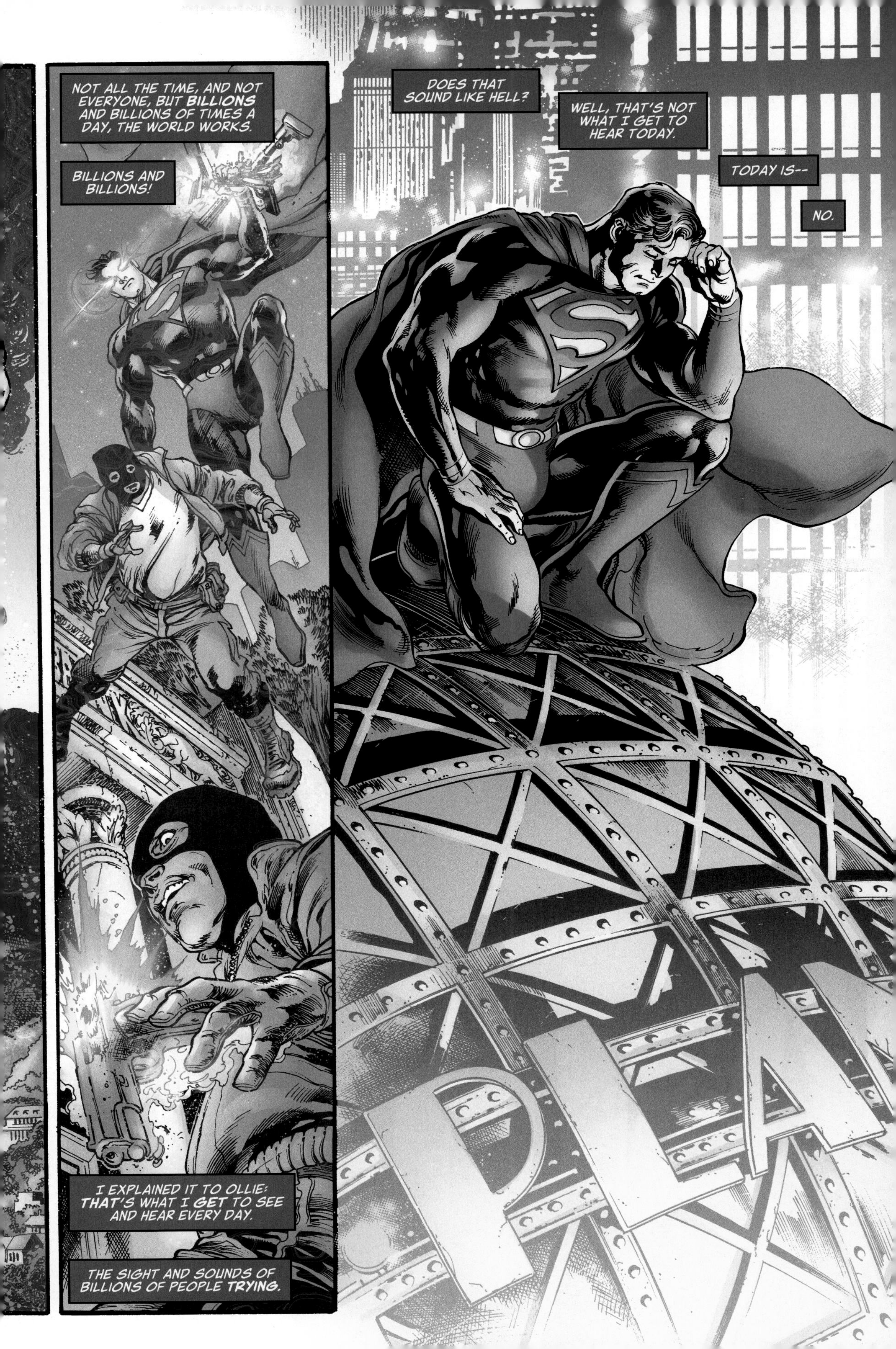
NOT ALL THE TIME, AND NOT EVERYONE, BUT BILLIONS AND BILLIONS OF TIMES A DAY, THE WORLD WORKS.
BILLIONS AND BILLIONS!
I EXPLAINED IT TO OLLIE: THAT'S WHAT I GET TO SEE AND HEAR EVERY DAY.
THE SIGHT AND SOUNDS OF BILLIONS OF PEOPLE TRYING.
DOES THAT SOUND LIKE HELL?
WELL, THAT'S NOT WHAT I GET TO HEAR TODAY.
TODAY IS--
NO.

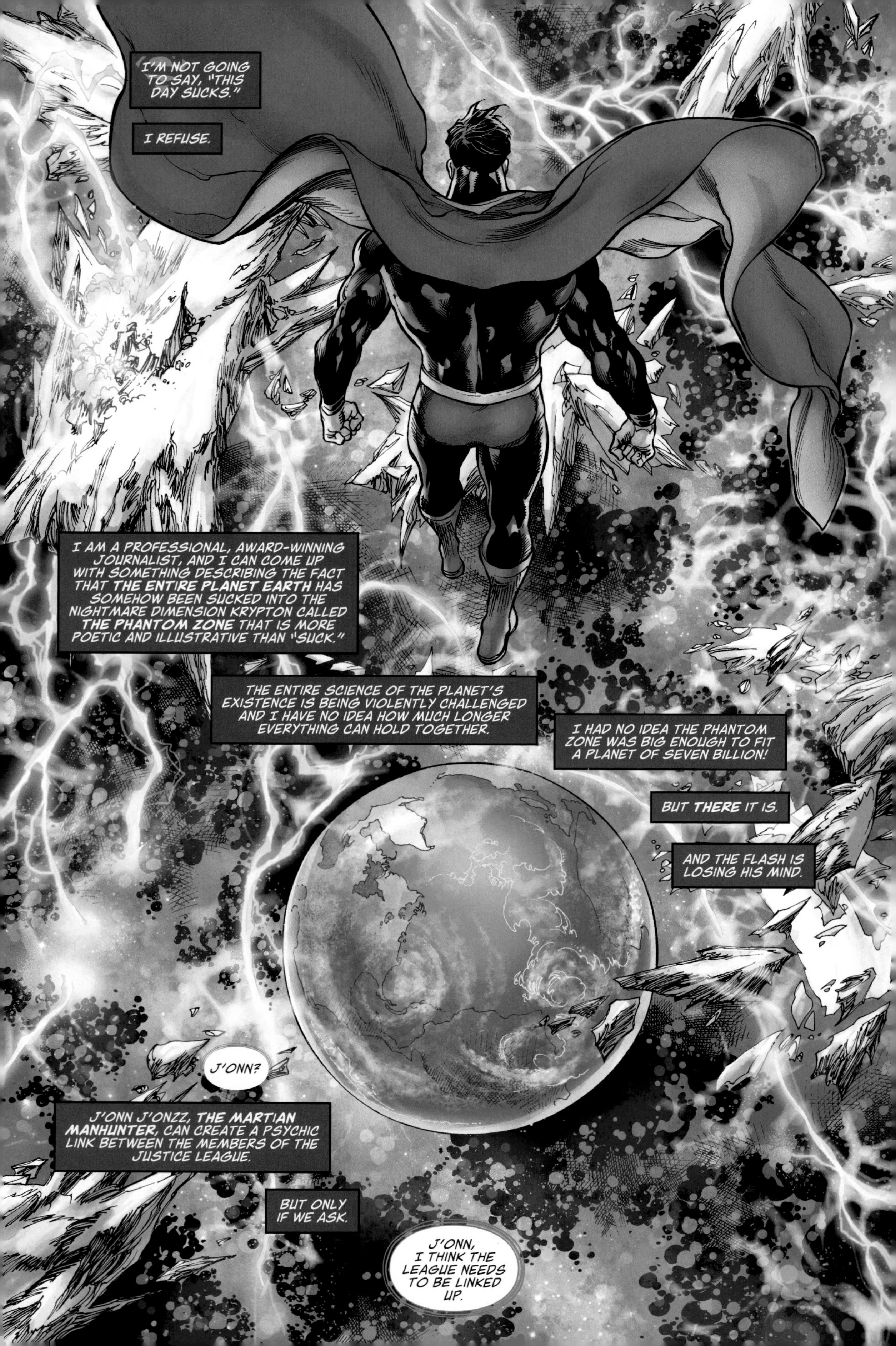
I'M NOT GOING TO SAY, "THIS DAY SUCKS."
I REFUSE.
I AM A PROFESSIONAL, AWARD-WINNING JOURNALIST, AND I CAN COME UP WITH SOMETHING DESCRIBING THE FACT THAT THE ENTIRE PLANET EARTH HAS SOMEHOW BEEN SUCKED INTO THE NIGHTMARE DIMENSION KRYPTON CALLED THE PHANTOM ZONE THAT IS MORE POETIC AND ILLUSTRATIVE THAN "SUCK."
THE ENTIRE SCIENCE OF THE PLANET'S EXISTENCE IS BEING VIOLENTLY CHALLENGED AND I HAVE NO IDEA HOW MUCH LONGER EVERYTHING CAN HOLD TOGETHER.
I HAD NO IDEA THE PHANTOM ZONE WAS BIG ENOUGH TO FIT A PLANET OF SEVEN BILLION!
BUT THERE IT IS.
AND THE FLASH IS LOSING HIS MIND.
J'ONN?
J'ONN J'ONZZ, THE MARTIAN MANHUNTER, CAN CREATE A PSYCHIC LINK BETWEEN THE MEMBERS OF THE JUSTICE LEAGUE.
BUT ONLY IF WE ASK.
J'ONN, I THINK THE LEAGUE NEEDS TO BE LINKED UP.

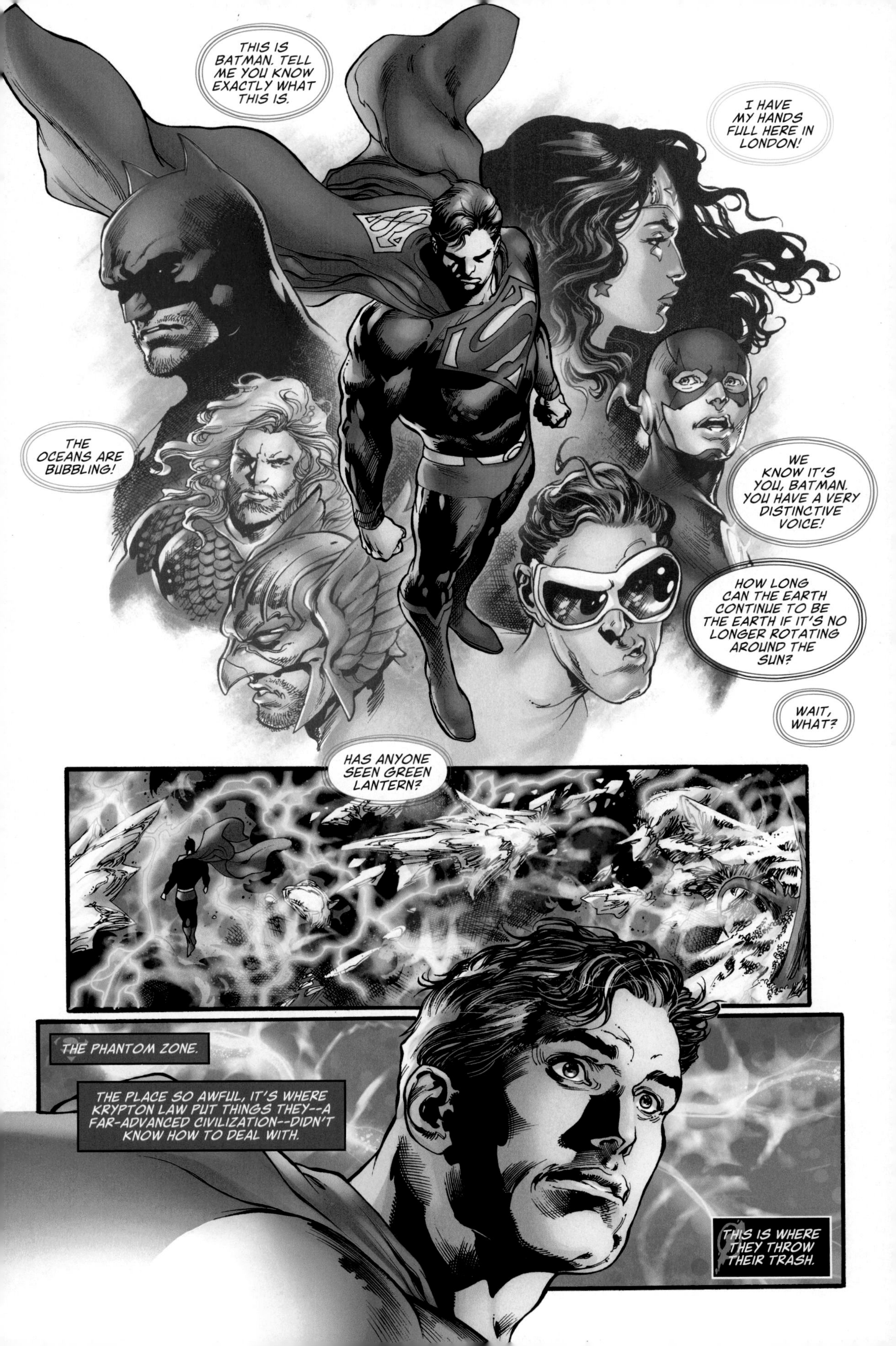
THIS IS BATMAN. TELL ME YOU KNOW EXACTLY WHAT THIS IS.
I HAVE MY HANDS FULL HERE IN LONDON!
THE OCEANS ARE BUBBLING!
WE KNOW IT'S YOU, BATMAN. YOU HAVE A VERY DISTINCTIVE VOICE!
HOW LONG CAN THE EARTH CONTINUE TO BE THE EARTH IF IT'S NO LONGER ROTATING AROUND THE SUN?
WAIT, WHAT?
HAS ANYONE SEEN GREEN LANTERN?
THE PHANTOM ZONE.
THE PLACE SO AWFUL, IT'S WHERE KRYPTON LAW PUT THINGS THEY--A FAR-ADVANCED CIVILIZATION--DIDN'T KNOW HOW TO DEAL WITH.
THIS IS WHERE THEY THROW THEIR TRASH.

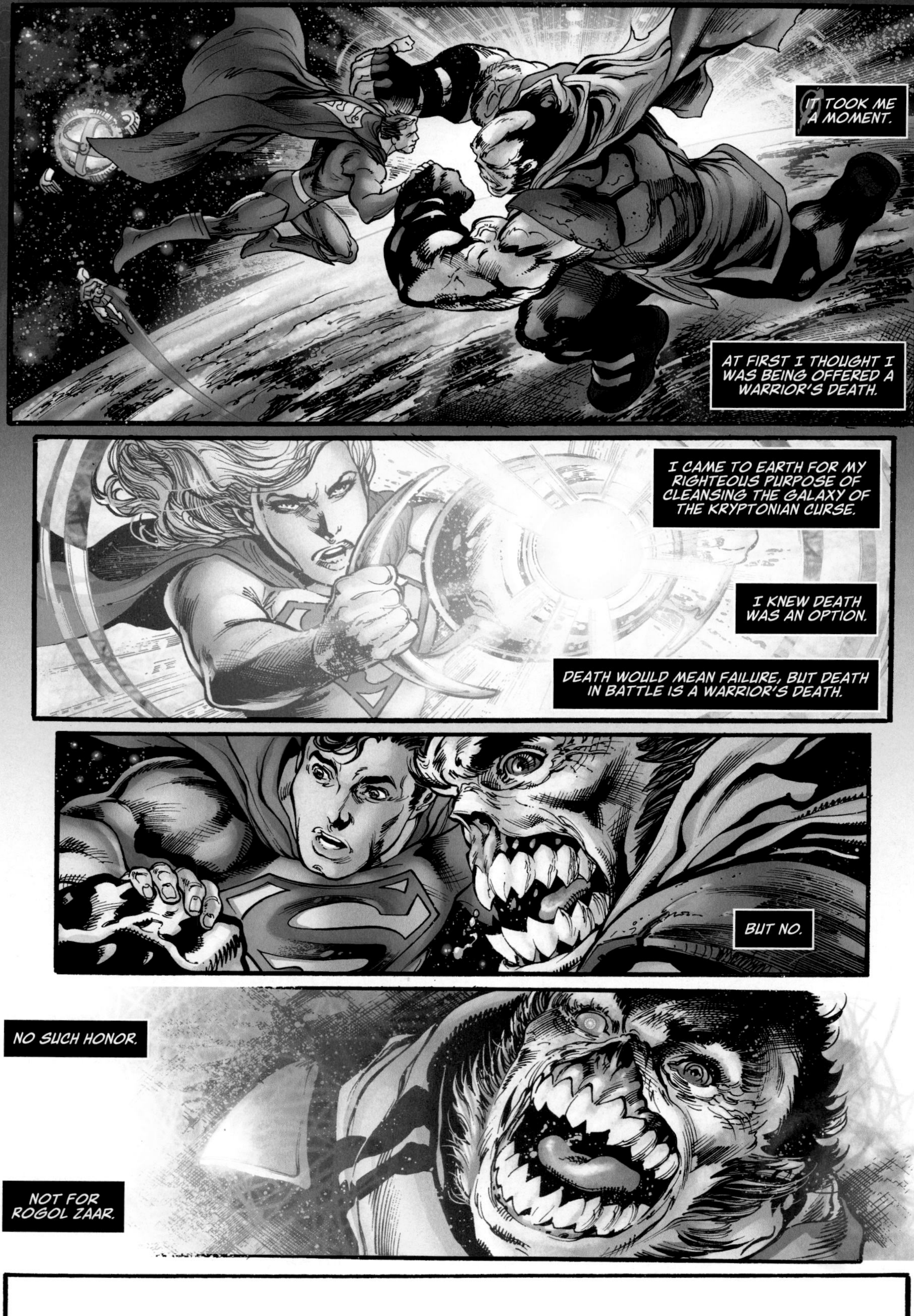
IT TOOK ME A MOMENT.
AT FIRST I THOUGHT I WAS BEING OFFERED A WARRIOR'S DEATH.
I CAME TO EARTH FOR MY RIGHTEOUS PURPOSE OF CLEANSING THE GALAXY OF THE KRYPTONIAN CURSE.
I KNEW DEATH WAS AN OPTION.
DEATH WOULD MEAN FAILURE, BUT DEATH IN BATTLE IS A WARRIOR'S DEATH.
BUT NO.
NO SUCH HONOR.
NOT FOR ROGOL ZAAR.
THIS IS NOT THE FIRST TIME THE WINDS OF WAR HAD THROWN ME FROM BATTLE...

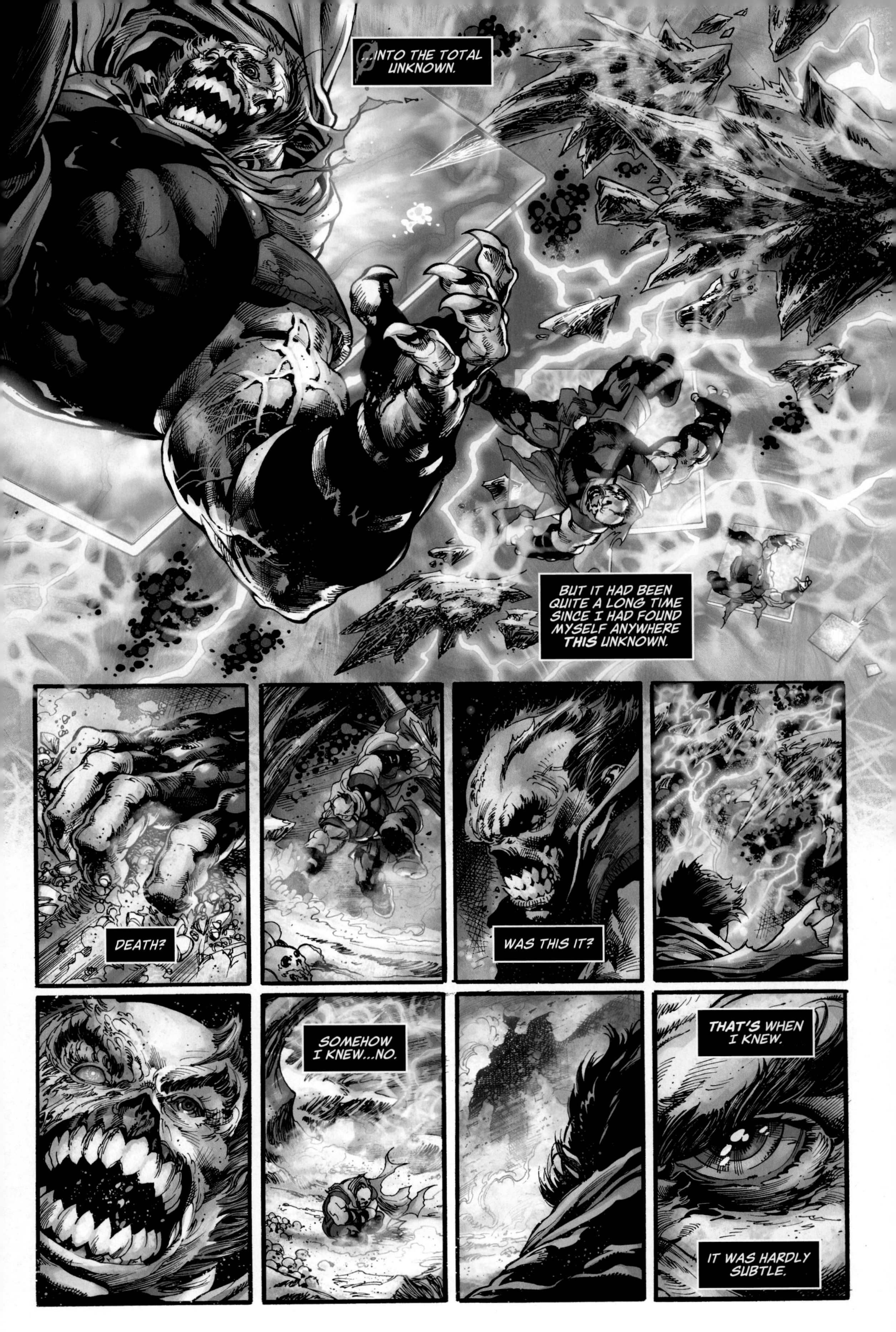
...INTO THE TOTAL UNKNOWN.
BUT IT HAD BEEN QUITE A LONG TIME SINCE I HAD FOUND MYSELF ANYWHERE THIS UNKNOWN.
DEATH?
WAS THIS IT?
SOMEHOW I KNEW...NO.
THAT'S WHEN I KNEW.
IT WAS HARDLY SUBTLE.

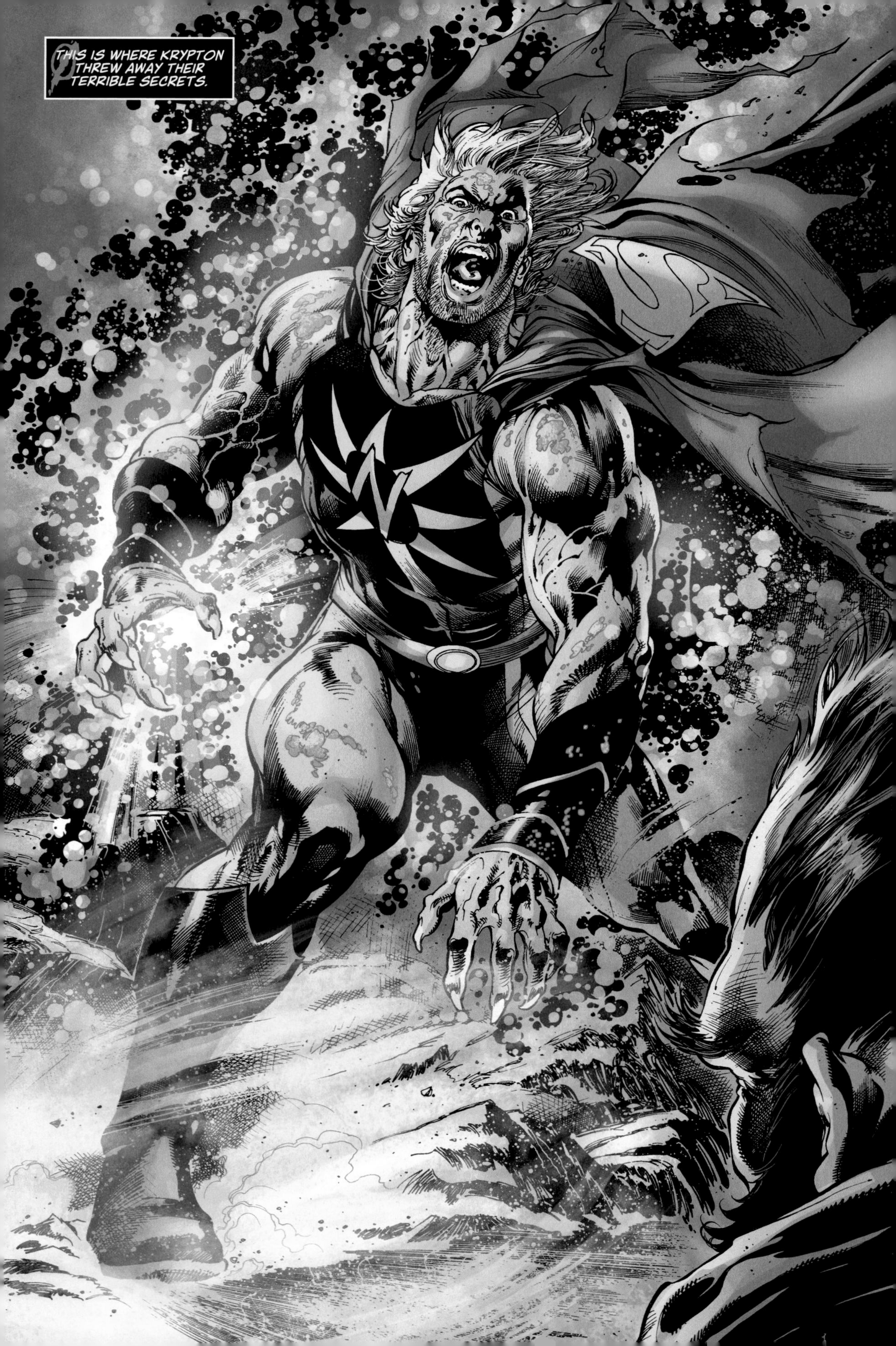
THIS IS WHERE KRYPTON THREW AWAY THEIR TERRIBLE SECRETS.

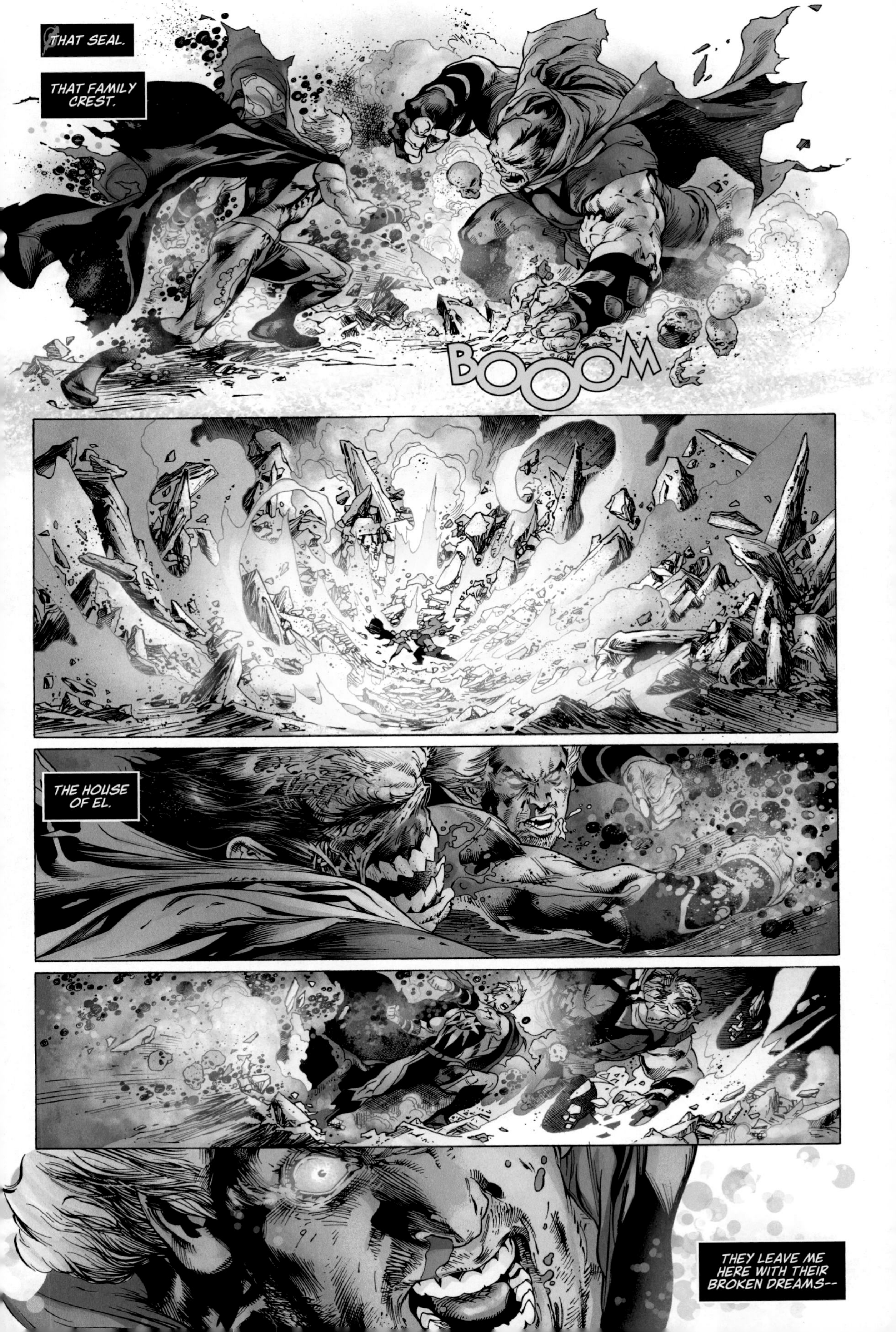
THAT SEAL.
THAT FAMILY CREST.
BOOOM
THE HOUSE OF EL.
THEY LEAVE ME HERE WITH THEIR BROKEN DREAMS--

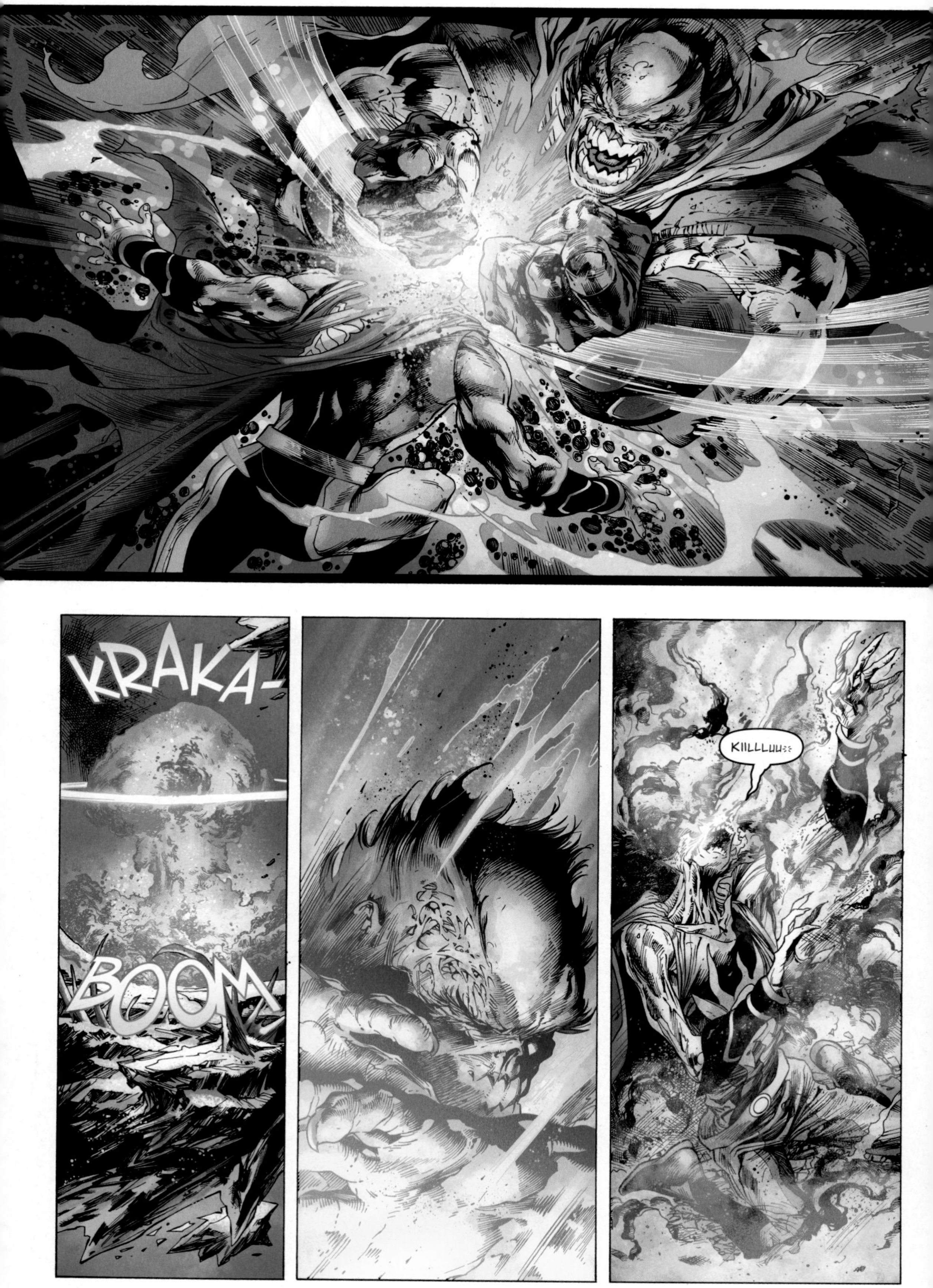
KRAKA-
BOOM
KIILLLUU

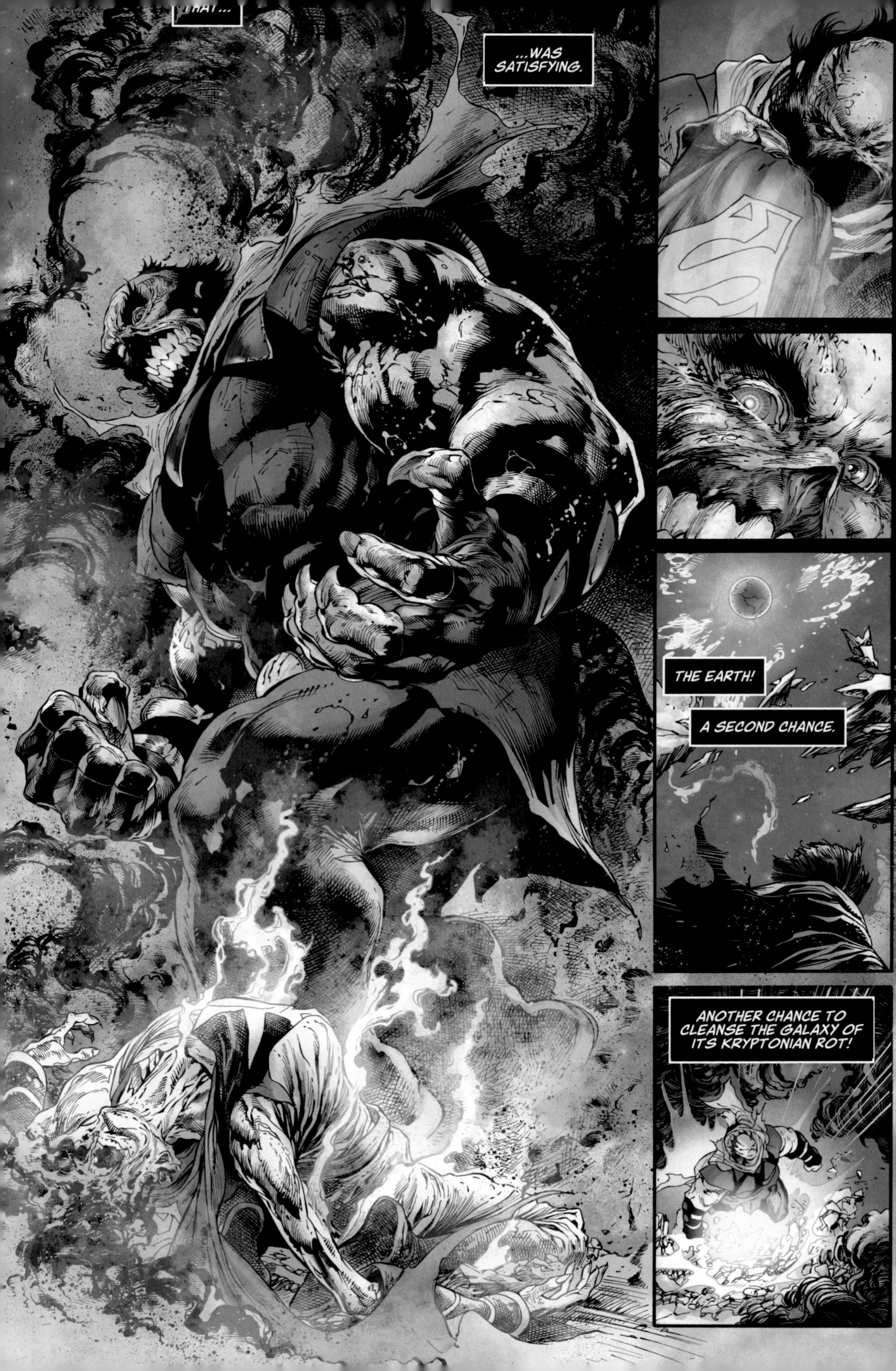
THAT...
...WAS SATISFYING.
THE EARTH!
A SECOND CHANCE.
ANOTHER CHANCE TO CLEANSE THE GALAXY OF ITS KRYPTONIAN ROT!

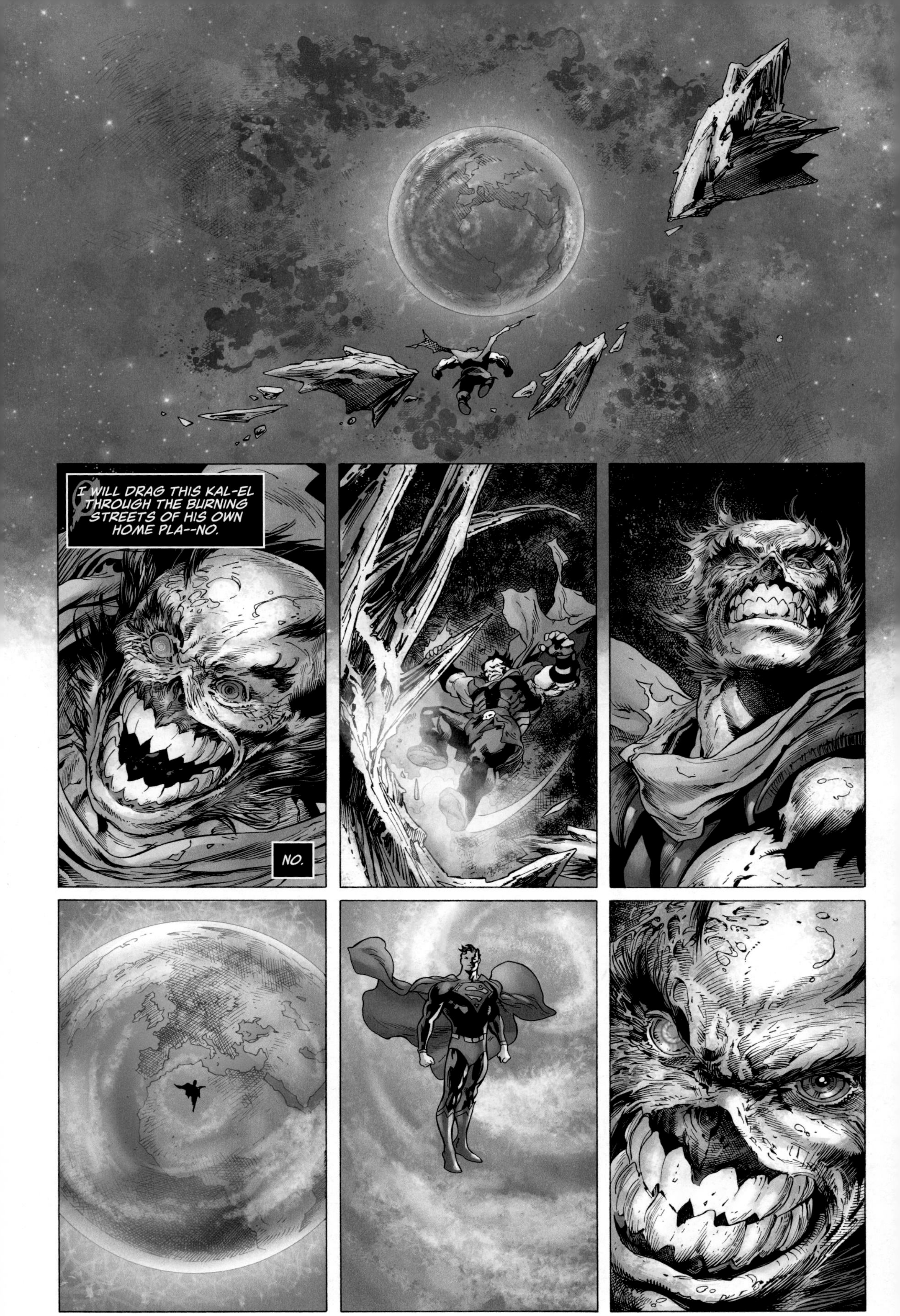
I WILL DRAG THIS KAL-EL THROUGH THE BURNING STREETS OF HIS OWN HOME PLA--NO.
NO.

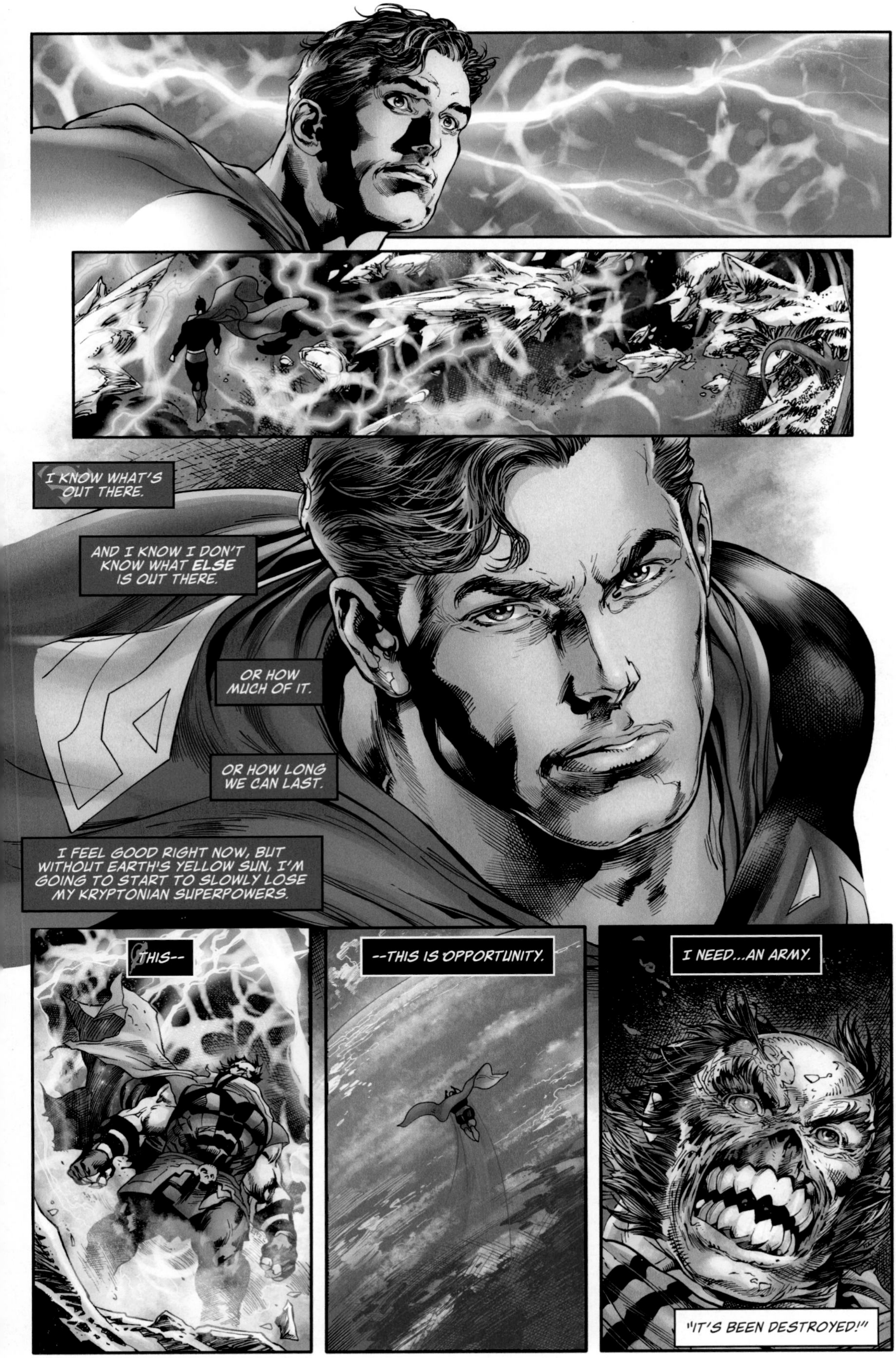
I KNOW WHAT'S OUT THERE.
AND I KNOW I DON'T KNOW WHAT ELSE IS OUT THERE.
OR HOW MUCH OF IT.
OR HOW LONG WE CAN LAST.
I FEEL GOOD RIGHT NOW, BUT WITHOUT EARTH'S YELLOW SUN, I'M GOING TO START TO SLOWLY LOSE MY KRYPTONIAN SUPERPOWERS.
THIS--
--THIS IS OPPORTUNITY.
I NEED...AN ARMY.
"IT'S BEEN DESTROYED!"

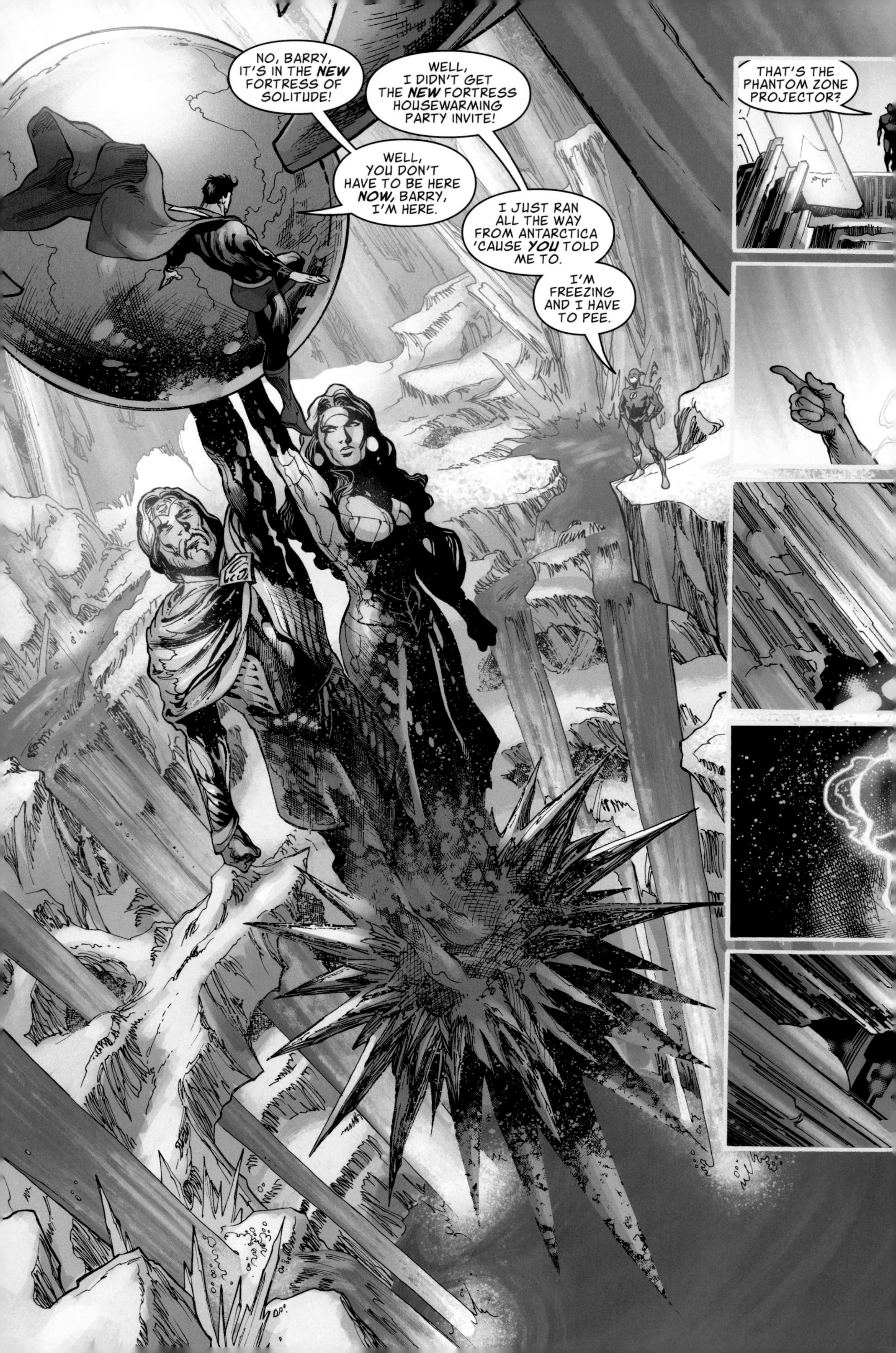

NO, BARRY, IT'S IN THE NEW FORTRESS OF SOLITUDE!
WELL, I DIDN'T GET THE NEW FORTRESS HOUSEWARMING PARTY INVITE!
WELL, YOU DON'T HAVE TO BE HERE NOW, BARRY, I'M HERE.
I JUST RAN ALL THE WAY FROM ANTARCTICA 'CAUSE YOU TOLD ME TO.
I'M FREEZING AND I HAVE TO PEE.
THAT'S THE PHANTOM ZONE PROJECTOR?

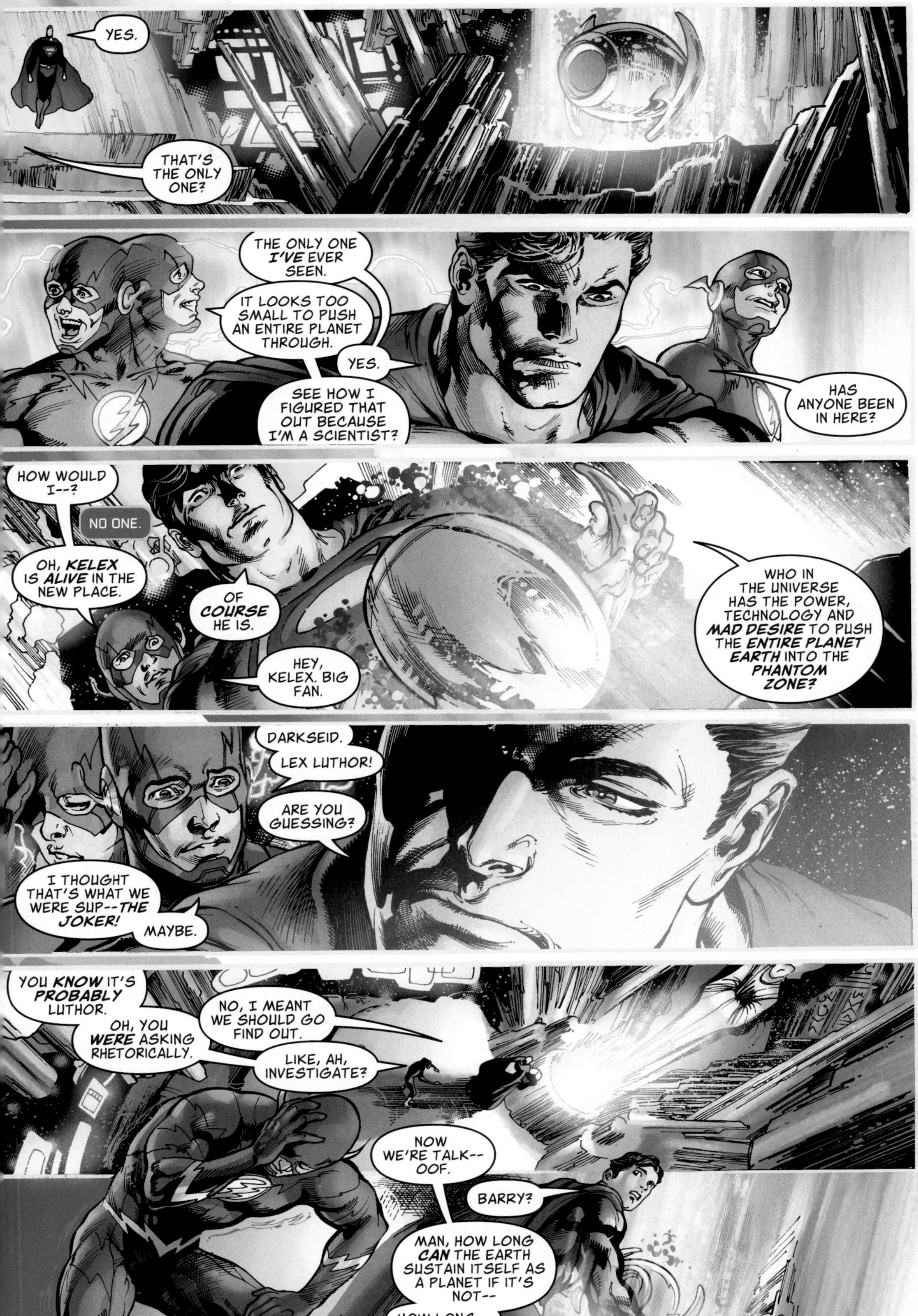
YES.
THAT'S THE ONLY ONE?
THE ONLY ONE I'VE EVER SEEN.
IT LOOKS TOO SMALL TO PUSH AN ENTIRE PLANET THROUGH.
YES.
SEE HOW I FIGURED THAT OUT BECAUSE I'M A SCIENTIST?
HAS ANYONE BEEN IN HERE?
HOW WOULD I--?
NO ONE.
OH, KELEX IS ALIVE IN THE NEW PLACE.
OF COURSE HE IS.
HEY, KELEX. BIG FAN.
WHO IN THE UNIVERSE HAS THE POWER, TECHNOLOGY AND MAD DESIRE TO PUSH THE ENTIRE PLANET EARTH INTO THE PHANTOM ZONE?
DARKSEID.
LEX LUTHOR!
ARE YOU GUESSING?
I THOUGHT THAT'S WHAT WE WERE SUP--THE JOKER!
MAYBE.
YOU KNOW IT'S PROBABLY LUTHOR.
OH, YOU WERE ASKING RHETORICALLY.
NO, I MEANT WE SHOULD GO FIND OUT.
LIKE, AH, INVESTIGATE?
NOW WE'RE TALK-- OOF.
BARRY?
MAN, HOW LONG CAN THE EARTH SUSTAIN ITSELF AS A PLANET IF IT'S NOT--
HOW LONG...
...TILL...

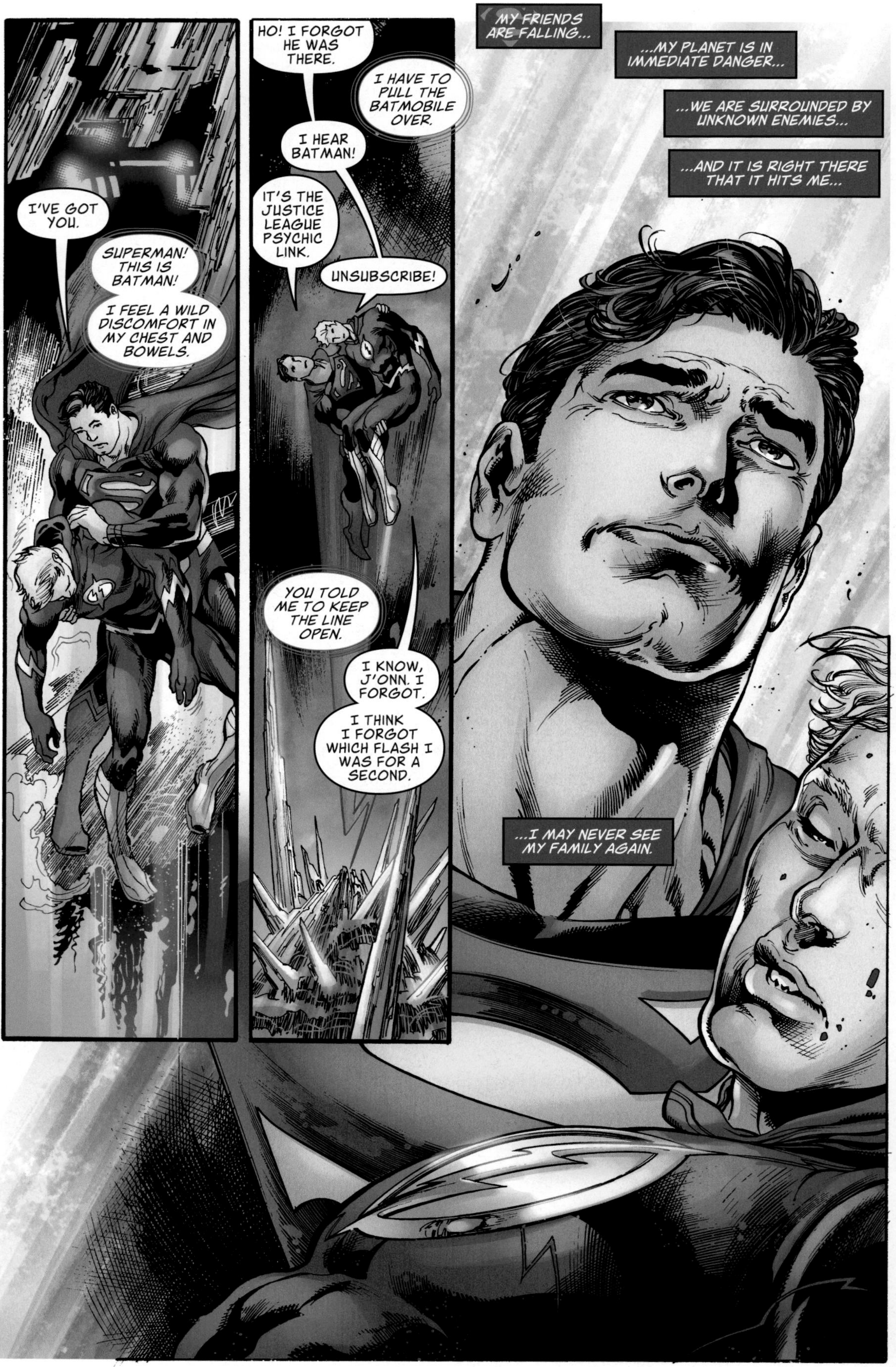
I'VE GOT YOU.
SUPERMAN! THIS IS BATMAN!
I FEEL A WILD DISCOMFORT IN MY CHEST AND BOWELS.
HO! I FORGOT HE WAS THERE.
I HAVE TO PULL THE BATMOBILE OVER.
I HEAR BATMAN!
IT'S THE JUSTICE LEAGUE PSYCHIC LINK.
UNSUBSCRIBE!
YOU TOLD ME TO KEEP THE LINE OPEN.
I KNOW, J'ONN. I FORGOT.
I THINK I FORGOT WHICH FLASH I WAS FOR A SECOND.
MY FRIENDS ARE FALLING...
...MY PLANET IS IN IMMEDIATE DANGER...
...WE ARE SURROUNDED BY UNKNOWN ENEMIES...
...AND IT IS RIGHT THERE THAT IT HITS ME...
...I MAY NEVER SEE MY FAMILY AGAIN.

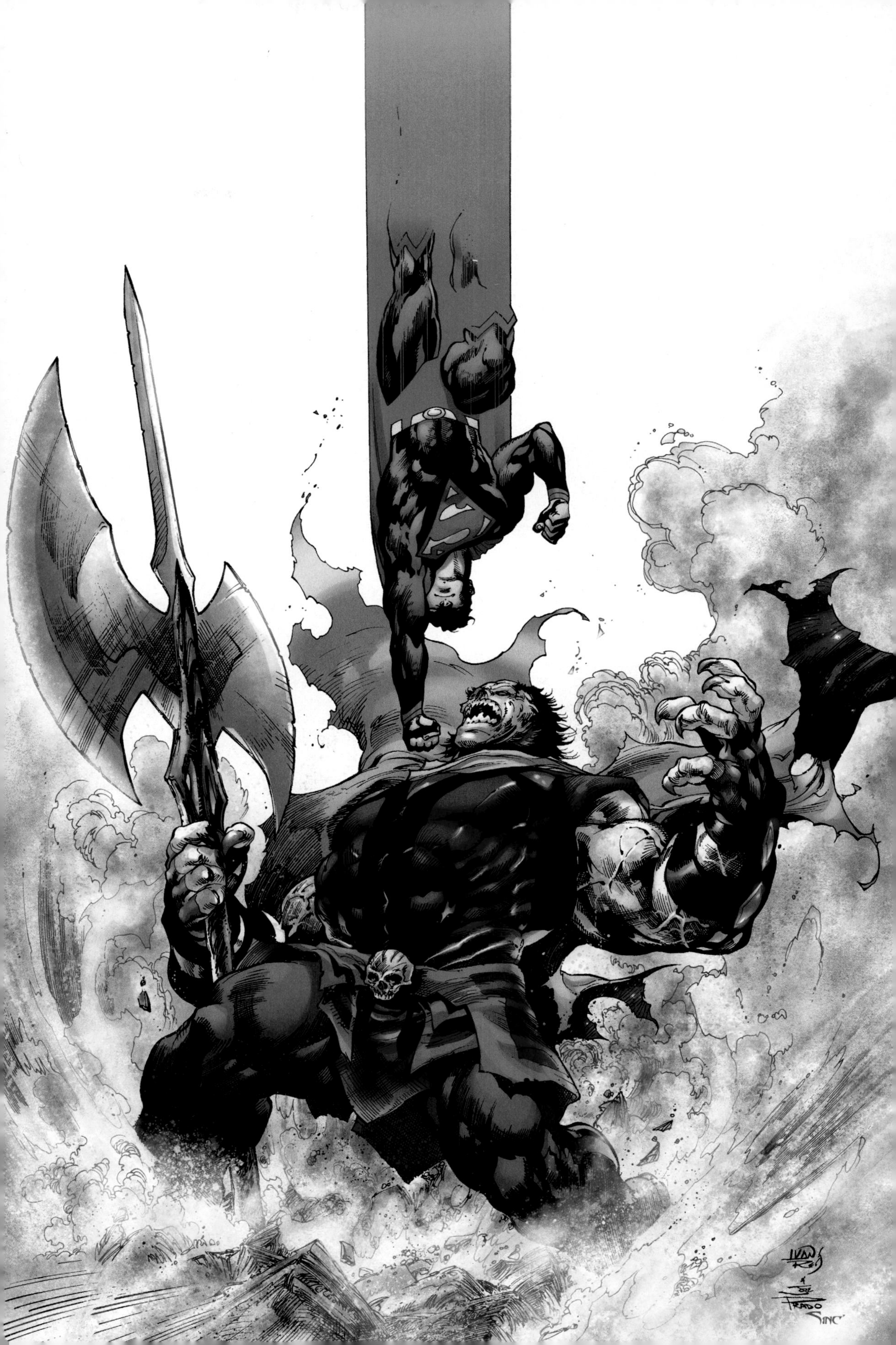

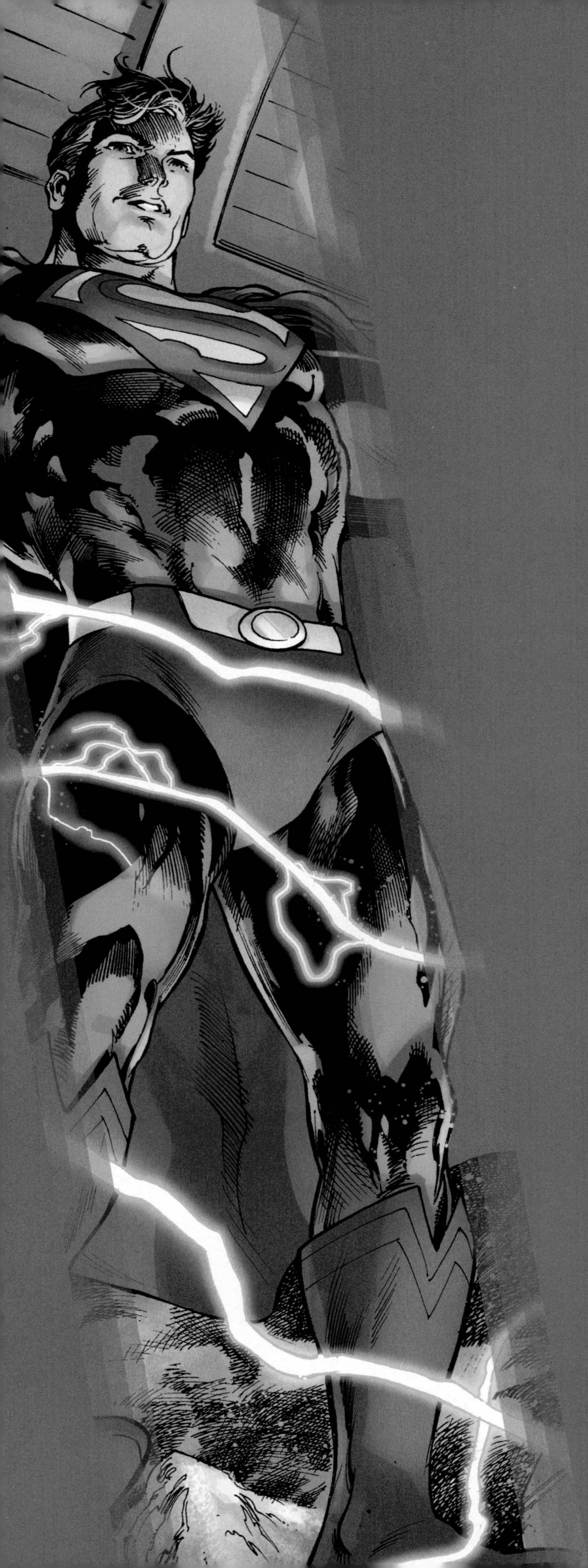

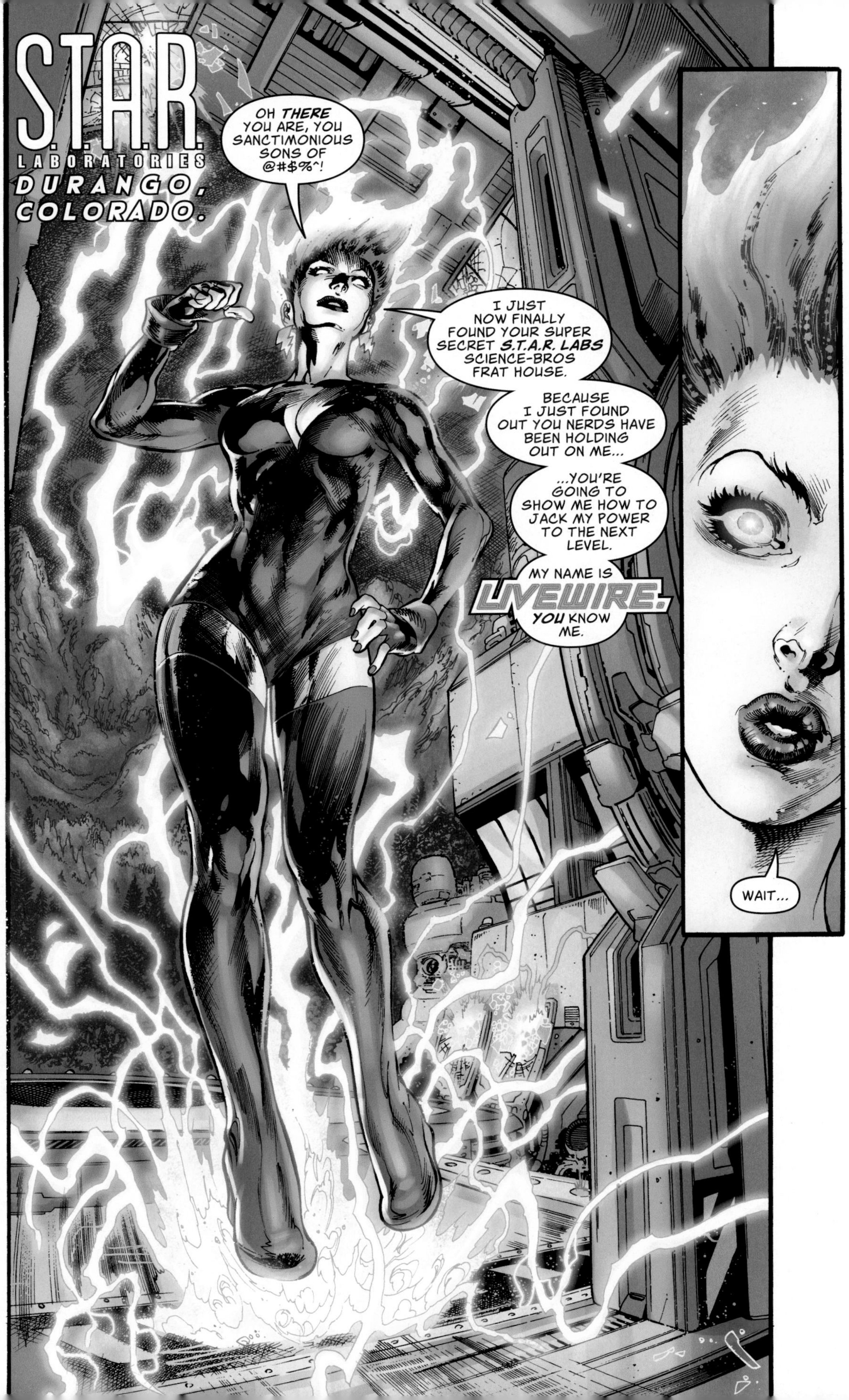
S.T.A.R. LABORATORIES DURANGO, COLORADO.
OH THERE YOU ARE, YOU SANCTIMONIOUS SONS OF @#$%^!
I JUST NOW FINALLY FOUND YOUR SUPER SECRET S.T.A.R. LABS SCIENCE-BROS FRAT HOUSE.
BECAUSE I JUST FOUND OUT YOU NERDS HAVE BEEN HOLDING OUT ON ME...
...YOU'RE GOING TO SHOW ME HOW TO JACK MY POWER TO THE NEXT LEVEL.
MY NAME IS LIVEWIRE. YOU KNOW ME.
WAIT...

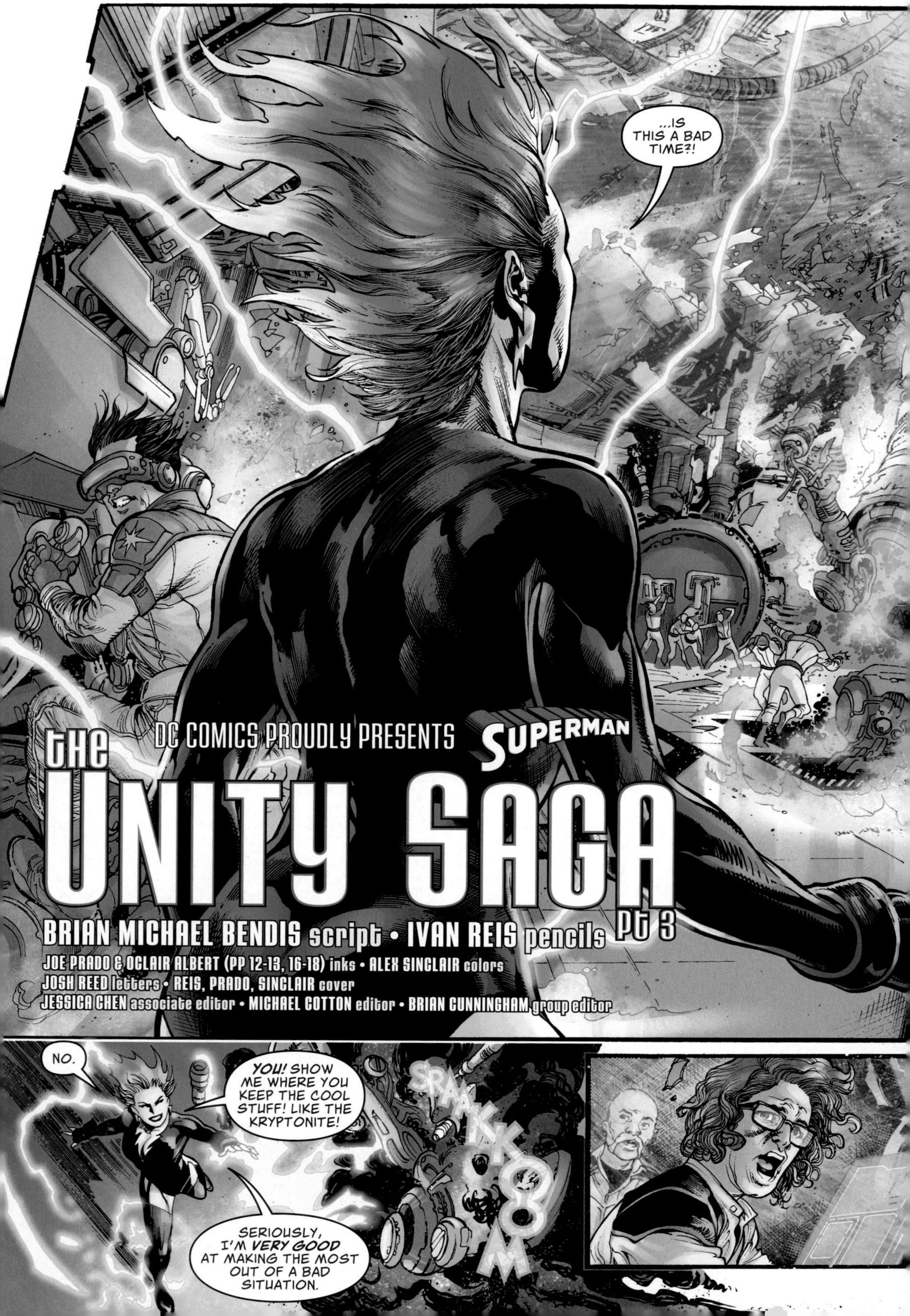
...IS THIS A BAD TIME?!
DC COMICS PROUDLY PRESENTS SUPERMAN
THE UNITY SAGA PT 3
BRIAN MICHAEL BENDIS script • IVAN REIS pencils
JOE PRADO & OCLAIR ALBERT (PP 12-13, 16-18) inks • ALEX SINCLAIR colors
JOSH REED letters • REIS, PRADO, SINCLAIR cover
JESSICA CHEN associate editor • MICHAEL COTTON editor • BRIAN CUNNINGHAM group editor
NO.
YOU! SHOW ME WHERE YOU KEEP THE COOL STUFF! LIKE THE KRYPTONITE!
SRAAKKOOM
SERIOUSLY, I'M VERY GOOD AT MAKING THE MOST OUT OF A BAD SITUATION.

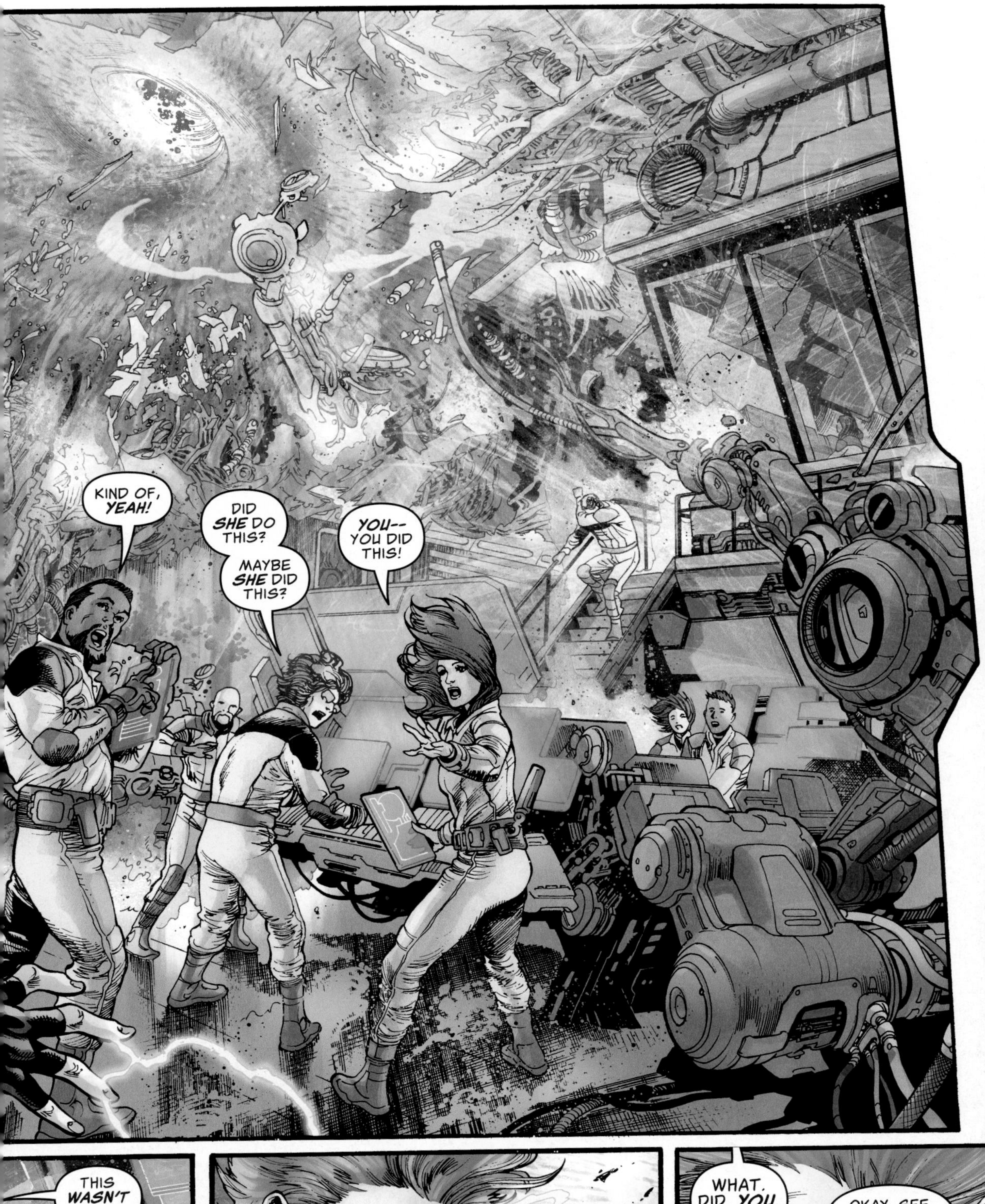
KIND OF, YEAH!
DID SHE DO THIS?
MAYBE SHE DID THIS?
YOU-- YOU DID THIS!

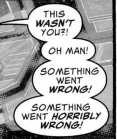

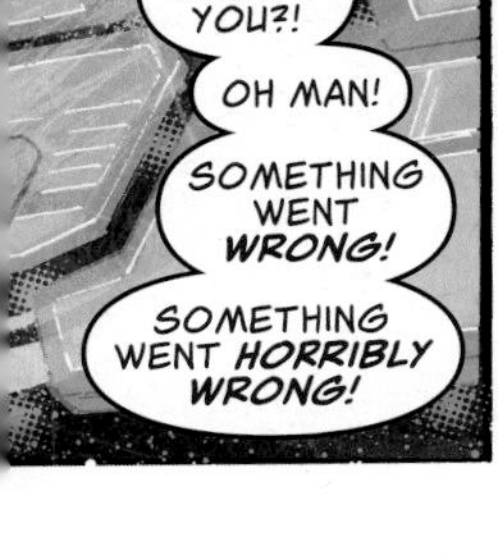
THIS WASN'T YOU?!
OH MAN!
SOMETHING WENT WRONG!
SOMETHING WENT HORRIBLY WRONG!

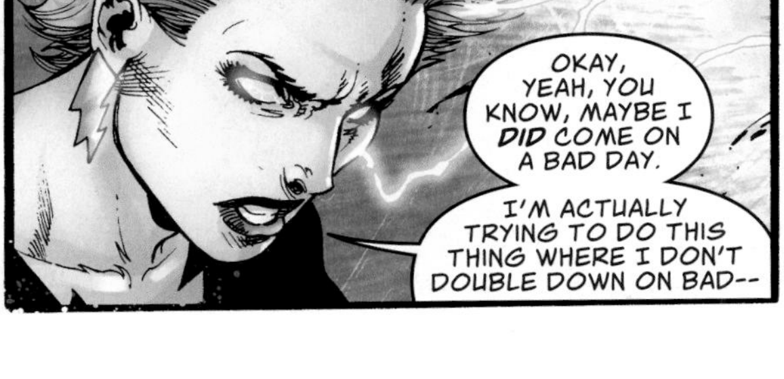
OKAY, YEAH, YOU KNOW, MAYBE I DID COME ON A BAD DAY.
I'M ACTUALLY TRYING TO DO THIS THING WHERE I DON'T DOUBLE DOWN ON BAD--

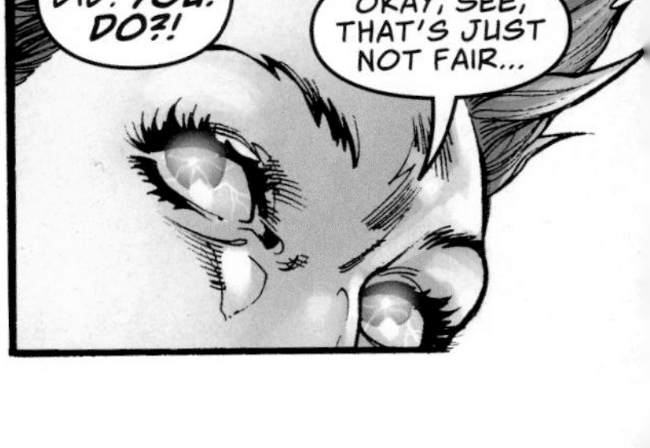
WHAT. DID. YOU. DO?!
OKAY, SEE, THAT'S JUST NOT FAIR...

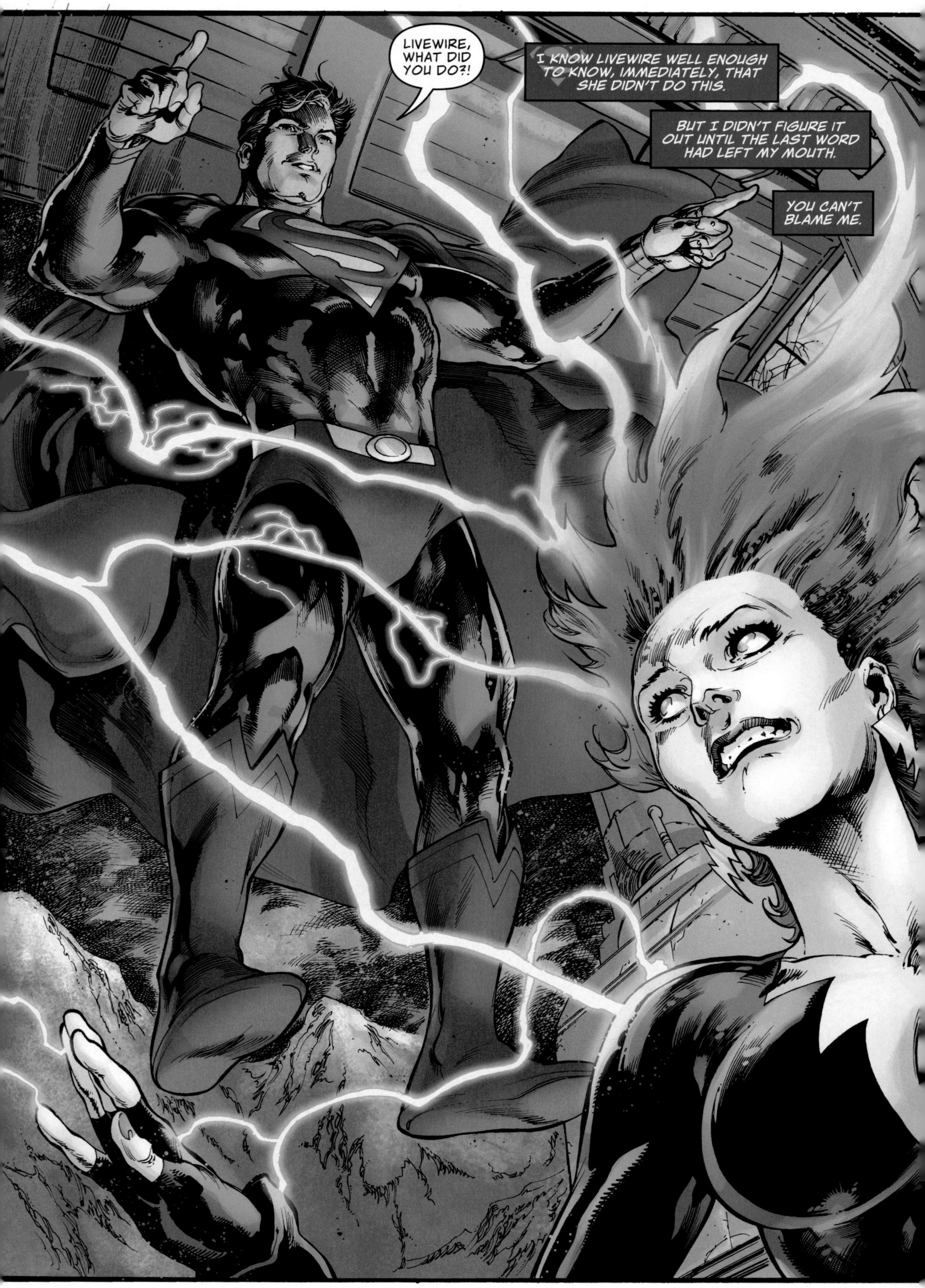
LIVEWIRE, WHAT DID YOU DO?!
I KNOW LIVEWIRE WELL ENOUGH TO KNOW, IMMEDIATELY, THAT SHE DIDN'T DO THIS.
BUT I DIDN'T FIGURE IT OUT UNTIL THE LAST WORD HAD LEFT MY MOUTH.
YOU CAN'T BLAME ME.

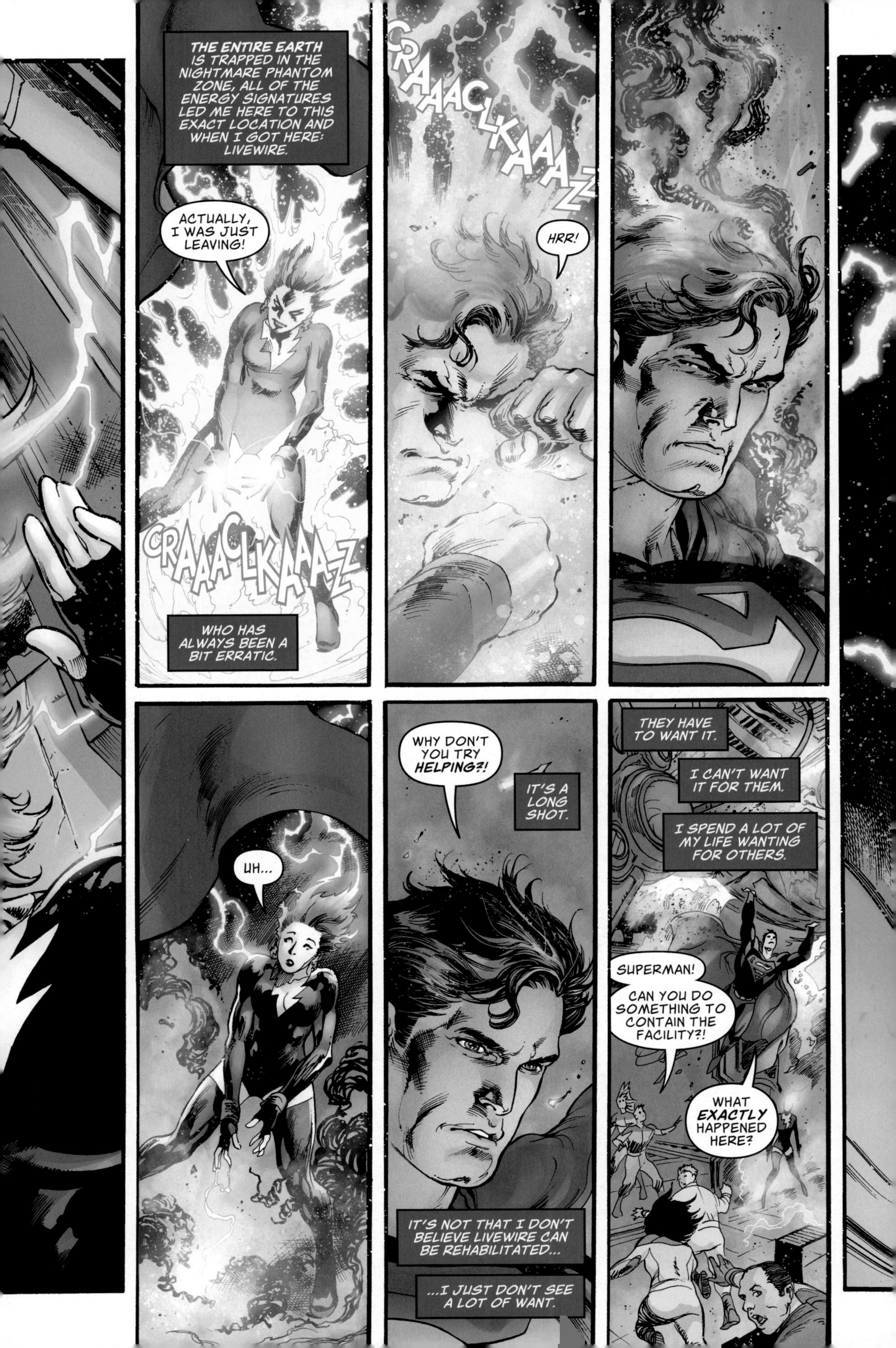
THE ENTIRE EARTH IS TRAPPED IN THE NIGHTMARE PHANTOM ZONE, ALL OF THE ENERGY SIGNATURES LED ME HERE TO THIS EXACT LOCATION AND WHEN I GOT HERE: LIVEWIRE.
ACTUALLY, I WAS JUST LEAVING!
CRAAACLKAAAZZ
WHO HAS ALWAYS BEEN A BIT ERRATIC.
CRAAACLKAAAZZ
HRR!
UH...
WHY DON'T YOU TRY HELPING?!
IT'S A LONG SHOT.
IT'S NOT THAT I DON'T BELIEVE LIVEWIRE CAN BE REHABILITATED...
...I JUST DON'T SEE A LOT OF WANT.
THEY HAVE TO WANT IT.
I CAN'T WANT IT FOR THEM.
I SPEND A LOT OF MY LIFE WANTING FOR OTHERS.
SUPERMAN!
CAN YOU DO SOMETHING TO CONTAIN THE FACILITY?!
WHAT EXACTLY HAPPENED HERE?

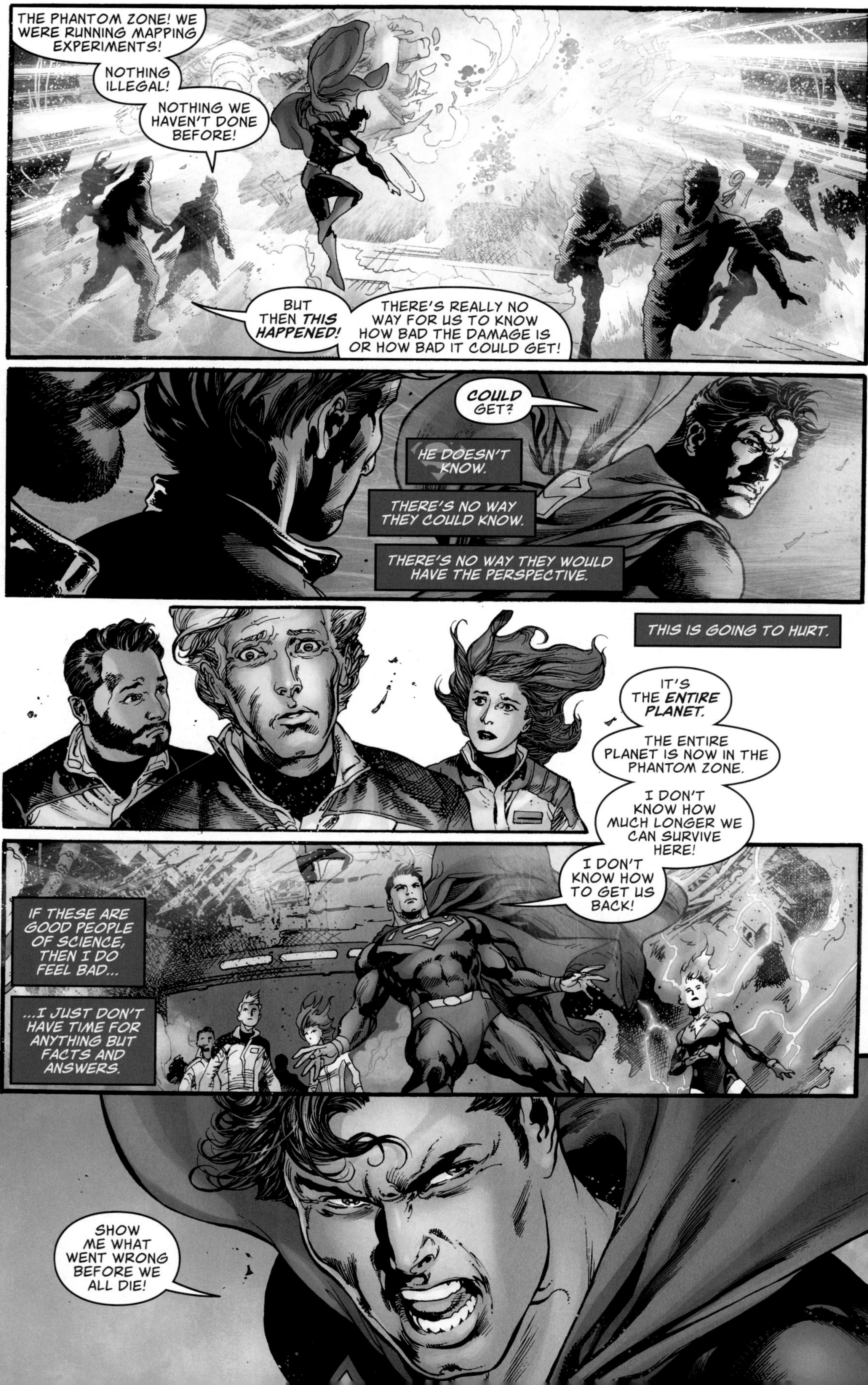
THE PHANTOM ZONE! WE WERE RUNNING MAPPING EXPERIMENTS!
NOTHING ILLEGAL!
NOTHING WE HAVEN'T DONE BEFORE!
BUT THEN THIS HAPPENED!
THERE'S REALLY NO WAY FOR US TO KNOW HOW BAD THE DAMAGE IS OR HOW BAD IT COULD GET!
COULD GET?
HE DOESN'T KNOW.
THERE'S NO WAY THEY COULD KNOW.
THERE'S NO WAY THEY WOULD HAVE THE PERSPECTIVE.
THIS IS GOING TO HURT.
IT'S THE ENTIRE PLANET.
THE ENTIRE PLANET IS NOW IN THE PHANTOM ZONE.
I DON'T KNOW HOW MUCH LONGER WE CAN SURVIVE HERE!
I DON'T KNOW HOW TO GET US BACK!
IF THESE ARE GOOD PEOPLE OF SCIENCE, THEN I DO FEEL BAD...
...I JUST DON'T HAVE TIME FOR ANYTHING BUT FACTS AND ANSWERS.
SHOW ME WHAT WENT WRONG BEFORE WE ALL DIE!

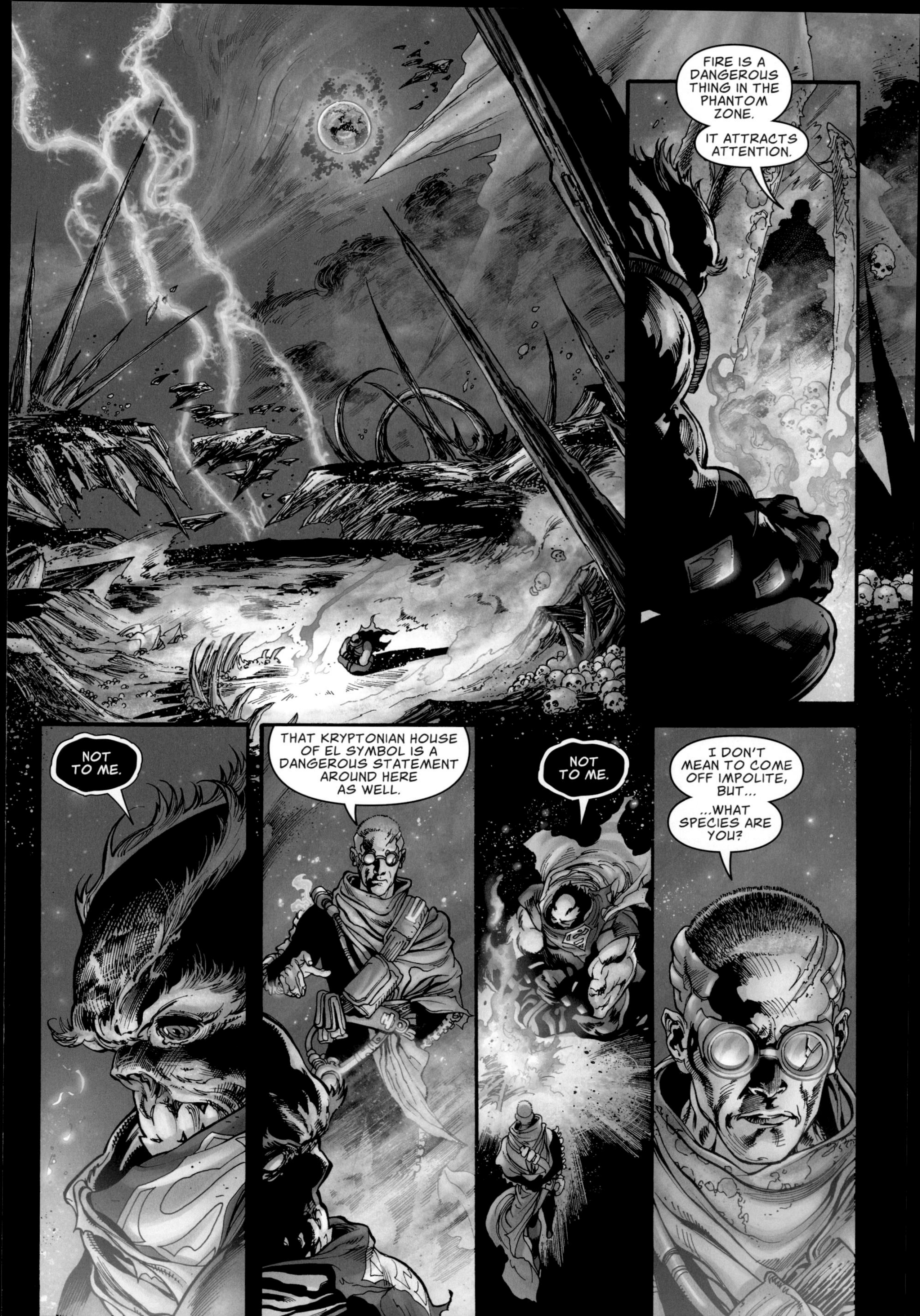
FIRE IS A DANGEROUS THING IN THE PHANTOM ZONE.
IT ATTRACTS ATTENTION.
NOT TO ME.
THAT KRYPTONIAN HOUSE OF EL SYMBOL IS A DANGEROUS STATEMENT AROUND HERE AS WELL.
NOT TO ME.
I DON'T MEAN TO COME OFF IMPOLITE, BUT...
...WHAT SPECIES ARE YOU?

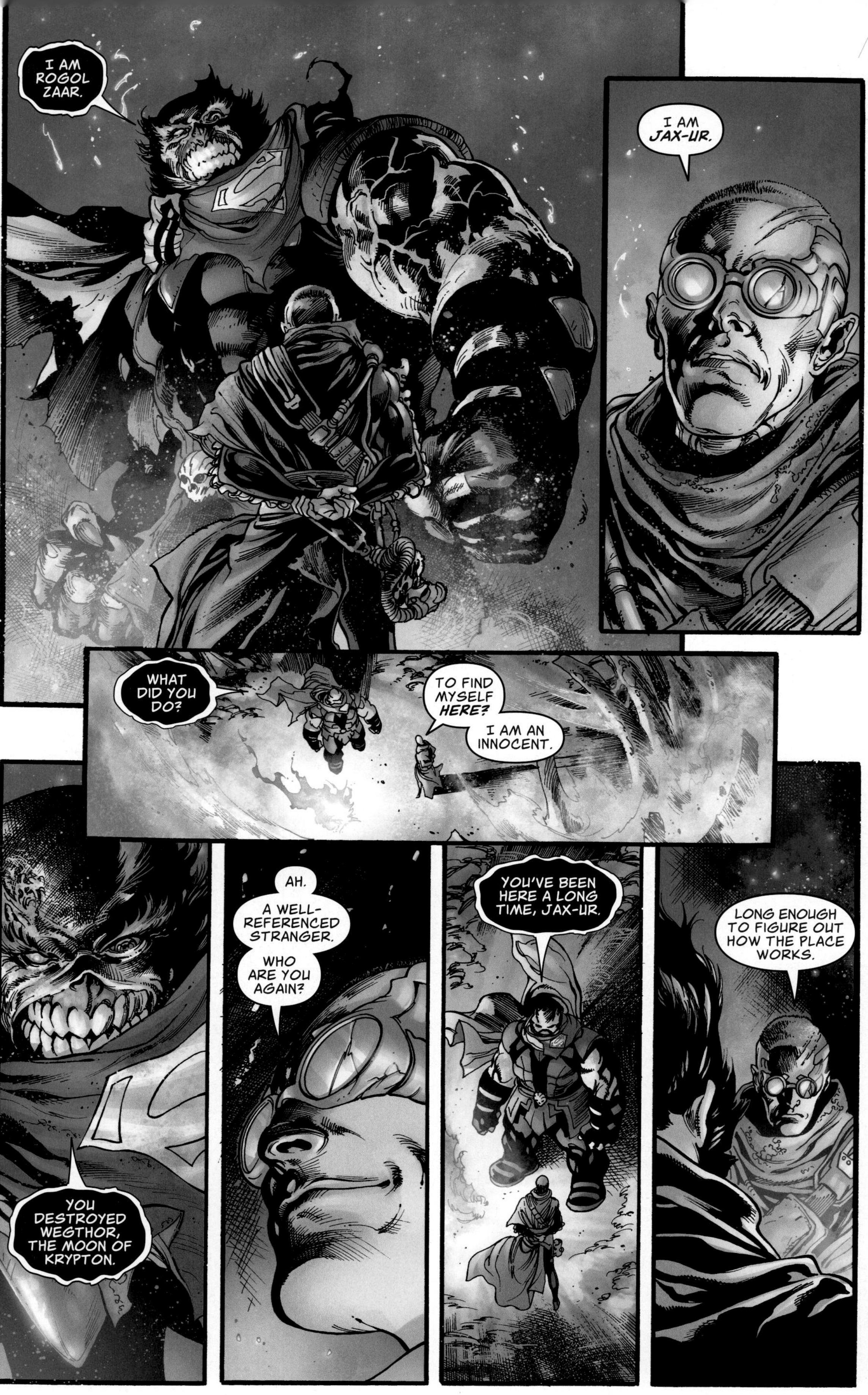
I AM ROGOL ZAAR.
I AM *JAX-UR.*
WHAT DID YOU DO?
TO FIND MYSELF *HERE?*
I AM AN INNOCENT.
YOU DESTROYED WEGTHOR, THE MOON OF KRYPTON.
AH.
A WELL-REFERENCED STRANGER.
WHO ARE YOU AGAIN?
YOU'VE BEEN HERE A LONG TIME, JAX-UR.
LONG ENOUGH TO FIGURE OUT HOW THE PLACE WORKS.

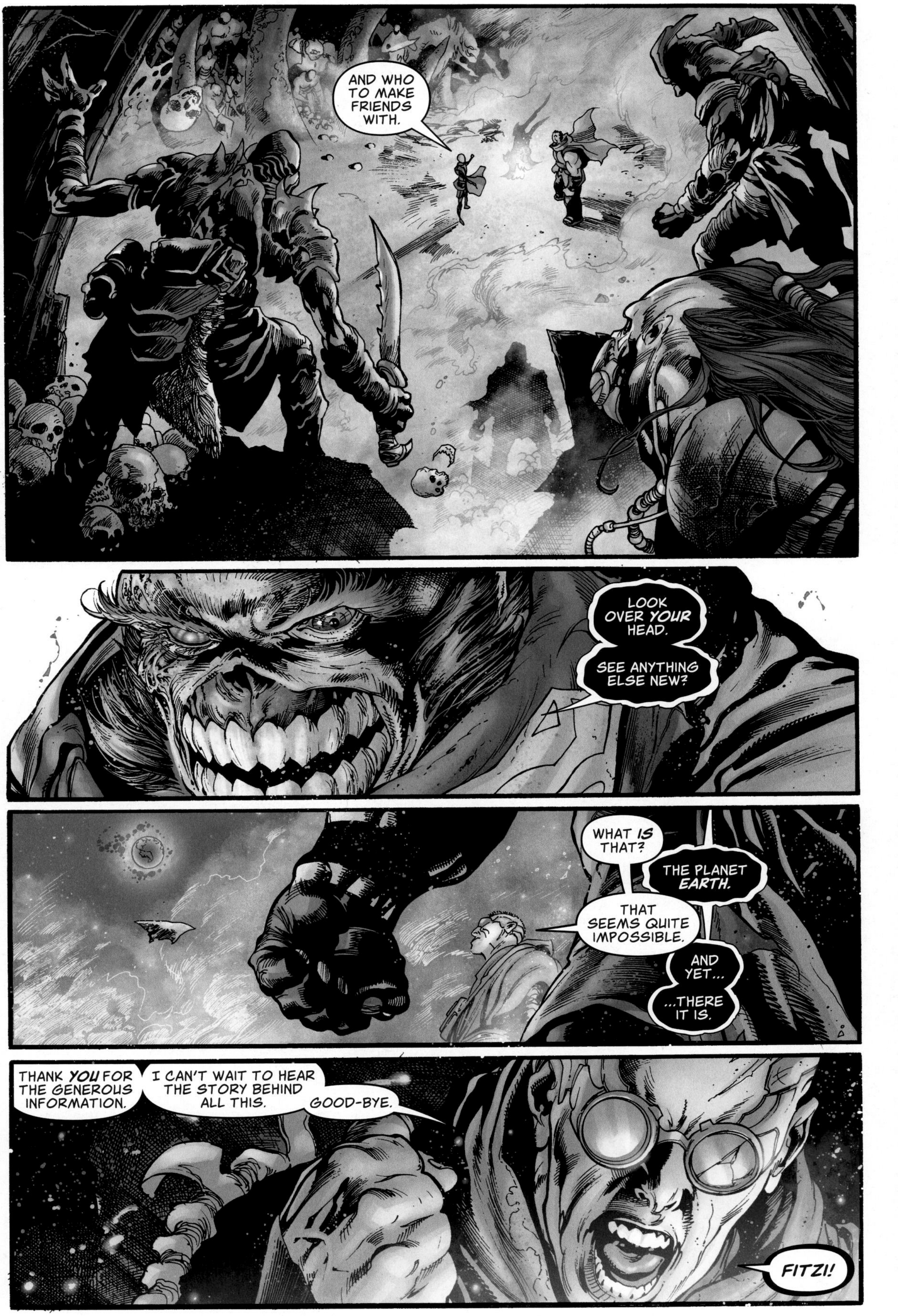

AND WHO TO MAKE FRIENDS WITH.
LOOK OVER YOUR HEAD.
SEE ANYTHING ELSE NEW?
WHAT IS THAT?
THE PLANET EARTH.
THAT SEEMS QUITE IMPOSSIBLE.
AND YET...
...THERE IT IS.
THANK YOU FOR THE GENEROUS INFORMATION.
I CAN'T WAIT TO HEAR THE STORY BEHIND ALL THIS.
GOOD-BYE.
FITZI!

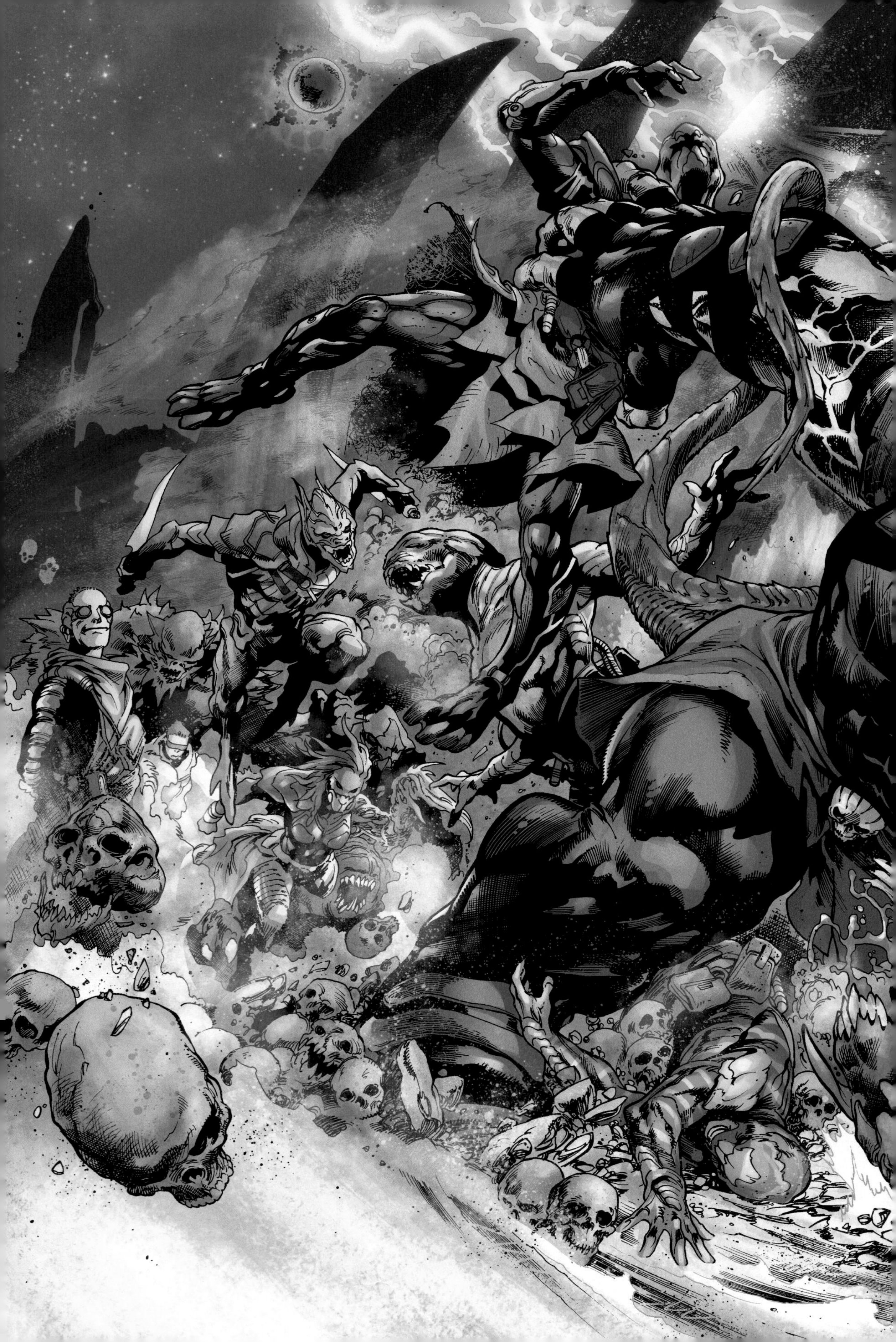

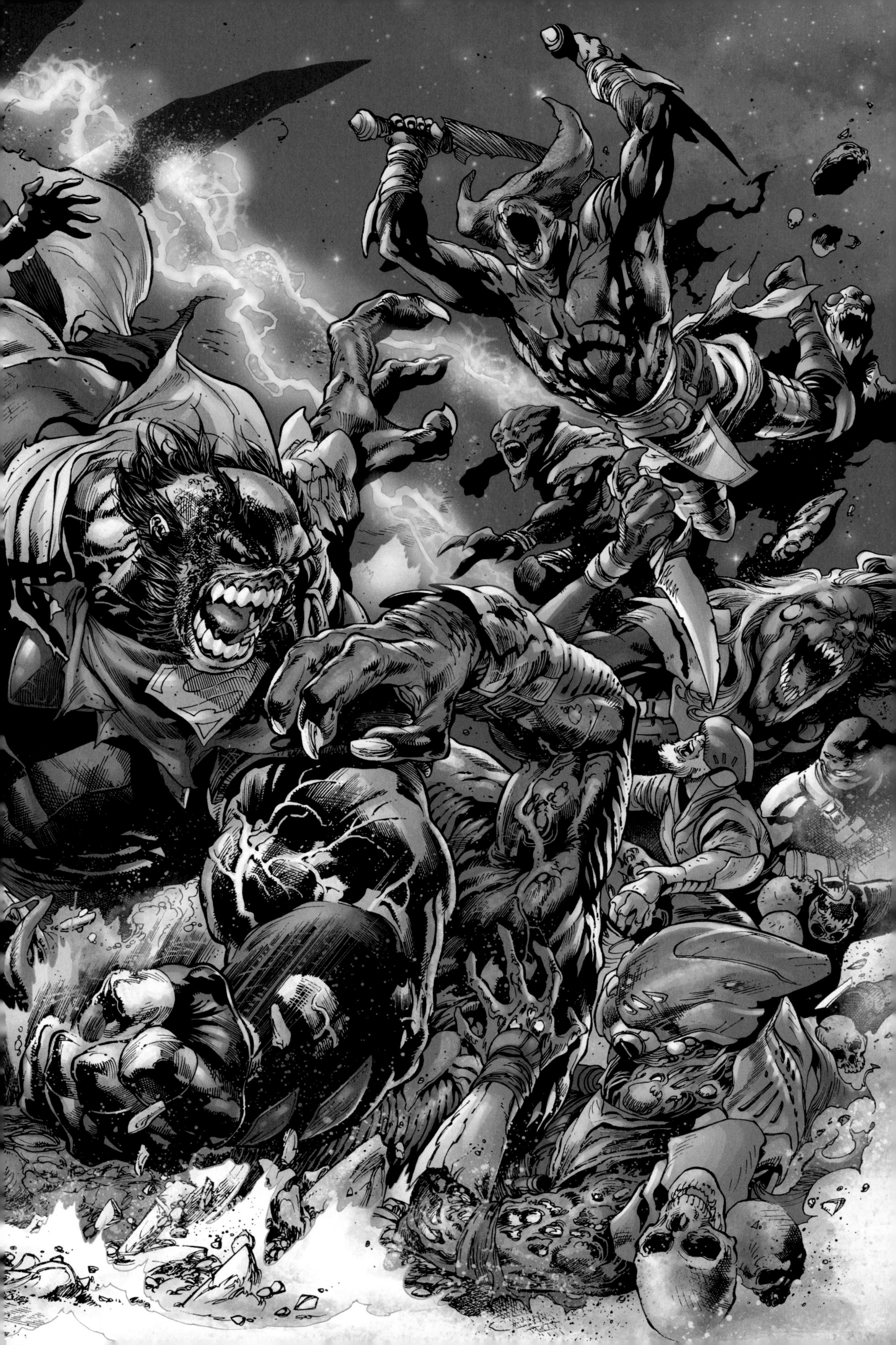

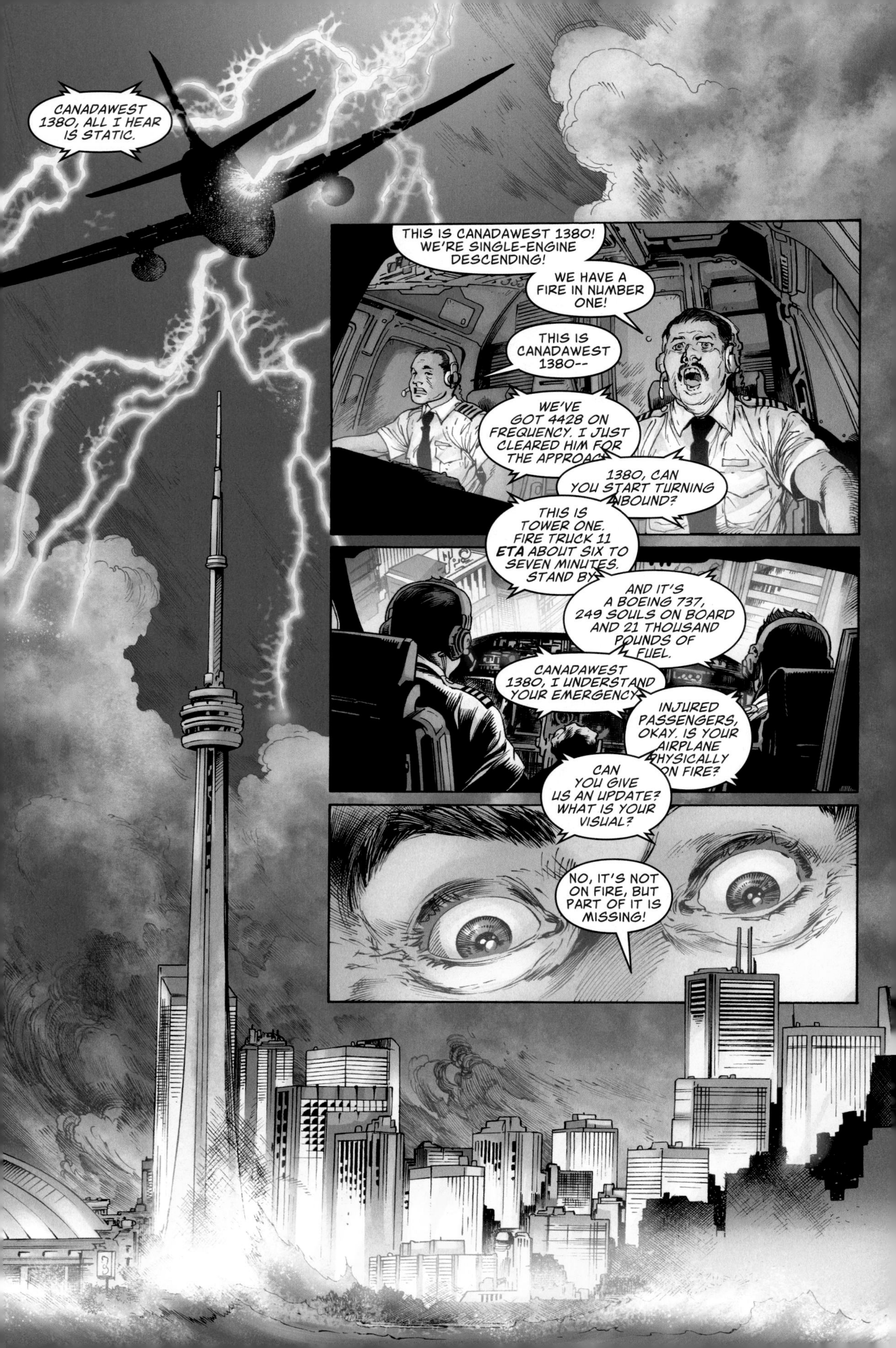
CANADAWEST 1380, ALL I HEAR IS STATIC.
THIS IS CANADAWEST 1380! WE'RE SINGLE-ENGINE DESCENDING!
WE HAVE A FIRE IN NUMBER ONE!
THIS IS CANADAWEST 1380--
WE'VE GOT 4428 ON FREQUENCY. I JUST CLEARED HIM FOR THE APPROACH.
1380, CAN YOU START TURNING INBOUND?
THIS IS TOWER ONE. FIRE TRUCK 11 ETA ABOUT SIX TO SEVEN MINUTES. STAND BY.
AND IT'S A BOEING 737, 249 SOULS ON BOARD AND 21 THOUSAND POUNDS OF FUEL.
CANADAWEST 1380, I UNDERSTAND YOUR EMERGENCY.
INJURED PASSENGERS, OKAY. IS YOUR AIRPLANE PHYSICALLY ON FIRE?
CAN YOU GIVE US AN UPDATE? WHAT IS YOUR VISUAL?
NO, IT'S NOT ON FIRE, BUT PART OF IT IS MISSING!

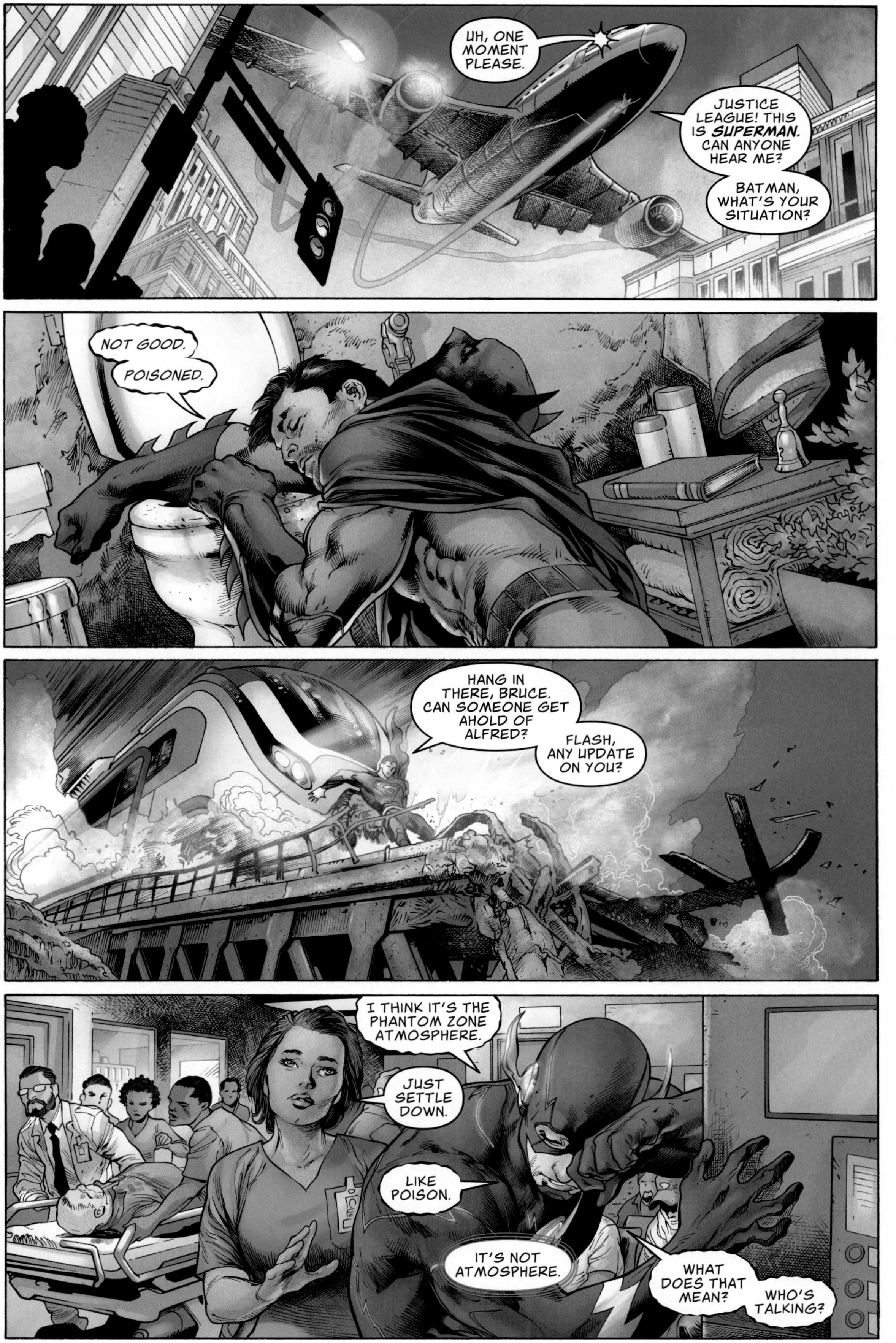
UH, ONE MOMENT PLEASE.
JUSTICE LEAGUE! THIS IS **SUPERMAN.** CAN ANYONE HEAR ME?
BATMAN, WHAT'S YOUR SITUATION?
NOT GOOD.
POISONED.
HANG IN THERE, BRUCE. CAN SOMEONE GET AHOLD OF ALFRED?
FLASH, ANY UPDATE ON YOU?
I THINK IT'S THE PHANTOM ZONE ATMOSPHERE.
JUST SETTLE DOWN.
LIKE POISON.
IT'S NOT ATMOSPHERE.
WHAT DOES THAT MEAN?
WHO'S TALKING?

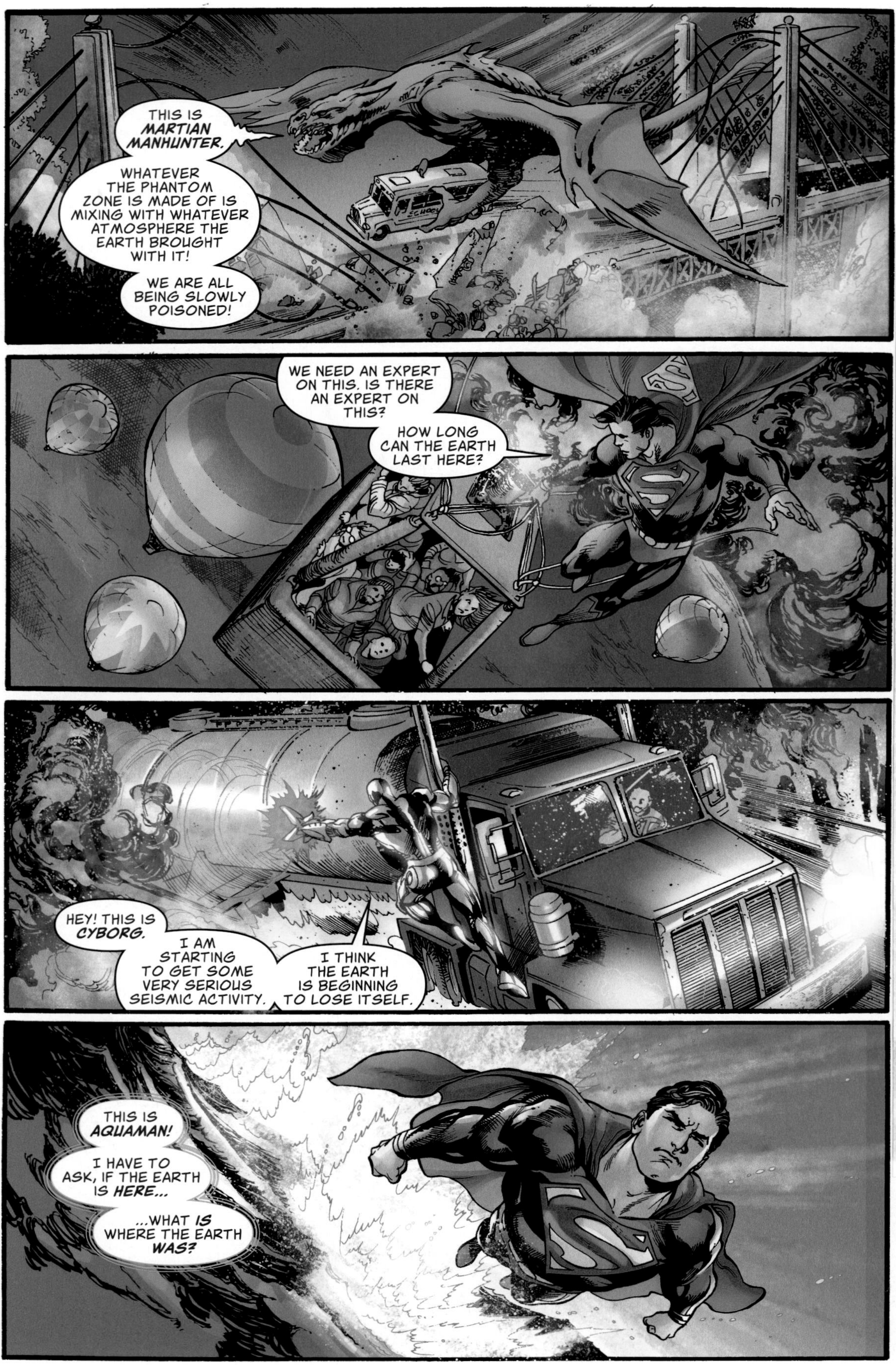
THIS IS MARTIAN MANHUNTER.
WHATEVER THE PHANTOM ZONE IS MADE OF IS MIXING WITH WHATEVER ATMOSPHERE THE EARTH BROUGHT WITH IT!
WE ARE ALL BEING SLOWLY POISONED!
SCHOOL
WE NEED AN EXPERT ON THIS. IS THERE AN EXPERT ON THIS?
HOW LONG CAN THE EARTH LAST HERE?
HEY! THIS IS CYBORG.
I AM STARTING TO GET SOME VERY SERIOUS SEISMIC ACTIVITY.
I THINK THE EARTH IS BEGINNING TO LOSE ITSELF.
THIS IS AQUAMAN!
I HAVE TO ASK, IF THE EARTH IS HERE...
...WHAT IS WHERE THE EARTH WAS?

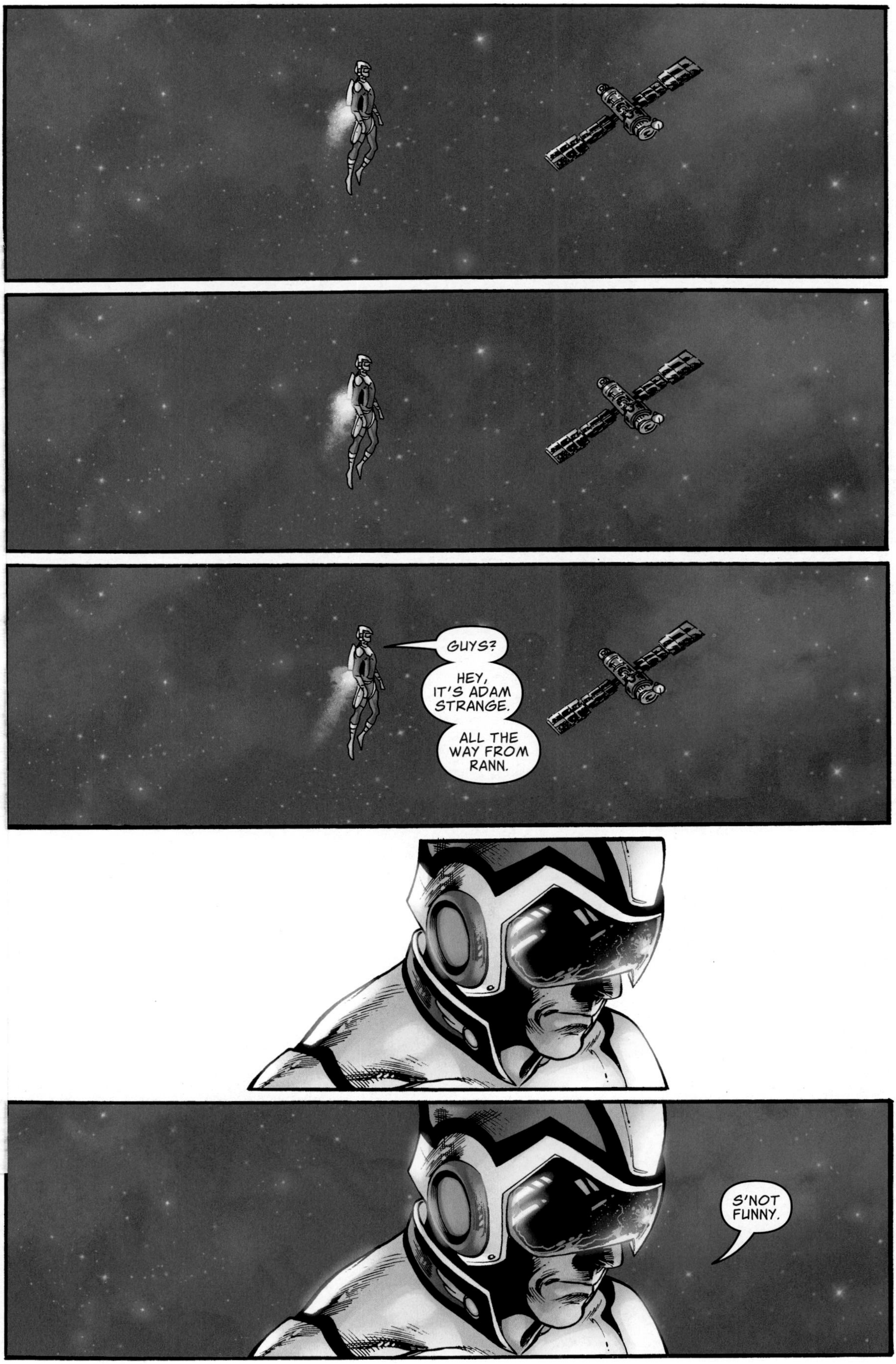
GUYS?
HEY, IT'S ADAM STRANGE.
ALL THE WAY FROM RANN.
S'NOT FUNNY.

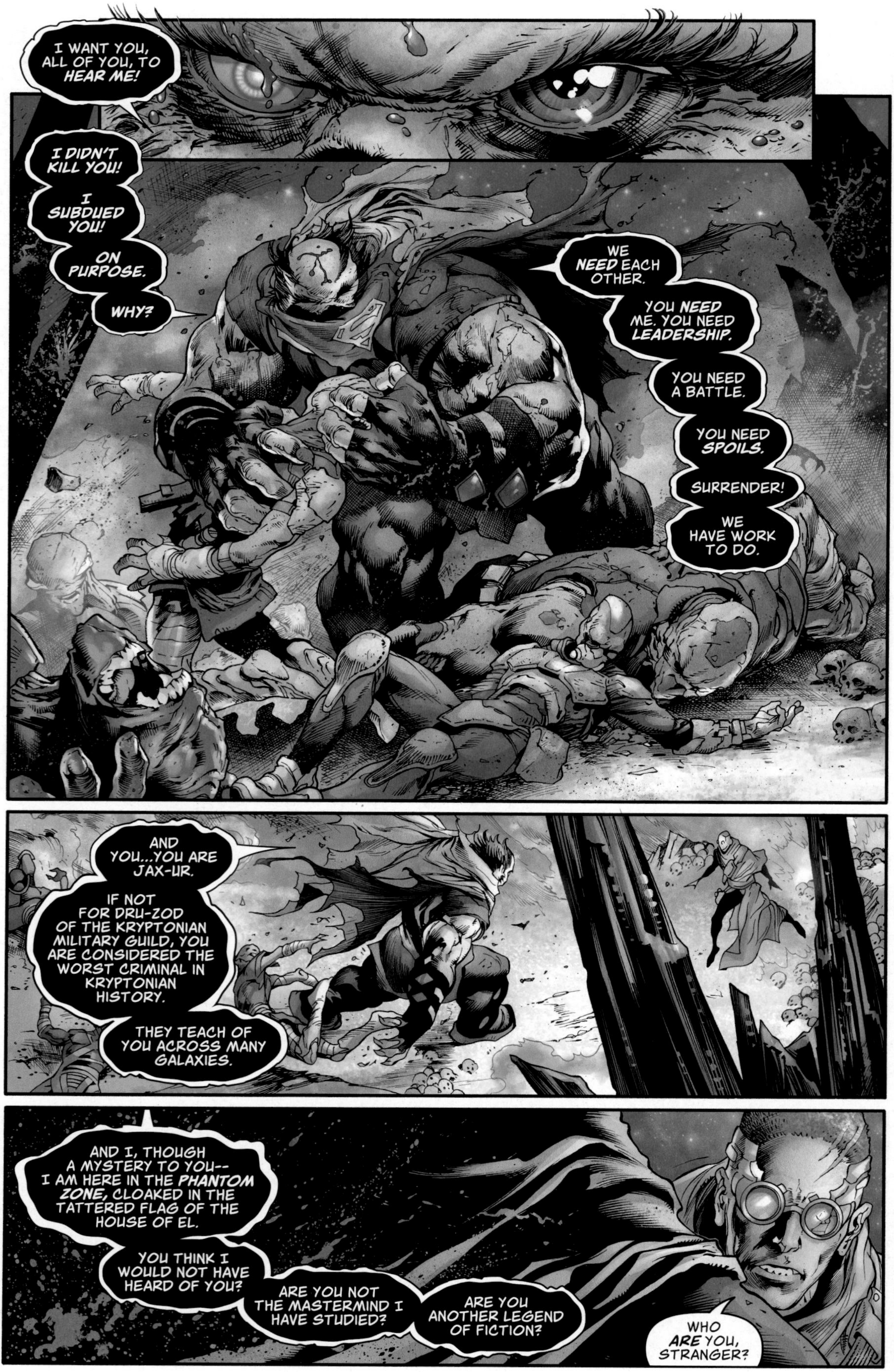
I WANT YOU, ALL OF YOU, TO HEAR ME!
I DIDN'T KILL YOU!
I SUBDUED YOU!
ON PURPOSE.
WHY?
WE NEED EACH OTHER.
YOU NEED ME. YOU NEED LEADERSHIP.
YOU NEED A BATTLE.
YOU NEED SPOILS.
SURRENDER!
WE HAVE WORK TO DO.
AND YOU...YOU ARE JAX-UR.
IF NOT FOR DRU-ZOD OF THE KRYPTONIAN MILITARY GUILD, YOU ARE CONSIDERED THE WORST CRIMINAL IN KRYPTONIAN HISTORY.
THEY TEACH OF YOU ACROSS MANY GALAXIES.
AND I, THOUGH A MYSTERY TO YOU-- I AM HERE IN THE PHANTOM ZONE, CLOAKED IN THE TATTERED FLAG OF THE HOUSE OF EL.
YOU THINK I WOULD NOT HAVE HEARD OF YOU?
ARE YOU NOT THE MASTERMIND I HAVE STUDIED?
ARE YOU ANOTHER LEGEND OF FICTION?
WHO ARE YOU, STRANGER?

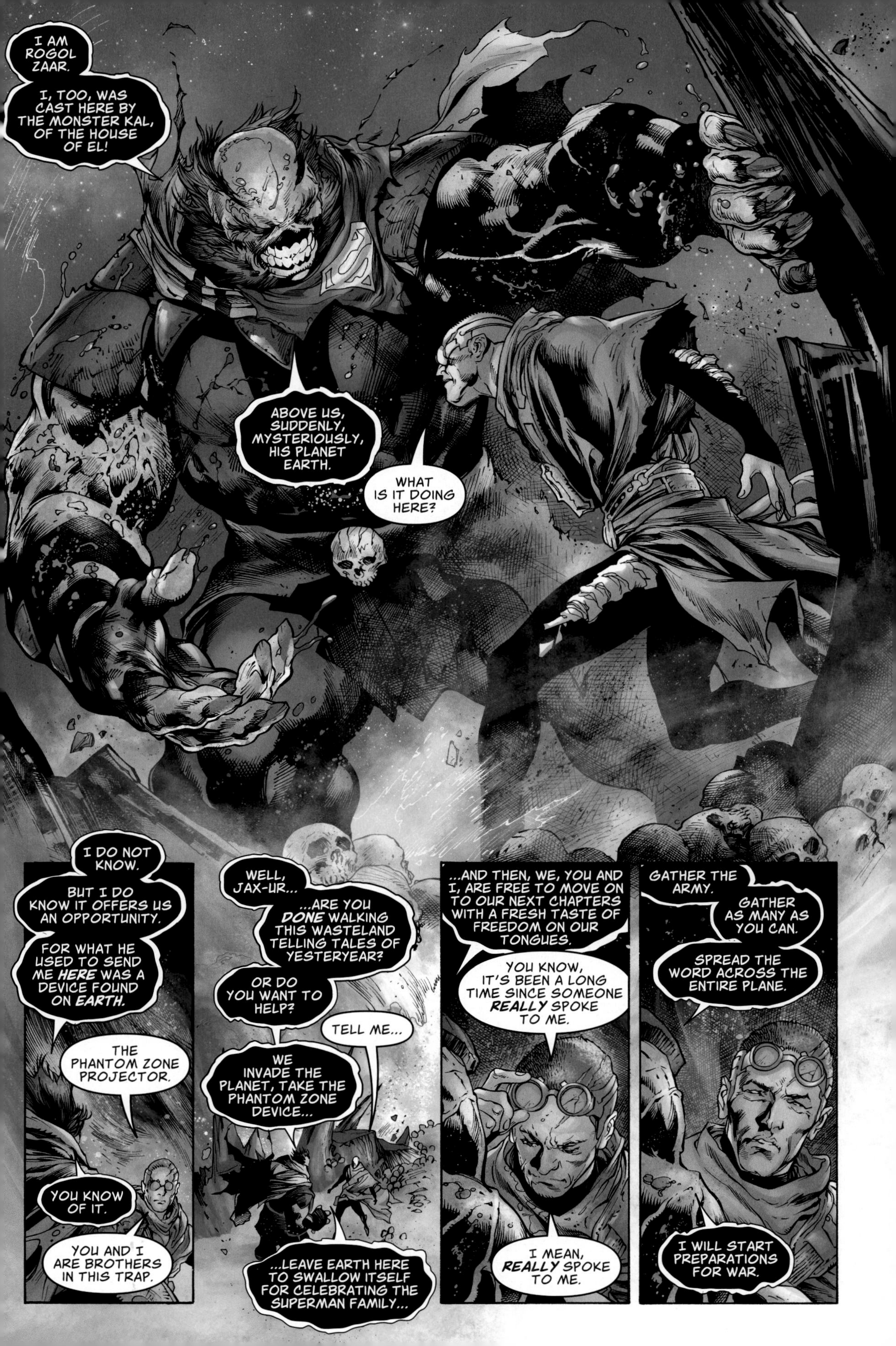
I AM ROGOL ZAAR.
I, TOO, WAS CAST HERE BY THE MONSTER KAL, OF THE HOUSE OF EL!
ABOVE US, SUDDENLY, MYSTERIOUSLY, HIS PLANET EARTH.
WHAT IS IT DOING HERE?
I DO NOT KNOW.
BUT I DO KNOW IT OFFERS US AN OPPORTUNITY.
FOR WHAT HE USED TO SEND ME HERE WAS A DEVICE FOUND ON EARTH.
THE PHANTOM ZONE PROJECTOR.
YOU KNOW OF IT.
YOU AND I ARE BROTHERS IN THIS TRAP.
WELL, JAX-UR...
...ARE YOU DONE WALKING THIS WASTELAND TELLING TALES OF YESTERYEAR?
OR DO YOU WANT TO HELP?
TELL ME...
WE INVADE THE PLANET, TAKE THE PHANTOM ZONE DEVICE...
...LEAVE EARTH HERE TO SWALLOW ITSELF FOR CELEBRATING THE SUPERMAN FAMILY...
...AND THEN, WE, YOU AND I, ARE FREE TO MOVE ON TO OUR NEXT CHAPTERS WITH A FRESH TASTE OF FREEDOM ON OUR TONGUES.
YOU KNOW, IT'S BEEN A LONG TIME SINCE SOMEONE REALLY SPOKE TO ME.
I MEAN, REALLY SPOKE TO ME.
GATHER THE ARMY.
GATHER AS MANY AS YOU CAN.
SPREAD THE WORD ACROSS THE ENTIRE PLANE.
I WILL START PREPARATIONS FOR WAR.

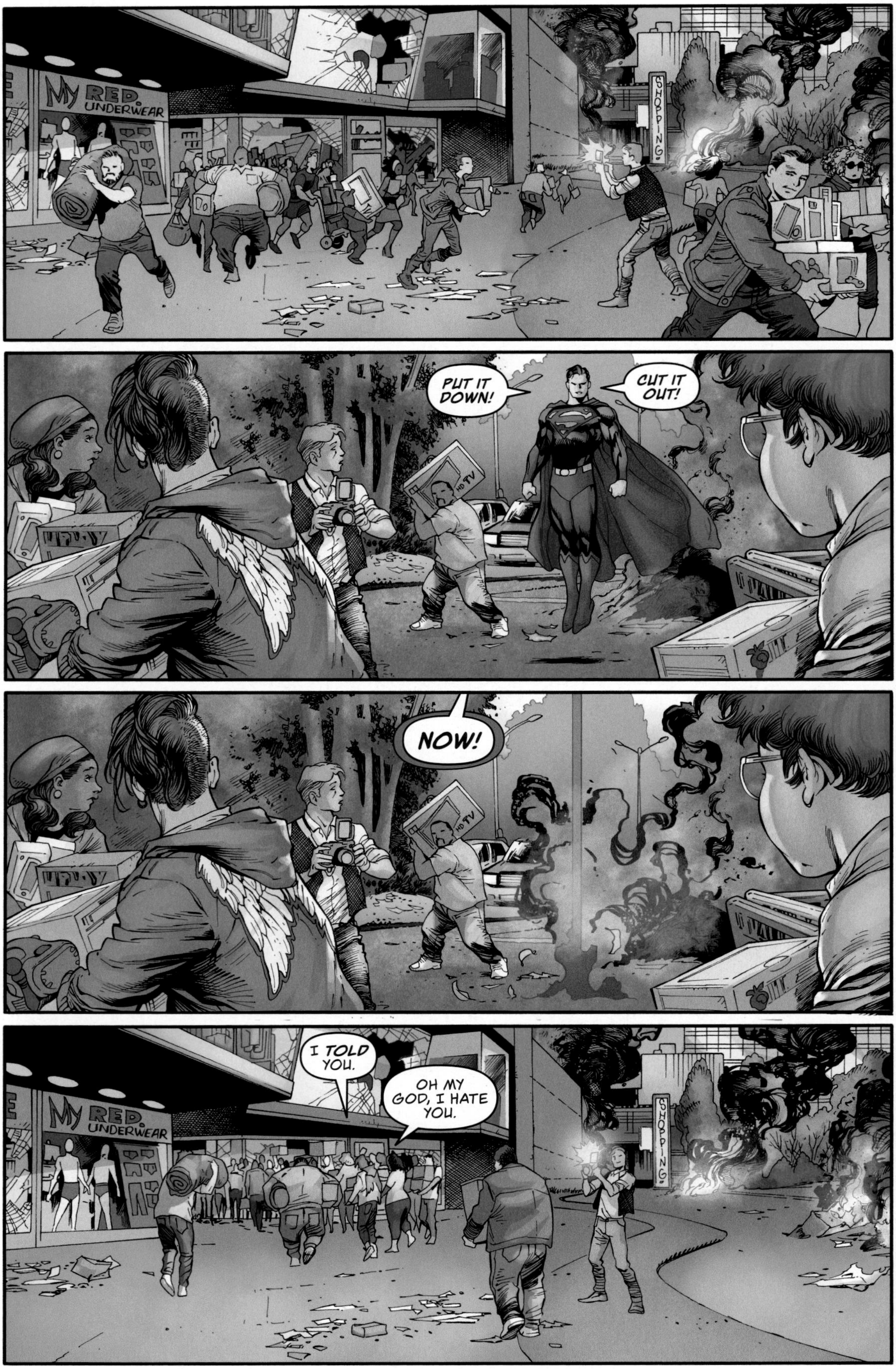
MY RED. UNDERWEAR
SHOPPING
PUT IT DOWN!
CUT IT OUT!
NOW!
I *TOLD* YOU.
OH MY GOD, I HATE YOU.

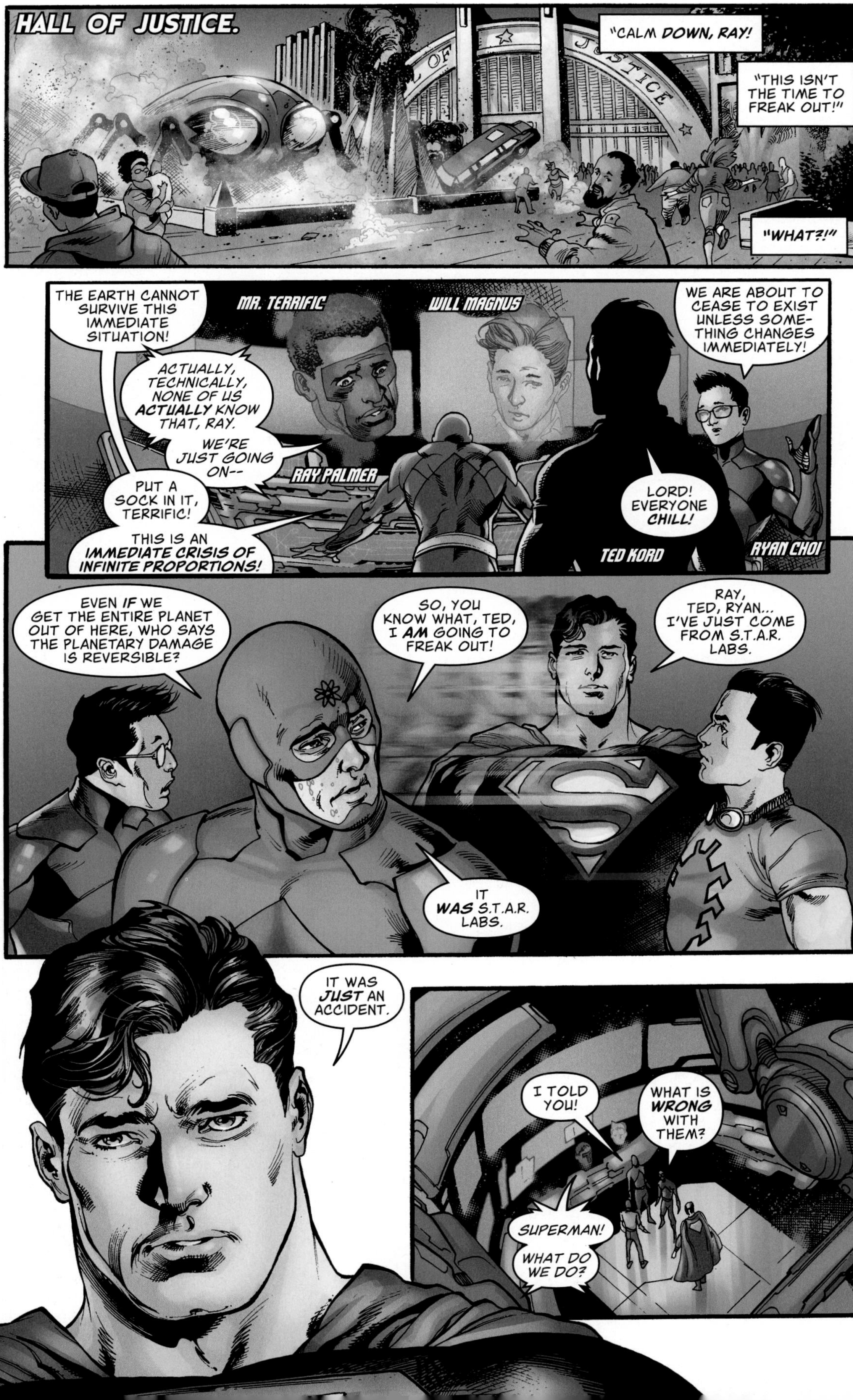
HALL OF JUSTICE.
"CALM DOWN, RAY!
"THIS ISN'T THE TIME TO FREAK OUT!"
"WHAT?!"
THE EARTH CANNOT SURVIVE THIS IMMEDIATE SITUATION!
MR. TERRIFIC
WILL MAGNUS
ACTUALLY, TECHNICALLY, NONE OF US ACTUALLY KNOW THAT, RAY.
WE'RE JUST GOING ON--
PUT A SOCK IN IT, TERRIFIC!
THIS IS AN IMMEDIATE CRISIS OF INFINITE PROPORTIONS!
RAY PALMER
WE ARE ABOUT TO CEASE TO EXIST UNLESS SOMETHING CHANGES IMMEDIATELY!
LORD! EVERYONE CHILL!
TED KORD
RYAN CHOI
EVEN IF WE GET THE ENTIRE PLANET OUT OF HERE, WHO SAYS THE PLANETARY DAMAGE IS REVERSIBLE?
SO, YOU KNOW WHAT, TED, I AM GOING TO FREAK OUT!
RAY, TED, RYAN... I'VE JUST COME FROM S.T.A.R. LABS.
IT WAS S.T.A.R. LABS.
IT WAS JUST AN ACCIDENT.
I TOLD YOU!
WHAT IS WRONG WITH THEM?
SUPERMAN!
WHAT DO WE DO?

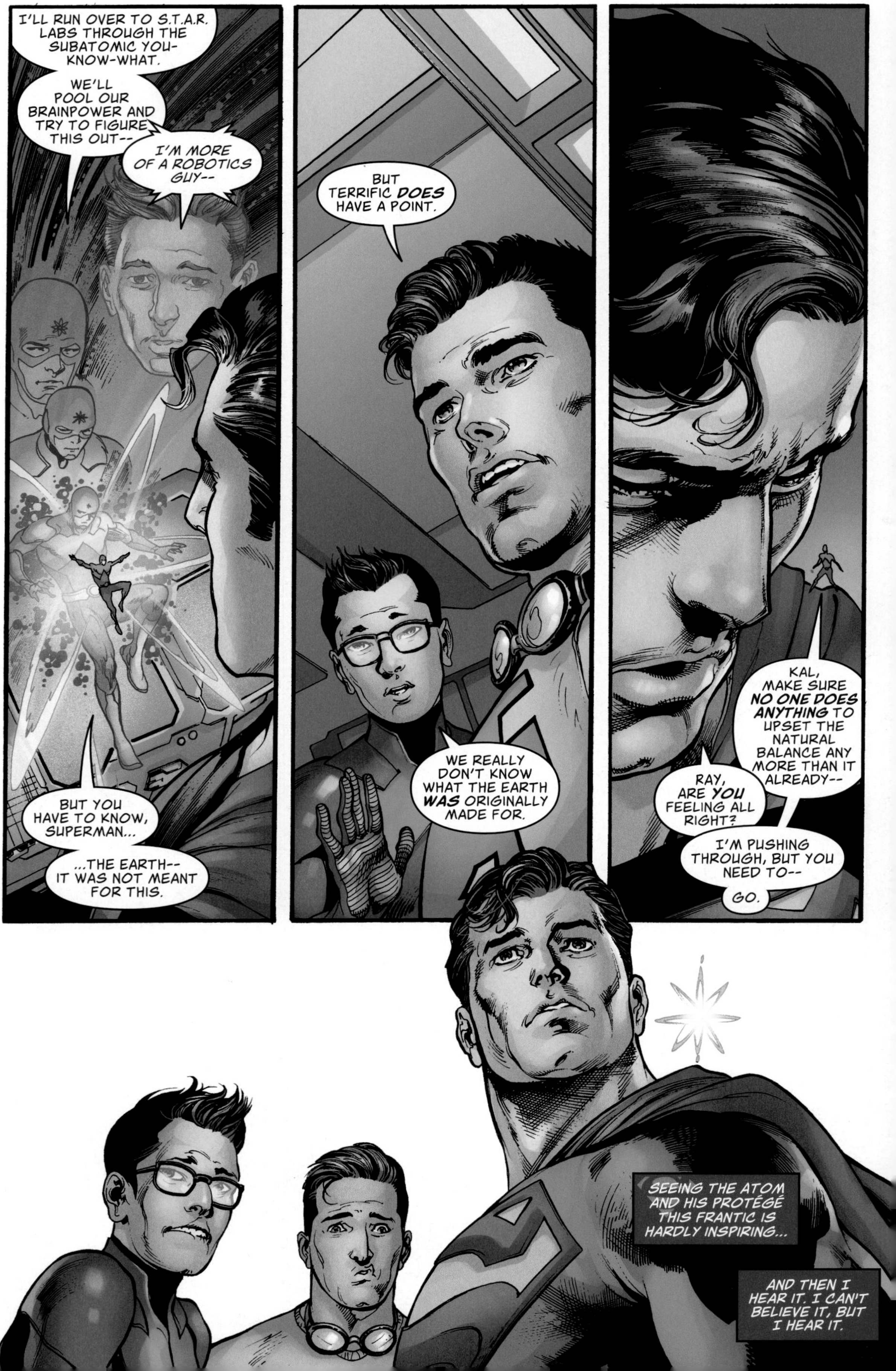

I'LL RUN OVER TO S.T.A.R. LABS THROUGH THE SUBATOMIC YOU-KNOW-WHAT.
WE'LL POOL OUR BRAINPOWER AND TRY TO FIGURE THIS OUT--
I'M MORE OF A ROBOTICS GUY--
BUT YOU HAVE TO KNOW, SUPERMAN...
...THE EARTH-- IT WAS NOT MEANT FOR THIS.
BUT TERRIFIC **DOES** HAVE A POINT.
WE REALLY DON'T KNOW WHAT THE EARTH **WAS** ORIGINALLY MADE FOR.
KAL, MAKE SURE **NO ONE DOES ANYTHING** TO UPSET THE NATURAL BALANCE ANY MORE THAN IT ALREADY--
RAY, ARE **YOU** FEELING ALL RIGHT?
I'M PUSHING THROUGH, BUT YOU NEED TO--
GO.
SEEING THE ATOM AND HIS PROTÉGÉ THIS FRANTIC IS HARDLY INSPIRING...
AND THEN I HEAR IT. I CAN'T BELIEVE IT, BUT I HEAR IT.

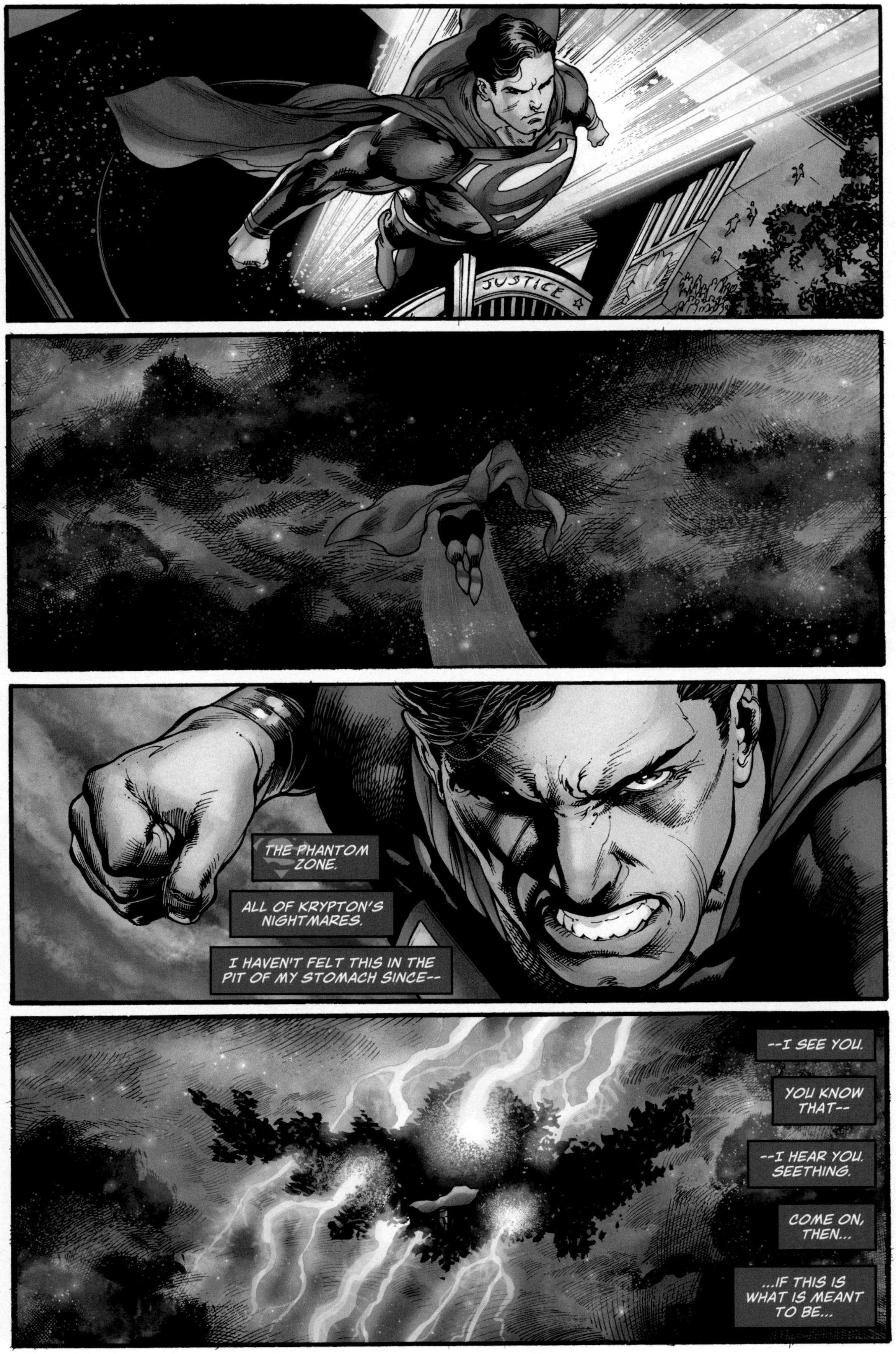
JUSTICE
THE PHANTOM ZONE.
ALL OF KRYPTON'S NIGHTMARES.
I HAVEN'T FELT THIS IN THE PIT OF MY STOMACH SINCE--
--I SEE YOU.
YOU KNOW THAT--
--I HEAR YOU. SEETHING.
COME ON, THEN...
...IF THIS IS WHAT IS MEANT TO BE...

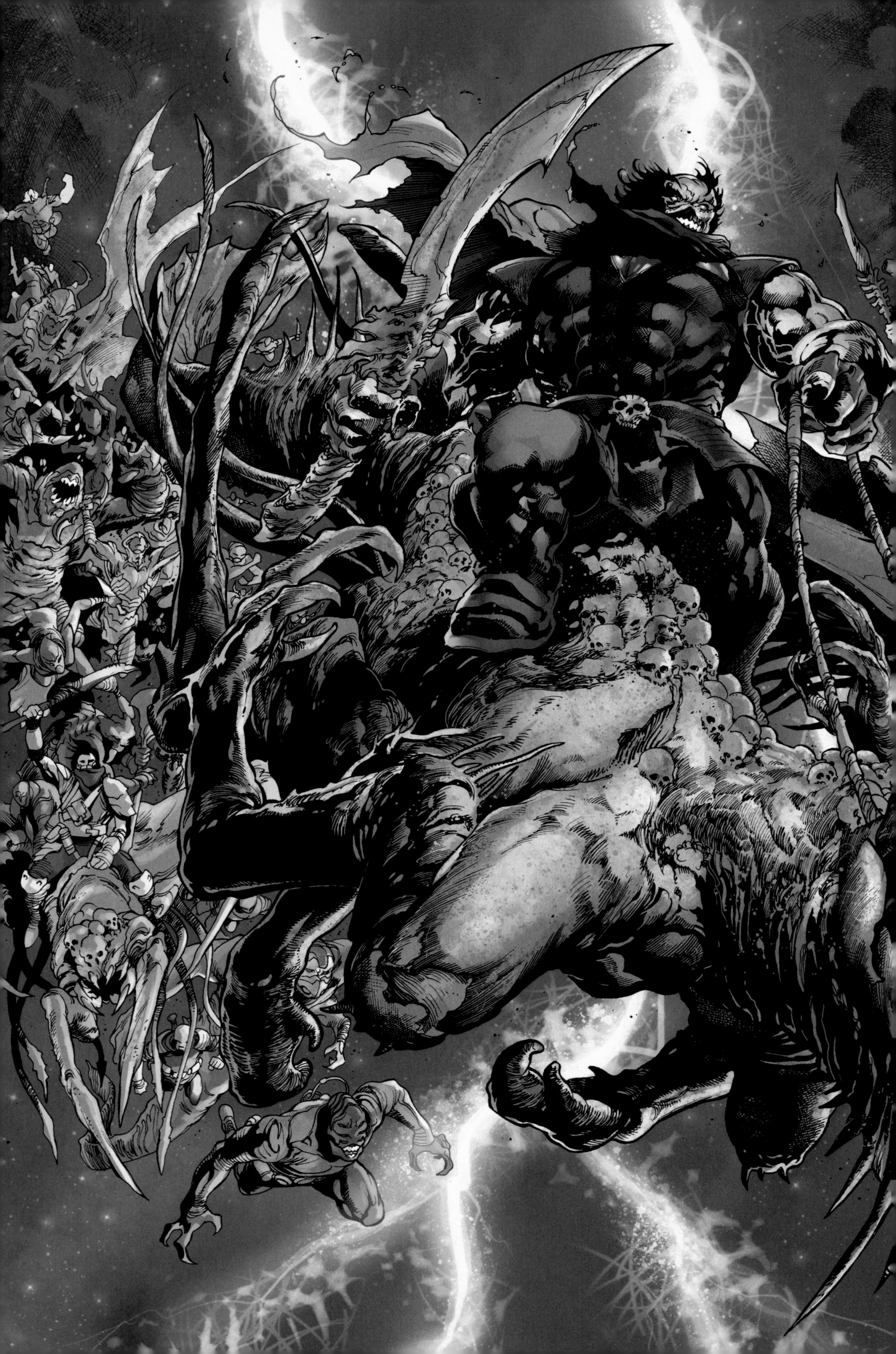

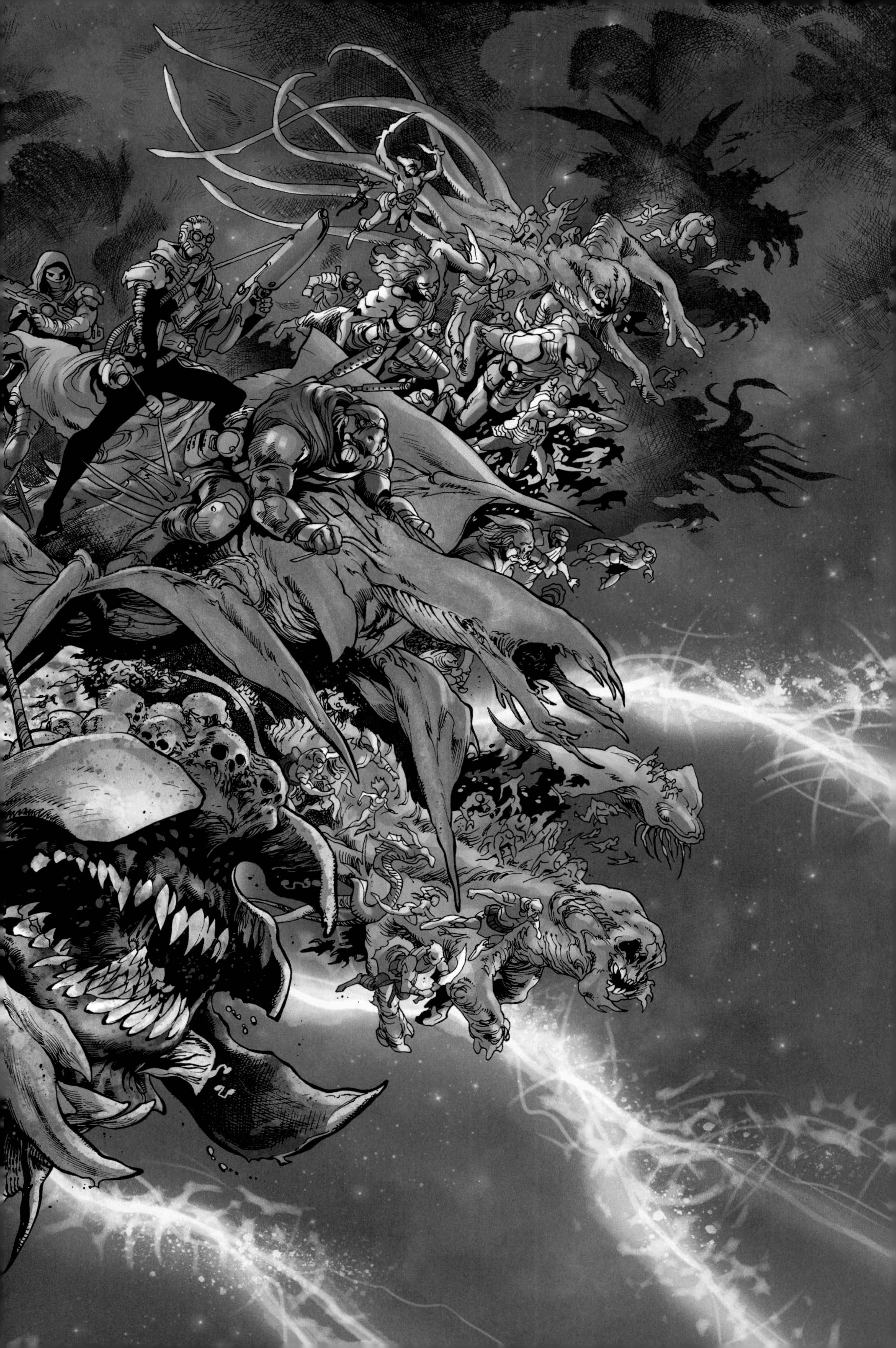

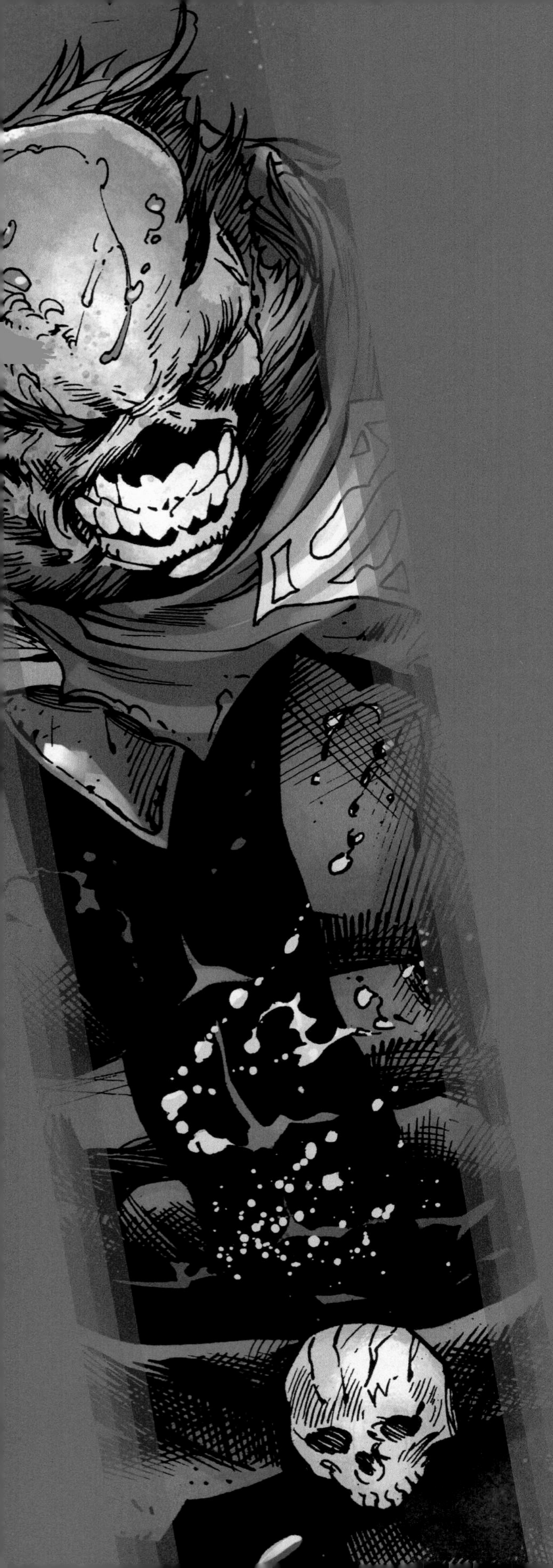

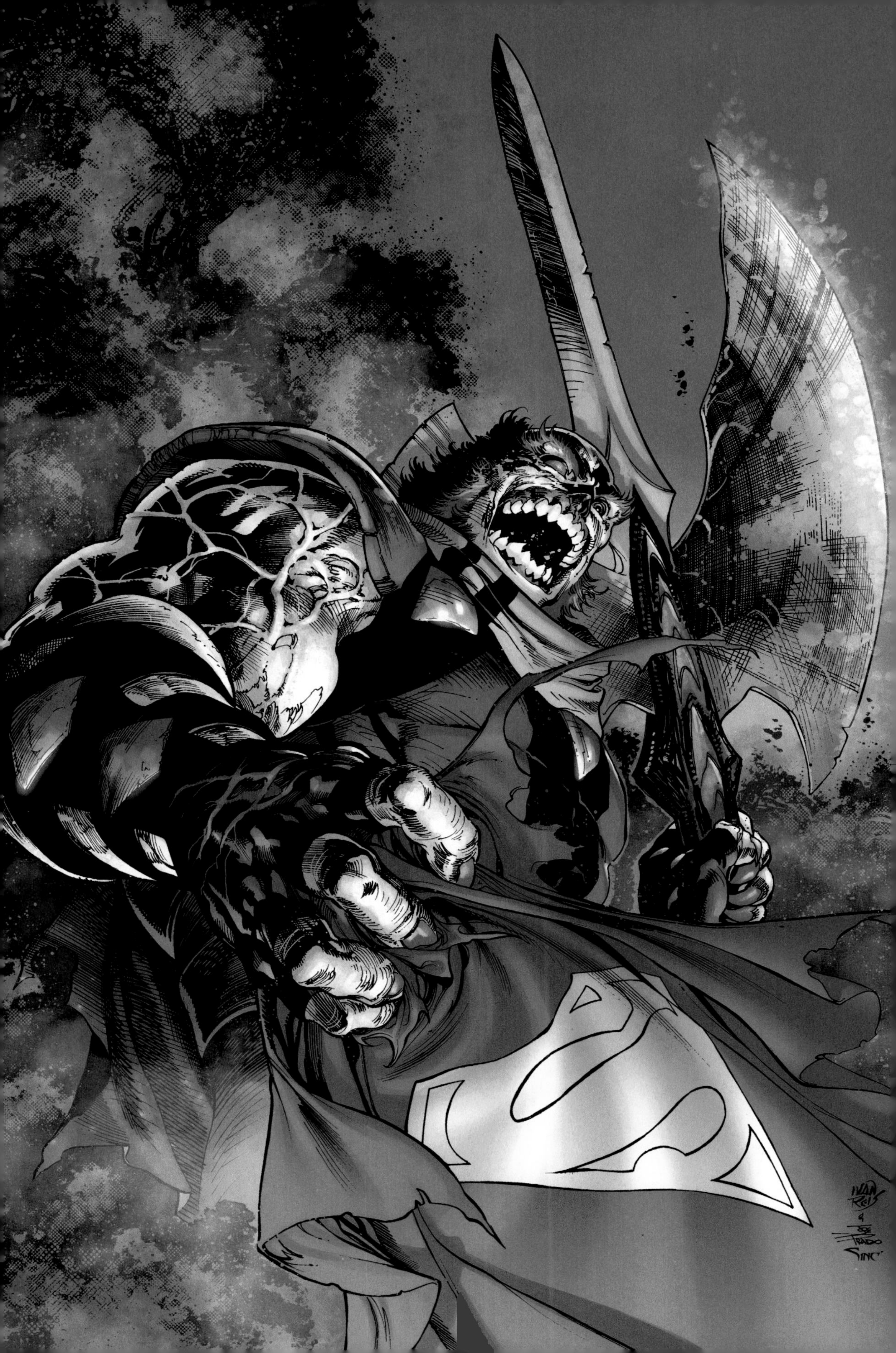

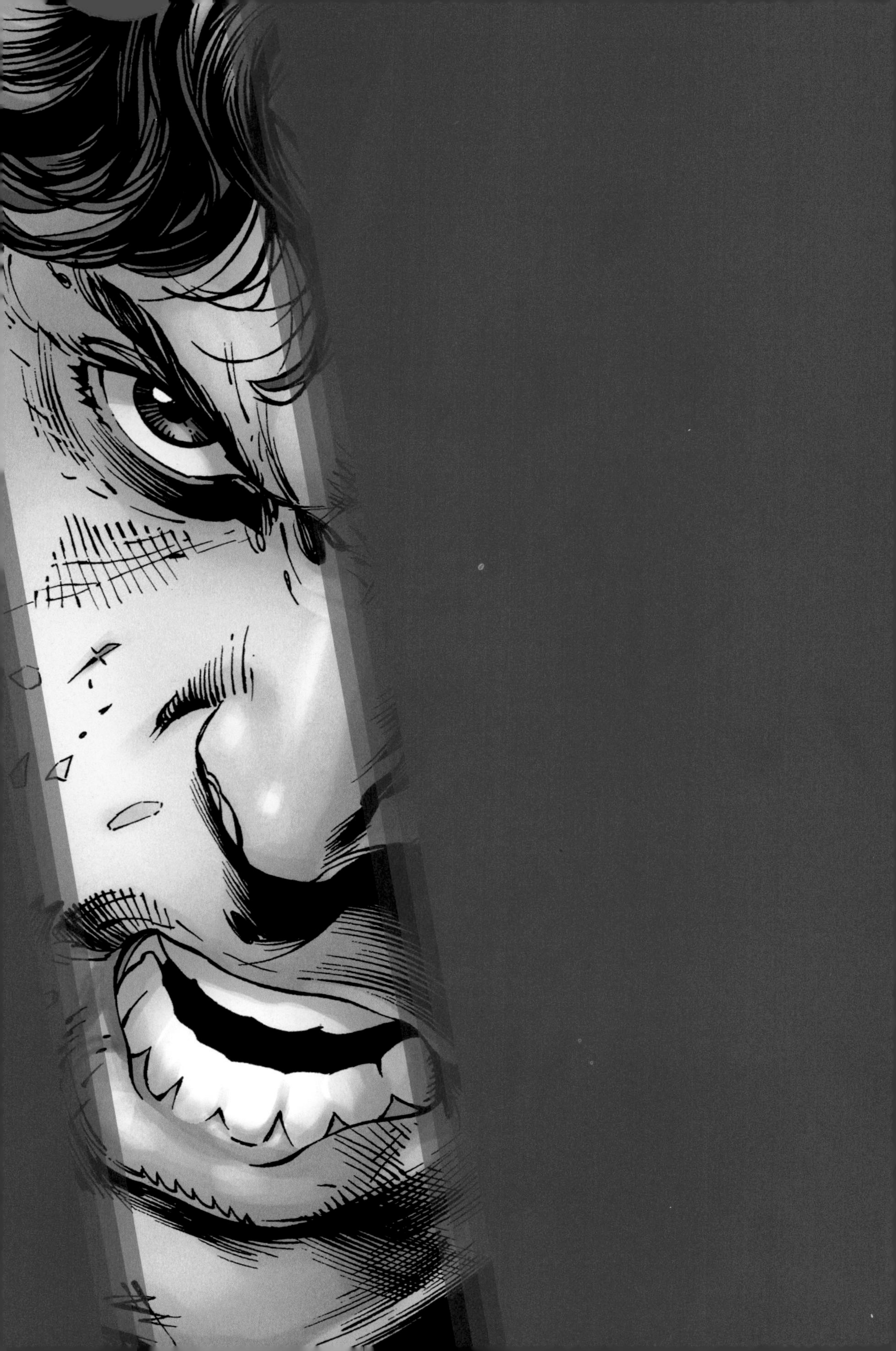

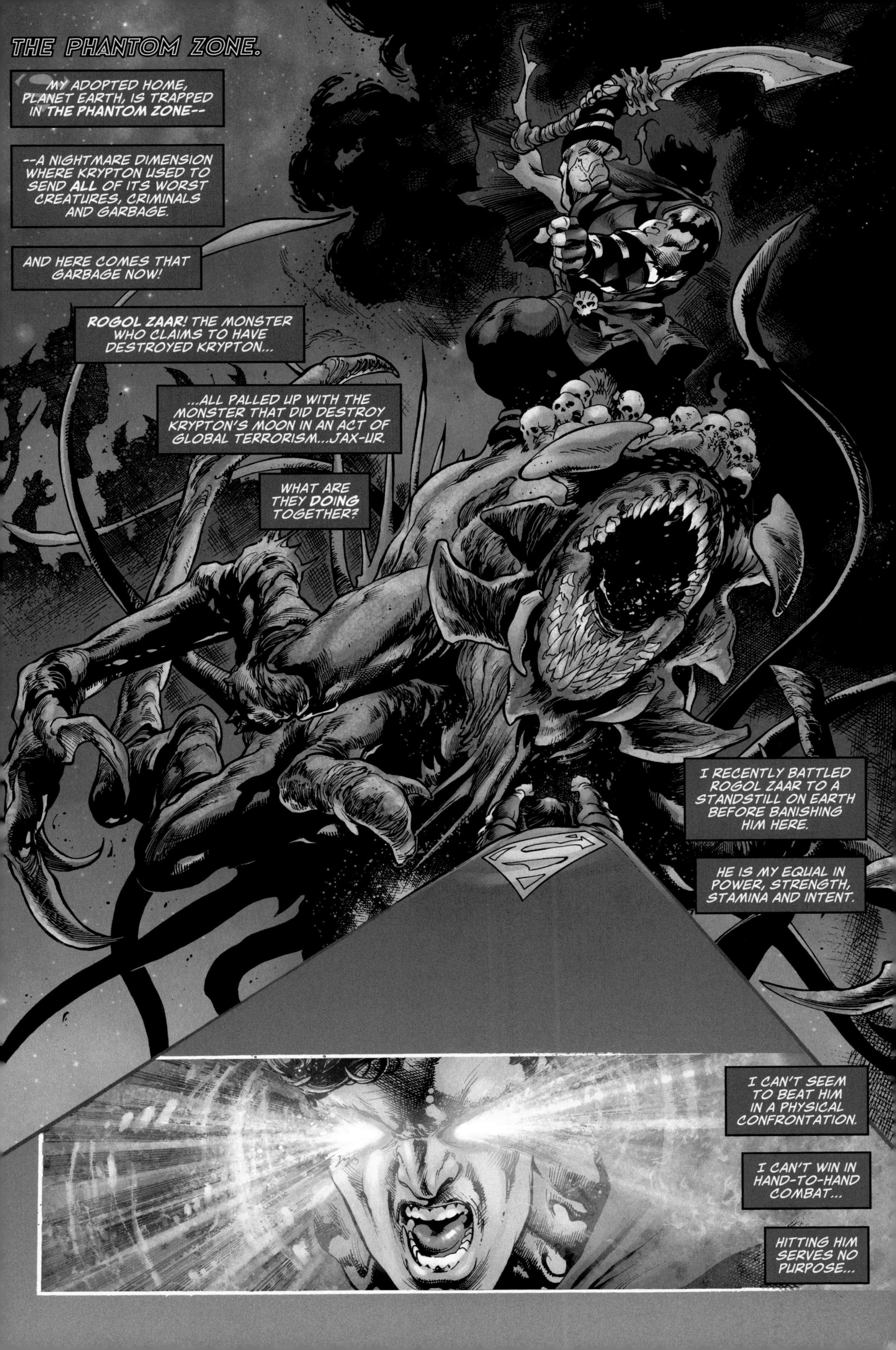
THE PHANTOM ZONE.
MY ADOPTED HOME, PLANET EARTH, IS TRAPPED IN THE PHANTOM ZONE--
--A NIGHTMARE DIMENSION WHERE KRYPTON USED TO SEND ALL OF ITS WORST CREATURES, CRIMINALS AND GARBAGE.
AND HERE COMES THAT GARBAGE NOW!
ROGOL ZAAR! THE MONSTER WHO CLAIMS TO HAVE DESTROYED KRYPTON...
...ALL PALLED UP WITH THE MONSTER THAT DID DESTROY KRYPTON'S MOON IN AN ACT OF GLOBAL TERRORISM...JAX-UR.
WHAT ARE THEY DOING TOGETHER?
I RECENTLY BATTLED ROGOL ZAAR TO A STANDSTILL ON EARTH BEFORE BANISHING HIM HERE.
HE IS MY EQUAL IN POWER, STRENGTH, STAMINA AND INTENT.
I CAN'T SEEM TO BEAT HIM IN A PHYSICAL CONFRONTATION.
I CAN'T WIN IN HAND-TO-HAND COMBAT...
HITTING HIM SERVES NO PURPOSE...

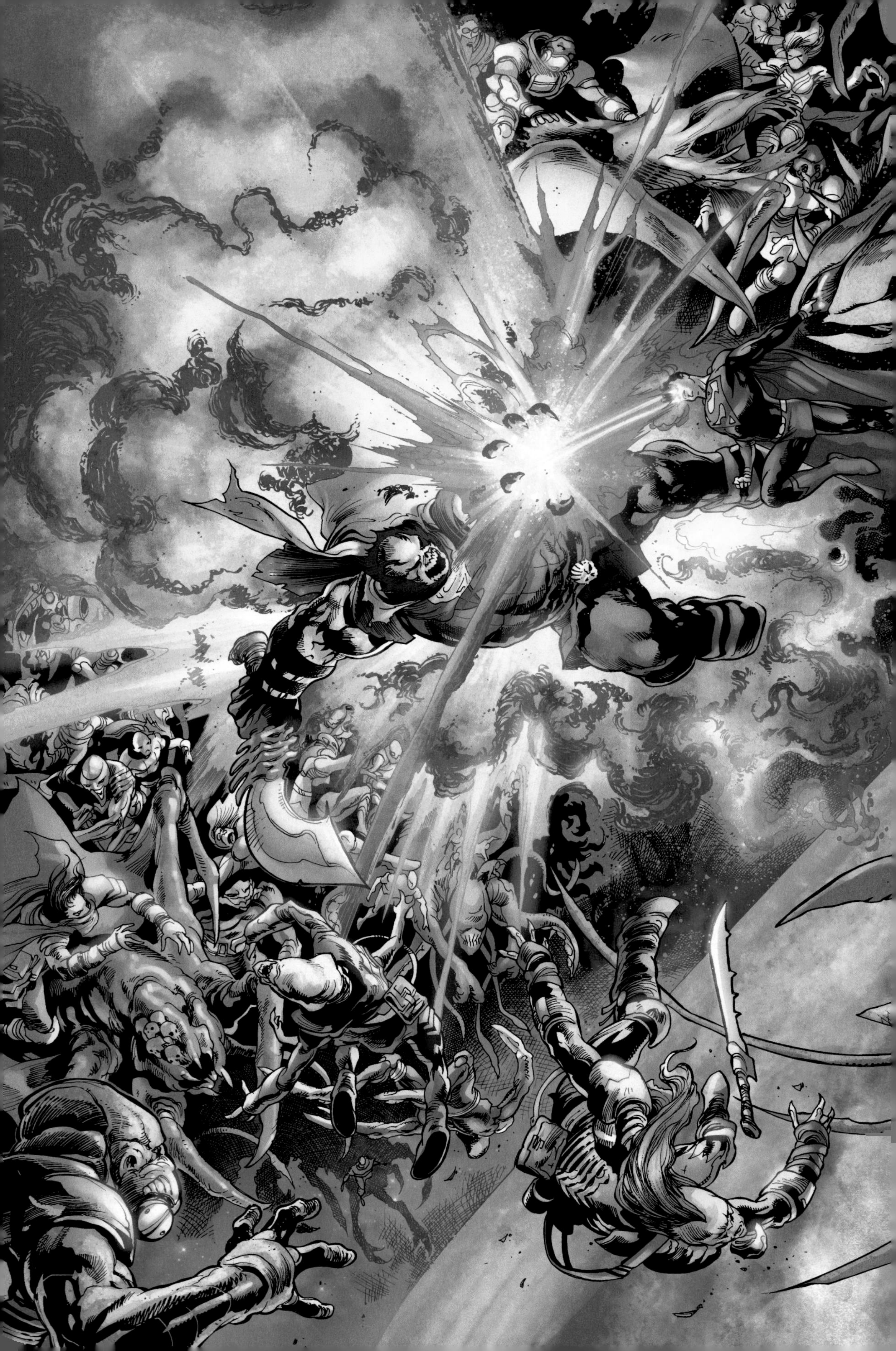

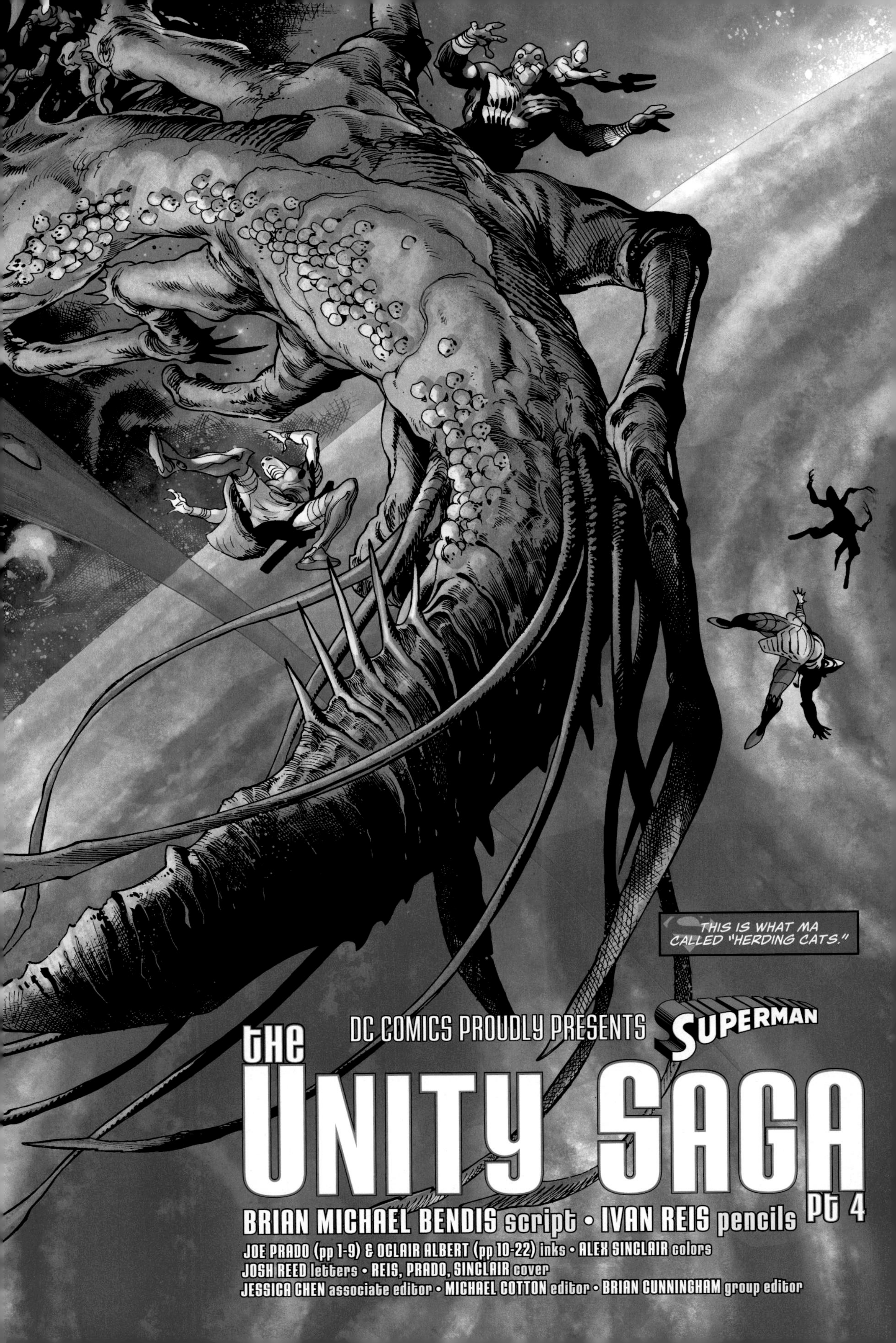
THIS IS WHAT MA CALLED "HERDING CATS."
DC COMICS PROUDLY PRESENTS SUPERMAN
THE UNITY SAGA PT 4
BRIAN MICHAEL BENDIS script • IVAN REIS pencils
JOE PRADO (pp 1-9) & OCLAIR ALBERT (pp 10-22) inks • ALEX SINCLAIR colors
JOSH REED letters • REIS, PRADO, SINCLAIR cover
JESSICA CHEN associate editor • MICHAEL COTTON editor • BRIAN CUNNINGHAM group editor

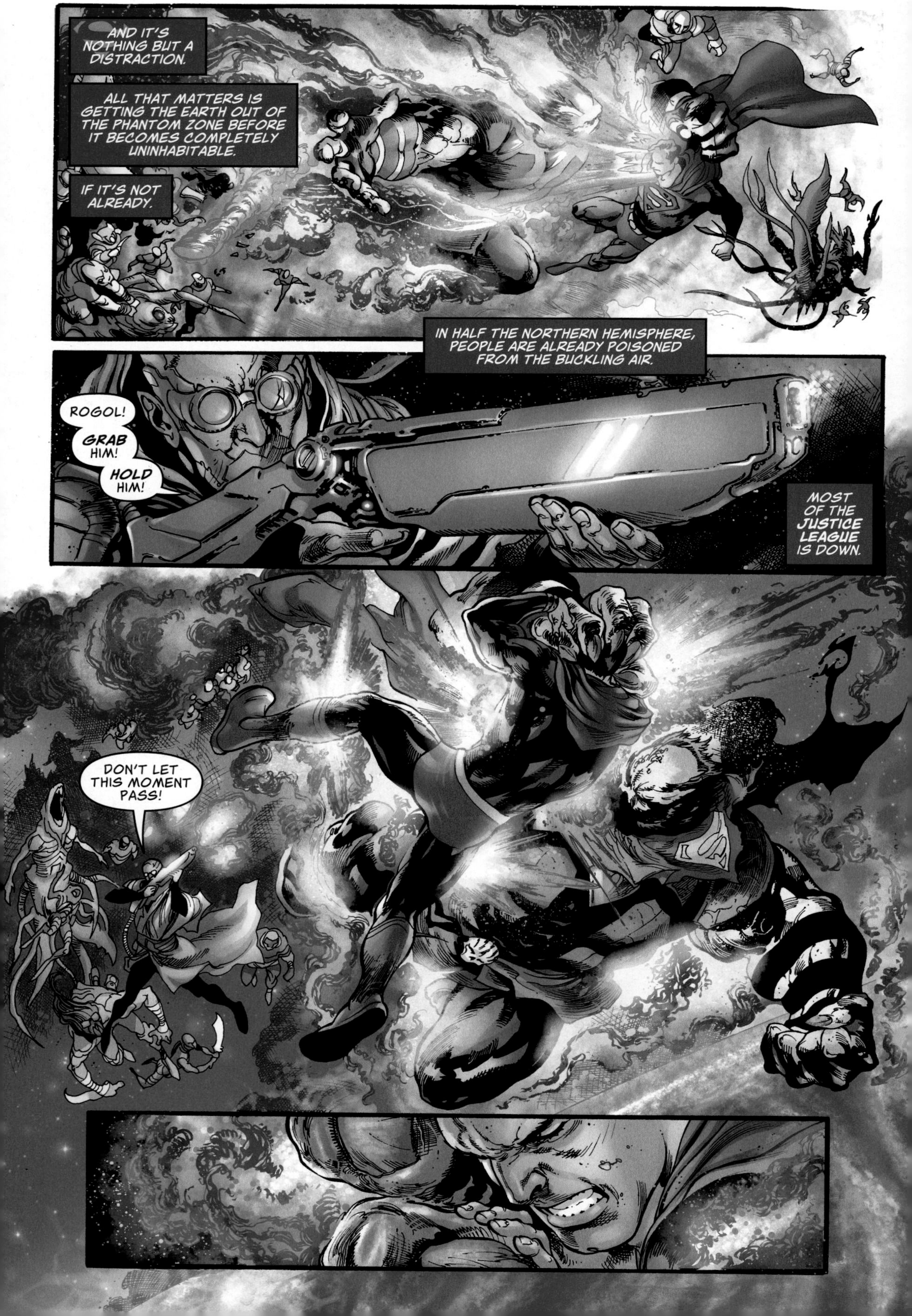
AND IT'S NOTHING BUT A DISTRACTION.
ALL THAT MATTERS IS GETTING THE EARTH OUT OF THE PHANTOM ZONE BEFORE IT BECOMES COMPLETELY UNINHABITABLE.
IF IT'S NOT ALREADY.
IN HALF THE NORTHERN HEMISPHERE, PEOPLE ARE ALREADY POISONED FROM THE BUCKLING AIR.
ROGOL!
GRAB HIM!
HOLD HIM!
MOST OF THE JUSTICE LEAGUE IS DOWN.
DON'T LET THIS MOMENT PASS!

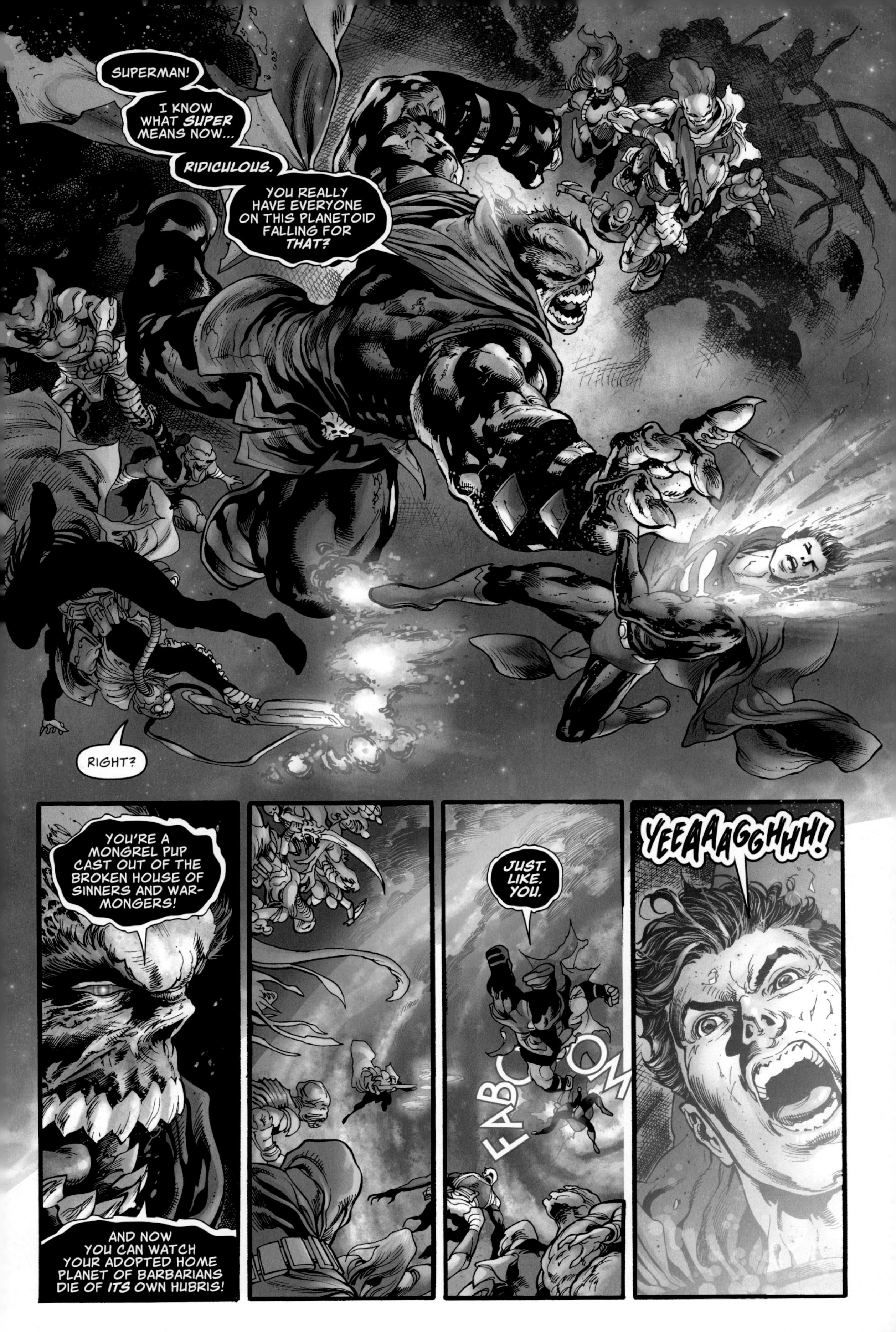
SUPERMAN!
I KNOW WHAT SUPER MEANS NOW...
RIDICULOUS.
YOU REALLY HAVE EVERYONE ON THIS PLANETOID FALLING FOR THAT?
RIGHT?
YOU'RE A MONGREL PUP CAST OUT OF THE BROKEN HOUSE OF SINNERS AND WAR-MONGERS!
AND NOW YOU CAN WATCH YOUR ADOPTED HOME PLANET OF BARBARIANS DIE OF ITS OWN HUBRIS!
JUST. LIKE. YOU.
FABOOOM
YEEAAAAGGHHH!

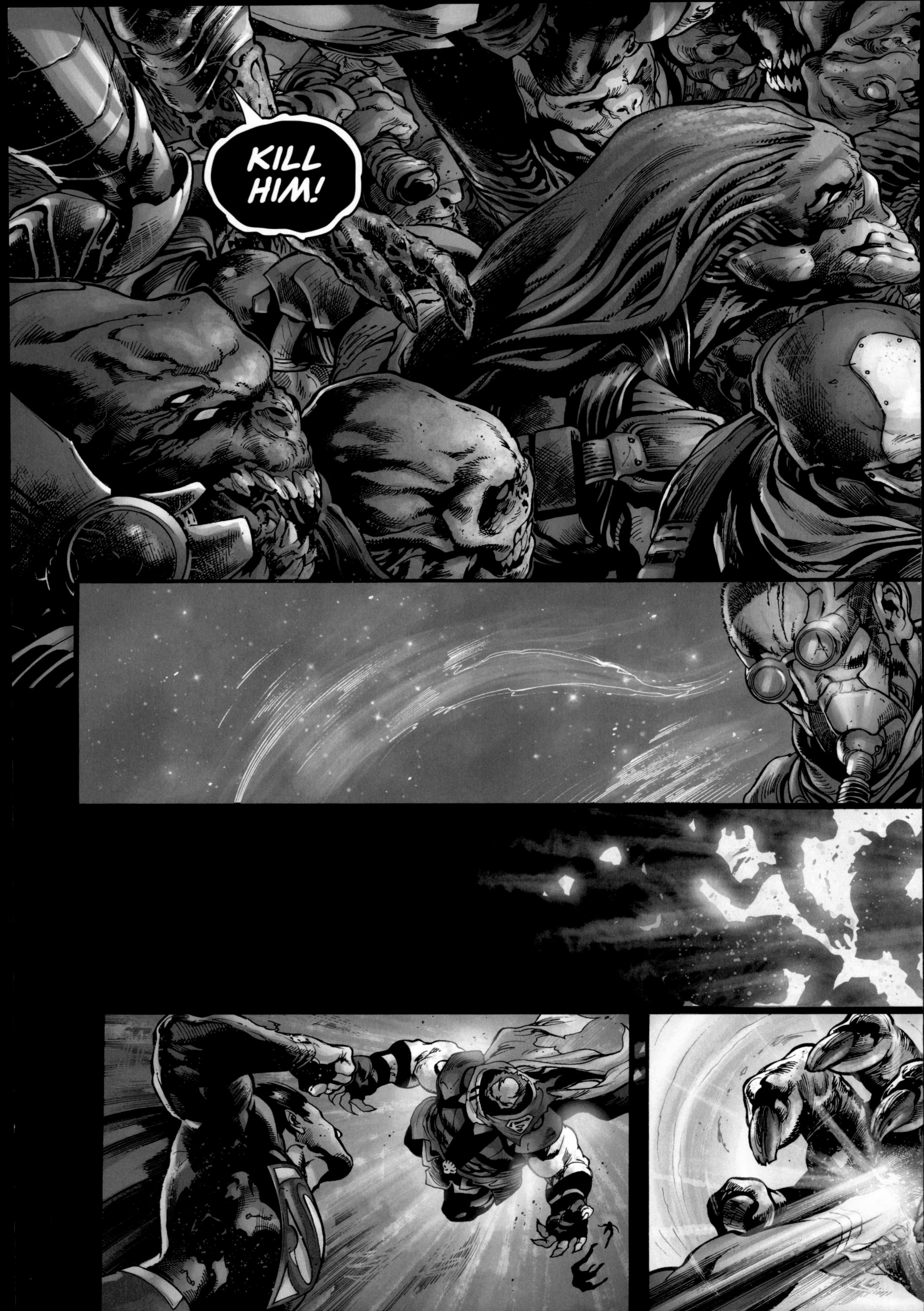
KILL HIM!

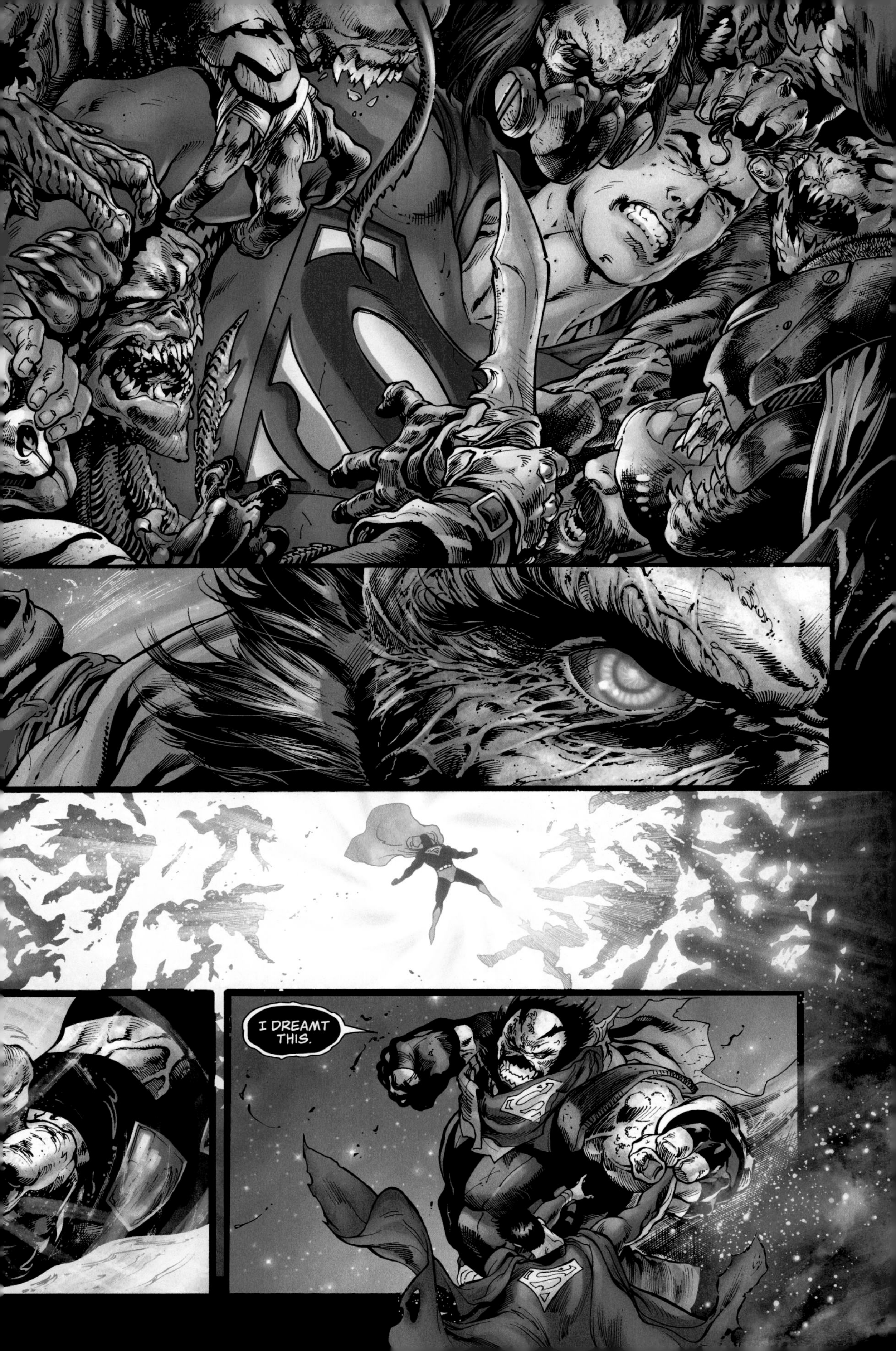
I DREAMT THIS.

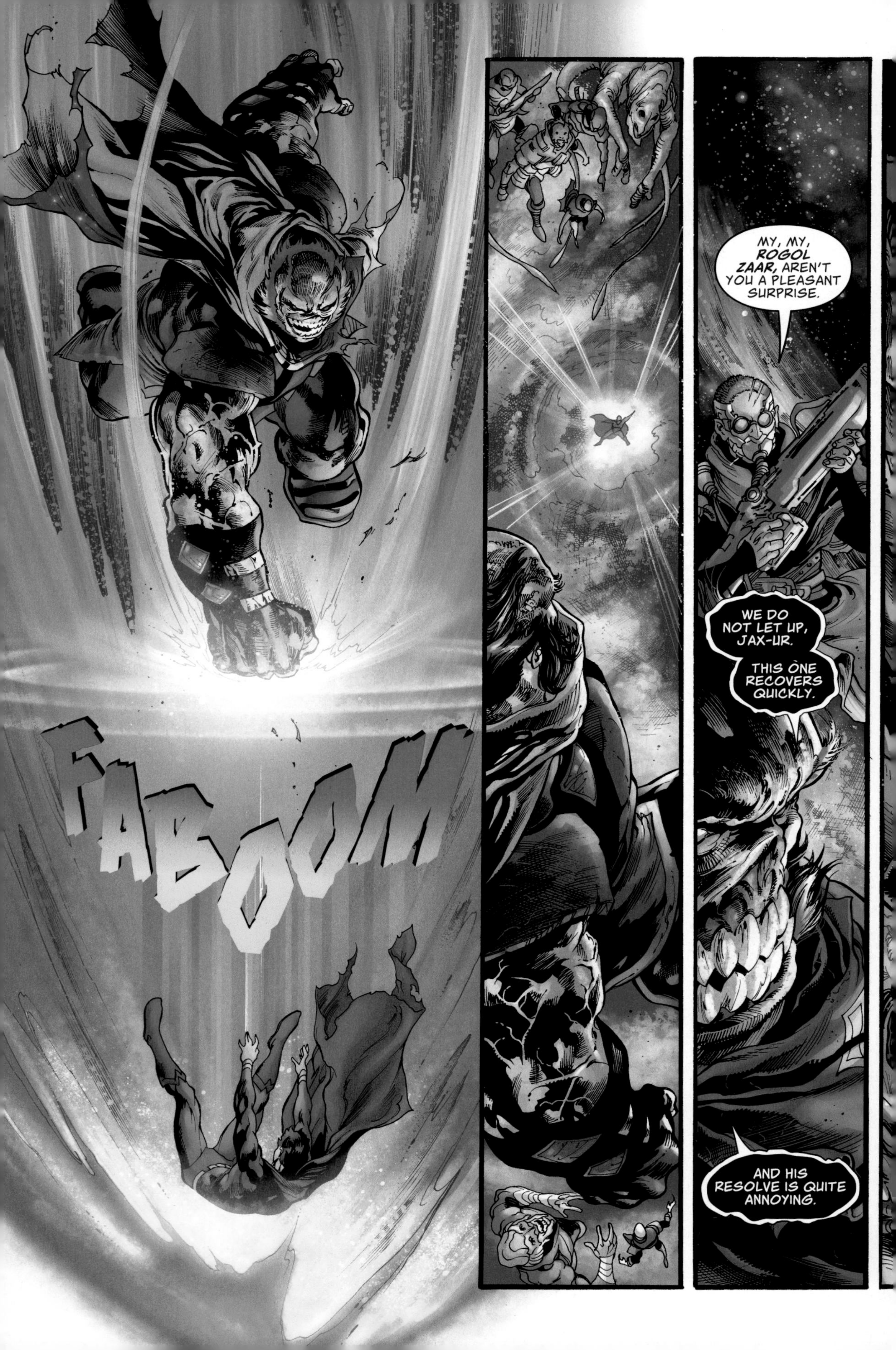
FABOOM
MY, MY, ROGOL ZAAR, AREN'T YOU A PLEASANT SURPRISE.
WE DO NOT LET UP, JAX-UR.
THIS ONE RECOVERS QUICKLY.
AND HIS RESOLVE IS QUITE ANNOYING.

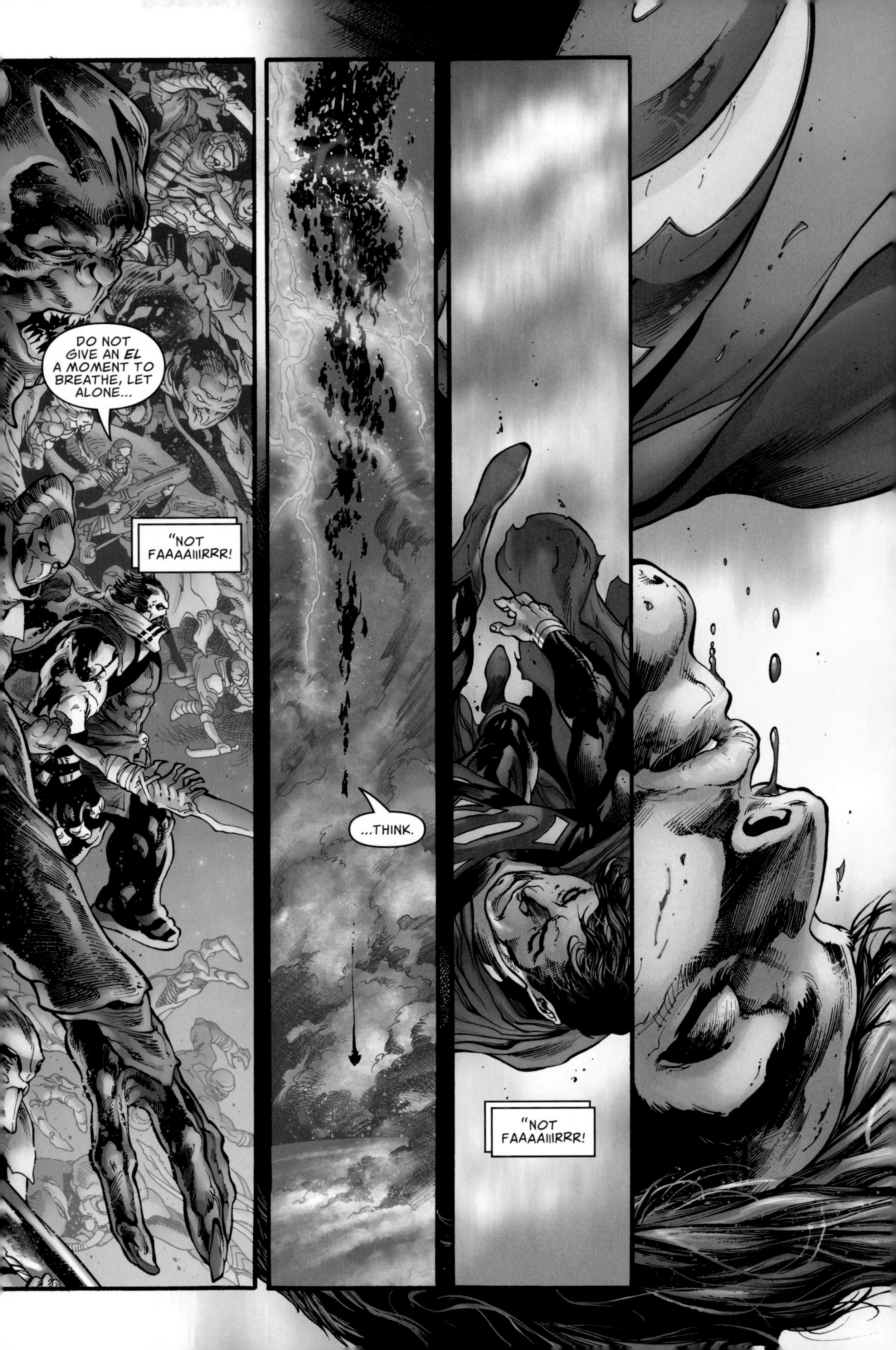
DO NOT GIVE AN EL A MOMENT TO BREATHE, LET ALONE...
"NOT FAAAAIIIRRR!
...THINK.
"NOT FAAAAIIIRRR!

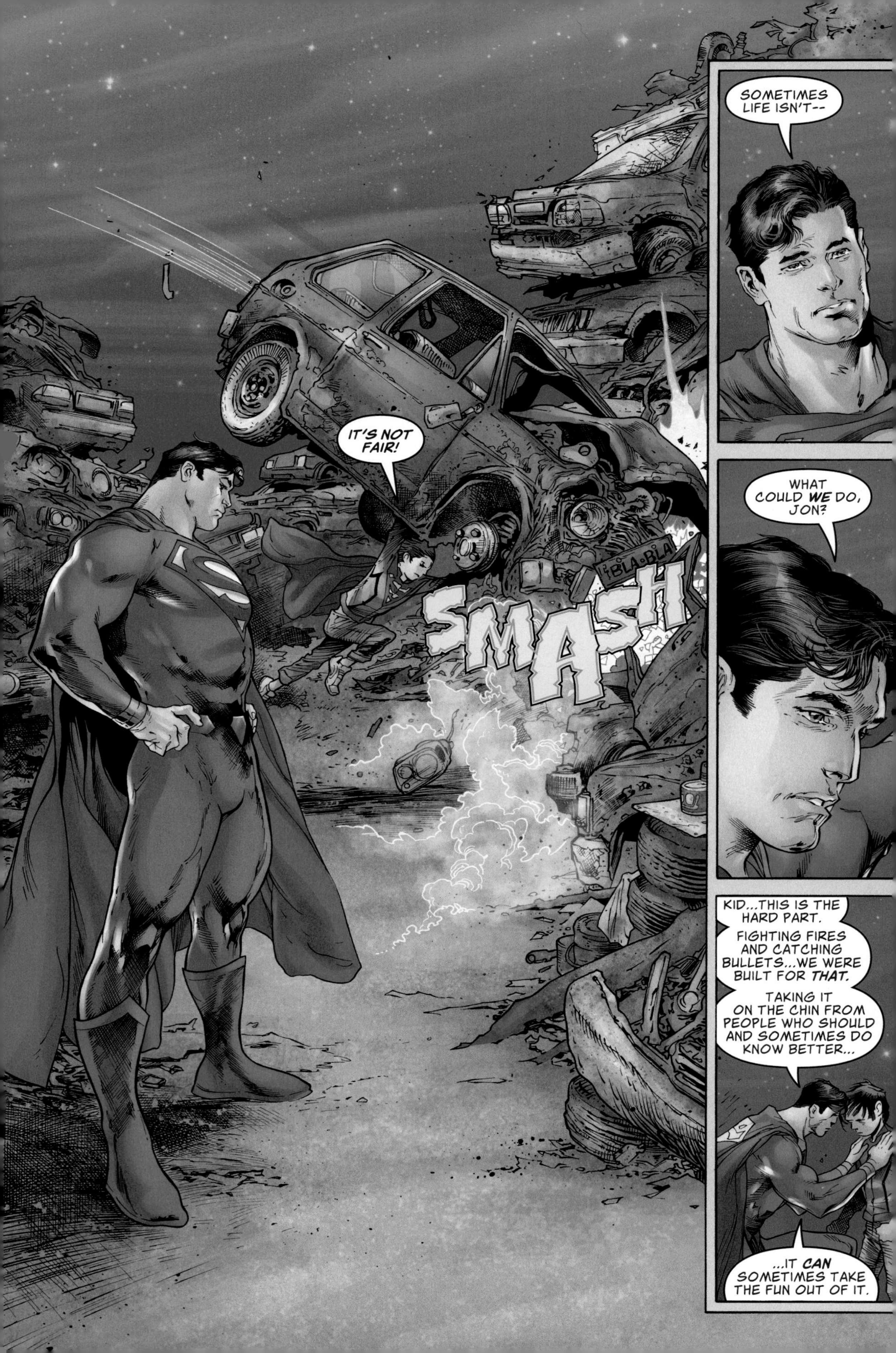
IT'S NOT FAIR!
SMASH
BLA-BLA
SOMETIMES LIFE ISN'T--
WHAT COULD *WE* DO, JON?
KID...THIS IS THE HARD PART.
FIGHTING FIRES AND CATCHING BULLETS...WE WERE BUILT FOR *THAT.*
TAKING IT ON THE CHIN FROM PEOPLE WHO SHOULD AND SOMETIMES DO KNOW BETTER...
...IT *CAN* SOMETIMES TAKE THE FUN OUT OF IT.

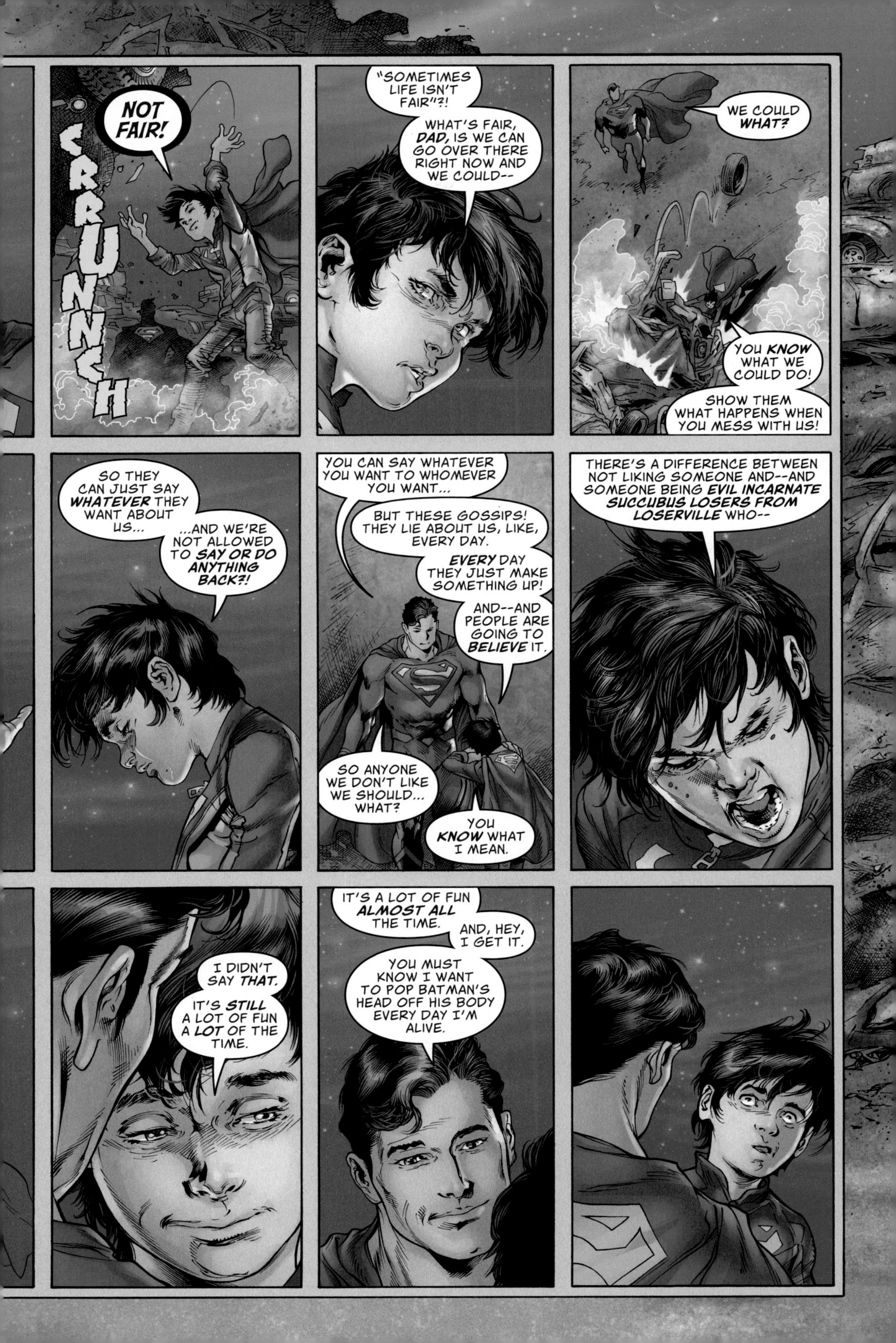

NOT FAIR!
CRRUNNCH
"SOMETIMES LIFE ISN'T FAIR"?!
WHAT'S FAIR, DAD, IS WE CAN GO OVER THERE RIGHT NOW AND WE COULD--
WE COULD WHAT?
YOU KNOW WHAT WE COULD DO!
SHOW THEM WHAT HAPPENS WHEN YOU MESS WITH US!
SO THEY CAN JUST SAY WHATEVER THEY WANT ABOUT US...
...AND WE'RE NOT ALLOWED TO SAY OR DO ANYTHING BACK?!
YOU CAN SAY WHATEVER YOU WANT TO WHOMEVER YOU WANT...
BUT THESE GOSSIPS! THEY LIE ABOUT US, LIKE, EVERY DAY.
EVERY DAY THEY JUST MAKE SOMETHING UP!
AND--AND PEOPLE ARE GOING TO BELIEVE IT.
SO ANYONE WE DON'T LIKE WE SHOULD... WHAT?
YOU KNOW WHAT I MEAN.
THERE'S A DIFFERENCE BETWEEN NOT LIKING SOMEONE AND--AND SOMEONE BEING EVIL INCARNATE SUCCUBUS LOSERS FROM LOSERVILLE WHO--
I DIDN'T SAY THAT.
IT'S STILL A LOT OF FUN A LOT OF THE TIME.
IT'S A LOT OF FUN ALMOST ALL THE TIME.
AND, HEY, I GET IT.
YOU MUST KNOW I WANT TO POP BATMAN'S HEAD OFF HIS BODY EVERY DAY I'M ALIVE.

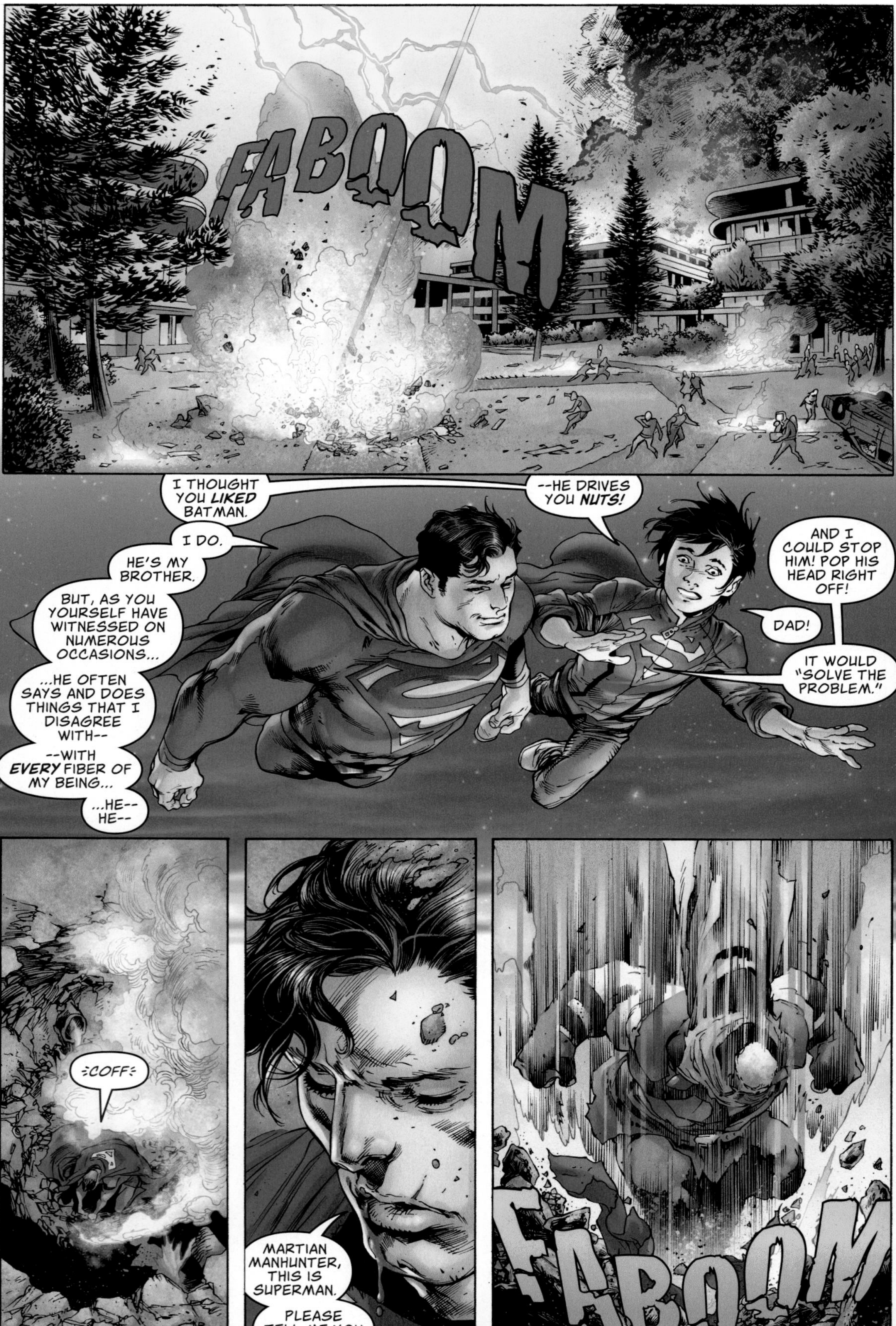
FABOOM
I THOUGHT YOU LIKED BATMAN.
--HE DRIVES YOU NUTS!
I DO.
HE'S MY BROTHER.
BUT, AS YOU YOURSELF HAVE WITNESSED ON NUMEROUS OCCASIONS...
...HE OFTEN SAYS AND DOES THINGS THAT I DISAGREE WITH--
--WITH EVERY FIBER OF MY BEING...
...HE-- HE--
AND I COULD STOP HIM! POP HIS HEAD RIGHT OFF!
DAD!
IT WOULD "SOLVE THE PROBLEM."
=COFF=
MARTIAN MANHUNTER, THIS IS SUPERMAN.
PLEASE TELL ME YOU CAN HEAR--
FABOOM

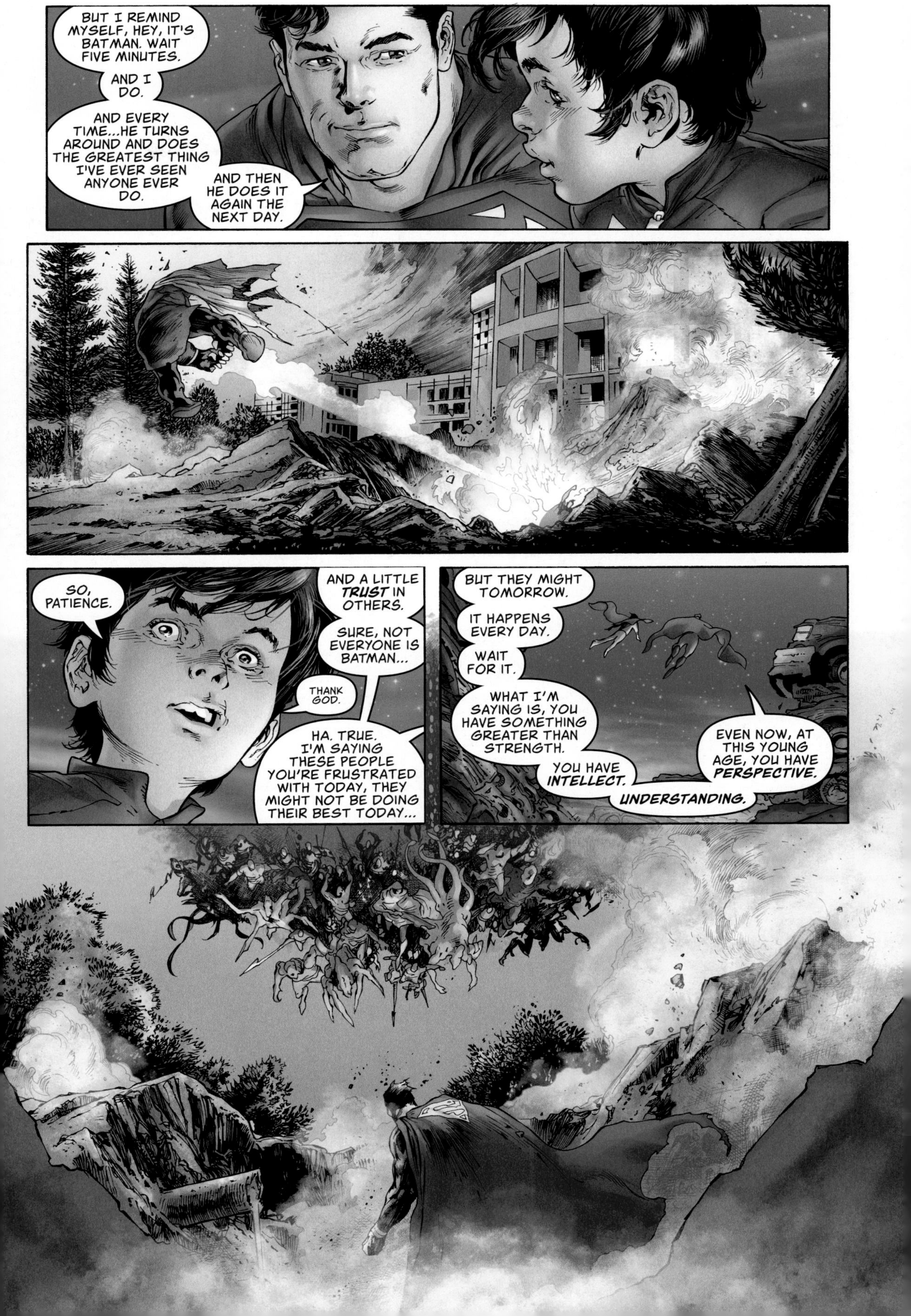
BUT I REMIND MYSELF, HEY, IT'S BATMAN. WAIT FIVE MINUTES.
AND I DO.
AND EVERY TIME...HE TURNS AROUND AND DOES THE GREATEST THING I'VE EVER SEEN ANYONE EVER DO.
AND THEN HE DOES IT AGAIN THE NEXT DAY.
SO, PATIENCE.
AND A LITTLE TRUST IN OTHERS.
SURE, NOT EVERYONE IS BATMAN...
THANK GOD.
HA. TRUE. I'M SAYING THESE PEOPLE YOU'RE FRUSTRATED WITH TODAY, THEY MIGHT NOT BE DOING THEIR BEST TODAY...
BUT THEY MIGHT TOMORROW.
IT HAPPENS EVERY DAY.
WAIT FOR IT.
WHAT I'M SAYING IS, YOU HAVE SOMETHING GREATER THAN STRENGTH.
YOU HAVE INTELLECT.
UNDERSTANDING.
EVEN NOW, AT THIS YOUNG AGE, YOU HAVE PERSPECTIVE.

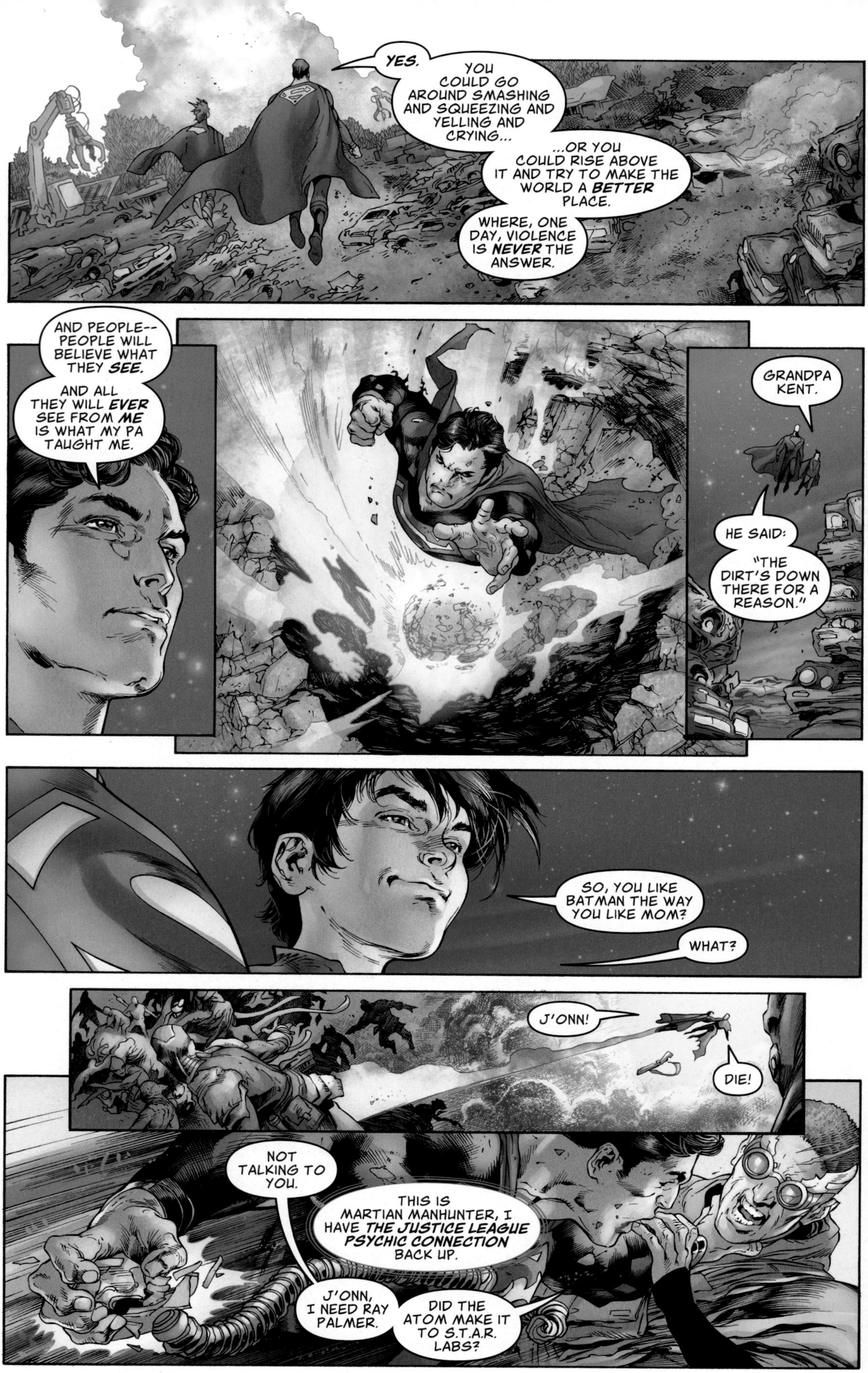
YES.
YOU COULD GO AROUND SMASHING AND SQUEEZING AND YELLING AND CRYING...
...OR YOU COULD RISE ABOVE IT AND TRY TO MAKE THE WORLD A BETTER PLACE.
WHERE, ONE DAY, VIOLENCE IS NEVER THE ANSWER.
AND PEOPLE--PEOPLE WILL BELIEVE WHAT THEY SEE.
AND ALL THEY WILL EVER SEE FROM ME IS WHAT MY PA TAUGHT ME.
GRANDPA KENT.
HE SAID:
"THE DIRT'S DOWN THERE FOR A REASON."
SO, YOU LIKE BATMAN THE WAY YOU LIKE MOM?
WHAT?
J'ONN!
DIE!
NOT TALKING TO YOU.
THIS IS MARTIAN MANHUNTER, I HAVE THE JUSTICE LEAGUE PSYCHIC CONNECTION BACK UP.
J'ONN, I NEED RAY PALMER.
DID THE ATOM MAKE IT TO S.T.A.R. LABS?

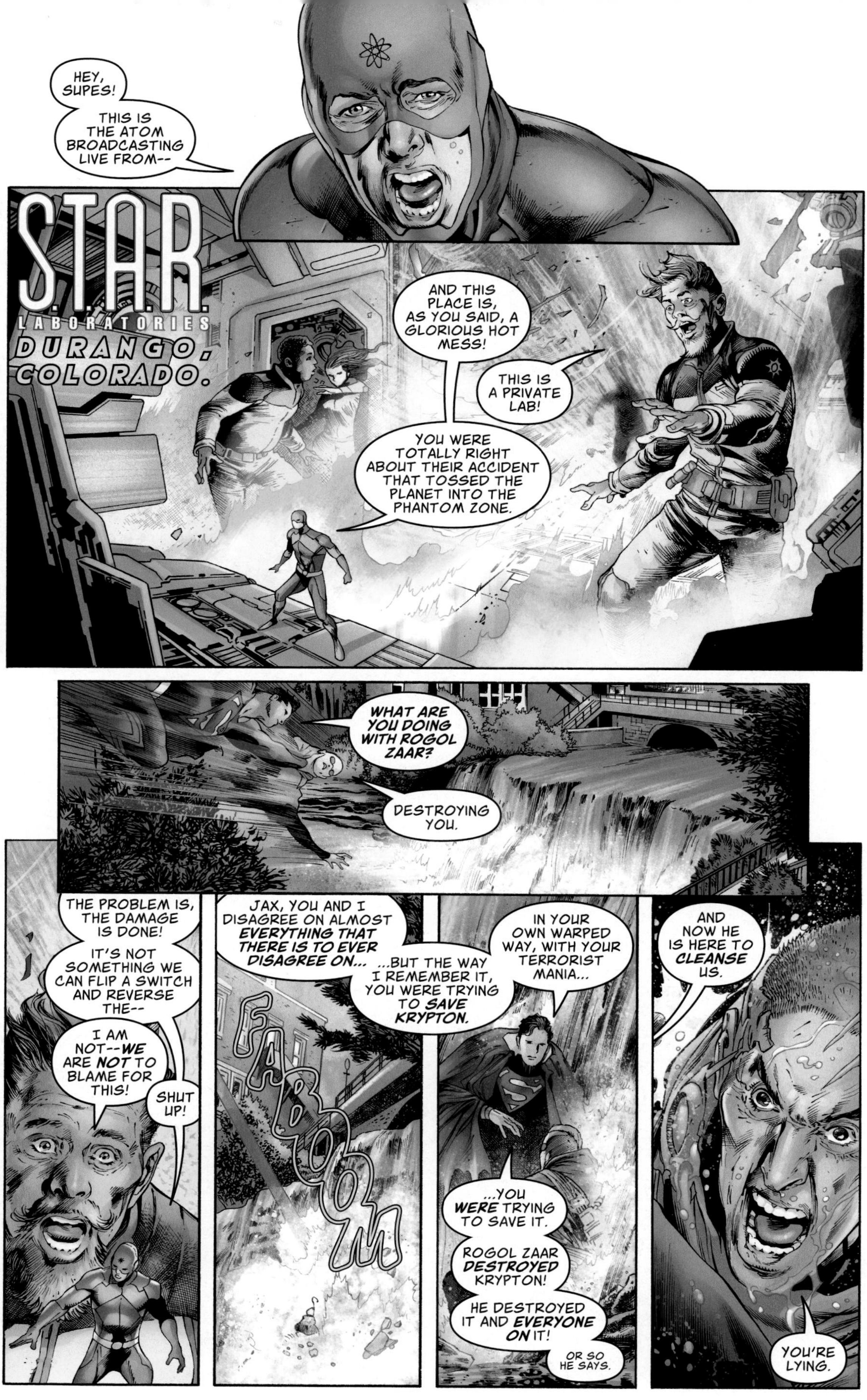

HEY, SUPES!
THIS IS THE ATOM BROADCASTING LIVE FROM--
S.T.A.R. LABORATORIES
DURANGO, COLORADO.
AND THIS PLACE IS, AS YOU SAID, A GLORIOUS HOT MESS!
THIS IS A PRIVATE LAB!
YOU WERE TOTALLY RIGHT ABOUT THEIR ACCIDENT THAT TOSSED THE PLANET INTO THE PHANTOM ZONE.
WHAT ARE YOU DOING WITH ROGOL ZAAR?
DESTROYING YOU.
THE PROBLEM IS, THE DAMAGE IS DONE!
IT'S NOT SOMETHING WE CAN FLIP A SWITCH AND REVERSE THE--
I AM NOT--WE ARE NOT TO BLAME FOR THIS!
SHUT UP!
JAX, YOU AND I DISAGREE ON ALMOST EVERYTHING THAT THERE IS TO EVER DISAGREE ON...
...BUT THE WAY I REMEMBER IT, YOU WERE TRYING TO SAVE KRYPTON.
FABOOM
IN YOUR OWN WARPED WAY, WITH YOUR TERRORIST MANIA...
...YOU WERE TRYING TO SAVE IT.
ROGOL ZAAR DESTROYED KRYPTON!
HE DESTROYED IT AND EVERYONE ON IT!
OR SO HE SAYS.
AND NOW HE IS HERE TO CLEANSE US.
YOU'RE LYING.

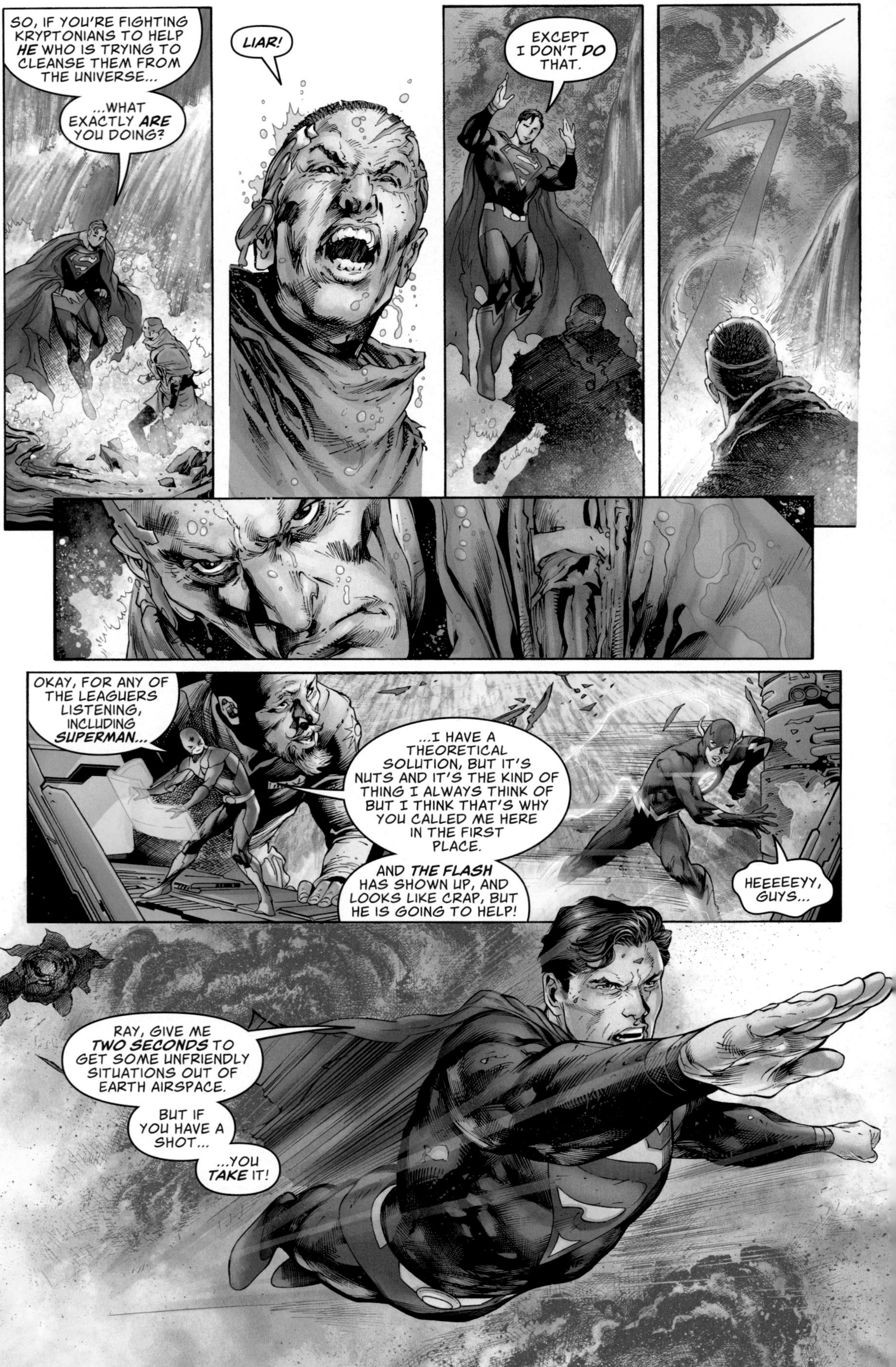

SO, IF YOU'RE FIGHTING KRYPTONIANS TO HELP HE WHO IS TRYING TO CLEANSE THEM FROM THE UNIVERSE...
...WHAT EXACTLY ARE YOU DOING?
LIAR!
EXCEPT I DON'T DO THAT.
OKAY, FOR ANY OF THE LEAGUERS LISTENING, INCLUDING SUPERMAN...
...I HAVE A THEORETICAL SOLUTION, BUT IT'S NUTS AND IT'S THE KIND OF THING I ALWAYS THINK OF BUT I THINK THAT'S WHY YOU CALLED ME HERE IN THE FIRST PLACE.
AND THE FLASH HAS SHOWN UP, AND LOOKS LIKE CRAP, BUT HE IS GOING TO HELP!
HEEEEEYY, GUYS...
RAY, GIVE ME TWO SECONDS TO GET SOME UNFRIENDLY SITUATIONS OUT OF EARTH AIRSPACE.
BUT IF YOU HAVE A SHOT...
...YOU TAKE IT!

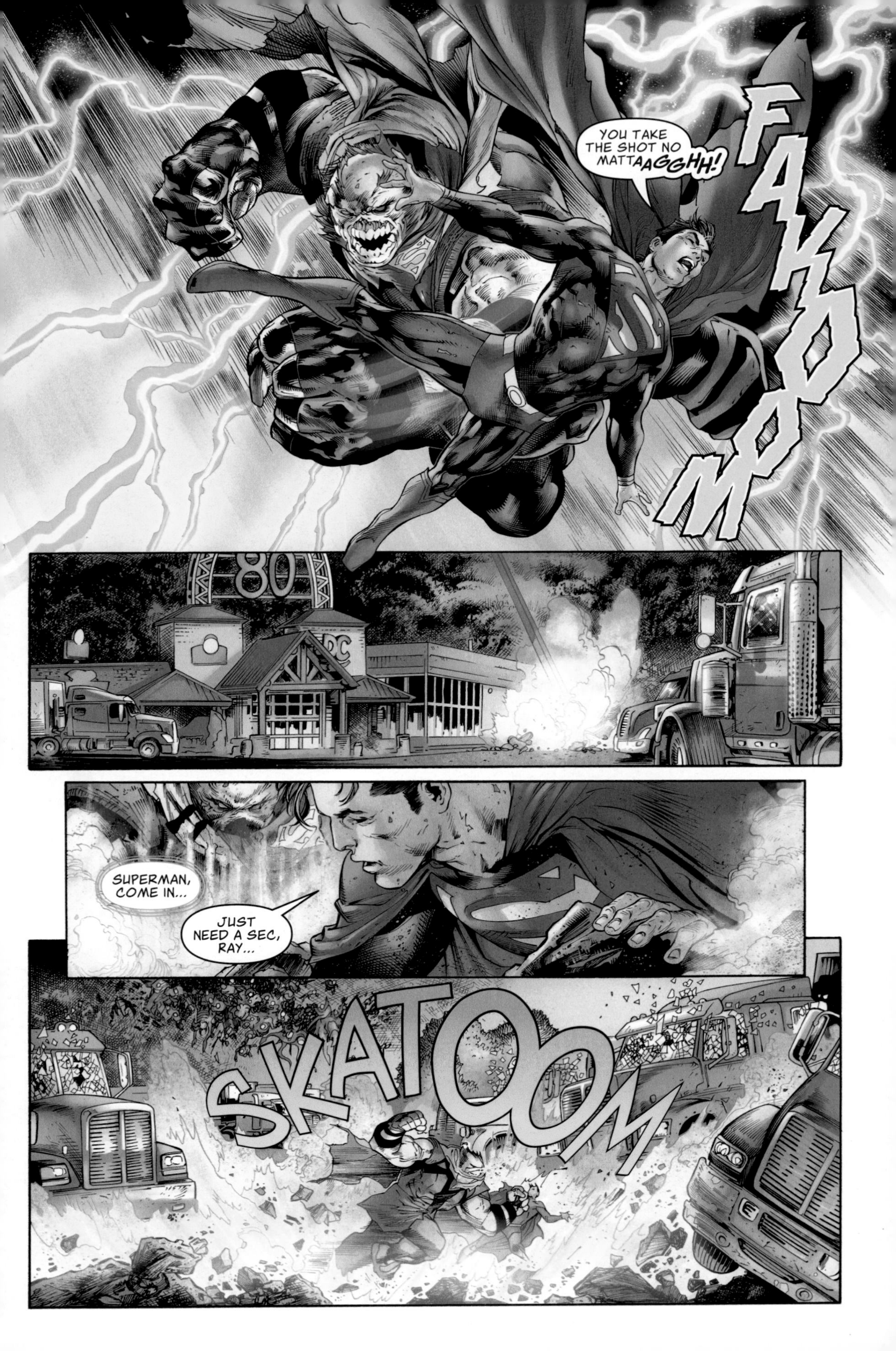

YOU TAKE THE SHOT NO MATTAAGGHH!
FAKOOOM
80
SUPERMAN, COME IN...
JUST NEED A SEC, RAY...
SKATOOOM

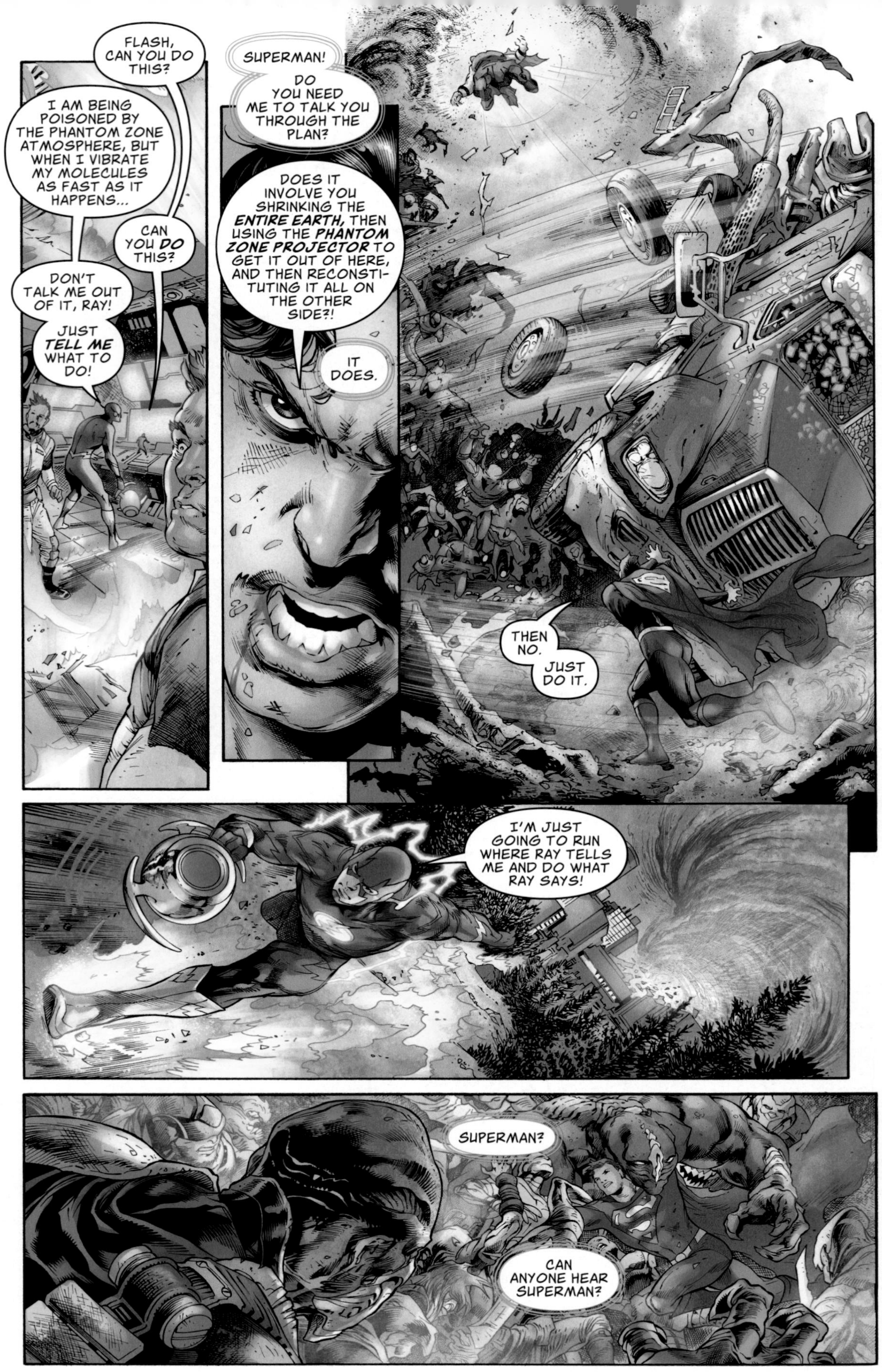
FLASH, CAN YOU DO THIS?
I AM BEING POISONED BY THE PHANTOM ZONE ATMOSPHERE, BUT WHEN I VIBRATE MY MOLECULES AS FAST AS IT HAPPENS...
CAN YOU DO THIS?
DON'T TALK ME OUT OF IT, RAY!
JUST TELL ME WHAT TO DO!
SUPERMAN!
DO YOU NEED ME TO TALK YOU THROUGH THE PLAN?
DOES IT INVOLVE YOU SHRINKING THE ENTIRE EARTH, THEN USING THE PHANTOM ZONE PROJECTOR TO GET IT OUT OF HERE, AND THEN RECONSTITUTING IT ALL ON THE OTHER SIDE?!
IT DOES.
THEN NO.
JUST DO IT.
I'M JUST GOING TO RUN WHERE RAY TELLS ME AND DO WHAT RAY SAYS!
SUPERMAN?
CAN ANYONE HEAR SUPERMAN?

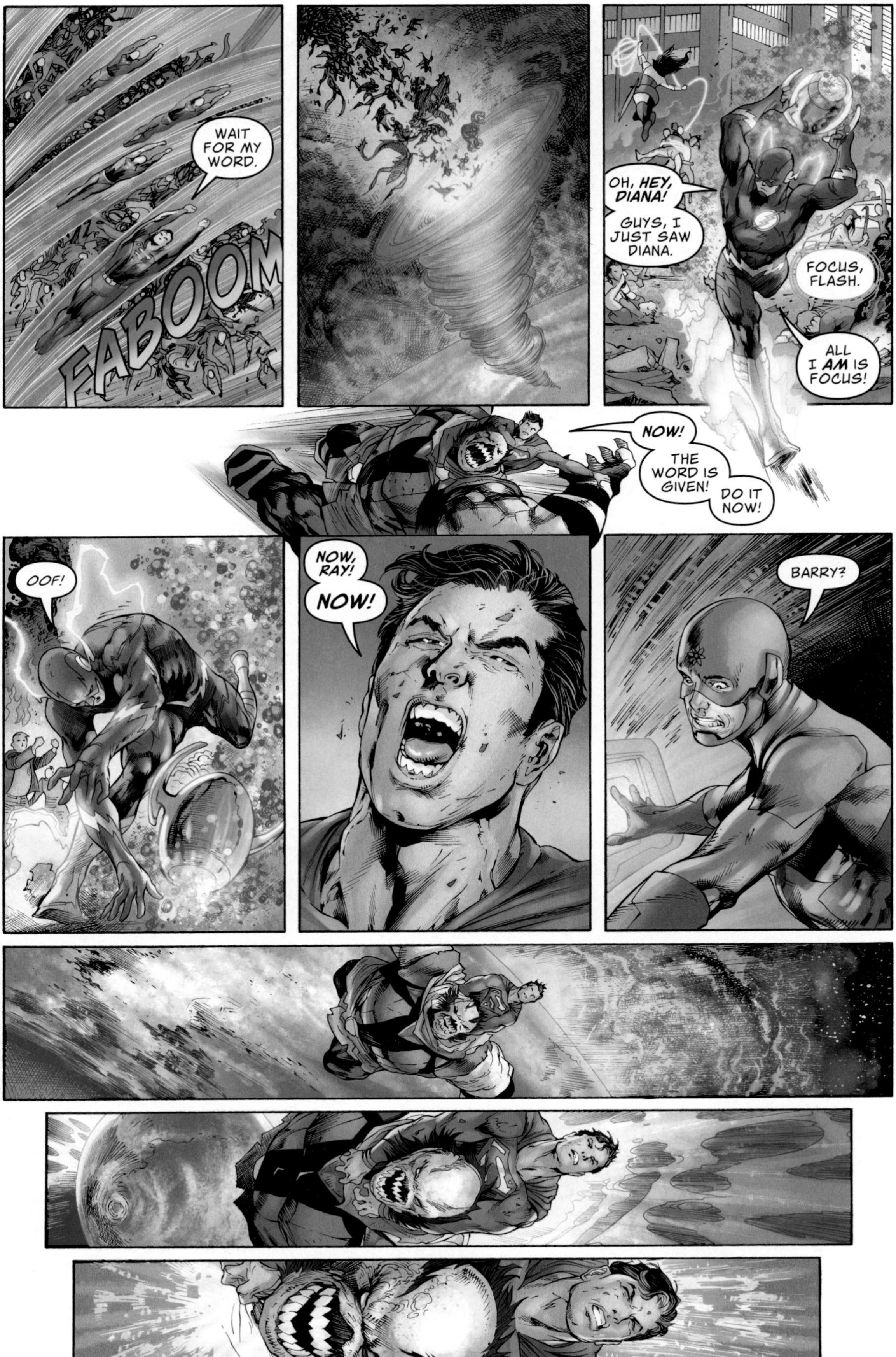
WAIT FOR MY WORD.
FABOOM
OH, HEY, DIANA!
GUYS, I JUST SAW DIANA.
FOCUS, FLASH.
ALL I AM IS FOCUS!
NOW!
THE WORD IS GIVEN!
DO IT NOW!
OOF!
NOW, RAY!
NOW!
BARRY?

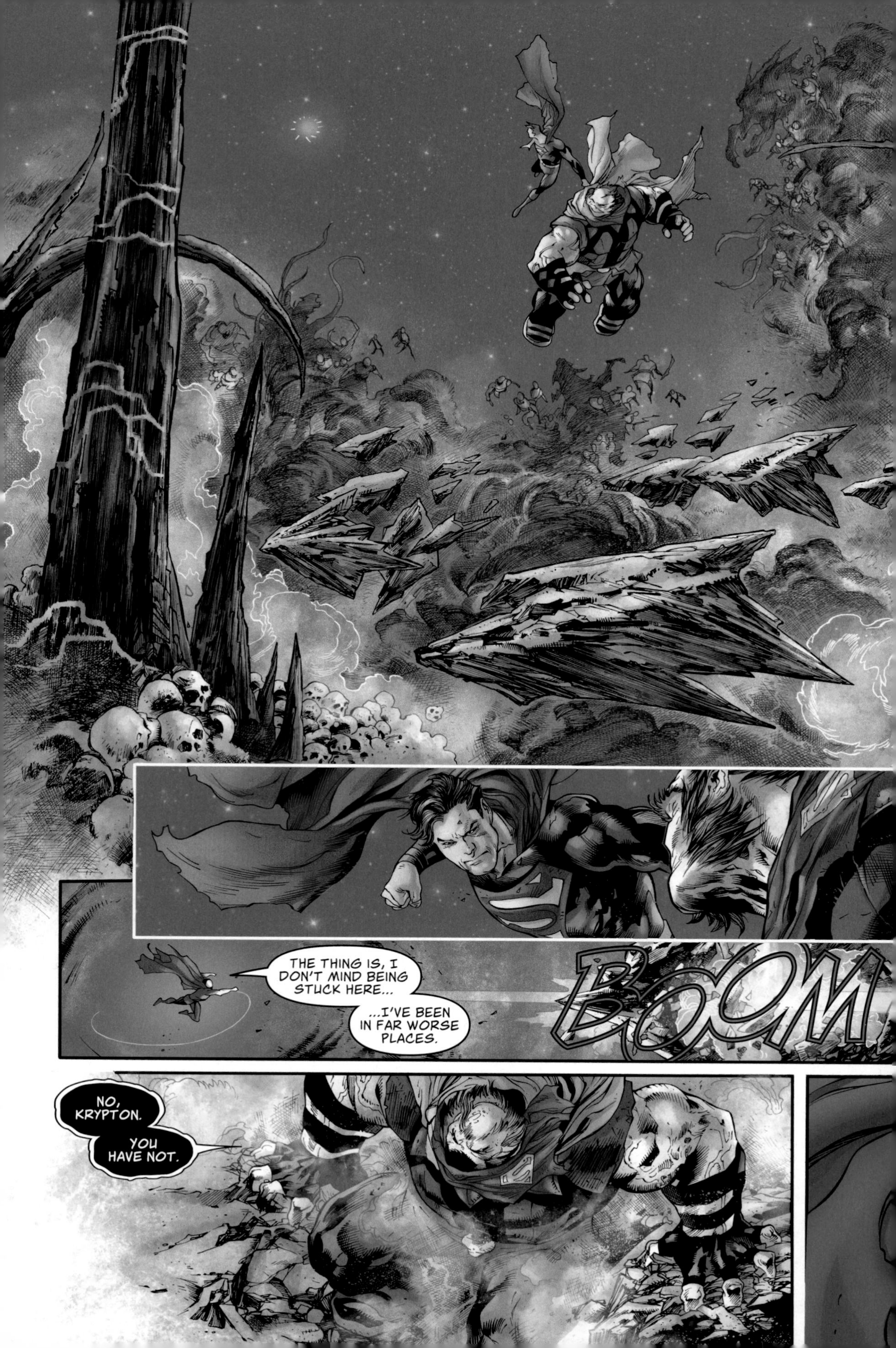
THE THING IS, I DON'T MIND BEING STUCK HERE...
...I'VE BEEN IN FAR WORSE PLACES.
BOOM
NO, KRYPTON.
YOU HAVE NOT.

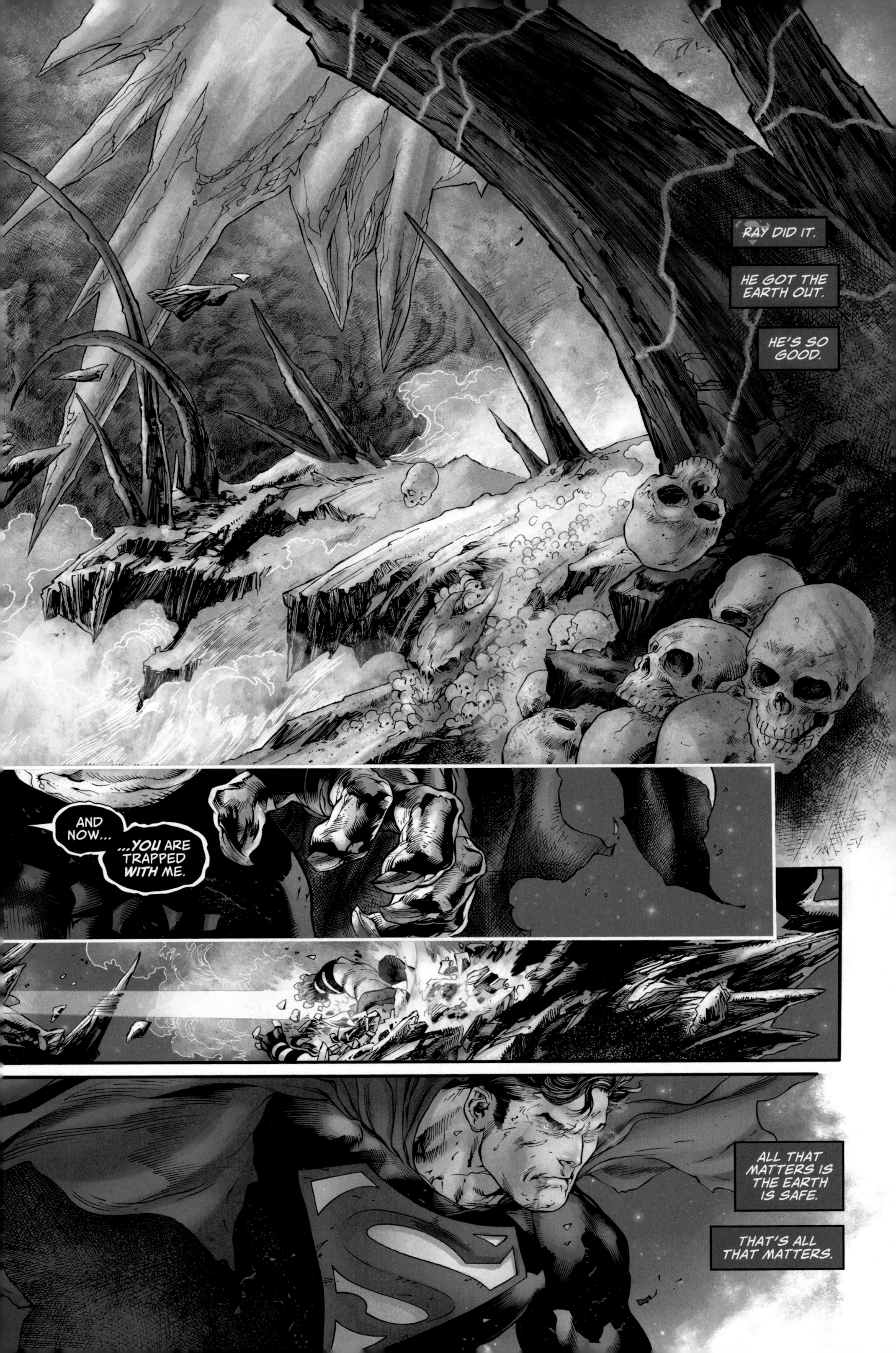
RAY DID IT.
HE GOT THE EARTH OUT.
HE'S SO GOOD.
AND NOW...
...YOU ARE TRAPPED WITH ME.
ALL THAT MATTERS IS THE EARTH IS SAFE.
THAT'S ALL THAT MATTERS.

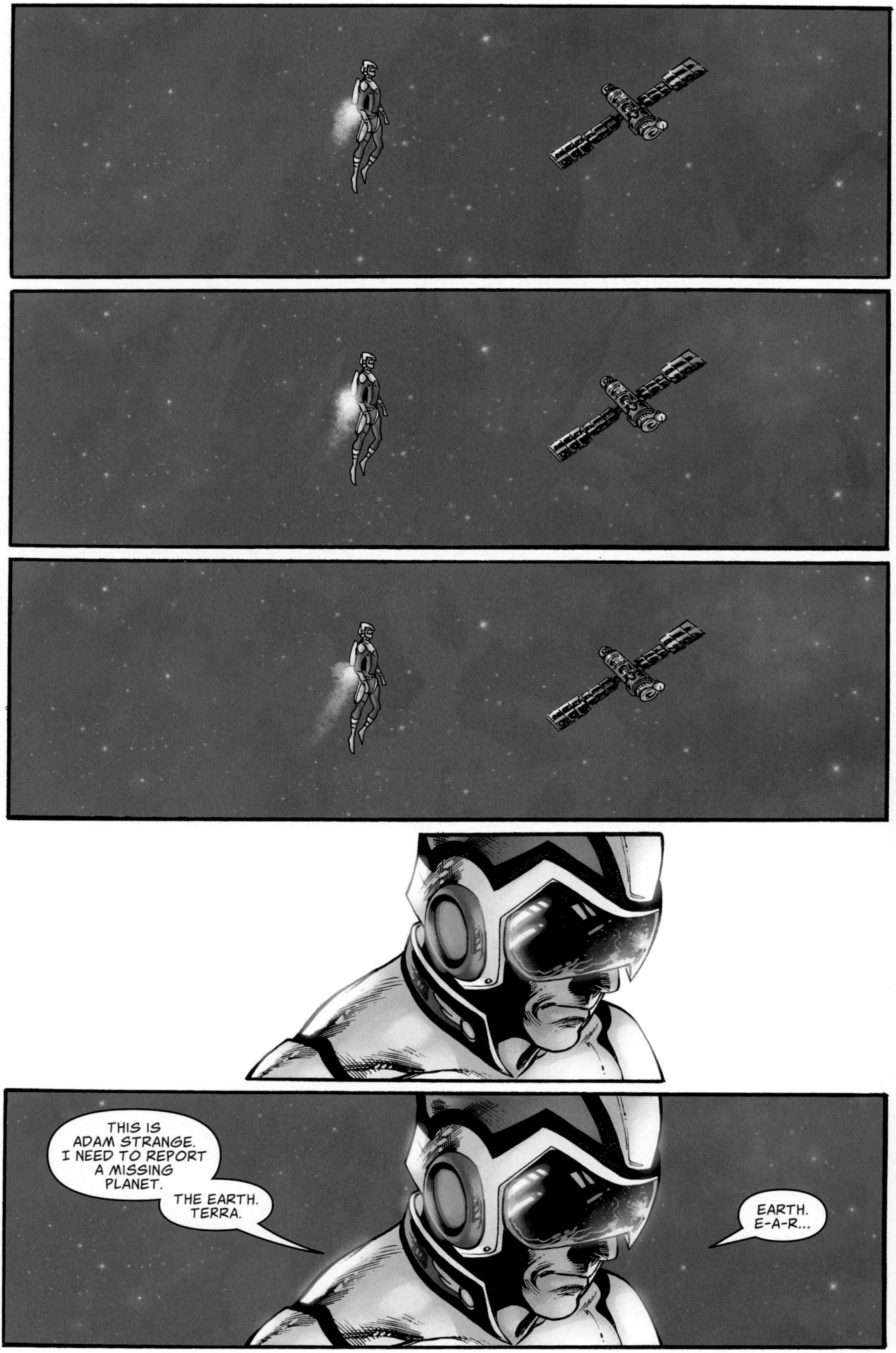
THIS IS ADAM STRANGE. I NEED TO REPORT A MISSING PLANET.
THE EARTH. TERRA.
EARTH. E-A-R...

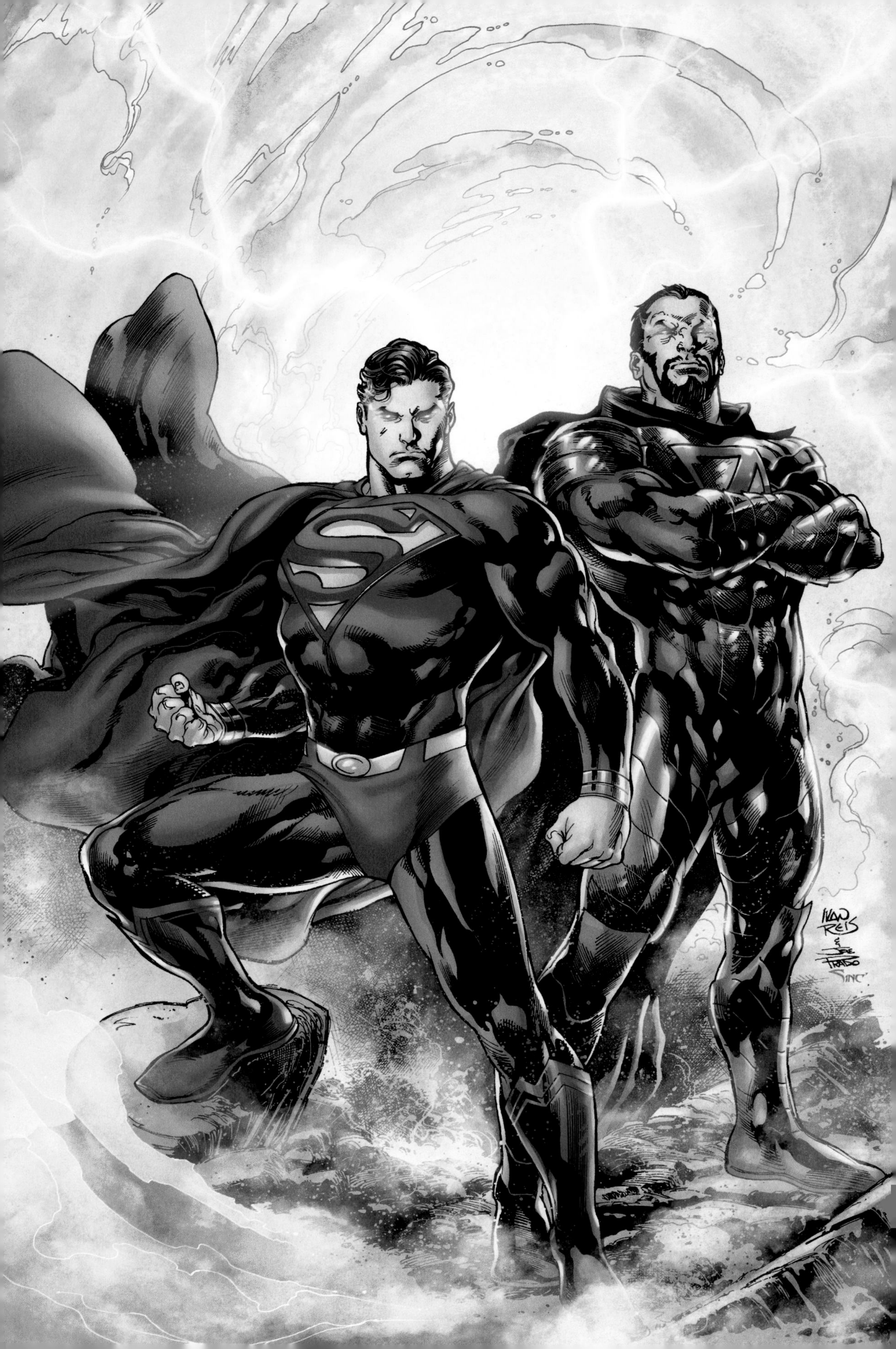

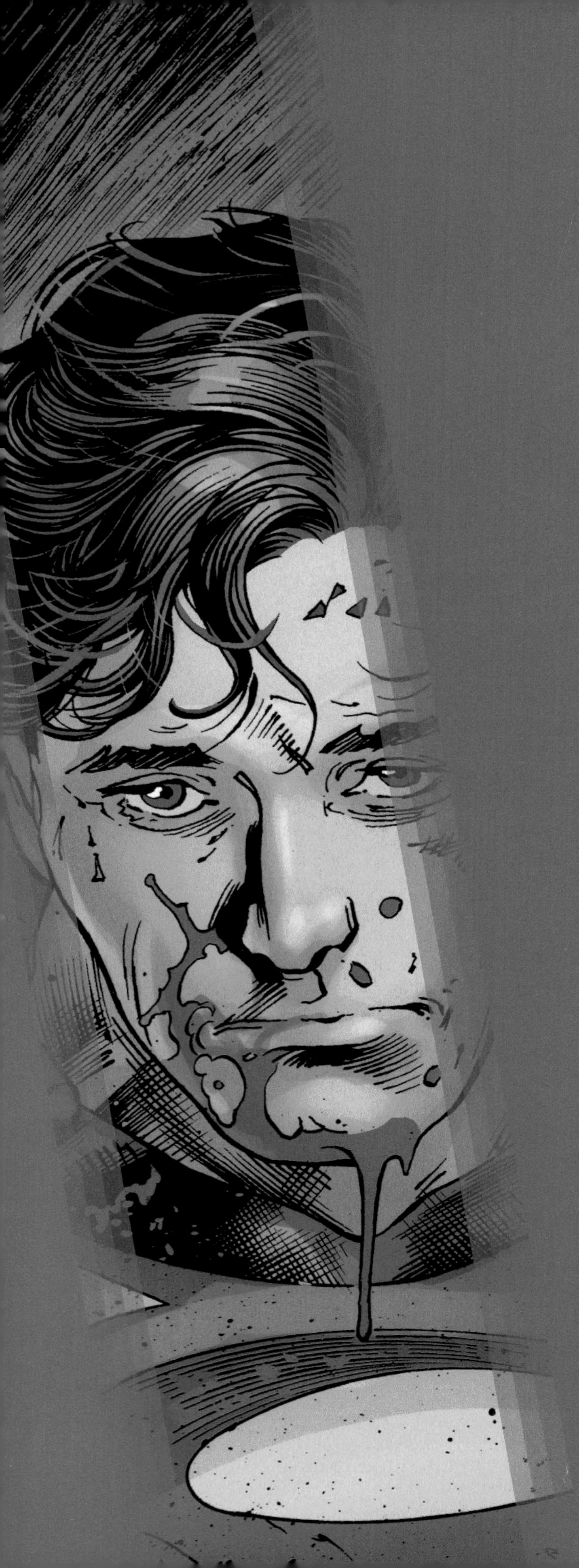

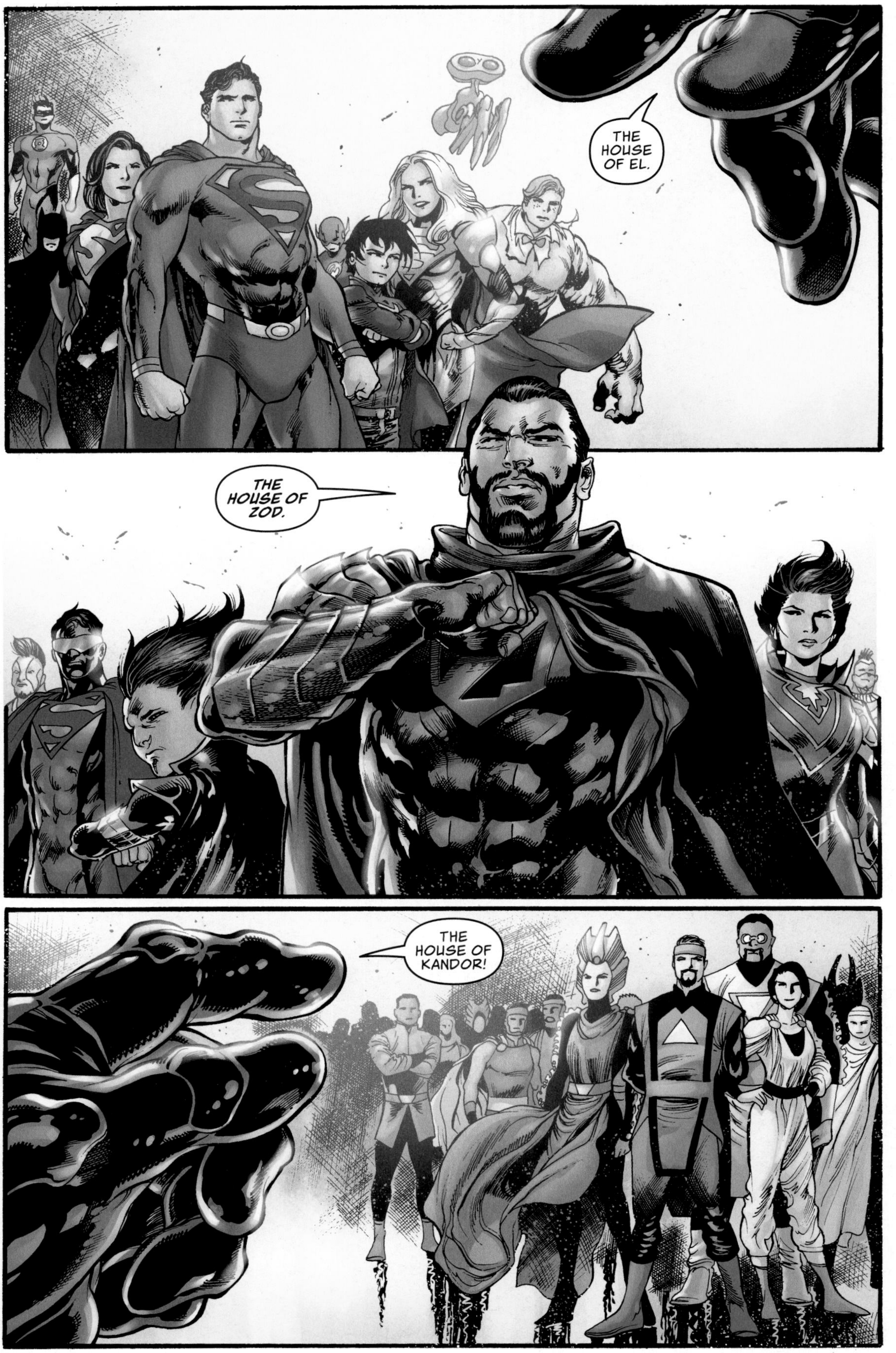
THE HOUSE OF EL.
THE HOUSE OF ZOD.
THE HOUSE OF KANDOR!

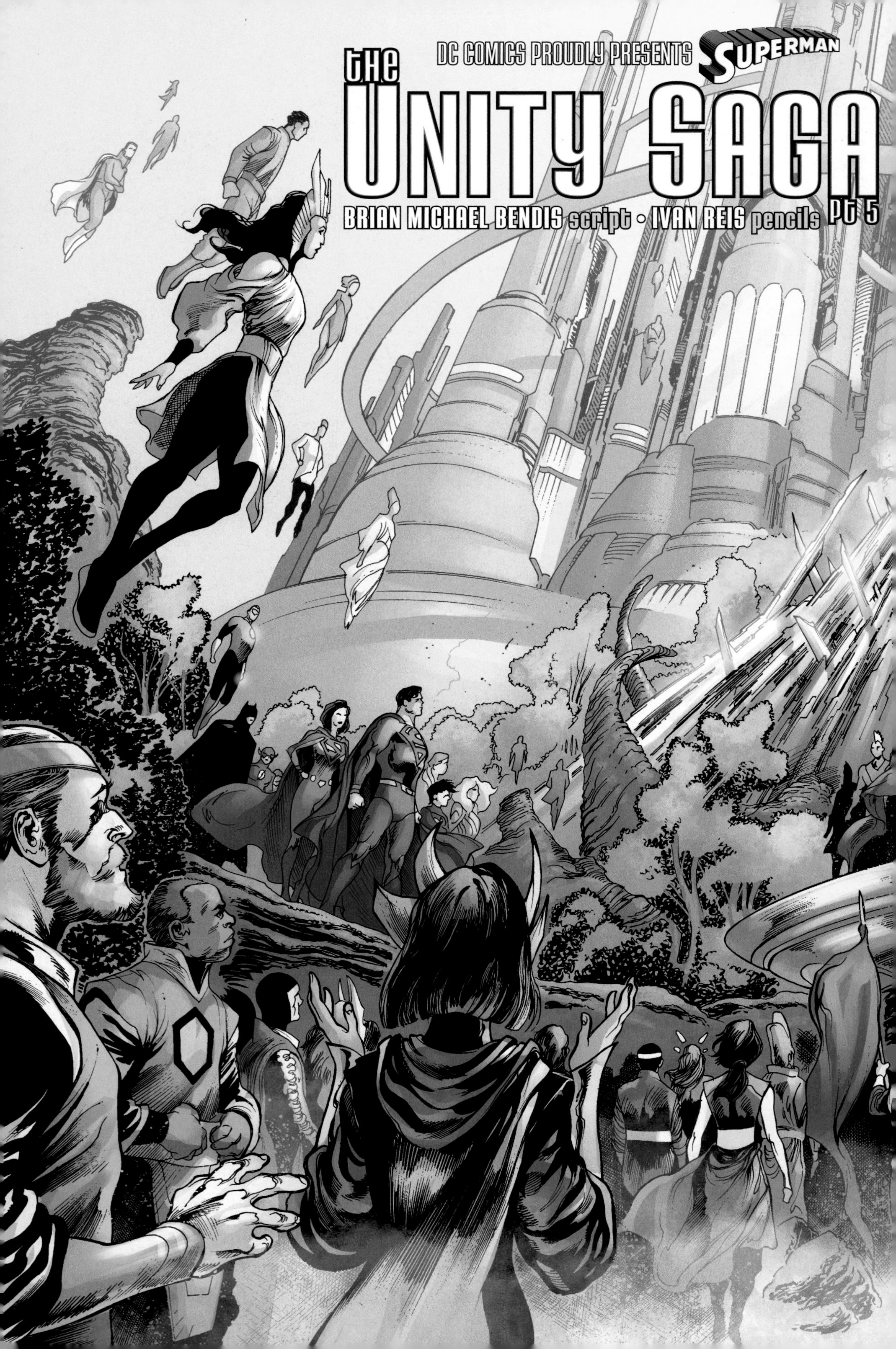
DC COMICS PROUDLY PRESENTS SUPERMAN
the UNITY SAGA pt 5
BRIAN MICHAEL BENDIS script • IVAN REIS pencils

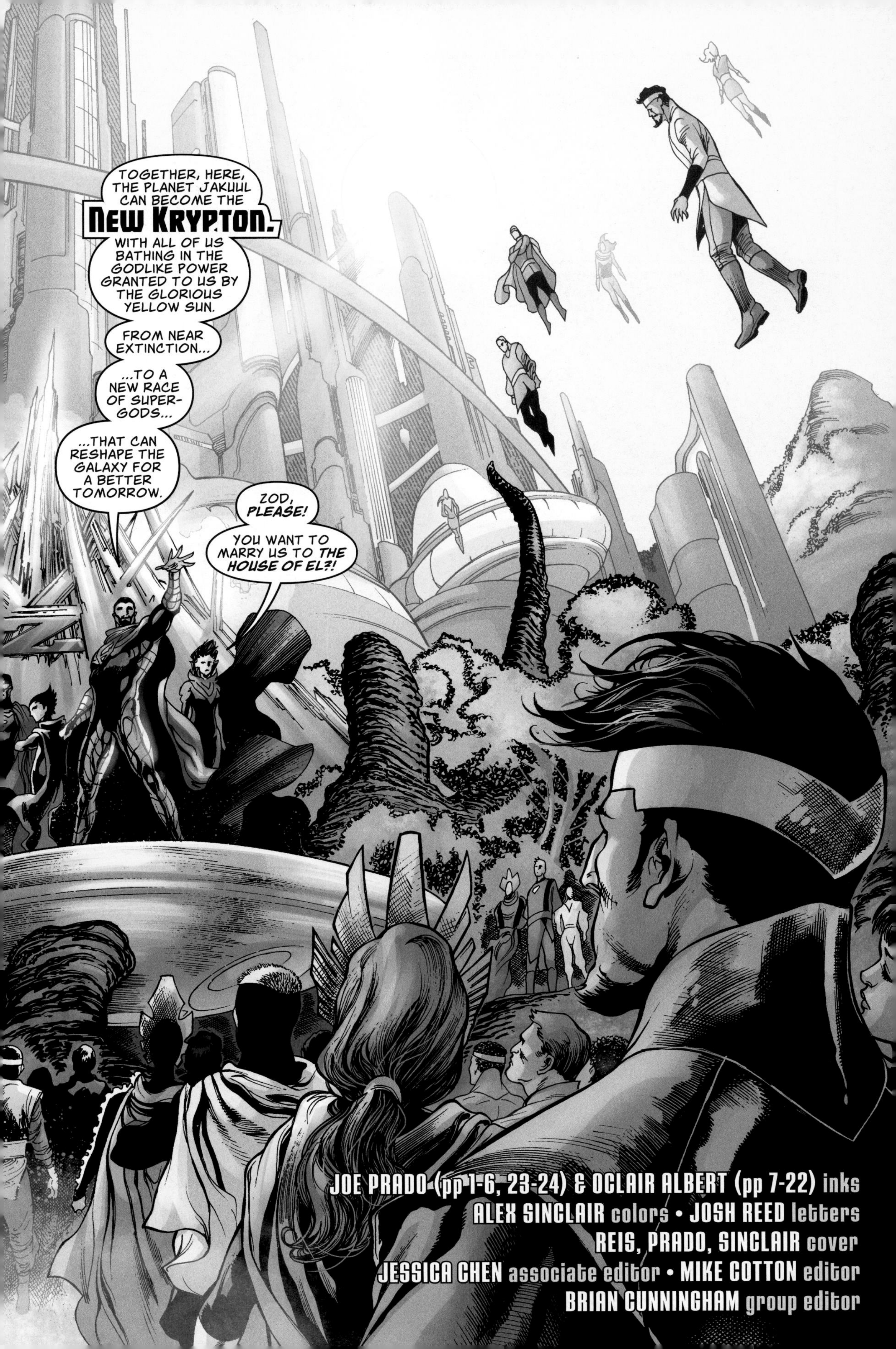
TOGETHER, HERE, THE PLANET JAKUUL CAN BECOME THE
NEW KRYPTON.
WITH ALL OF US BATHING IN THE GODLIKE POWER GRANTED TO US BY THE GLORIOUS YELLOW SUN.
FROM NEAR EXTINCTION...
...TO A NEW RACE OF SUPER-GODS...
...THAT CAN RESHAPE THE GALAXY FOR A BETTER TOMORROW.
ZOD, PLEASE!
YOU WANT TO MARRY US TO THE HOUSE OF EL?!
JOE PRADO (pp 1-6, 23-24) & OCLAIR ALBERT (pp 7-22) inks
ALEX SINCLAIR colors • JOSH REED letters
REIS, PRADO, SINCLAIR cover
JESSICA CHEN associate editor • MIKE COTTON editor
BRIAN CUNNINGHAM group editor

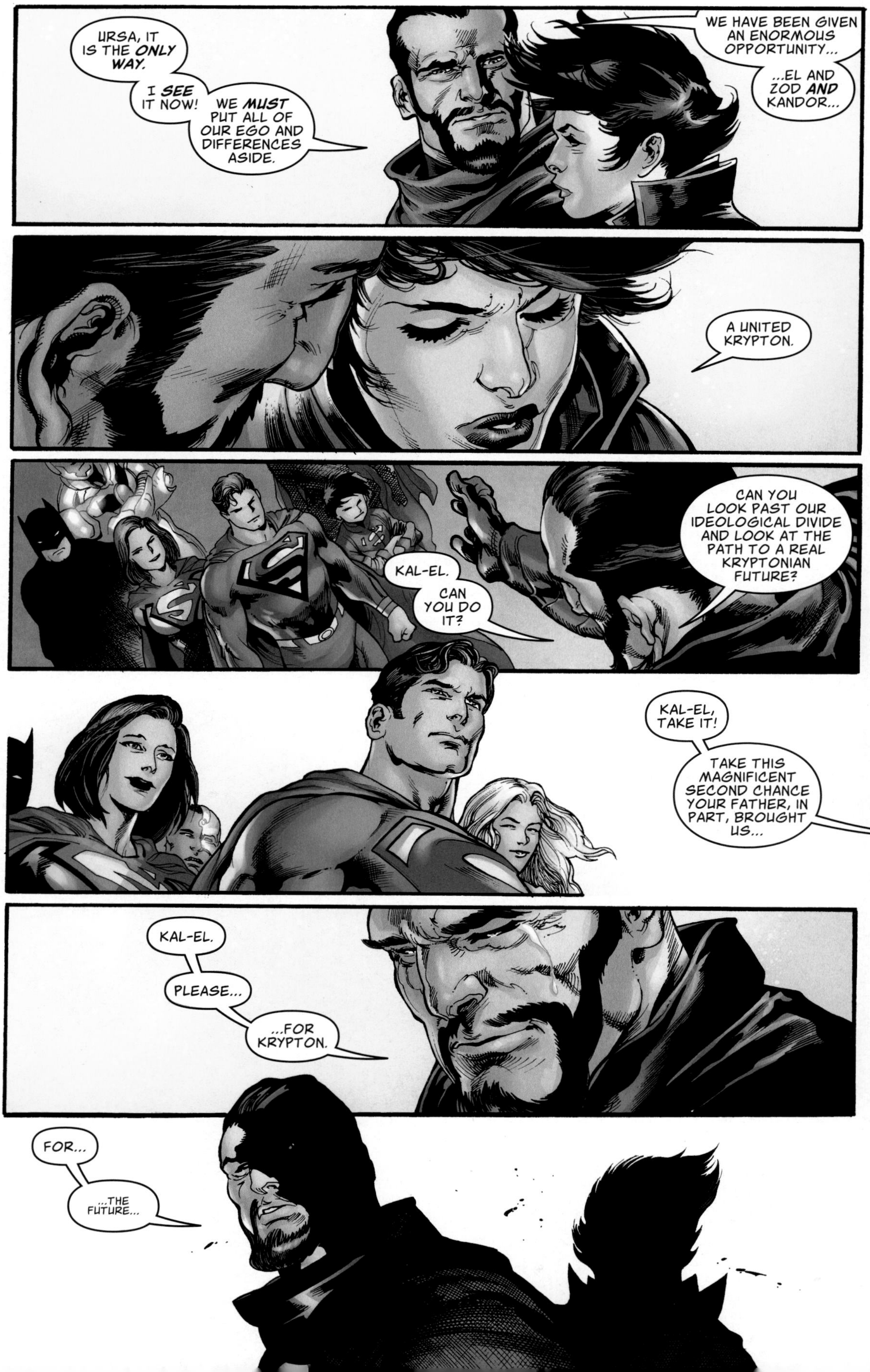
URSA, IT IS THE ONLY WAY.
I SEE IT NOW!
WE MUST PUT ALL OF OUR EGO AND DIFFERENCES ASIDE.
WE HAVE BEEN GIVEN AN ENORMOUS OPPORTUNITY...
...EL AND ZOD AND KANDOR...
A UNITED KRYPTON.
CAN YOU LOOK PAST OUR IDEOLOGICAL DIVIDE AND LOOK AT THE PATH TO A REAL KRYPTONIAN FUTURE?
KAL-EL.
CAN YOU DO IT?
KAL-EL, TAKE IT!
TAKE THIS MAGNIFICENT SECOND CHANCE YOUR FATHER, IN PART, BROUGHT US...
KAL-EL.
PLEASE...
...FOR KRYPTON.
FOR...
...THE FUTURE...

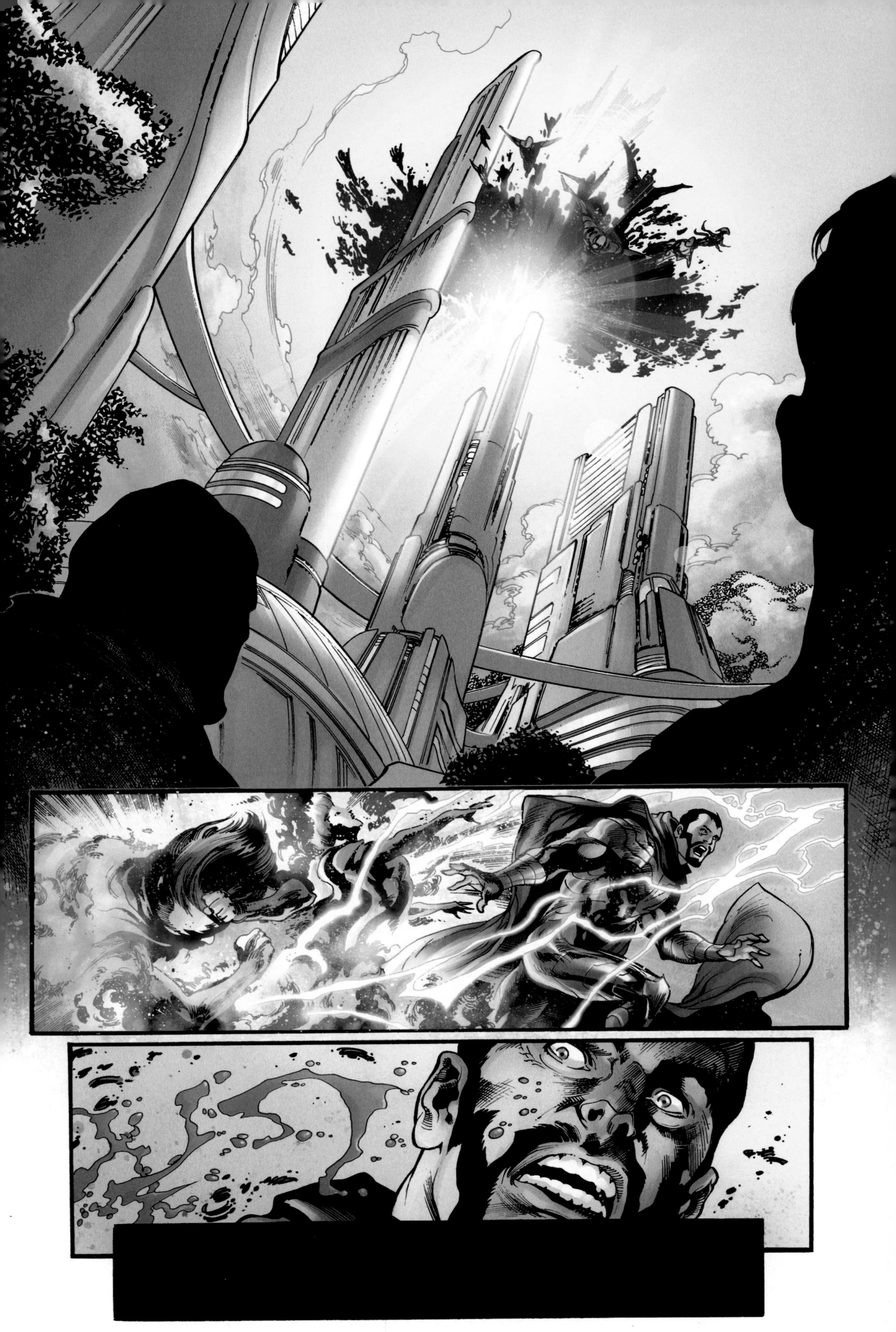
[redacted]

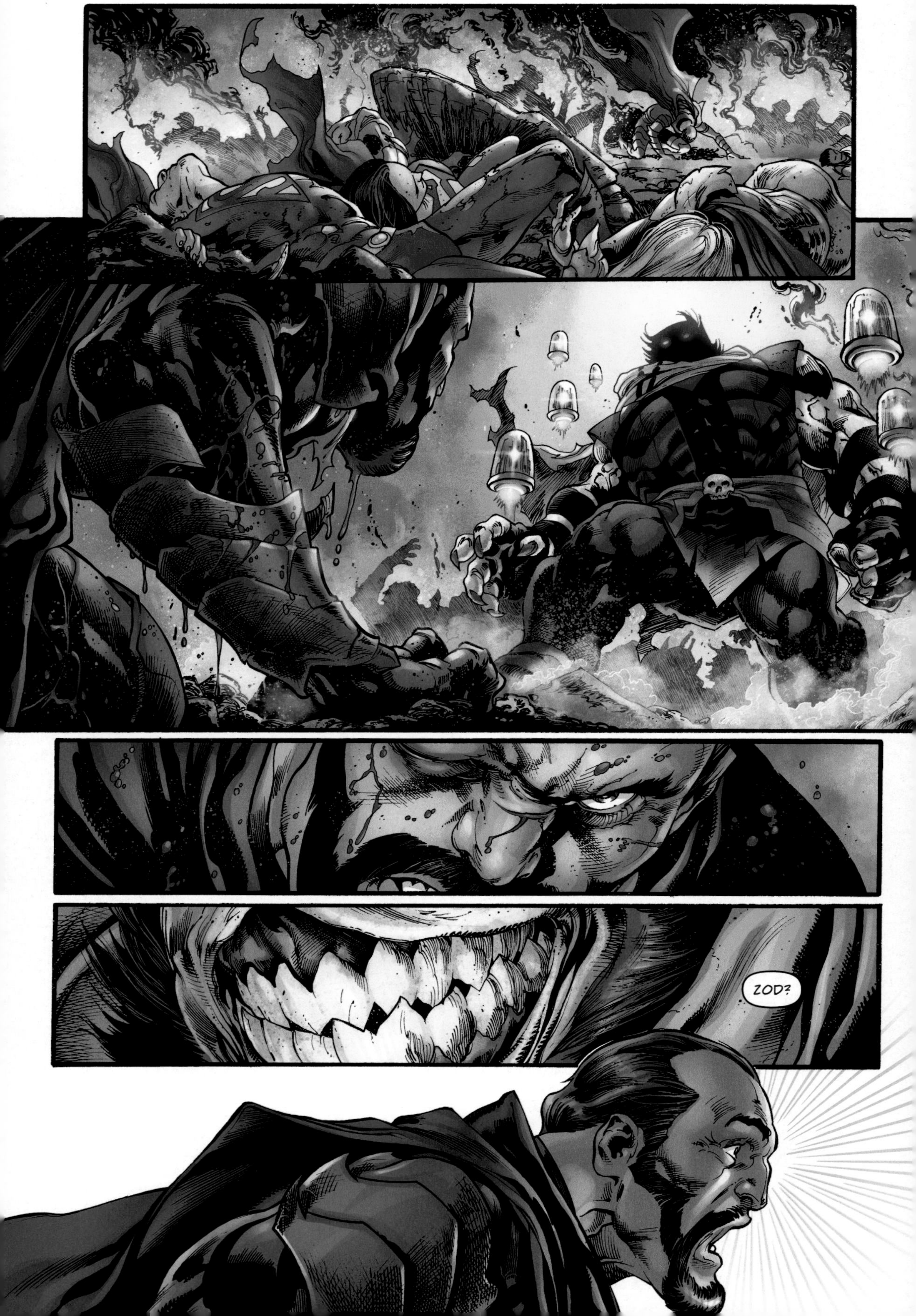
ZOD?

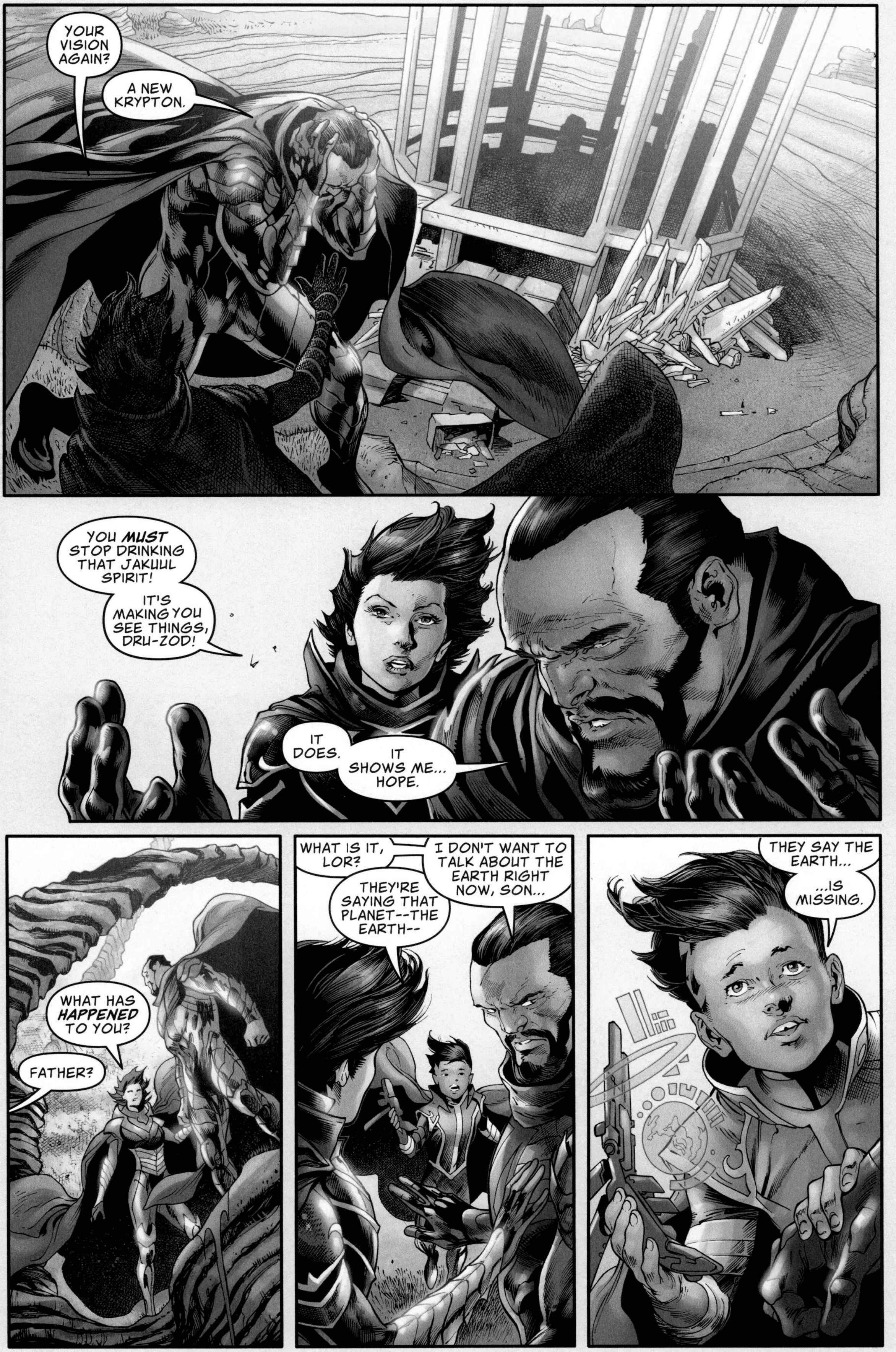
YOUR VISION AGAIN?
A NEW KRYPTON.
YOU **MUST** STOP DRINKING THAT JAKUUL SPIRIT!
IT'S MAKING YOU SEE THINGS, DRU-ZOD!
IT DOES.
IT SHOWS ME... HOPE.
WHAT HAS **HAPPENED** TO YOU?
FATHER?
WHAT IS IT, LOR?
THEY'RE SAYING THAT PLANET--THE EARTH--
I DON'T WANT TO TALK ABOUT THE EARTH RIGHT NOW, SON...
THEY SAY THE EARTH...
...IS MISSING.

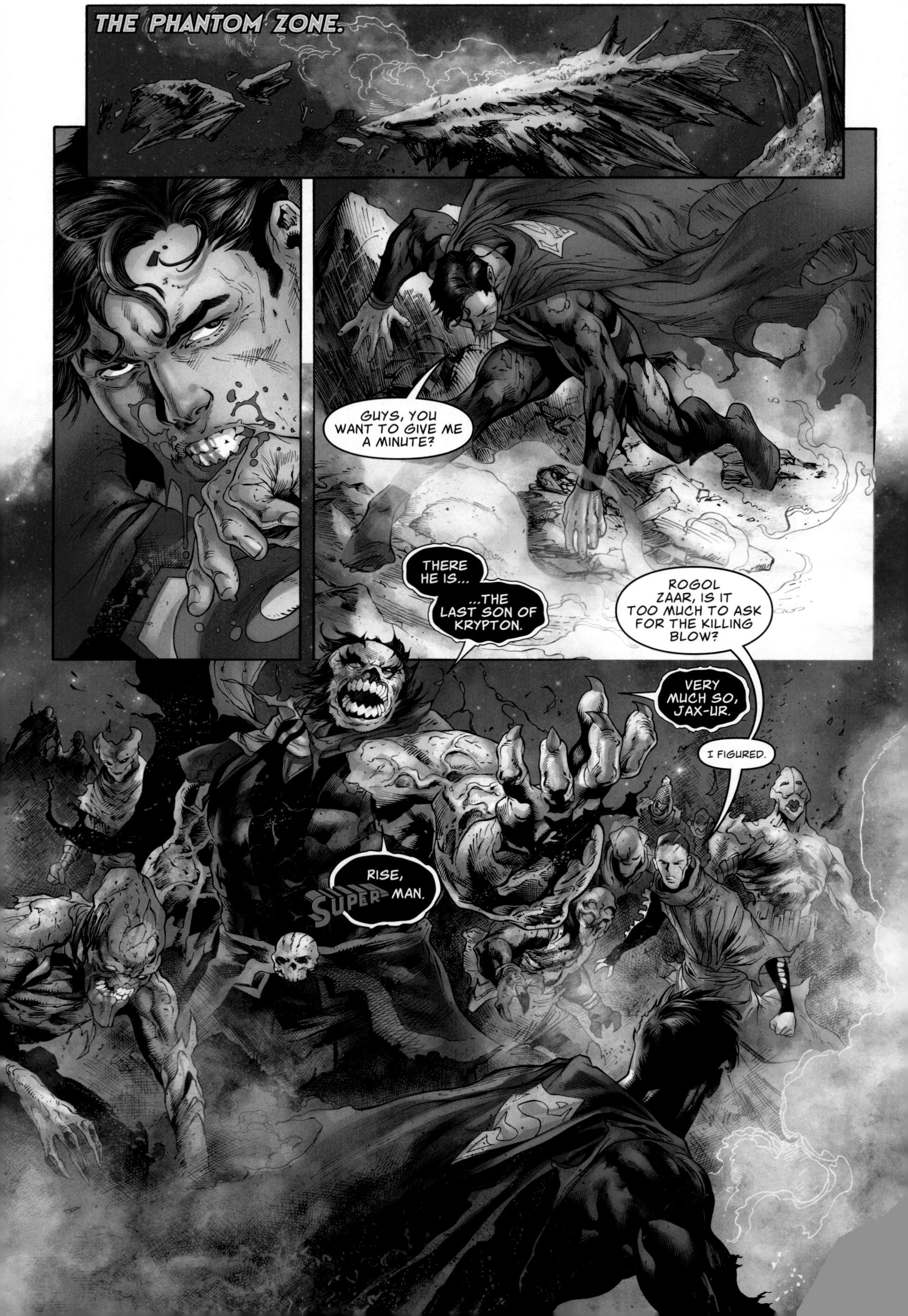
THE PHANTOM ZONE.
GUYS, YOU WANT TO GIVE ME A MINUTE?
THERE HE IS...
...THE LAST SON OF KRYPTON.
ROGOL ZAAR, IS IT TOO MUCH TO ASK FOR THE KILLING BLOW?
VERY MUCH SO, JAX-UR.
I FIGURED.
RISE, SUPER-MAN.

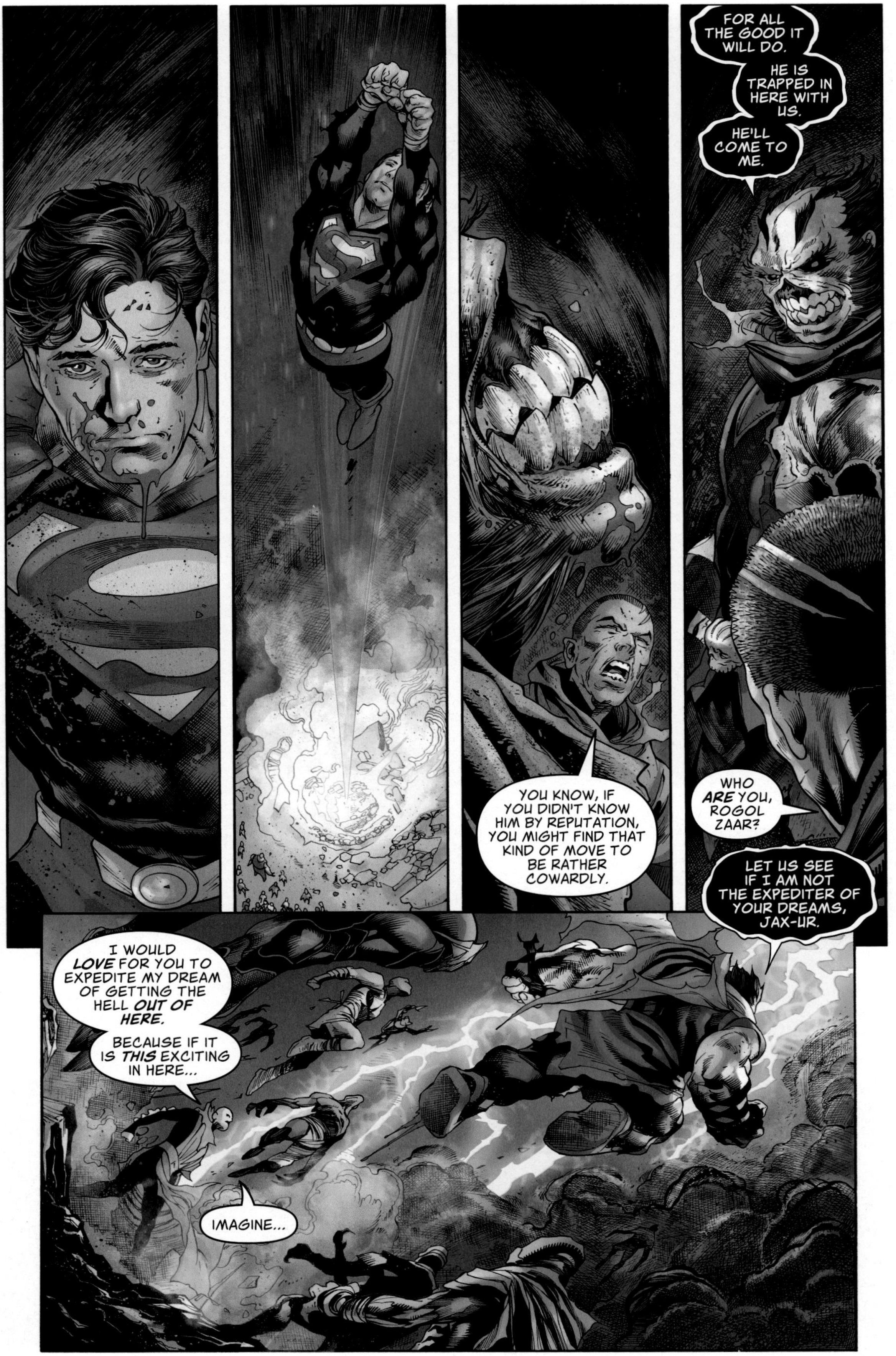
FOR ALL THE GOOD IT WILL DO.
HE IS TRAPPED IN HERE WITH US.
HE'LL COME TO ME.
YOU KNOW, IF YOU DIDN'T KNOW HIM BY REPUTATION, YOU MIGHT FIND THAT KIND OF MOVE TO BE RATHER COWARDLY.
WHO ARE YOU, ROGOL ZAAR?
LET US SEE IF I AM NOT THE EXPEDITER OF YOUR DREAMS, JAX-UR.
I WOULD LOVE FOR YOU TO EXPEDITE MY DREAM OF GETTING THE HELL OUT OF HERE.
BECAUSE IF IT IS THIS EXCITING IN HERE...
IMAGINE...

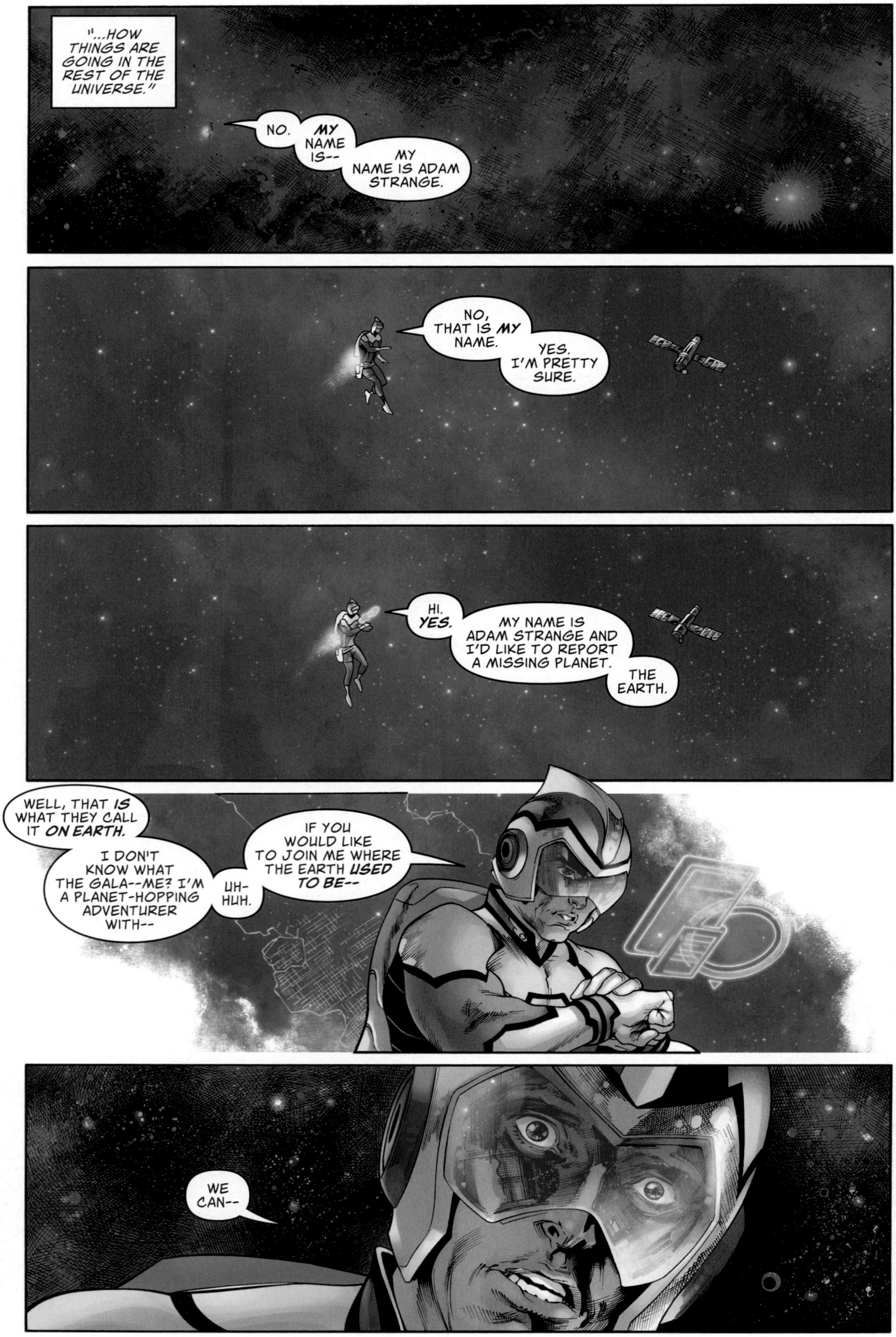

"...HOW THINGS ARE GOING IN THE REST OF THE UNIVERSE."
NO. MY NAME IS--
MY NAME IS ADAM STRANGE.
NO, THAT IS MY NAME.
YES. I'M PRETTY SURE.
HI. YES.
MY NAME IS ADAM STRANGE AND I'D LIKE TO REPORT A MISSING PLANET.
THE EARTH.
WELL, THAT IS WHAT THEY CALL IT ON EARTH.
I DON'T KNOW WHAT THE GALA--ME? I'M A PLANET-HOPPING ADVENTURER WITH--
UH-HUH.
IF YOU WOULD LIKE TO JOIN ME WHERE THE EARTH USED TO BE--
WE CAN--

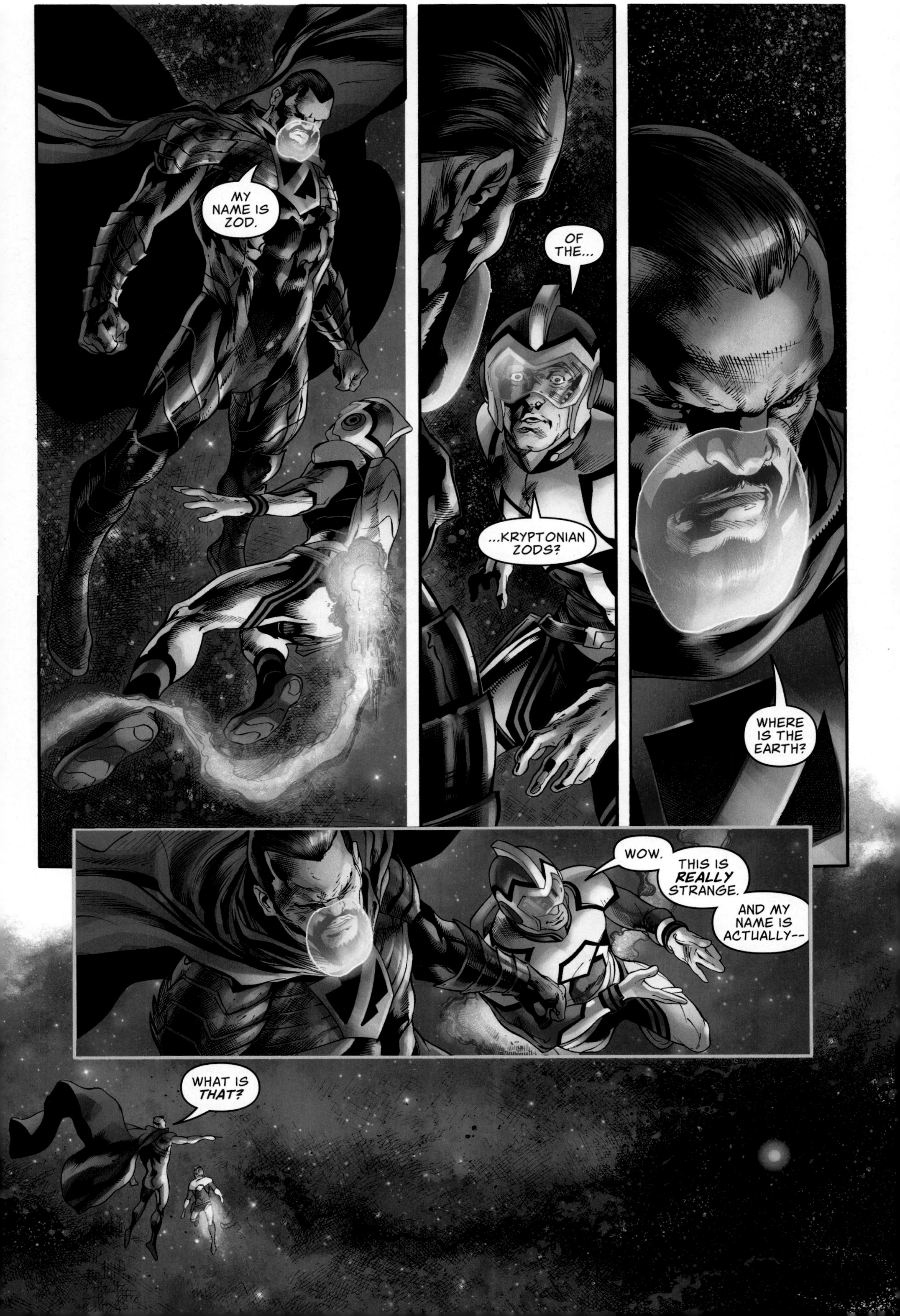
MY NAME IS ZOD.
OF THE...
...KRYPTONIAN ZODS?
WHERE IS THE EARTH?
WOW.
THIS IS *REALLY* STRANGE.
AND MY NAME IS ACTUALLY--
WHAT IS *THAT?*

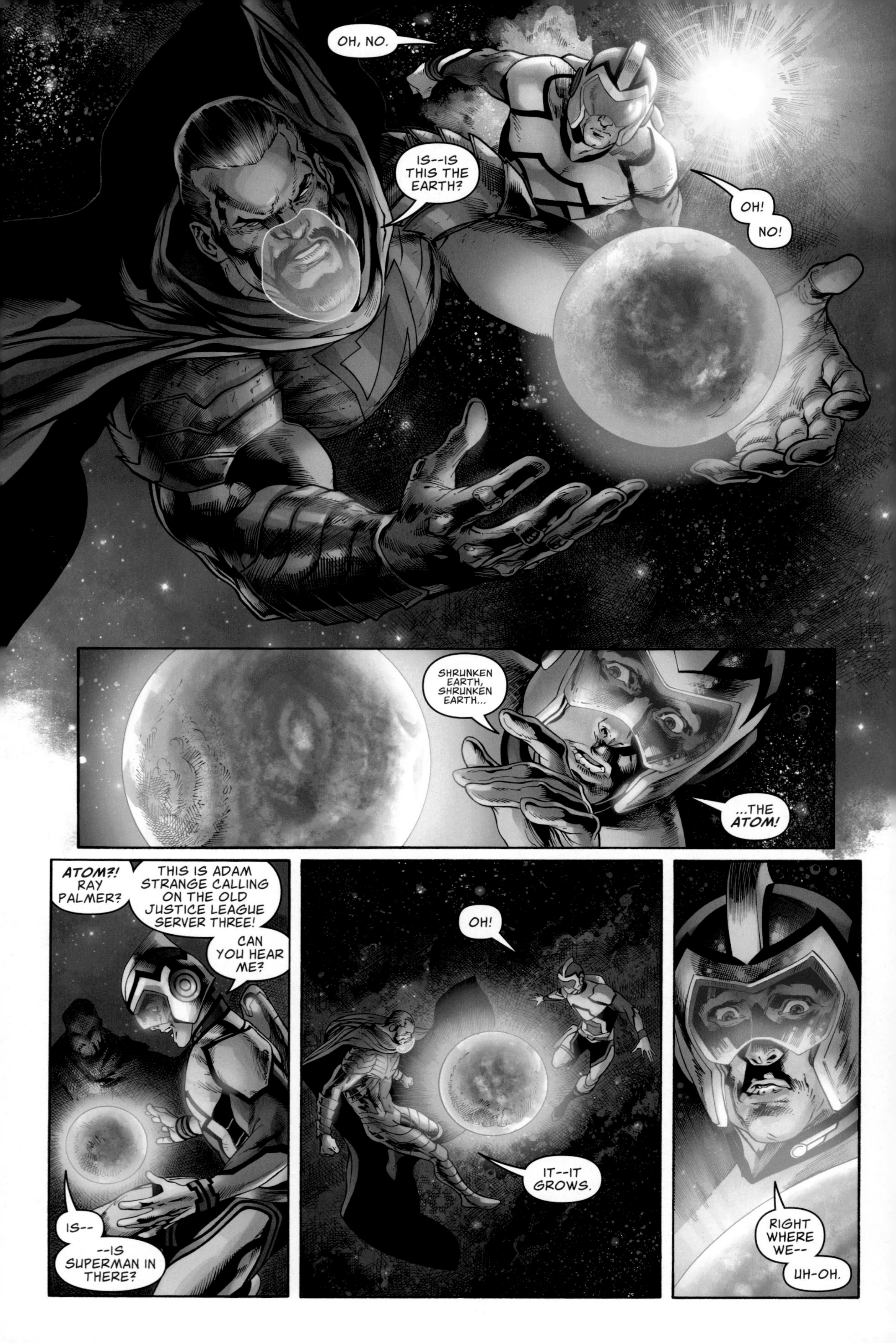
OH, NO.
IS--IS THIS THE EARTH?
OH!
NO!
SHRUNKEN EARTH, SHRUNKEN EARTH...
...THE ATOM!
ATOM?! RAY PALMER?
THIS IS ADAM STRANGE CALLING ON THE OLD JUSTICE LEAGUE SERVER THREE!
CAN YOU HEAR ME?
IS--
--IS SUPERMAN IN THERE?
OH!
IT--IT GROWS.
RIGHT WHERE WE--
UH-OH.

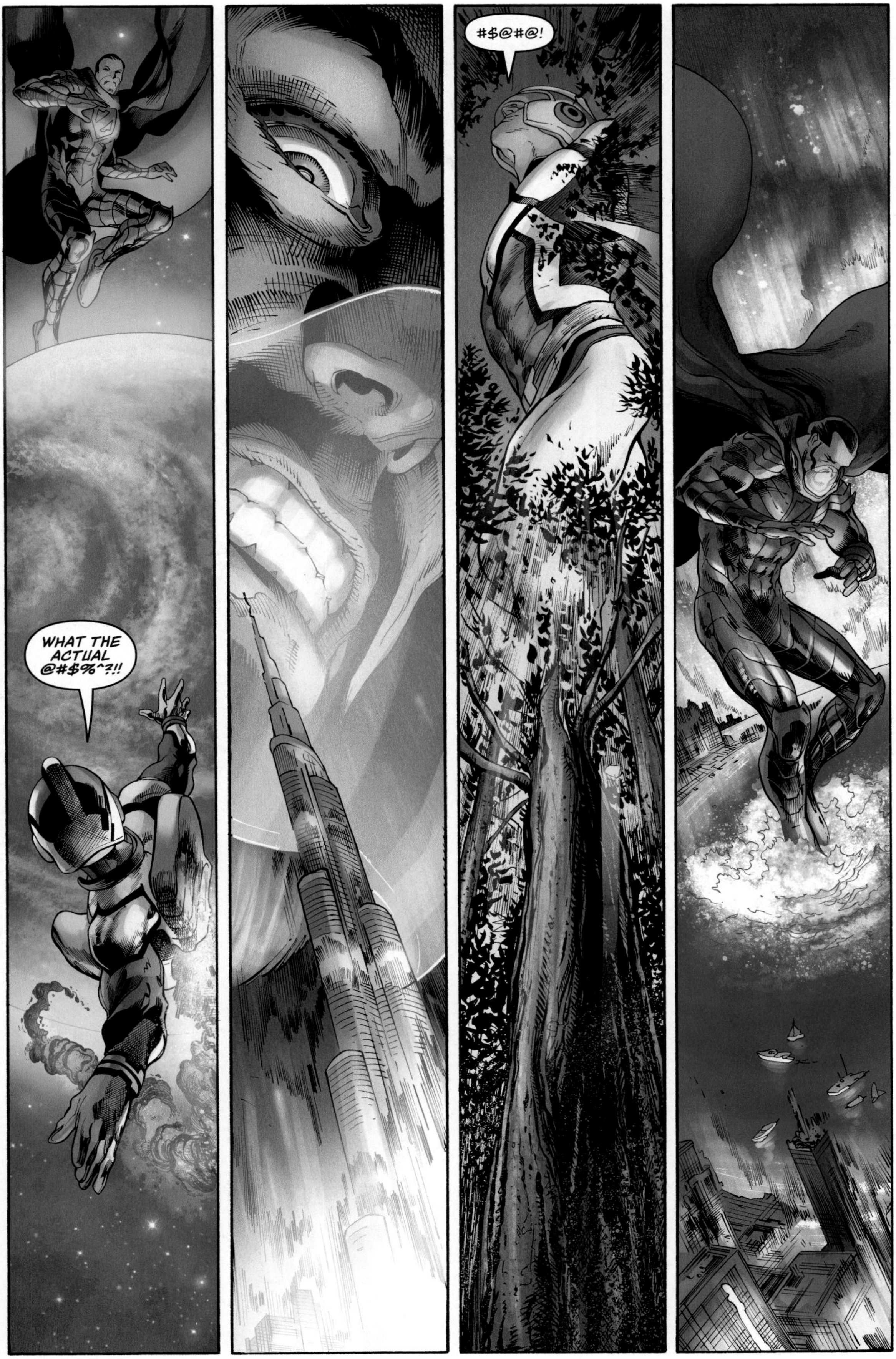
WHAT THE ACTUAL @#$%^?!!
#$@#@!

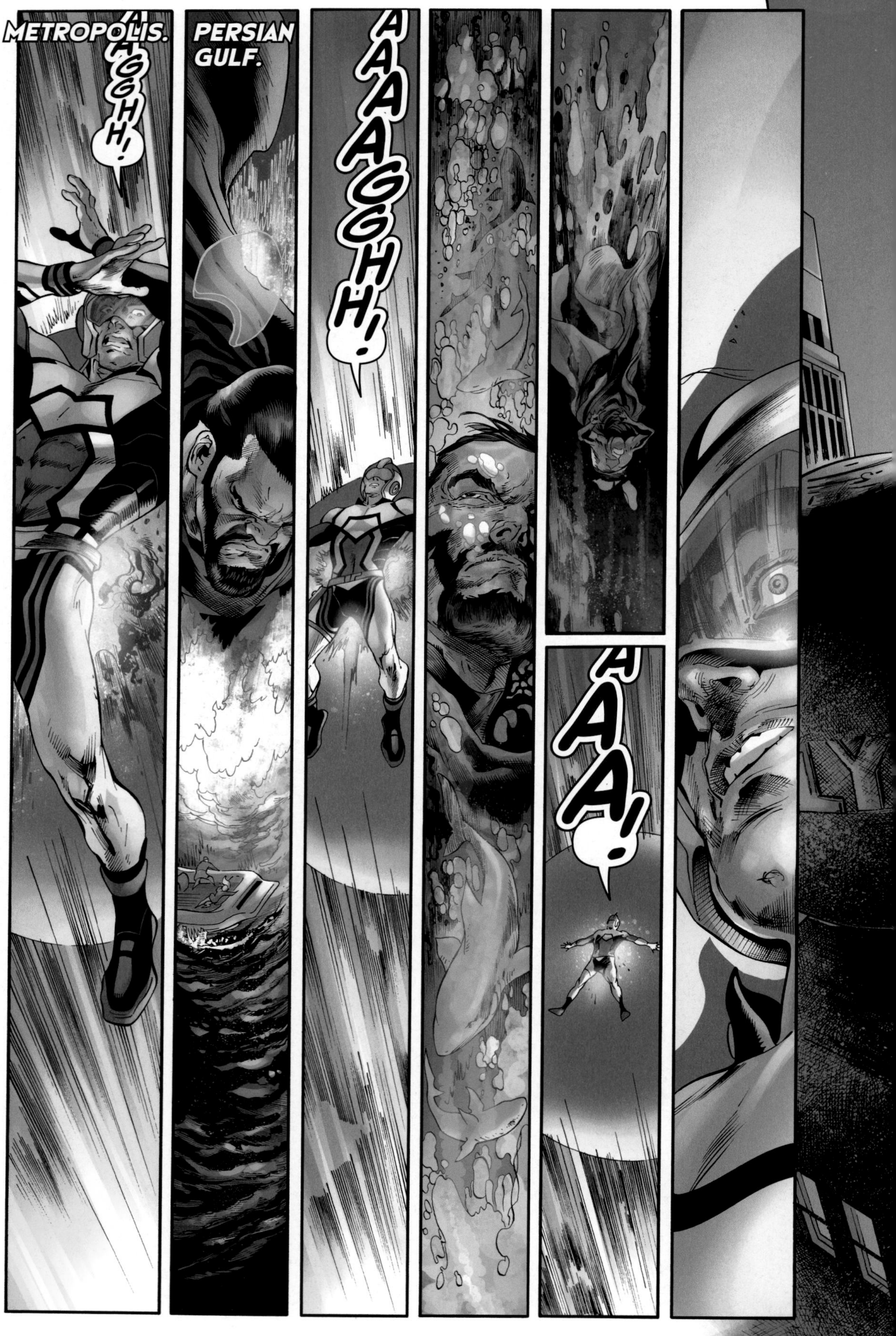
METROPOLIS.
AAGGHH!
PERSIAN GULF.
AAAAAGGHH!
AAA!

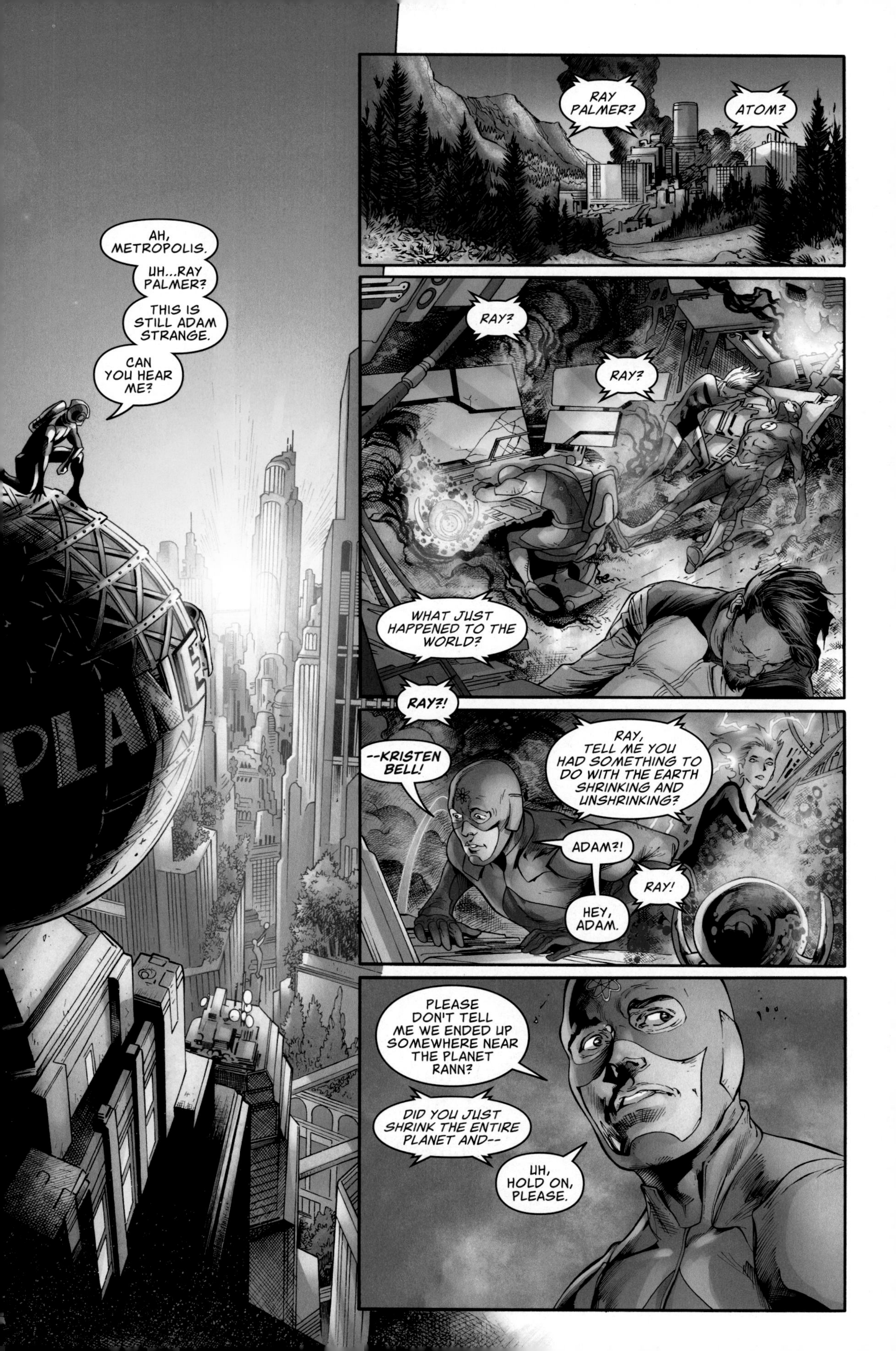
AH, METROPOLIS.
UH...RAY PALMER?
THIS IS STILL ADAM STRANGE.
CAN YOU HEAR ME?
RAY PALMER?
ATOM?
RAY?
RAY?
WHAT JUST HAPPENED TO THE WORLD?
RAY?!
--KRISTEN BELL!
RAY, TELL ME YOU HAD SOMETHING TO DO WITH THE EARTH SHRINKING AND UNSHRINKING?
ADAM?!
RAY!
HEY, ADAM.
PLEASE DON'T TELL ME WE ENDED UP SOMEWHERE NEAR THE PLANET RANN?
DID YOU JUST SHRINK THE ENTIRE PLANET AND--
UH, HOLD ON, PLEASE.

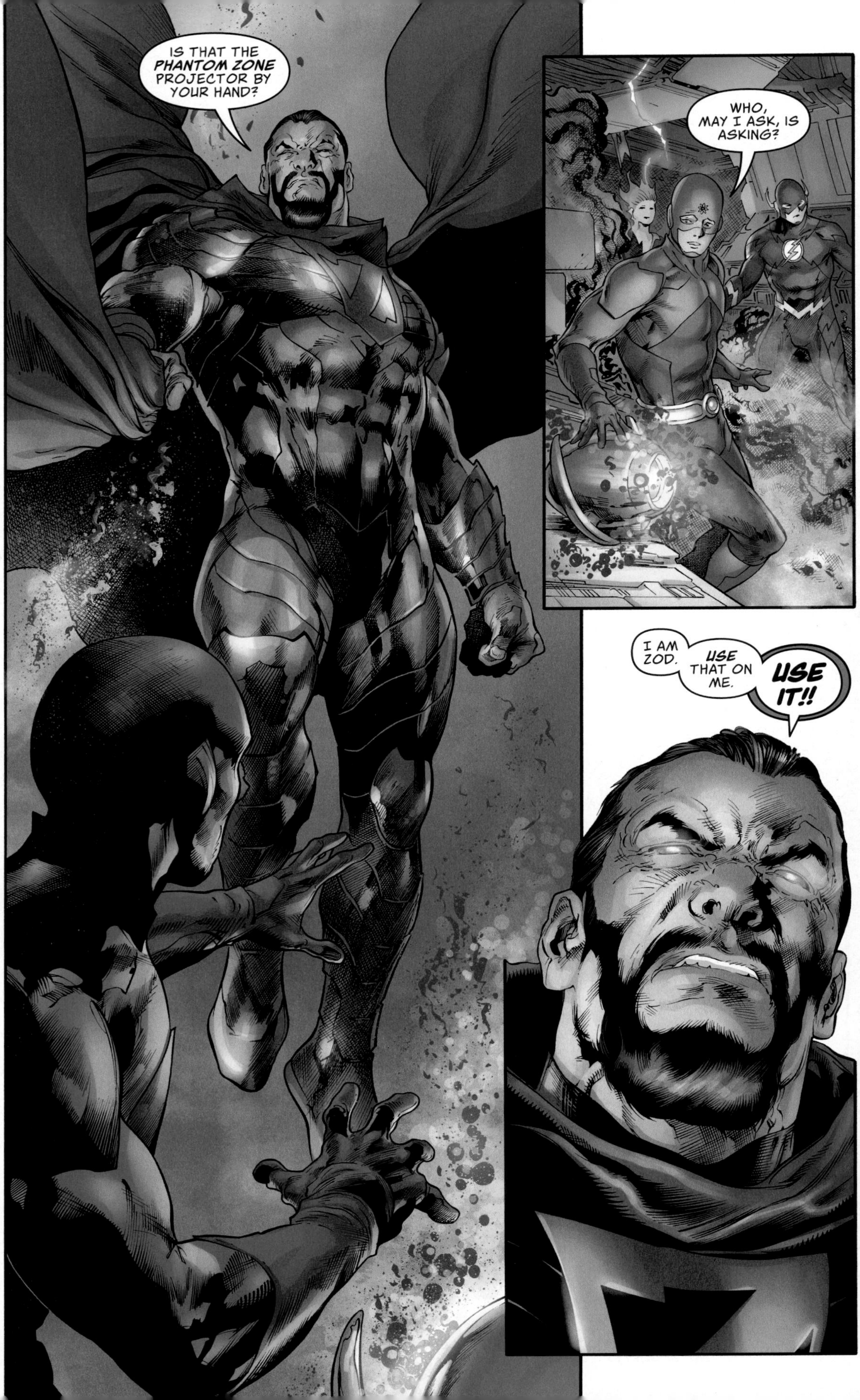
IS THAT THE PHANTOM ZONE PROJECTOR BY YOUR HAND?
WHO, MAY I ASK, IS ASKING?
I AM ZOD.
USE THAT ON ME.
USE IT!!

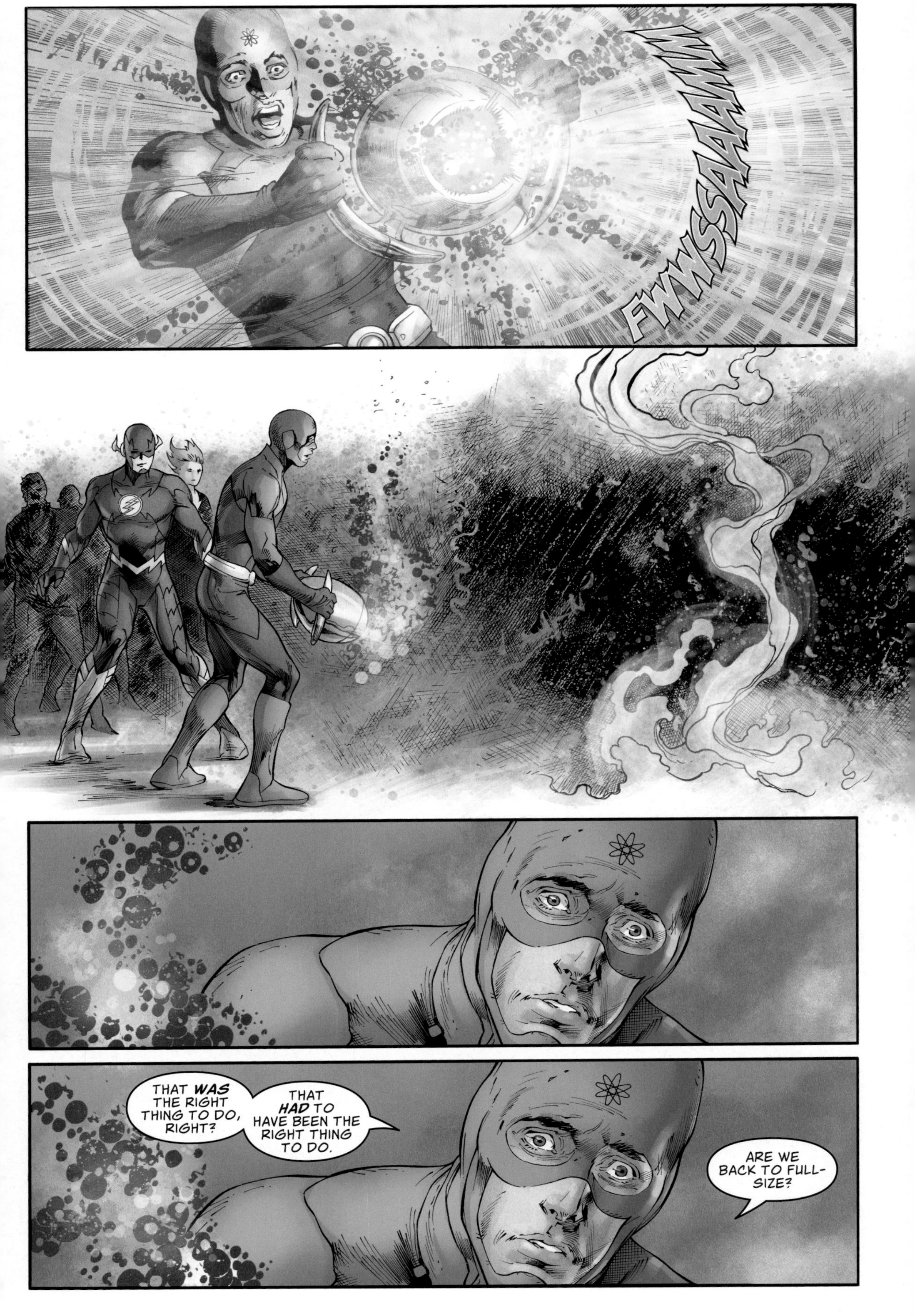
FWWSSAAAAWWM
THAT WAS THE RIGHT THING TO DO, RIGHT?
THAT HAD TO HAVE BEEN THE RIGHT THING TO DO.
ARE WE BACK TO FULL-SIZE?

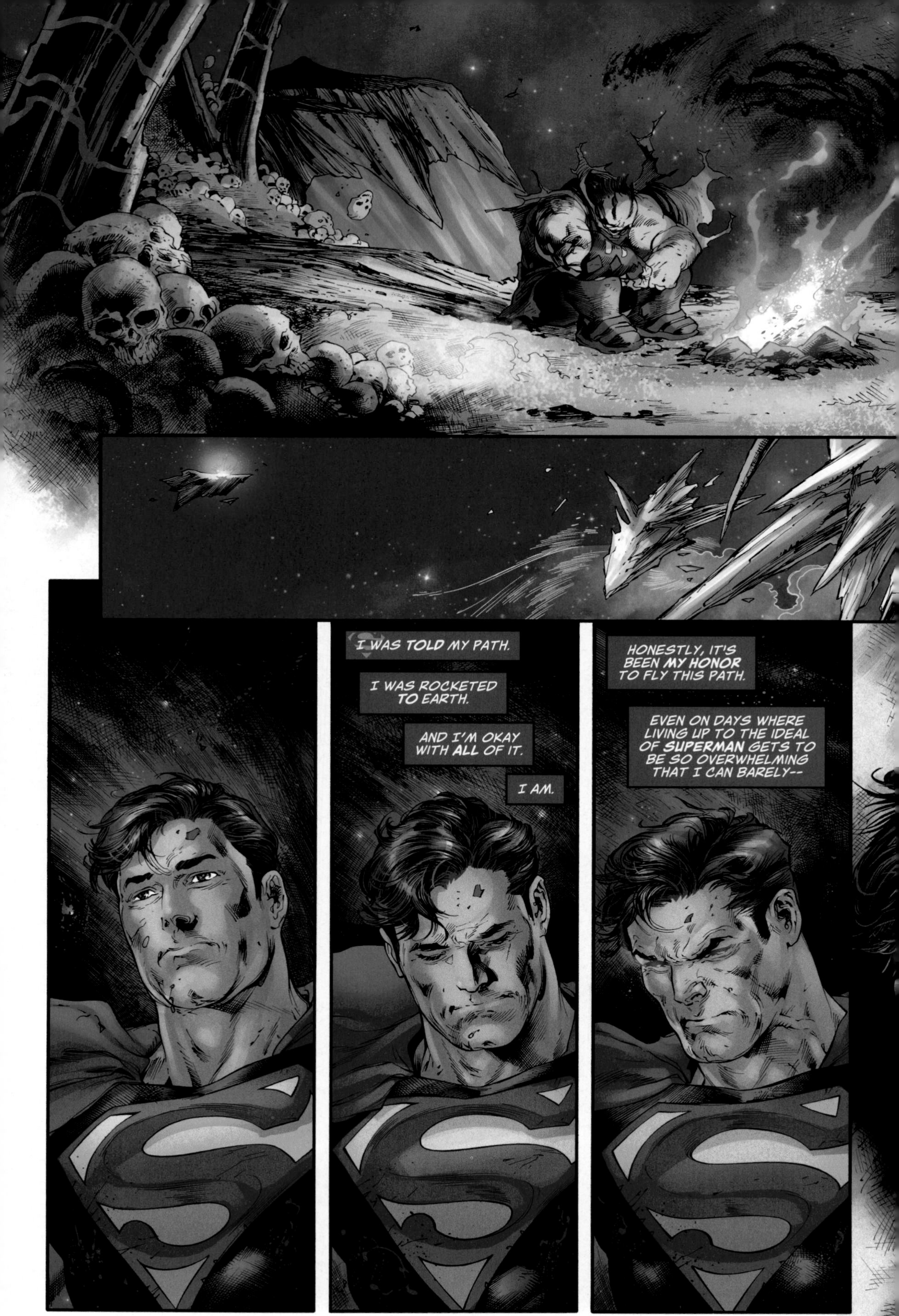

I WAS TOLD MY PATH.
I WAS ROCKETED TO EARTH.
AND I'M OKAY WITH ALL OF IT.
I AM.
HONESTLY, IT'S BEEN MY HONOR TO FLY THIS PATH.
EVEN ON DAYS WHERE LIVING UP TO THE IDEAL OF SUPERMAN GETS TO BE SO OVERWHELMING THAT I CAN BARELY--

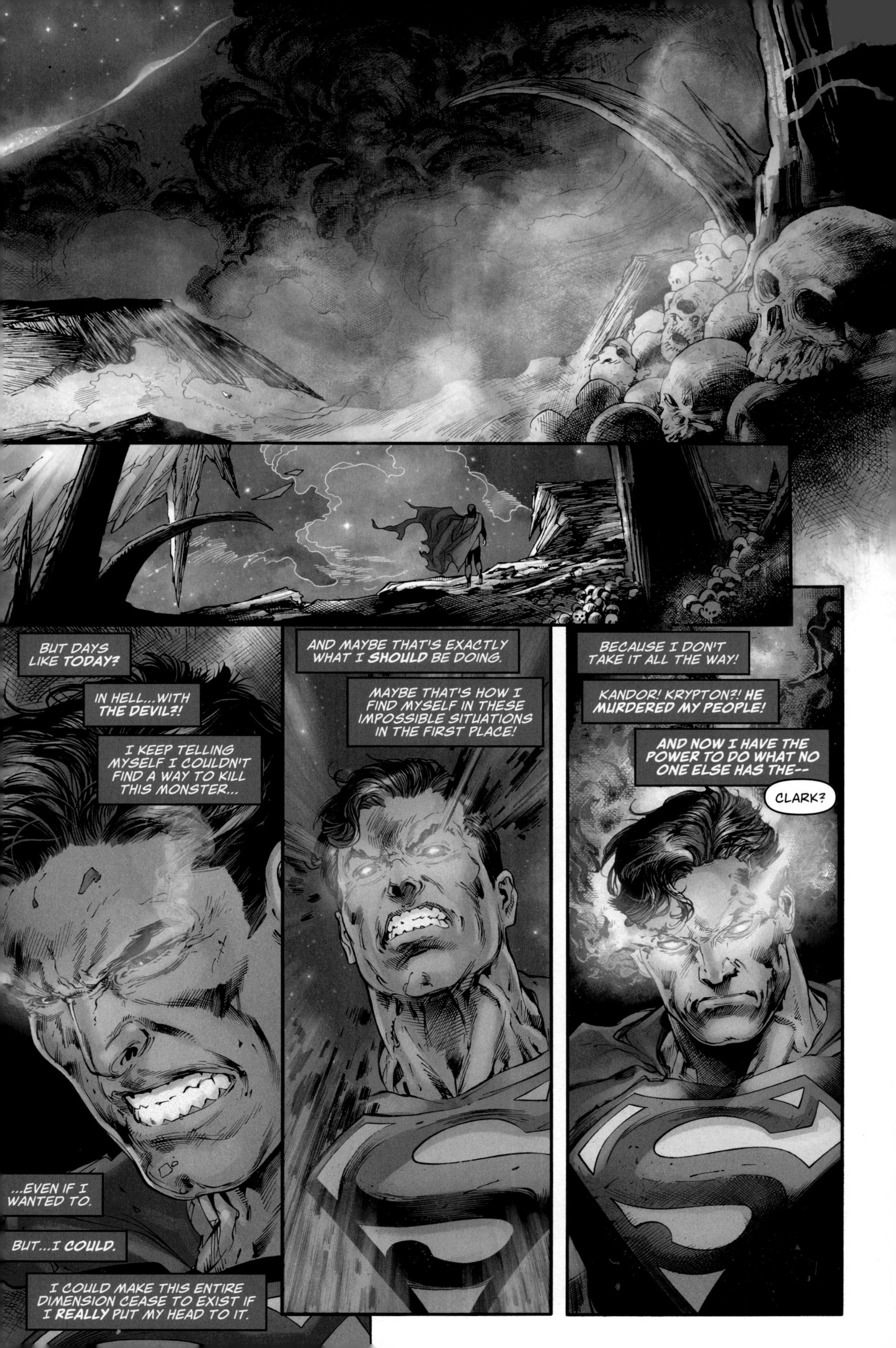

BUT DAYS LIKE TODAY?
IN HELL...WITH THE DEVIL?!
I KEEP TELLING MYSELF I COULDN'T FIND A WAY TO KILL THIS MONSTER...
...EVEN IF I WANTED TO.
BUT...I COULD.
I COULD MAKE THIS ENTIRE DIMENSION CEASE TO EXIST IF I REALLY PUT MY HEAD TO IT.
AND MAYBE THAT'S EXACTLY WHAT I SHOULD BE DOING.
MAYBE THAT'S HOW I FIND MYSELF IN THESE IMPOSSIBLE SITUATIONS IN THE FIRST PLACE!
BECAUSE I DON'T TAKE IT ALL THE WAY!
KANDOR! KRYPTON?! HE MURDERED MY PEOPLE!
AND NOW I HAVE THE POWER TO DO WHAT NO ONE ELSE HAS THE--
CLARK?

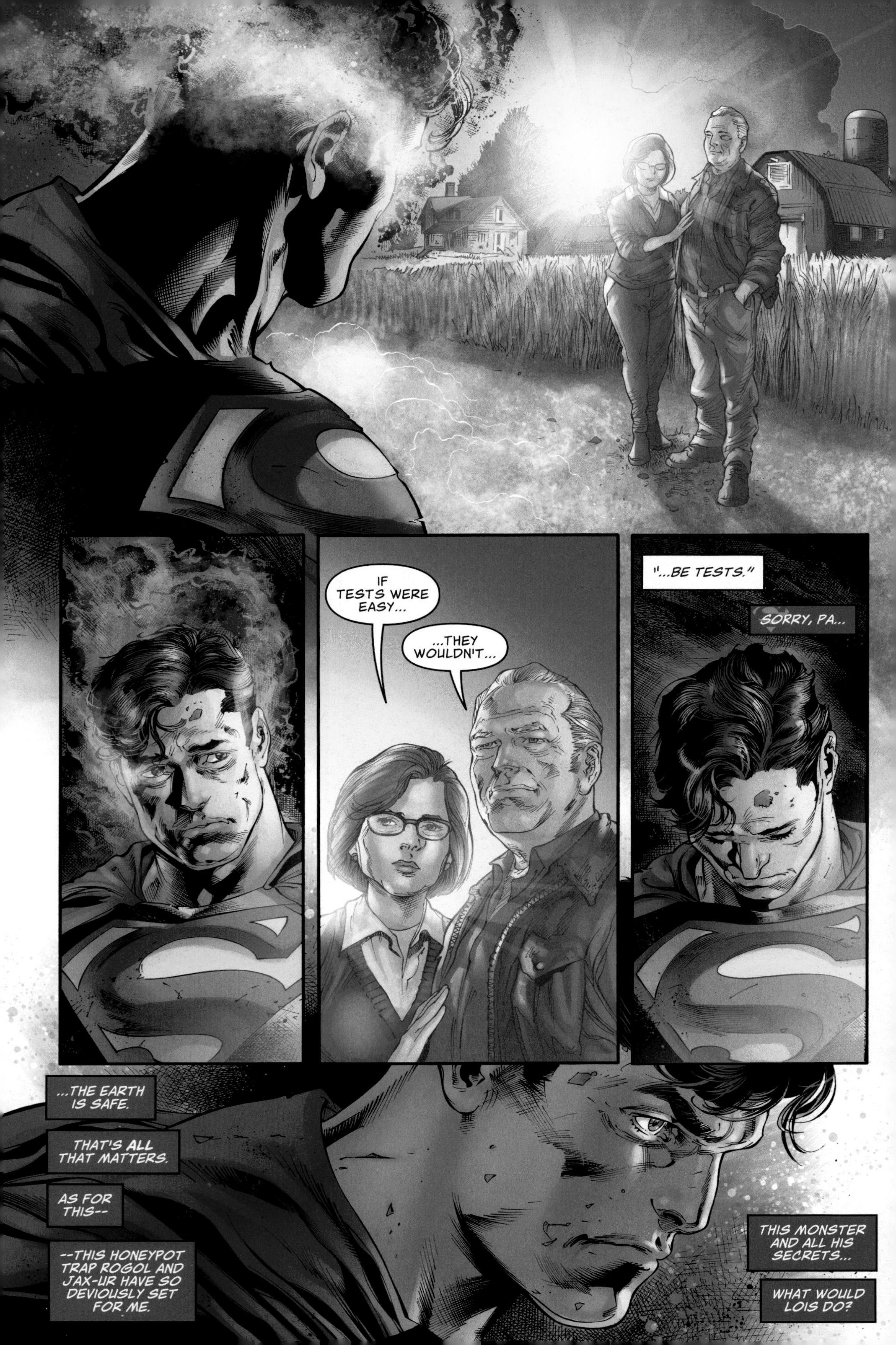
IF TESTS WERE EASY...
...THEY WOULDN'T...
"...BE TESTS."
SORRY, PA...
...THE EARTH IS SAFE.
THAT'S ALL THAT MATTERS.
AS FOR THIS--
--THIS HONEYPOT TRAP ROGOL AND JAX-UR HAVE SO DEVIOUSLY SET FOR ME.
THIS MONSTER AND ALL HIS SECRETS...
WHAT WOULD LOIS DO?

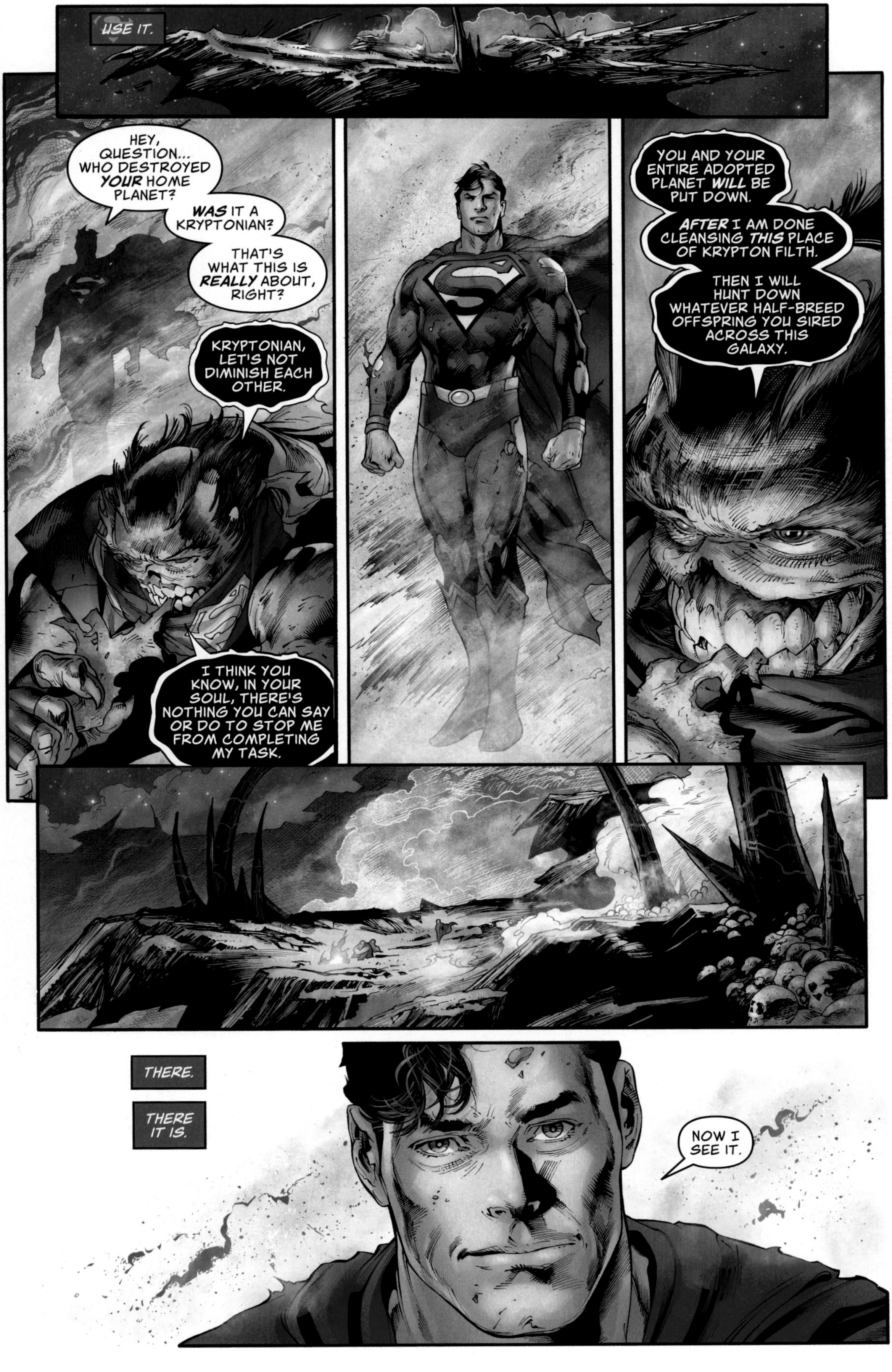
USE IT.
HEY, QUESTION... WHO DESTROYED YOUR HOME PLANET?
WAS IT A KRYPTONIAN?
THAT'S WHAT THIS IS REALLY ABOUT, RIGHT?
KRYPTONIAN, LET'S NOT DIMINISH EACH OTHER.
I THINK YOU KNOW, IN YOUR SOUL, THERE'S NOTHING YOU CAN SAY OR DO TO STOP ME FROM COMPLETING MY TASK.
YOU AND YOUR ENTIRE ADOPTED PLANET WILL BE PUT DOWN.
AFTER I AM DONE CLEANSING THIS PLACE OF KRYPTON FILTH.
THEN I WILL HUNT DOWN WHATEVER HALF-BREED OFFSPRING YOU SIRED ACROSS THIS GALAXY.
THERE.
THERE IT IS.
NOW I SEE IT.

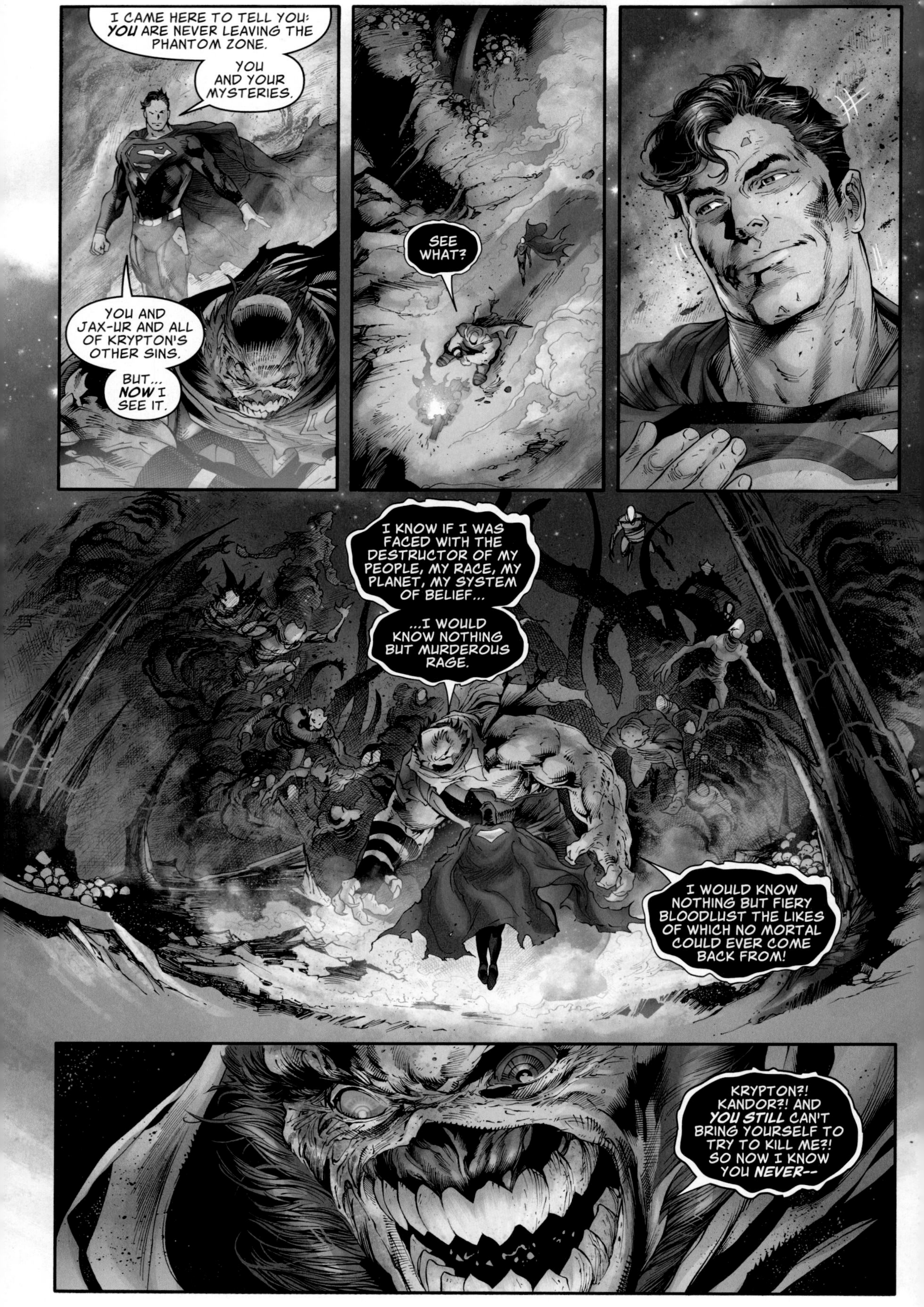
I CAME HERE TO TELL YOU: **YOU** ARE NEVER LEAVING THE PHANTOM ZONE.
YOU AND YOUR MYSTERIES.
YOU AND JAX-UR AND ALL OF KRYPTON'S OTHER SINS.
BUT... **NOW** I SEE IT.
SEE WHAT?
I KNOW IF I WAS FACED WITH THE DESTRUCTOR OF MY PEOPLE, MY RACE, MY PLANET, MY SYSTEM OF BELIEF...
...I WOULD KNOW NOTHING BUT MURDEROUS RAGE.
I WOULD KNOW NOTHING BUT FIERY BLOODLUST THE LIKES OF WHICH NO MORTAL COULD EVER COME BACK FROM!
KRYPTON?! KANDOR?! AND **YOU STILL** CAN'T BRING YOURSELF TO TRY TO KILL ME?! SO NOW I KNOW YOU **NEVER--**

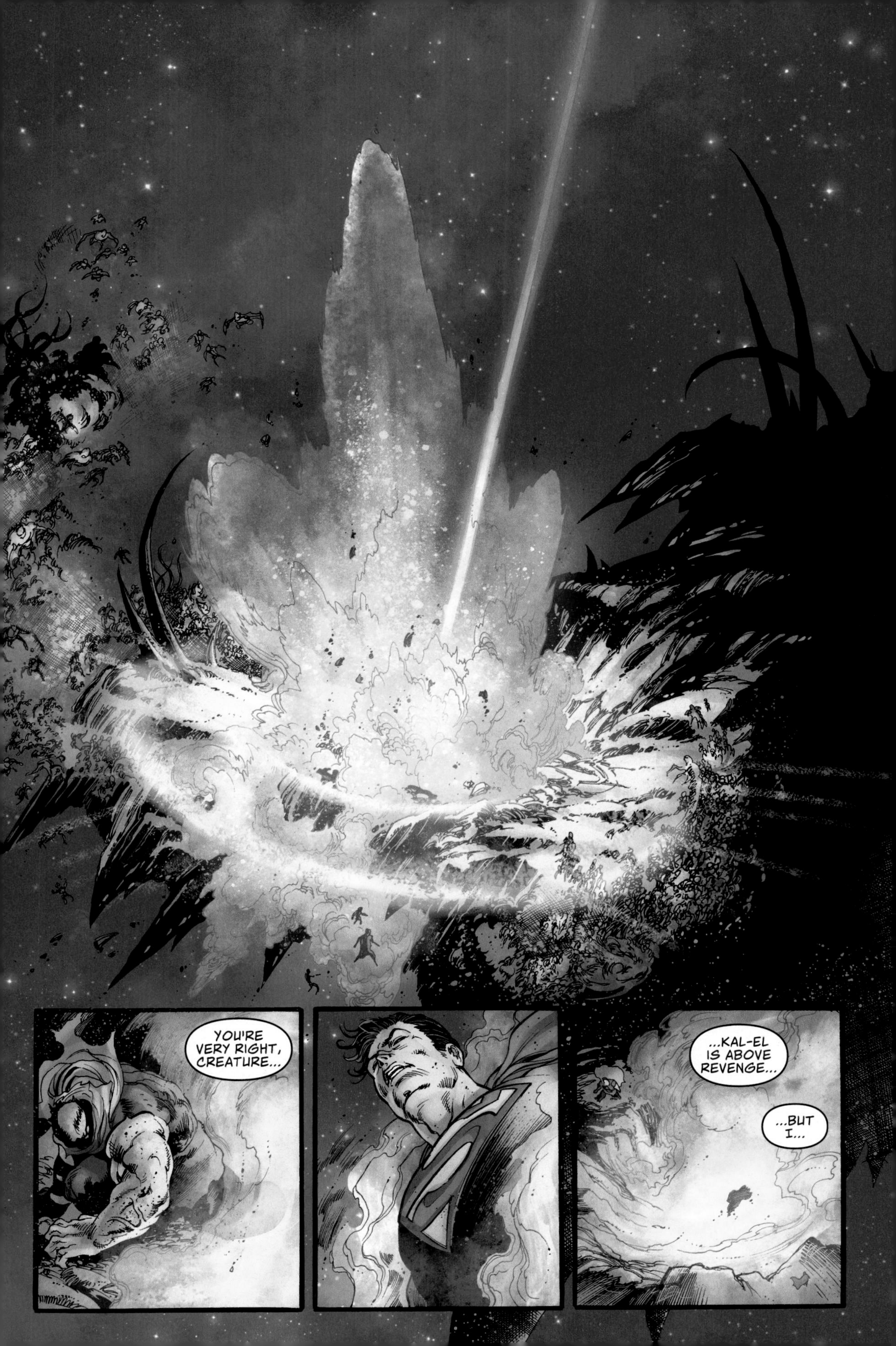
YOU'RE VERY RIGHT, CREATURE...
...KAL-EL IS ABOVE REVENGE...
...BUT I...

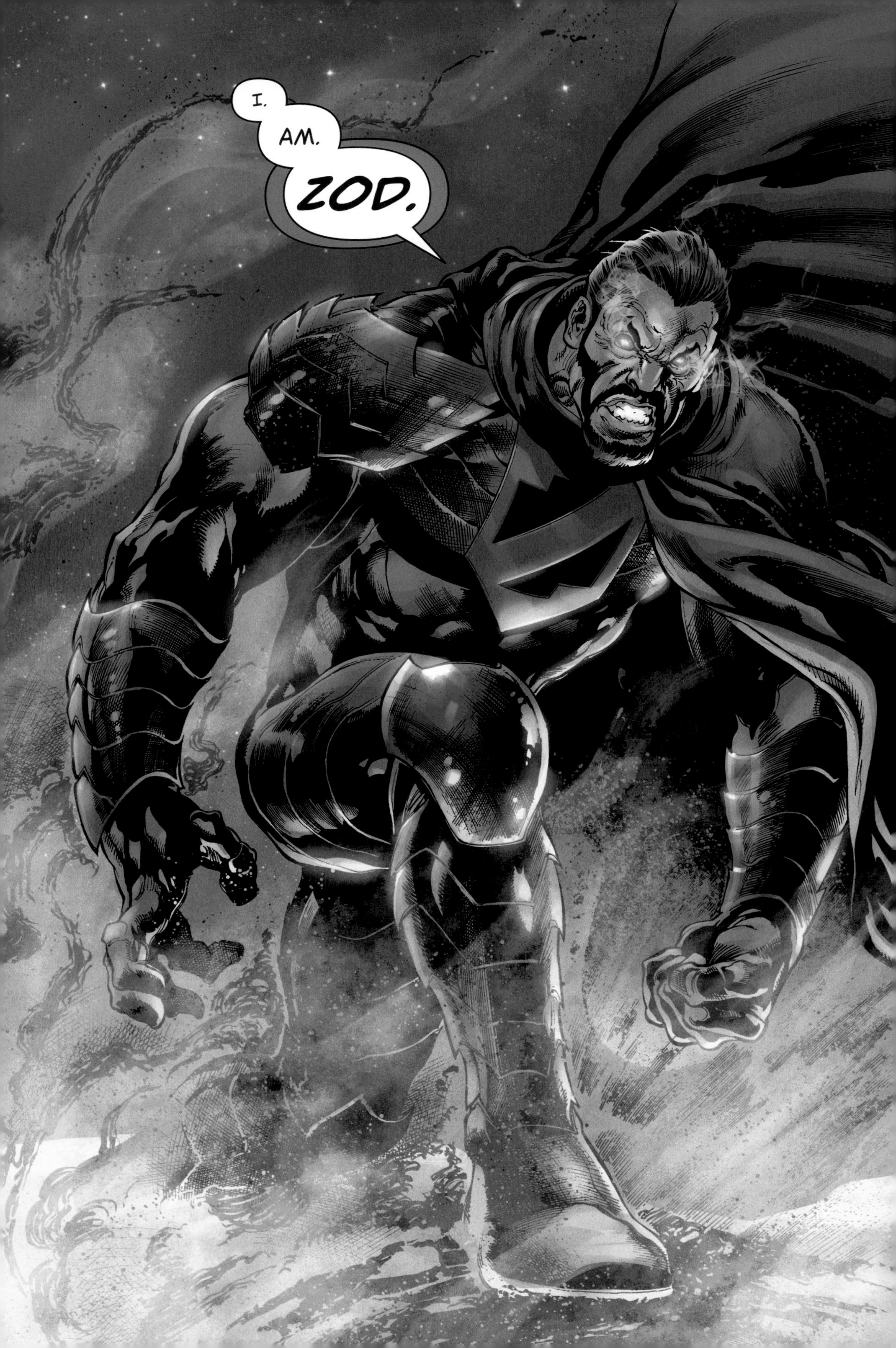
I.
AM.
ZOD.

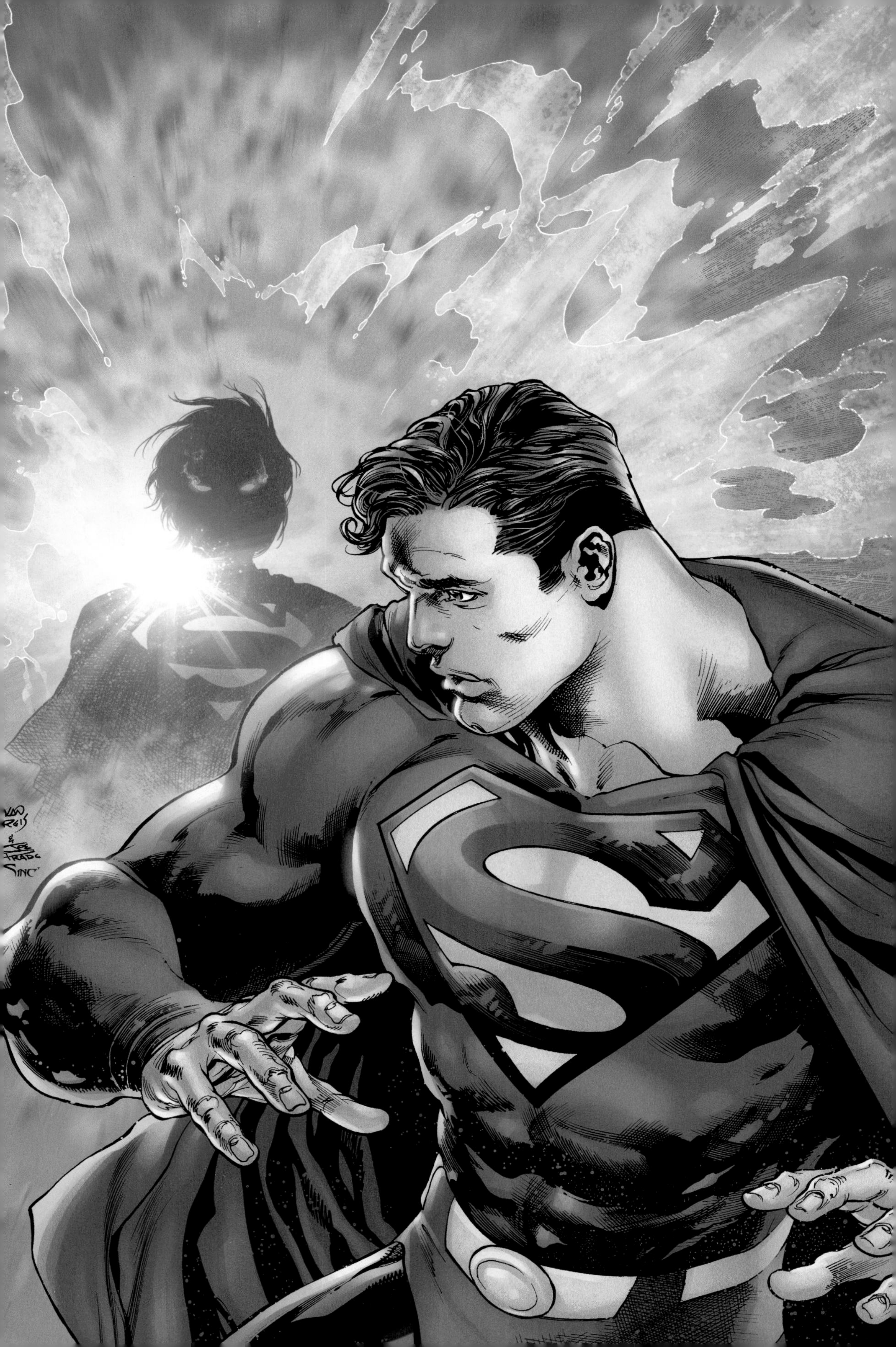

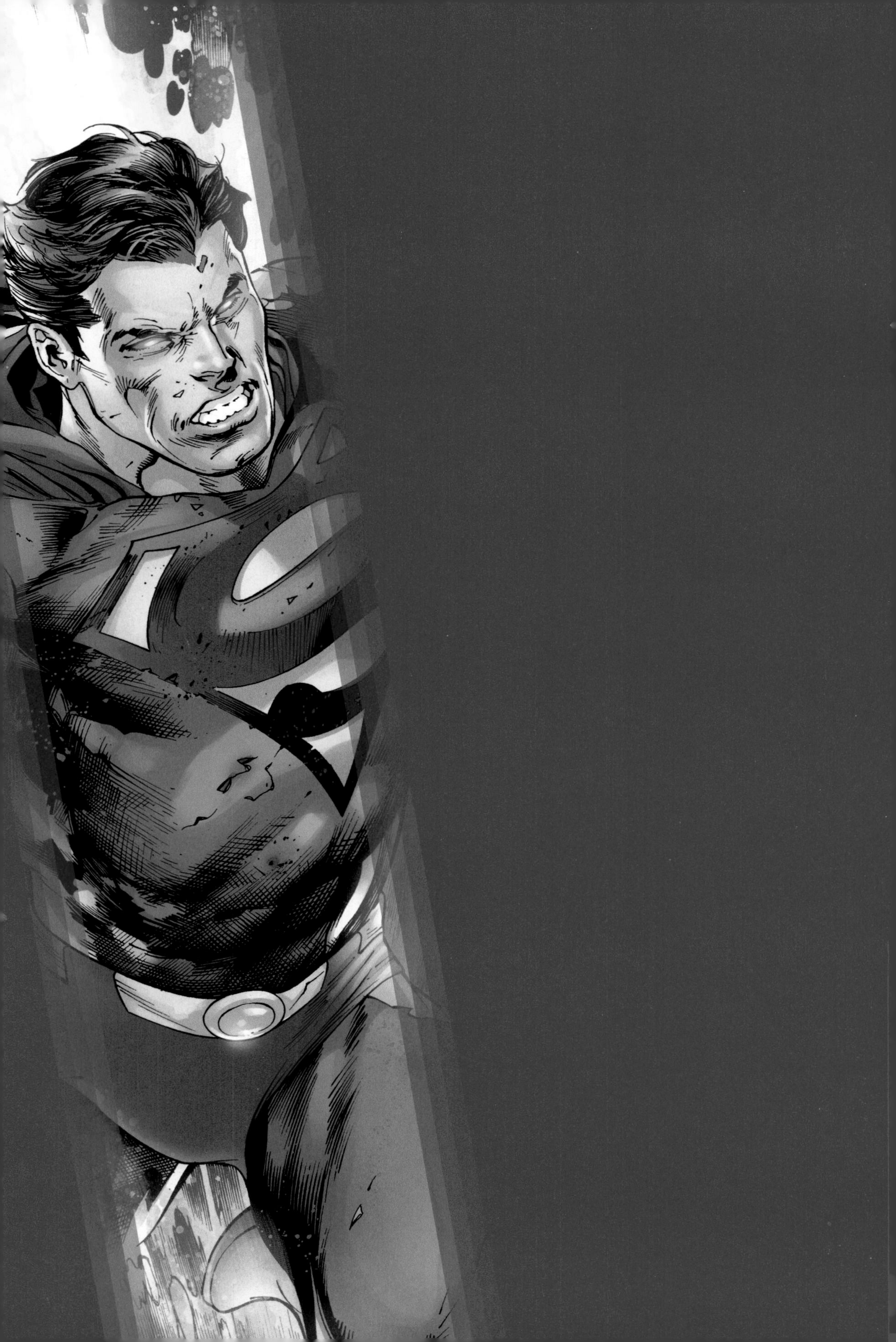

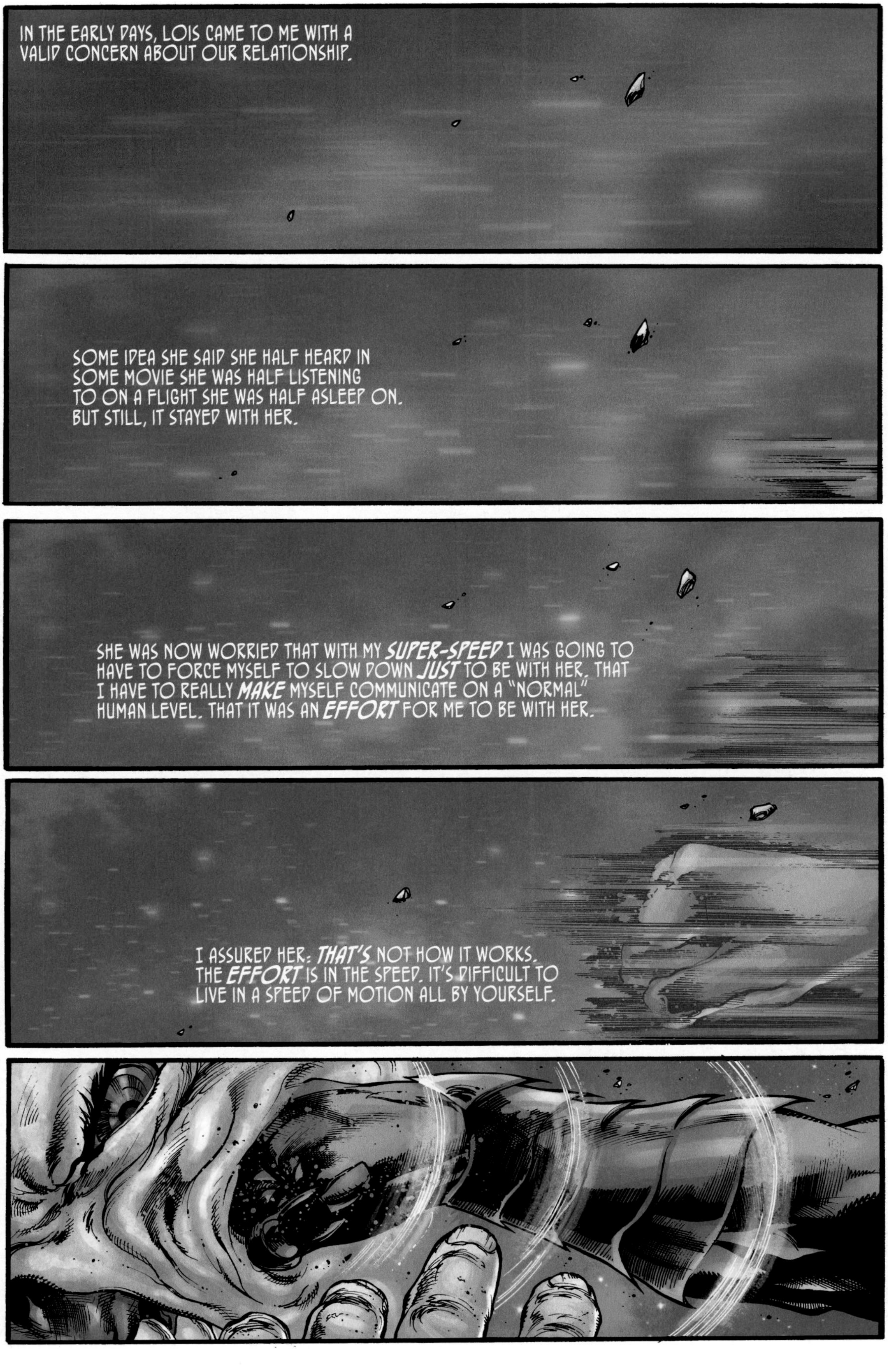
IN THE EARLY DAYS, LOIS CAME TO ME WITH A VALID CONCERN ABOUT OUR RELATIONSHIP.
SOME IDEA SHE SAID SHE HALF HEARD IN SOME MOVIE SHE WAS HALF LISTENING TO ON A FLIGHT SHE WAS HALF ASLEEP ON. BUT STILL, IT STAYED WITH HER.
SHE WAS NOW WORRIED THAT WITH MY SUPER-SPEED I WAS GOING TO HAVE TO FORCE MYSELF TO SLOW DOWN JUST TO BE WITH HER. THAT I HAVE TO REALLY MAKE MYSELF COMMUNICATE ON A "NORMAL" HUMAN LEVEL. THAT IT WAS AN EFFORT FOR ME TO BE WITH HER.
I ASSURED HER: THAT'S NOT HOW IT WORKS. THE EFFORT IS IN THE SPEED. IT'S DIFFICULT TO LIVE IN A SPEED OF MOTION ALL BY YOURSELF.

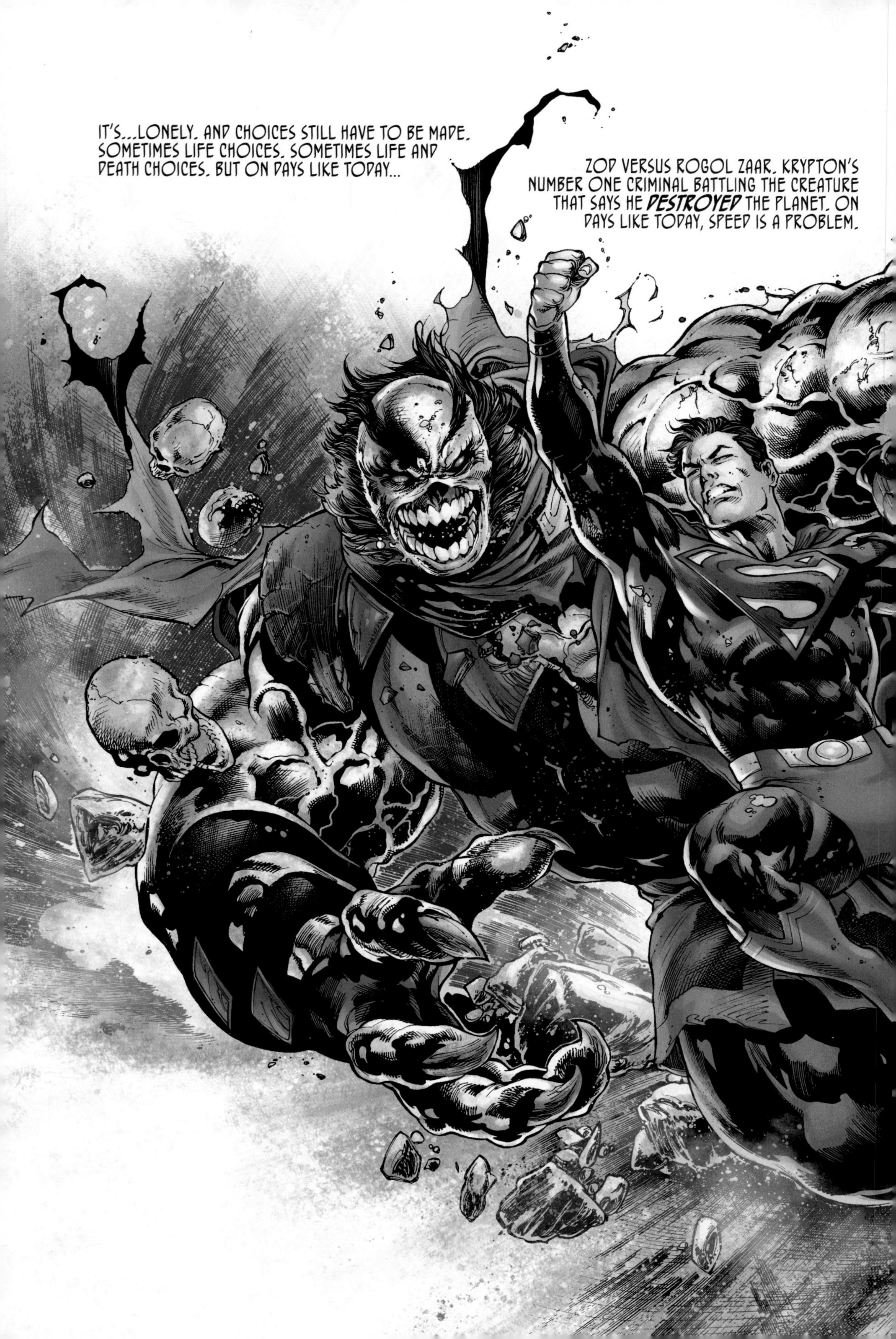
IT'S...LONELY. AND CHOICES STILL HAVE TO BE MADE. SOMETIMES LIFE CHOICES. SOMETIMES LIFE AND DEATH CHOICES. BUT ON DAYS LIKE TODAY...
ZOD VERSUS ROGOL ZAAR. KRYPTON'S NUMBER ONE CRIMINAL BATTLING THE CREATURE THAT SAYS HE DESTROYED THE PLANET. ON DAYS LIKE TODAY, SPEED IS A PROBLEM.

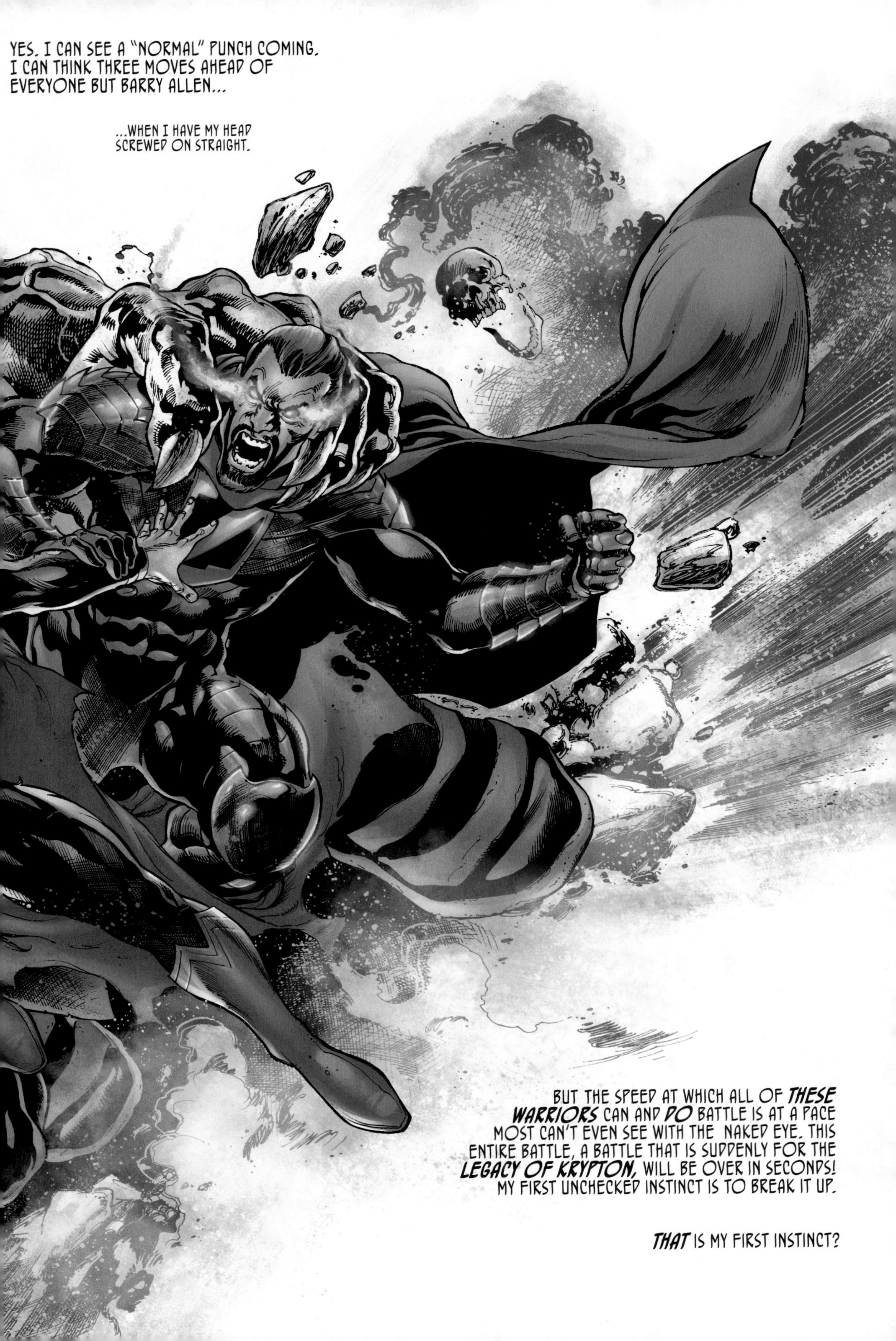
YES. I CAN SEE A "NORMAL" PUNCH COMING. I CAN THINK THREE MOVES AHEAD OF EVERYONE BUT BARRY ALLEN...
...WHEN I HAVE MY HEAD SCREWED ON STRAIGHT.
BUT THE SPEED AT WHICH ALL OF THESE WARRIORS CAN AND DO BATTLE IS AT A PACE MOST CAN'T EVEN SEE WITH THE NAKED EYE. THIS ENTIRE BATTLE, A BATTLE THAT IS SUDDENLY FOR THE LEGACY OF KRYPTON, WILL BE OVER IN SECONDS! MY FIRST UNCHECKED INSTINCT IS TO BREAK IT UP.
THAT IS MY FIRST INSTINCT?

DC COMICS PROUDLY PRESENTS

SUPERMAN

the UNITY SAGA pt 6

BRIAN MICHAEL BENDIS script
IVAN REIS pencils

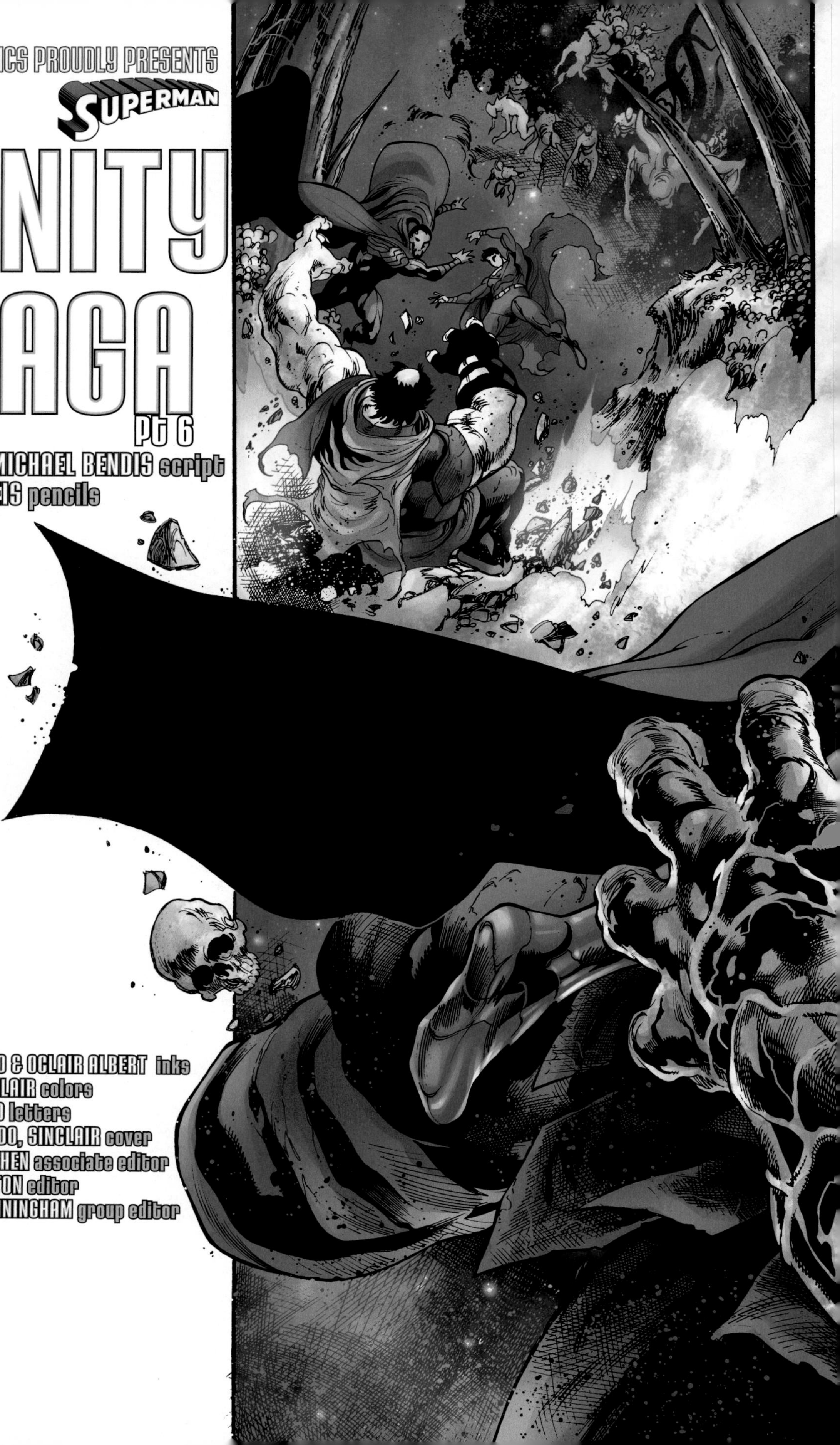

JOE PRADO & OCLAIR ALBERT inks
ALEX SINCLAIR colors
JOSH REED letters
REIS, PRADO, SINCLAIR cover
JESSICA CHEN associate editor
MIKE COTTON editor
BRIAN CUNNINGHAM group editor

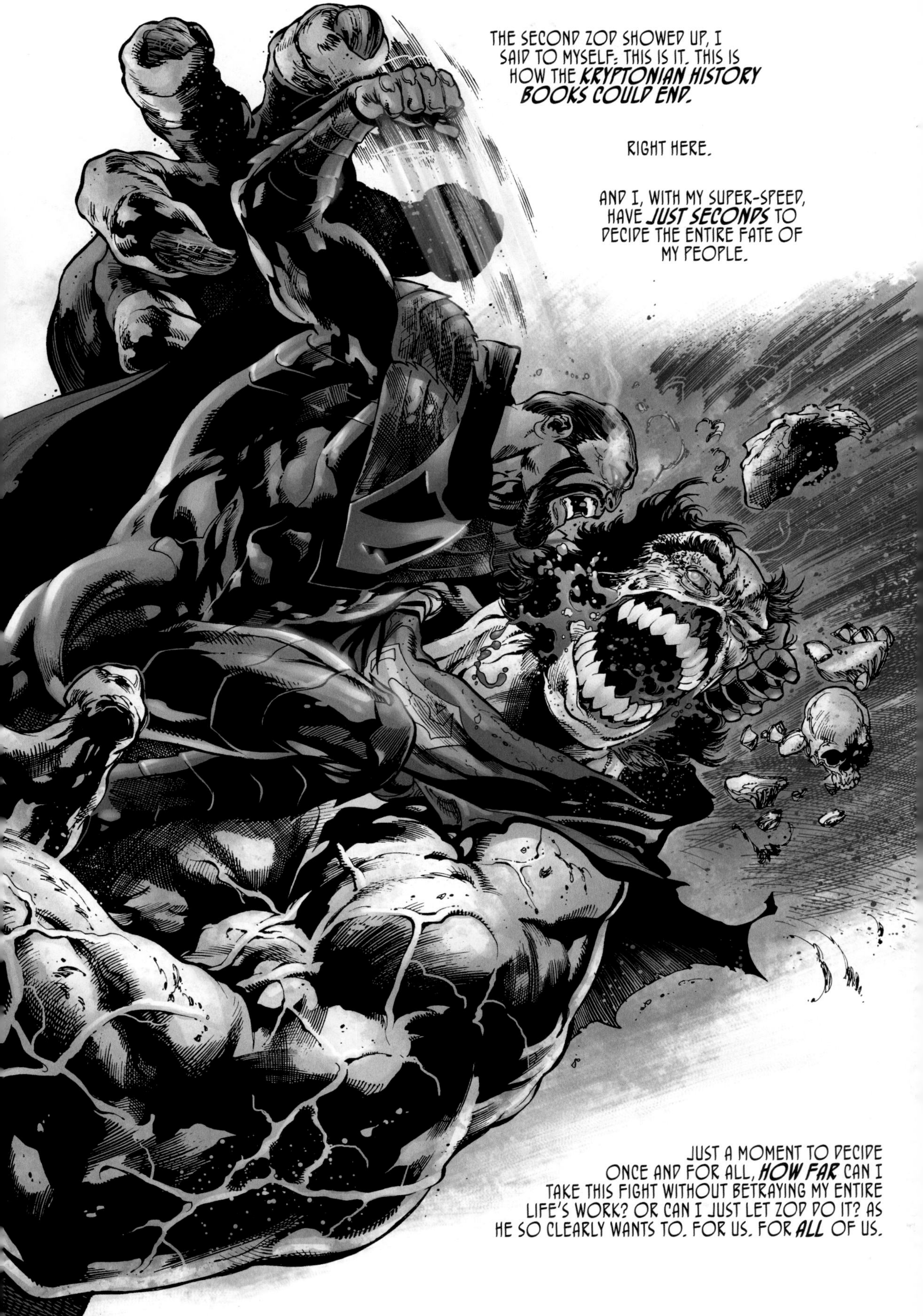
THE SECOND ZOD SHOWED UP, I SAID TO MYSELF: THIS IS IT. THIS IS HOW THE KRYPTONIAN HISTORY BOOKS COULD END.
RIGHT HERE.
AND I, WITH MY SUPER-SPEED, HAVE JUST SECONDS TO DECIDE THE ENTIRE FATE OF MY PEOPLE.
JUST A MOMENT TO DECIDE ONCE AND FOR ALL, HOW FAR CAN I TAKE THIS FIGHT WITHOUT BETRAYING MY ENTIRE LIFE'S WORK? OR CAN I JUST LET ZOD DO IT? AS HE SO CLEARLY WANTS TO. FOR US. FOR ALL OF US.

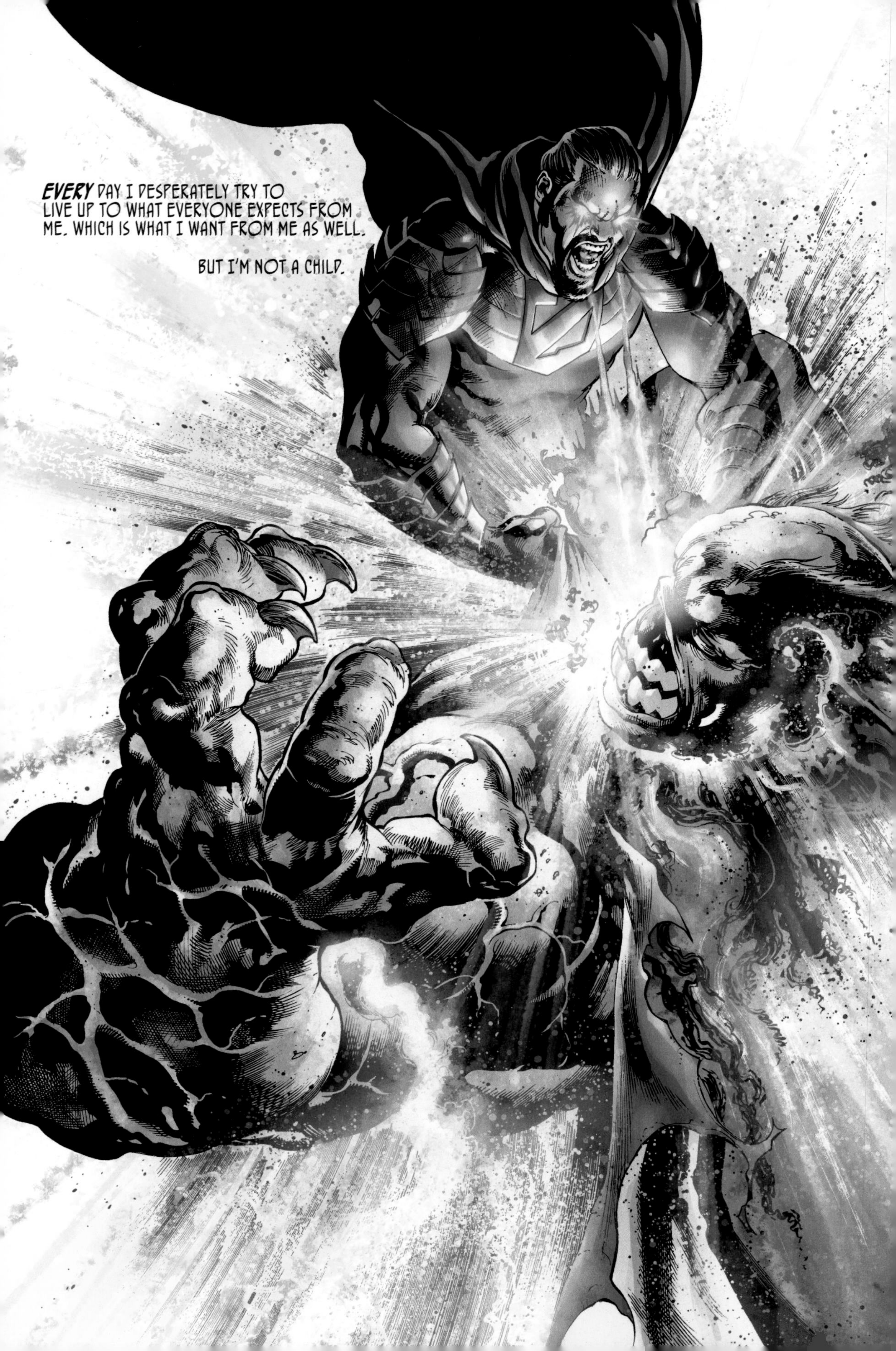

EVERY DAY I DESPERATELY TRY TO LIVE UP TO WHAT EVERYONE EXPECTS FROM ME. WHICH IS WHAT I WANT FROM ME AS WELL.
BUT I'M NOT A CHILD.

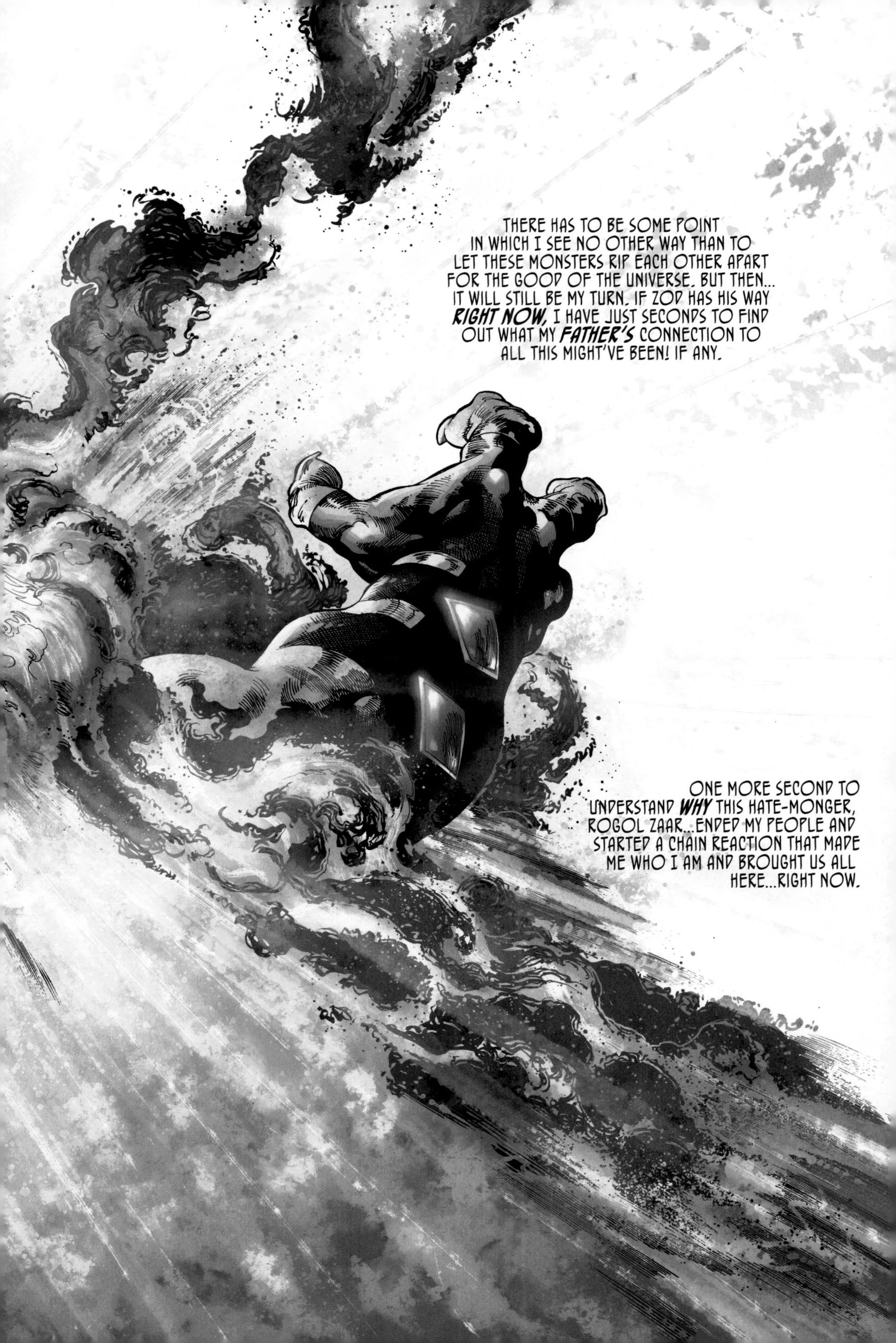
THERE HAS TO BE SOME POINT IN WHICH I SEE NO OTHER WAY THAN TO LET THESE MONSTERS RIP EACH OTHER APART FOR THE GOOD OF THE UNIVERSE. BUT THEN... IT WILL STILL BE MY TURN. IF ZOD HAS HIS WAY ***RIGHT NOW,*** I HAVE JUST SECONDS TO FIND OUT WHAT MY ***FATHER'S*** CONNECTION TO ALL THIS MIGHT'VE BEEN! IF ANY.
ONE MORE SECOND TO UNDERSTAND ***WHY*** THIS HATE-MONGER, ROGOL ZAAR...ENDED MY PEOPLE AND STARTED A CHAIN REACTION THAT MADE ME WHO I AM AND BROUGHT US ALL HERE...RIGHT NOW.

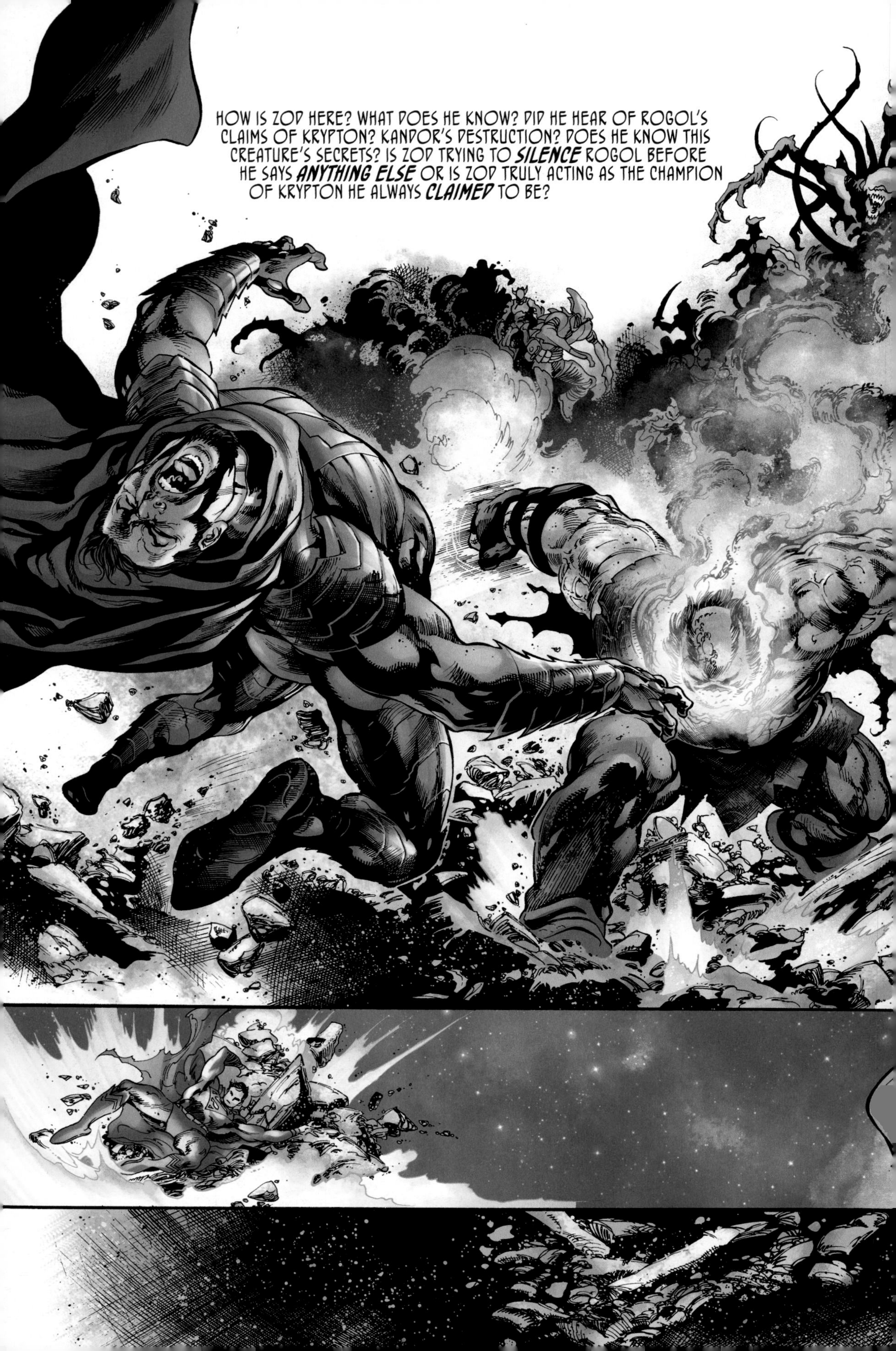
HOW IS ZOD HERE? WHAT DOES HE KNOW? DID HE HEAR OF ROGOL'S CLAIMS OF KRYPTON? KANDOR'S DESTRUCTION? DOES HE KNOW THIS CREATURE'S SECRETS? IS ZOD TRYING TO SILENCE ROGOL BEFORE HE SAYS ANYTHING ELSE OR IS ZOD TRULY ACTING AS THE CHAMPION OF KRYPTON HE ALWAYS CLAIMED TO BE?

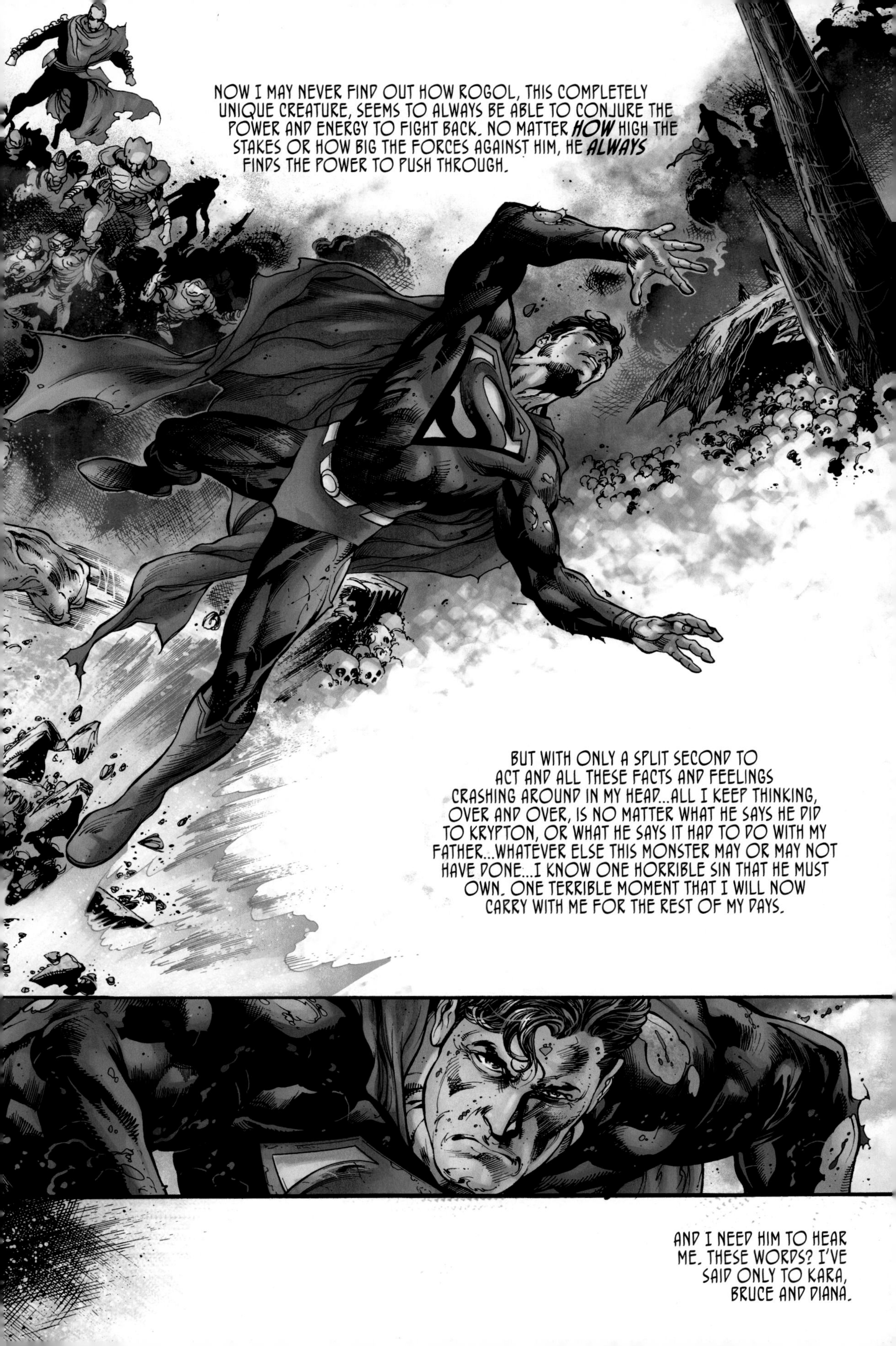
NOW I MAY NEVER FIND OUT HOW ROGOL, THIS COMPLETELY UNIQUE CREATURE, SEEMS TO ALWAYS BE ABLE TO CONJURE THE POWER AND ENERGY TO FIGHT BACK. NO MATTER HOW HIGH THE STAKES OR HOW BIG THE FORCES AGAINST HIM, HE ALWAYS FINDS THE POWER TO PUSH THROUGH.
BUT WITH ONLY A SPLIT SECOND TO ACT AND ALL THESE FACTS AND FEELINGS CRASHING AROUND IN MY HEAD...ALL I KEEP THINKING, OVER AND OVER, IS NO MATTER WHAT HE SAYS HE DID TO KRYPTON, OR WHAT HE SAYS IT HAD TO DO WITH MY FATHER...WHATEVER ELSE THIS MONSTER MAY OR MAY NOT HAVE DONE...I KNOW ONE HORRIBLE SIN THAT HE MUST OWN. ONE TERRIBLE MOMENT THAT I WILL NOW CARRY WITH ME FOR THE REST OF MY DAYS.
AND I NEED HIM TO HEAR ME. THESE WORDS? I'VE SAID ONLY TO KARA, BRUCE AND DIANA.

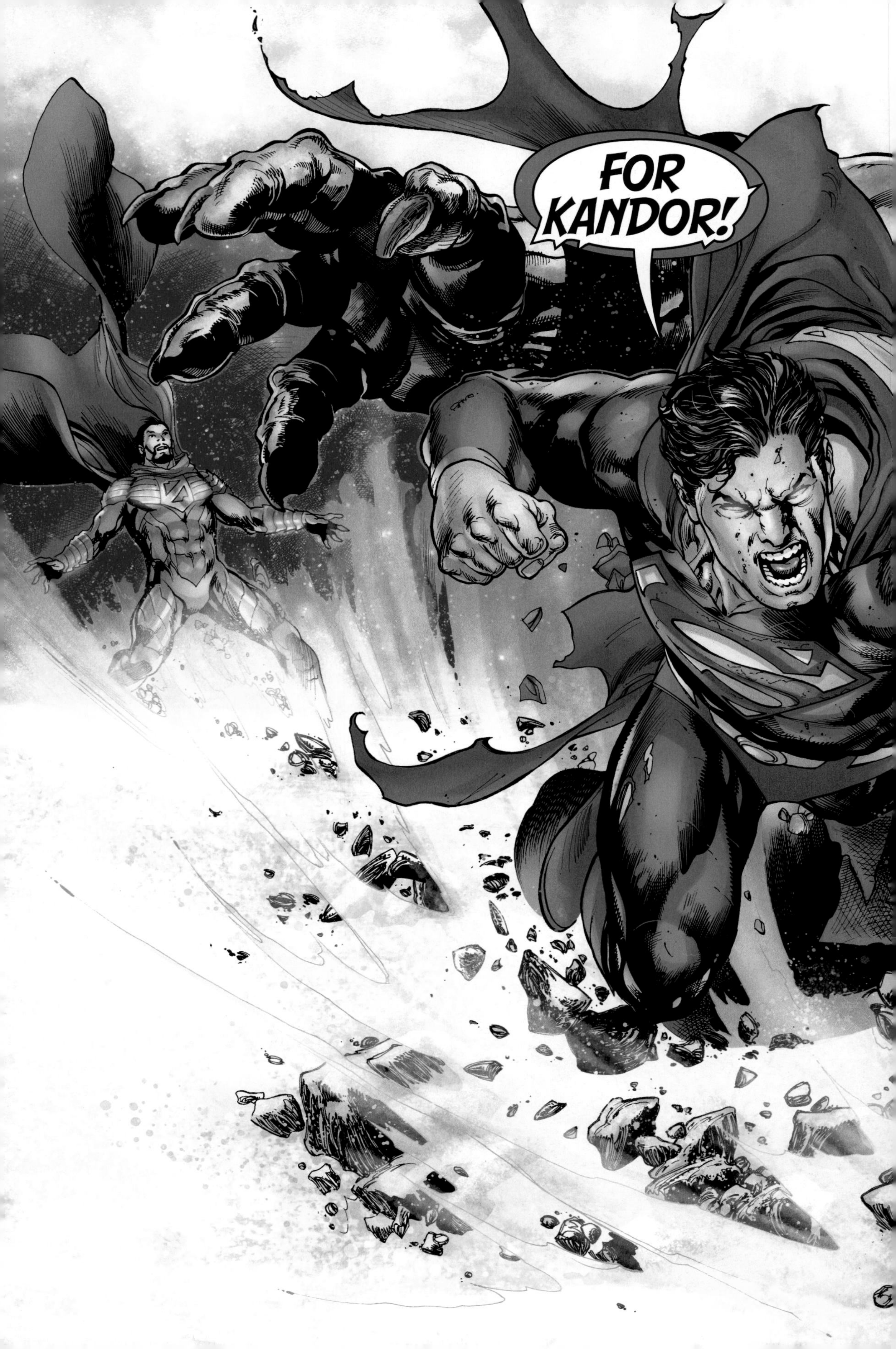
FOR KANDOR!

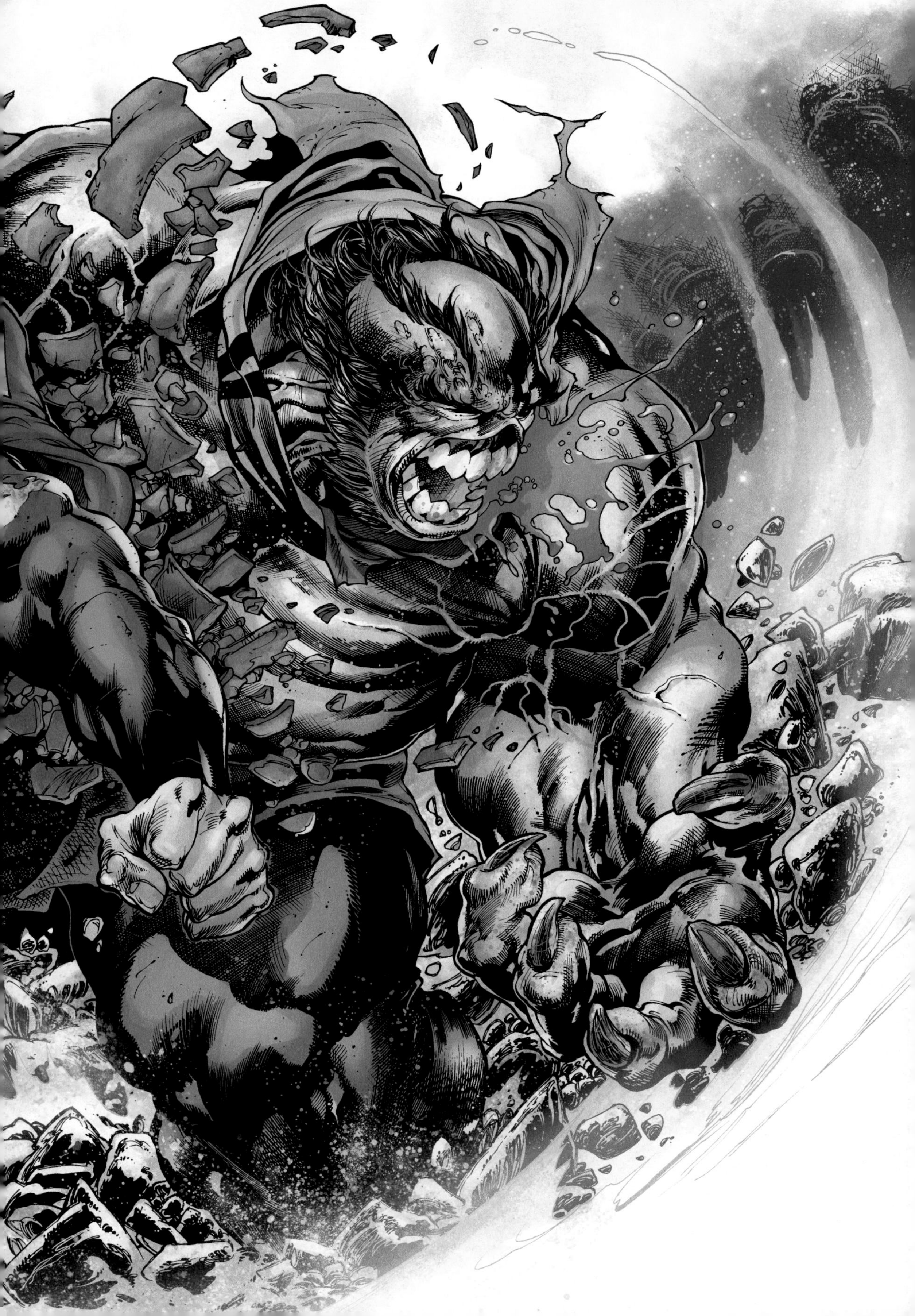

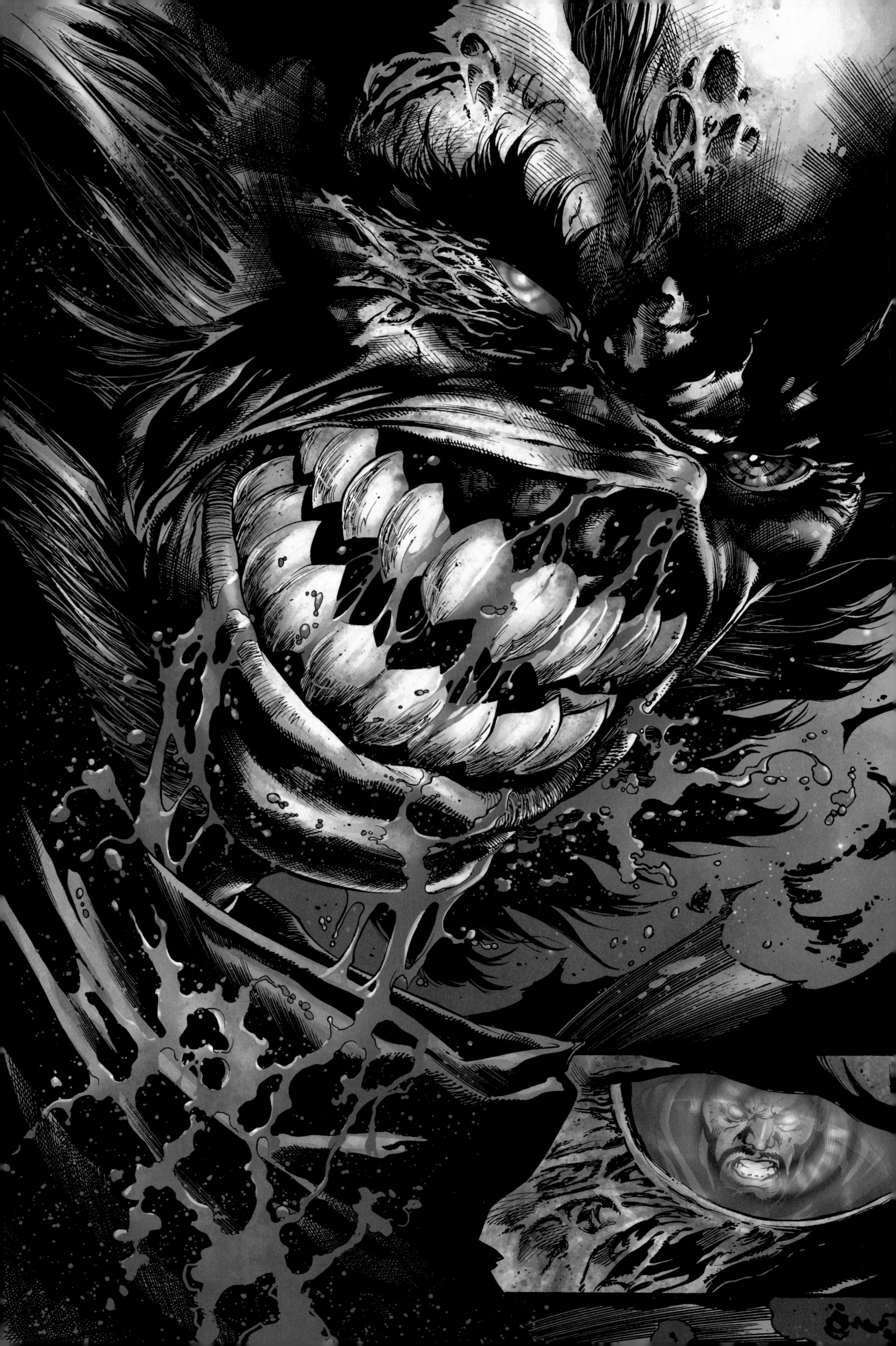

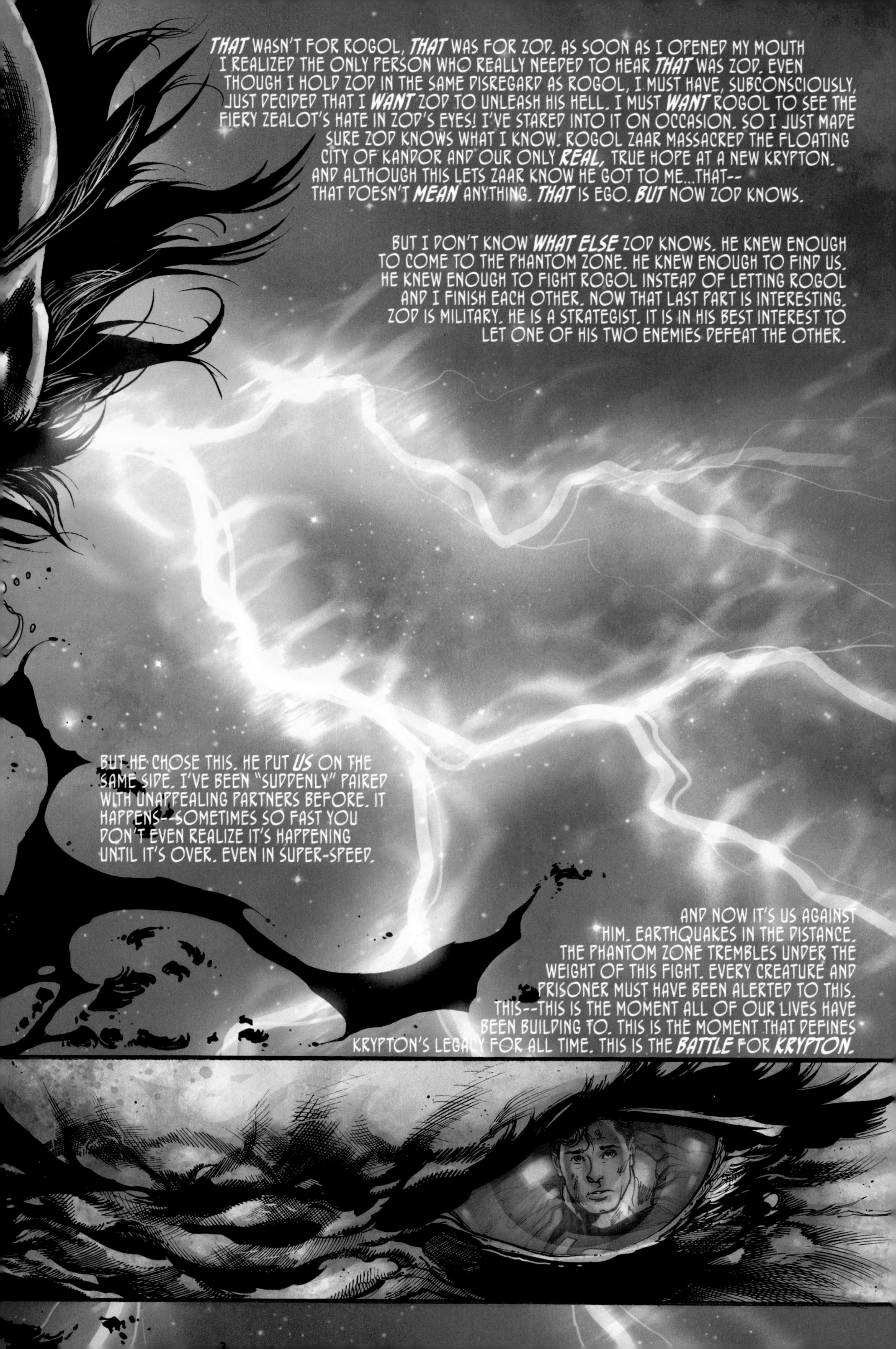
THAT WASN'T FOR ROGOL, THAT WAS FOR ZOD. AS SOON AS I OPENED MY MOUTH I REALIZED THE ONLY PERSON WHO REALLY NEEDED TO HEAR THAT WAS ZOD. EVEN THOUGH I HOLD ZOD IN THE SAME DISREGARD AS ROGOL, I MUST HAVE, SUBCONSCIOUSLY, JUST DECIDED THAT I WANT ZOD TO UNLEASH HIS HELL. I MUST WANT ROGOL TO SEE THE FIERY ZEALOT'S HATE IN ZOD'S EYES! I'VE STARED INTO IT ON OCCASION. SO I JUST MADE SURE ZOD KNOWS WHAT I KNOW. ROGOL ZAAR MASSACRED THE FLOATING CITY OF KANDOR AND OUR ONLY REAL, TRUE HOPE AT A NEW KRYPTON. AND ALTHOUGH THIS LETS ZAAR KNOW HE GOT TO ME...THAT-- THAT DOESN'T MEAN ANYTHING. THAT IS EGO. BUT NOW ZOD KNOWS.
BUT I DON'T KNOW WHAT ELSE ZOD KNOWS. HE KNEW ENOUGH TO COME TO THE PHANTOM ZONE. HE KNEW ENOUGH TO FIND US. HE KNEW ENOUGH TO FIGHT ROGOL INSTEAD OF LETTING ROGOL AND I FINISH EACH OTHER. NOW THAT LAST PART IS INTERESTING. ZOD IS MILITARY. HE IS A STRATEGIST. IT IS IN HIS BEST INTEREST TO LET ONE OF HIS TWO ENEMIES DEFEAT THE OTHER.
BUT HE CHOSE THIS. HE PUT US ON THE SAME SIDE. I'VE BEEN "SUDDENLY" PAIRED WITH UNAPPEALING PARTNERS BEFORE. IT HAPPENS--SOMETIMES SO FAST YOU DON'T EVEN REALIZE IT'S HAPPENING UNTIL IT'S OVER. EVEN IN SUPER-SPEED.
AND NOW IT'S US AGAINST HIM. EARTHQUAKES IN THE DISTANCE. THE PHANTOM ZONE TREMBLES UNDER THE WEIGHT OF THIS FIGHT. EVERY CREATURE AND PRISONER MUST HAVE BEEN ALERTED TO THIS. THIS--THIS IS THE MOMENT ALL OF OUR LIVES HAVE BEEN BUILDING TO. THIS IS THE MOMENT THAT DEFINES KRYPTON'S LEGACY FOR ALL TIME. THIS IS THE BATTLE FOR KRYPTON.

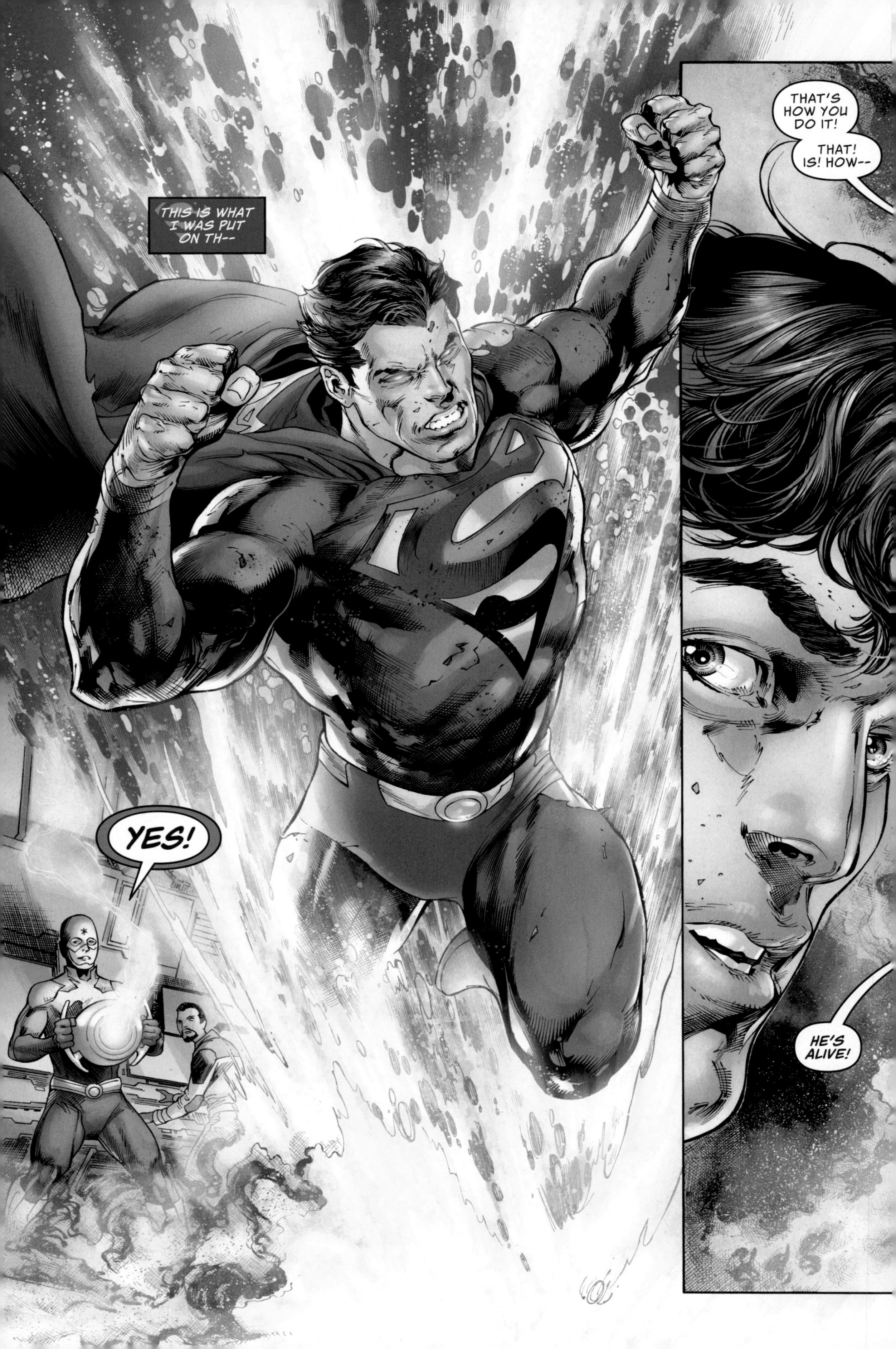

THIS IS WHAT I WAS PUT ON TH--
YES!
THAT'S HOW YOU DO IT!
THAT! IS! HOW--
HE'S ALIVE!

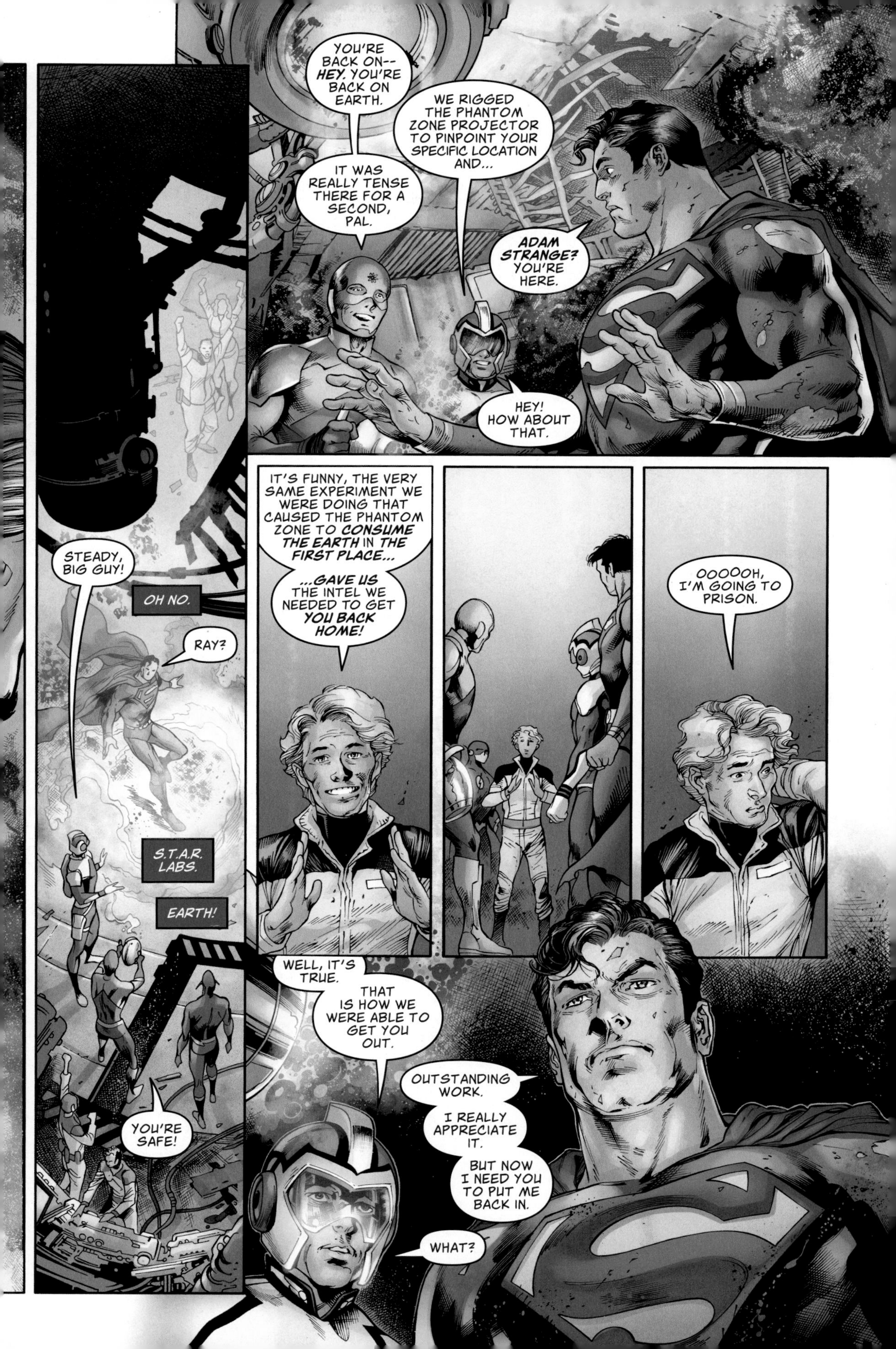
STEADY, BIG GUY!
OH NO.
RAY?
S.T.A.R. LABS.
EARTH!
YOU'RE SAFE!
YOU'RE BACK ON-- HEY. YOU'RE BACK ON EARTH.
IT WAS REALLY TENSE THERE FOR A SECOND, PAL.
WE RIGGED THE PHANTOM ZONE PROJECTOR TO PINPOINT YOUR SPECIFIC LOCATION AND...
ADAM STRANGE? YOU'RE HERE.
HEY! HOW ABOUT THAT.
IT'S FUNNY, THE VERY SAME EXPERIMENT WE WERE DOING THAT CAUSED THE PHANTOM ZONE TO CONSUME THE EARTH IN THE FIRST PLACE...
...GAVE US THE INTEL WE NEEDED TO GET YOU BACK HOME!
OOOOOH, I'M GOING TO PRISON.
WELL, IT'S TRUE.
THAT IS HOW WE WERE ABLE TO GET YOU OUT.
OUTSTANDING WORK.
I REALLY APPRECIATE IT.
BUT NOW I NEED YOU TO PUT ME BACK IN.
WHAT?

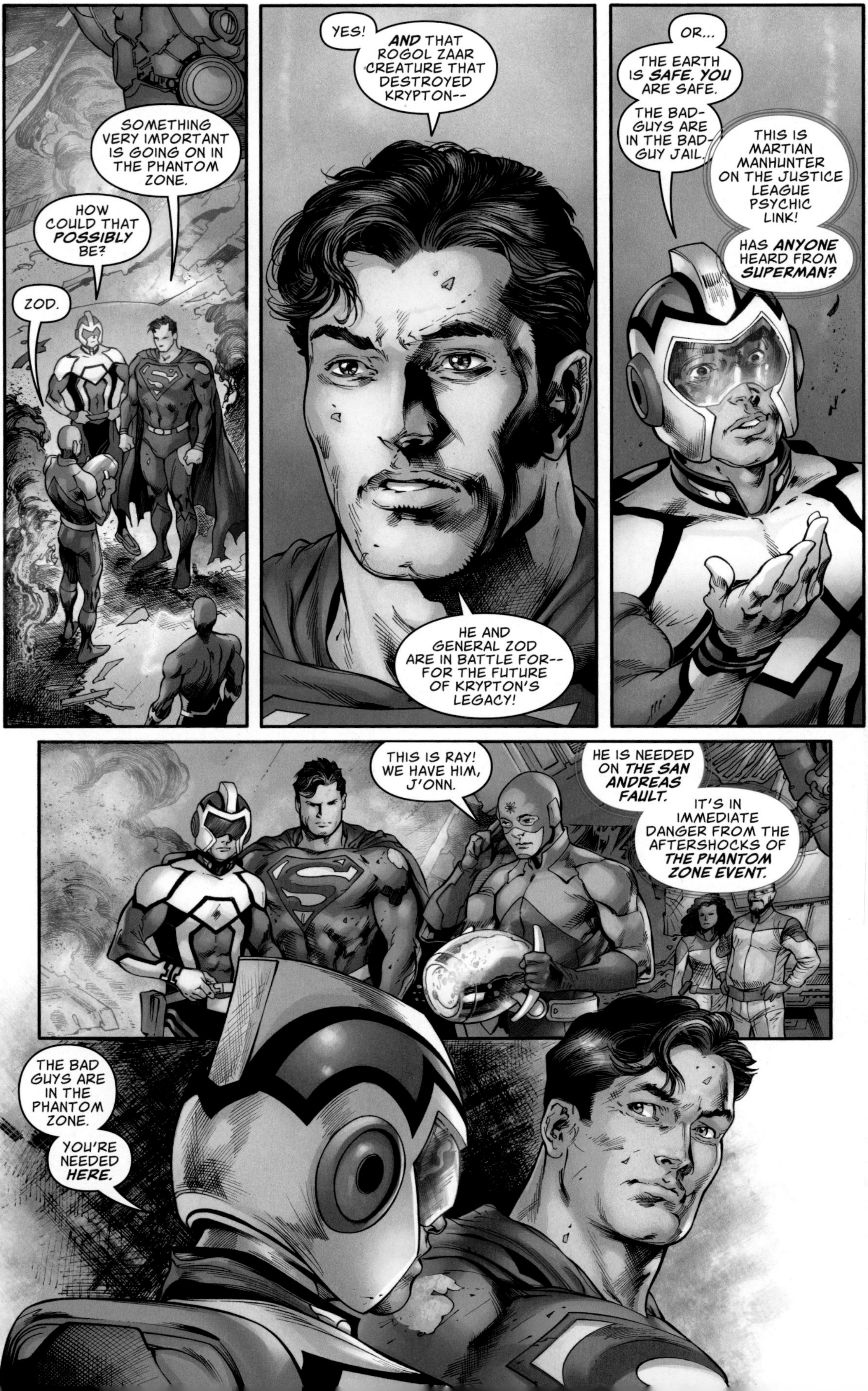
SOMETHING VERY IMPORTANT IS GOING ON IN THE PHANTOM ZONE.
HOW COULD THAT POSSIBLY BE?
ZOD.
YES!
AND THAT ROGOL ZAAR CREATURE THAT DESTROYED KRYPTON--
HE AND GENERAL ZOD ARE IN BATTLE FOR-- FOR THE FUTURE OF KRYPTON'S LEGACY!
OR...
THE EARTH IS SAFE. YOU ARE SAFE.
THE BAD-GUYS ARE IN THE BAD-GUY JAIL.
THIS IS MARTIAN MANHUNTER ON THE JUSTICE LEAGUE PSYCHIC LINK!
HAS ANYONE HEARD FROM SUPERMAN?
THIS IS RAY! WE HAVE HIM, J'ONN.
HE IS NEEDED ON THE SAN ANDREAS FAULT.
IT'S IN IMMEDIATE DANGER FROM THE AFTERSHOCKS OF THE PHANTOM ZONE EVENT.
THE BAD GUYS ARE IN THE PHANTOM ZONE.
YOU'RE NEEDED HERE.

YOU'RE RIGHT, ADAM. OF *COURSE* YOU'RE RIGHT.

HEY, IT'S BEEN A LONG DAY.

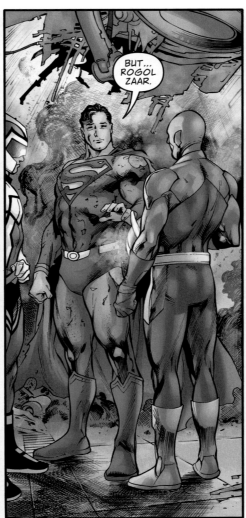

BUT... ROGOL ZAAR.

ROGOL ZAAR.

#$@@!

ZAAR! ZAAR!

ZAAR!

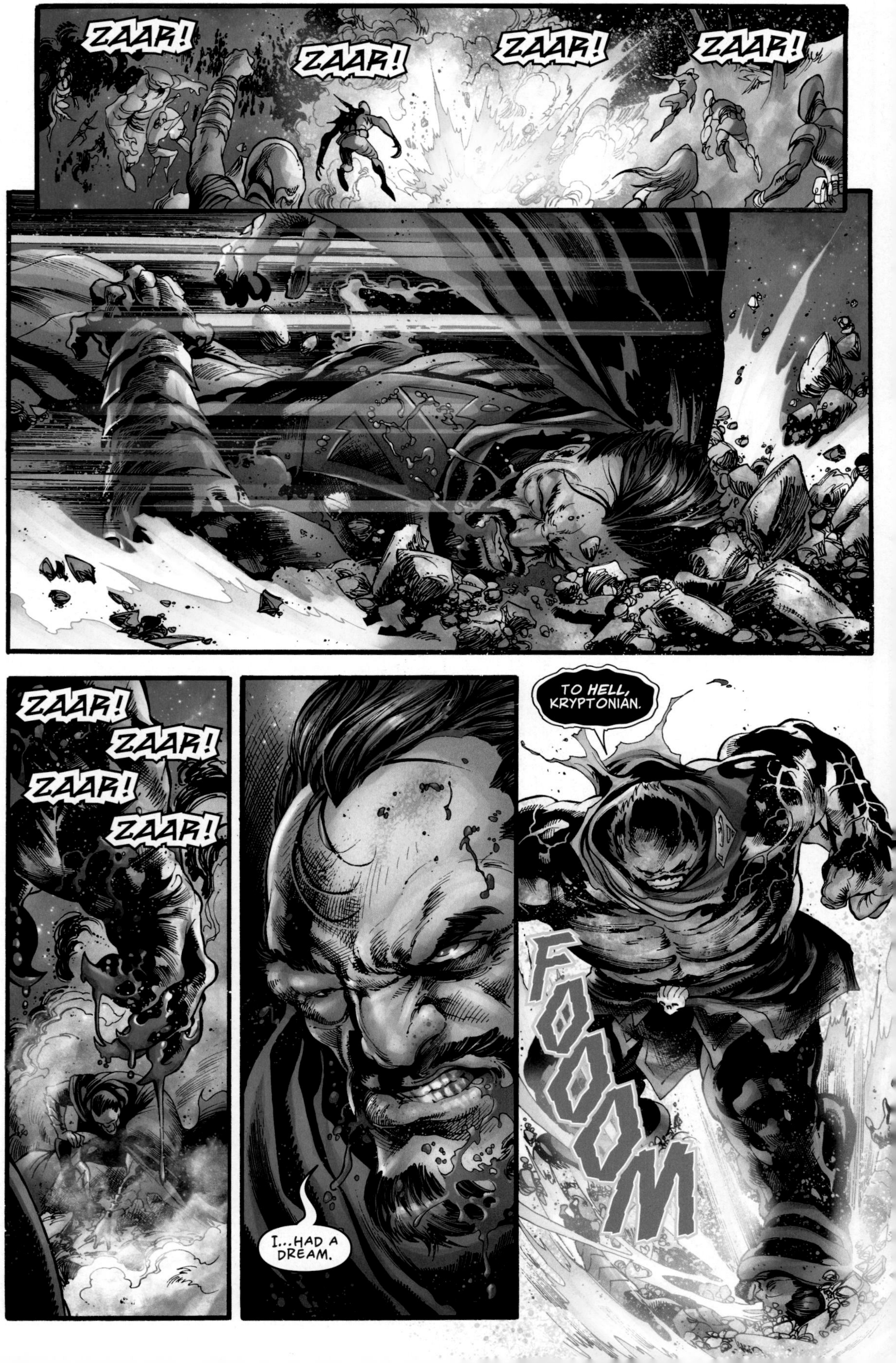
ZAAR!
ZAAR!
ZAAR!
ZAAR!
ZAAR!
ZAAR!
ZAAR!
ZAAR!
I...HAD A DREAM.
TO HELL, KRYPTONIAN.
FOOOM

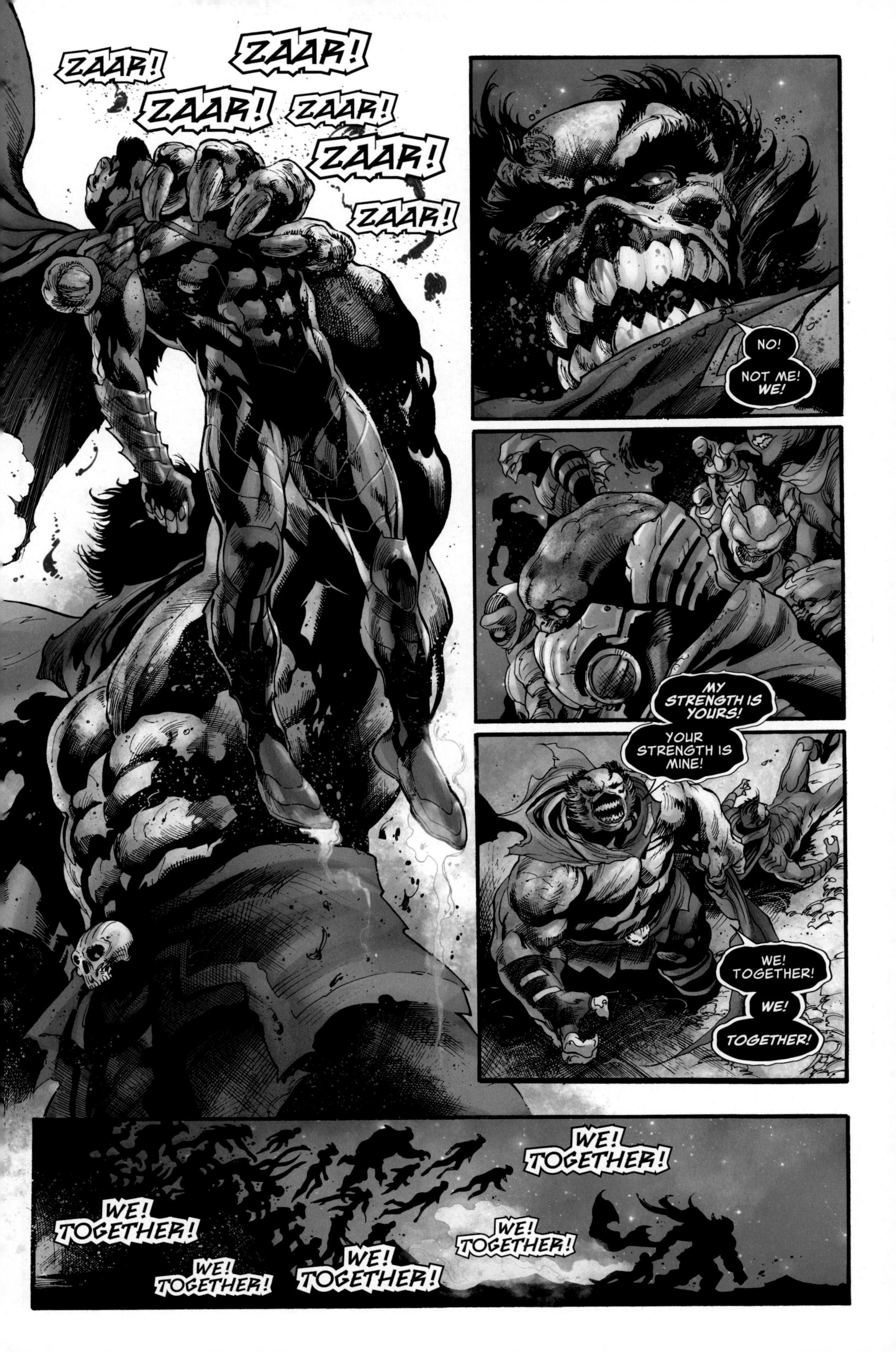
ZAAR!
ZAAR!
ZAAR!
ZAAR!
ZAAR!
ZAAR!
NO!
NOT ME! WE!
MY STRENGTH IS YOURS!
YOUR STRENGTH IS MINE!
WE! TOGETHER!
WE!
TOGETHER!
WE! TOGETHER!
WE! TOGETHER!
WE! TOGETHER!
WE! TOGETHER!
WE! TOGETHER!

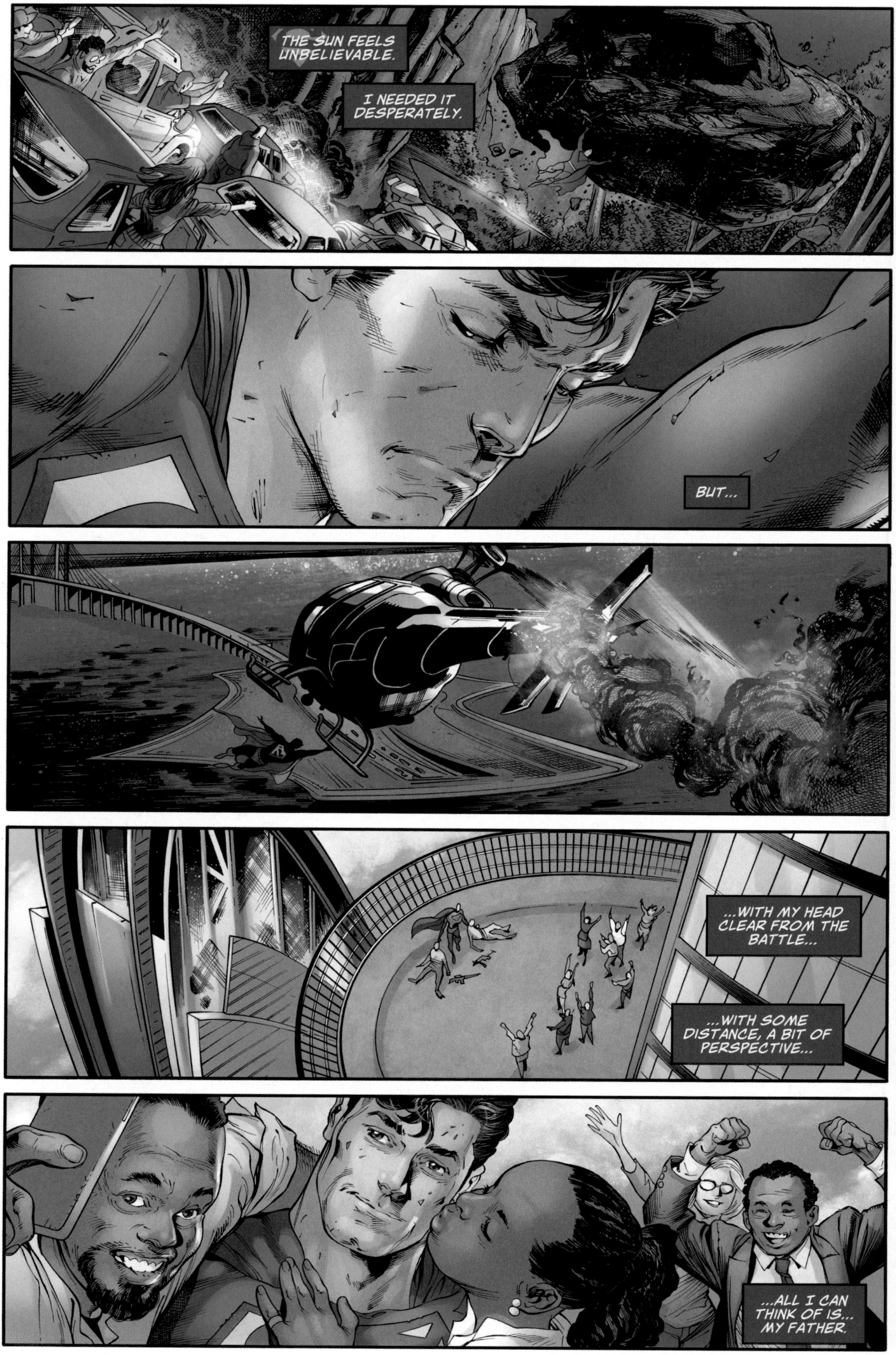
THE SUN FEELS UNBELIEVABLE.
I NEEDED IT DESPERATELY.
BUT...
...WITH MY HEAD CLEAR FROM THE BATTLE...
...WITH SOME DISTANCE, A BIT OF PERSPECTIVE...
...ALL I CAN THINK OF IS... MY FATHER.

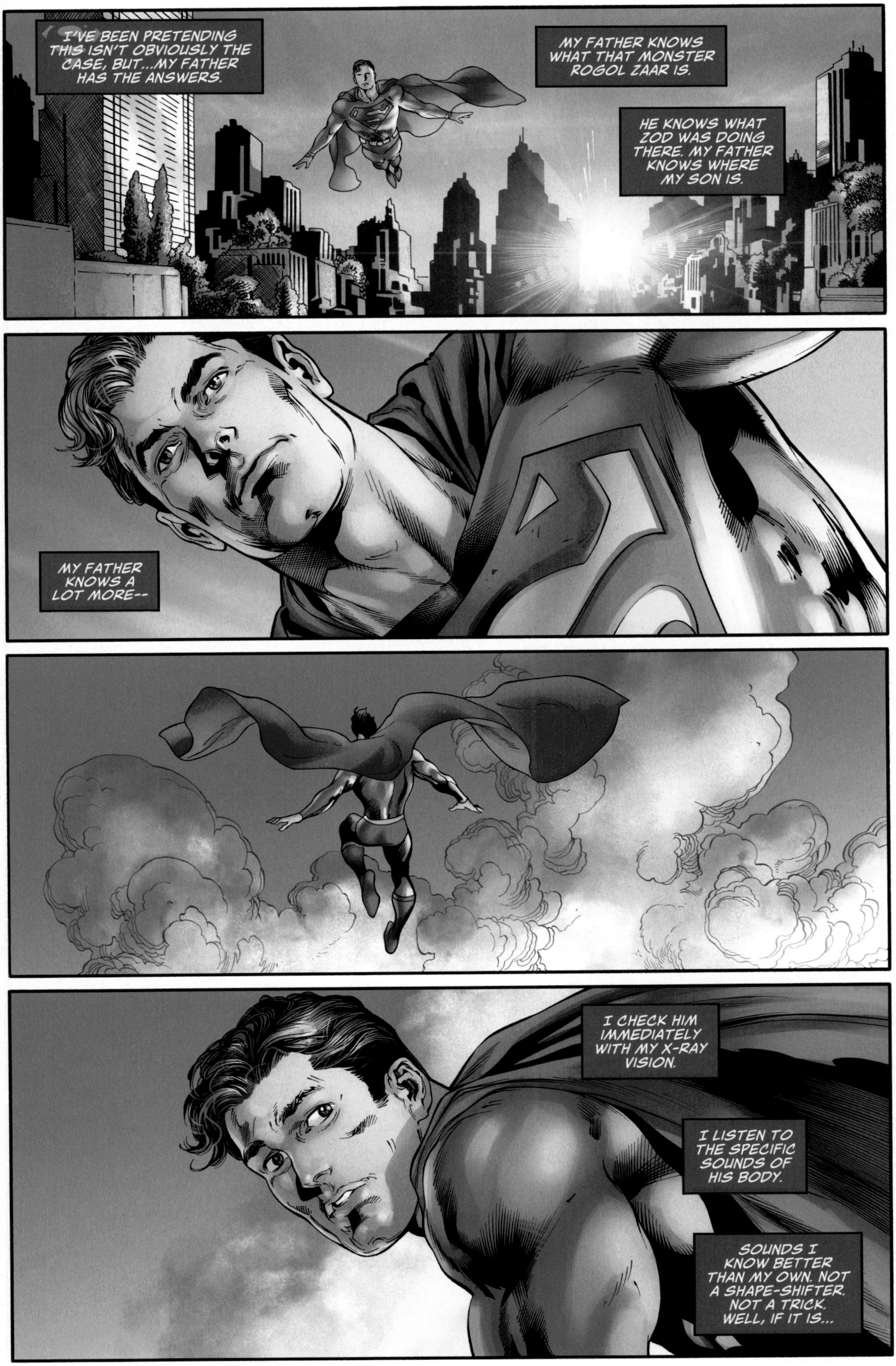
I'VE BEEN PRETENDING THIS ISN'T OBVIOUSLY THE CASE, BUT...MY FATHER HAS THE ANSWERS.
MY FATHER KNOWS WHAT THAT MONSTER ROGOL ZAAR IS.
HE KNOWS WHAT ZOD WAS DOING THERE. MY FATHER KNOWS WHERE MY SON IS.
MY FATHER KNOWS A LOT MORE--
I CHECK HIM IMMEDIATELY WITH MY X-RAY VISION.
I LISTEN TO THE SPECIFIC SOUNDS OF HIS BODY.
SOUNDS I KNOW BETTER THAN MY OWN. NOT A SHAPE-SHIFTER. NOT A TRICK. WELL, IF IT IS...

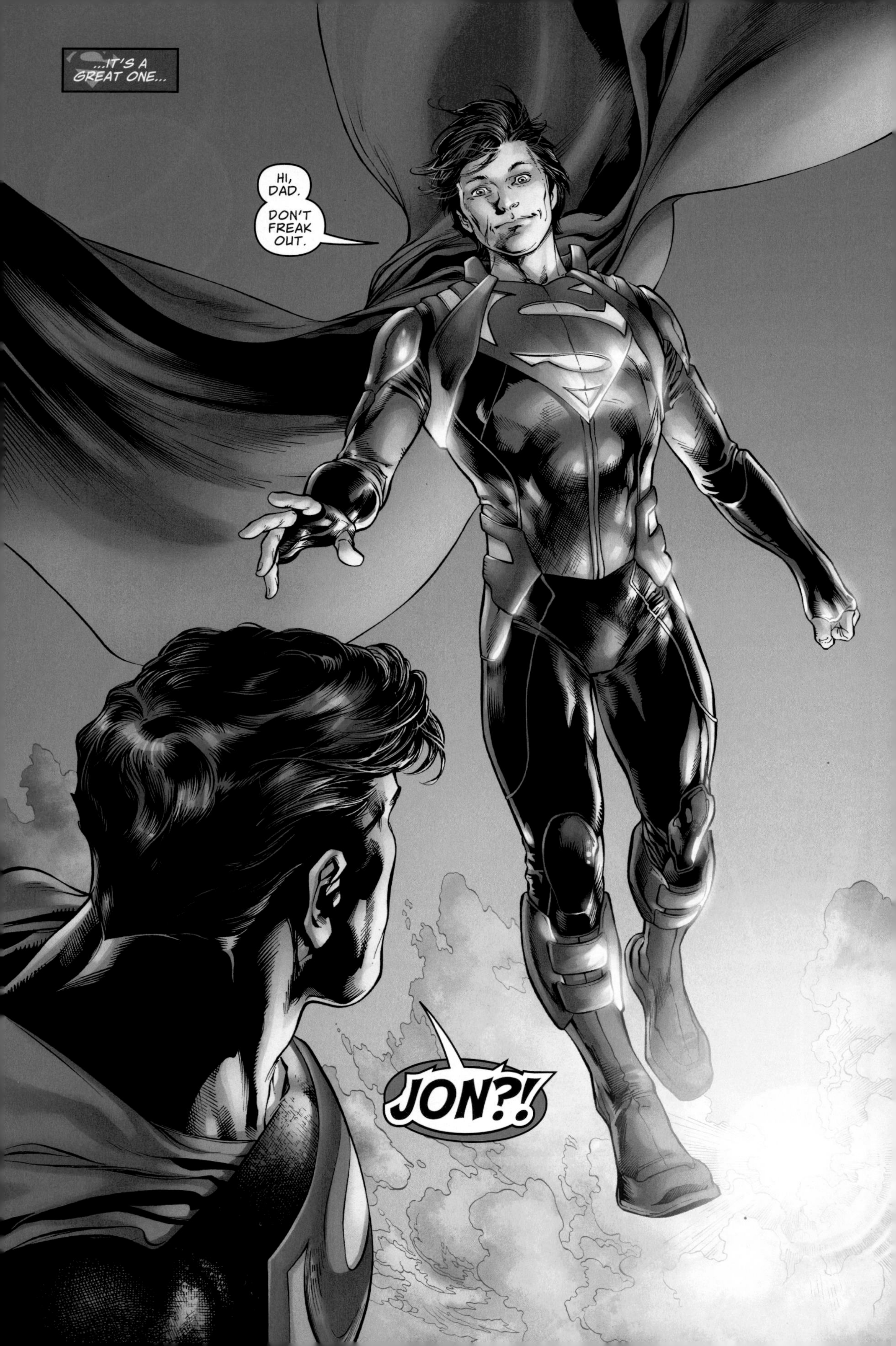
...IT'S A GREAT ONE...
HI, DAD.
DON'T FREAK OUT.
JON?!

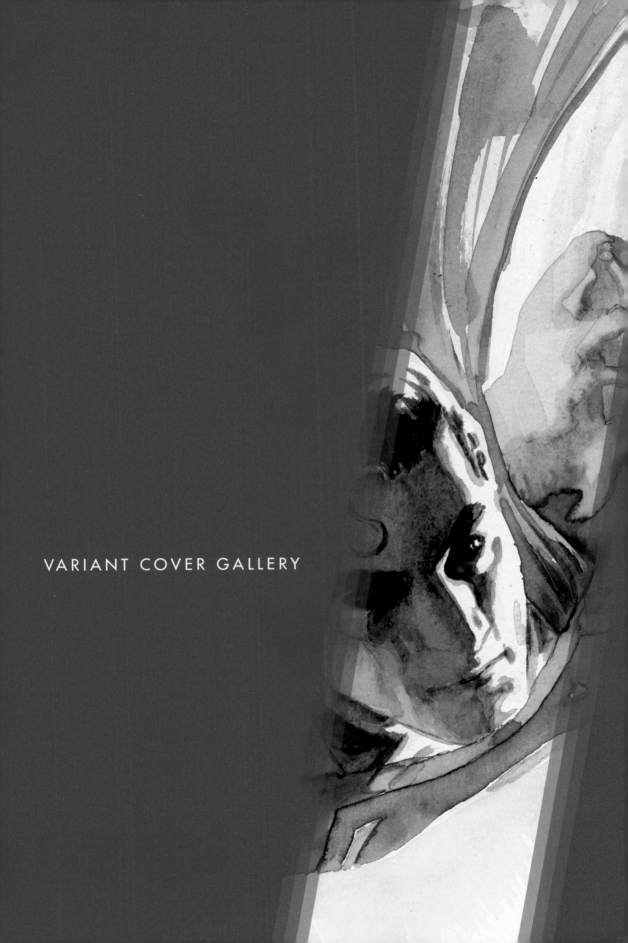

VARIANT COVER GALLERY

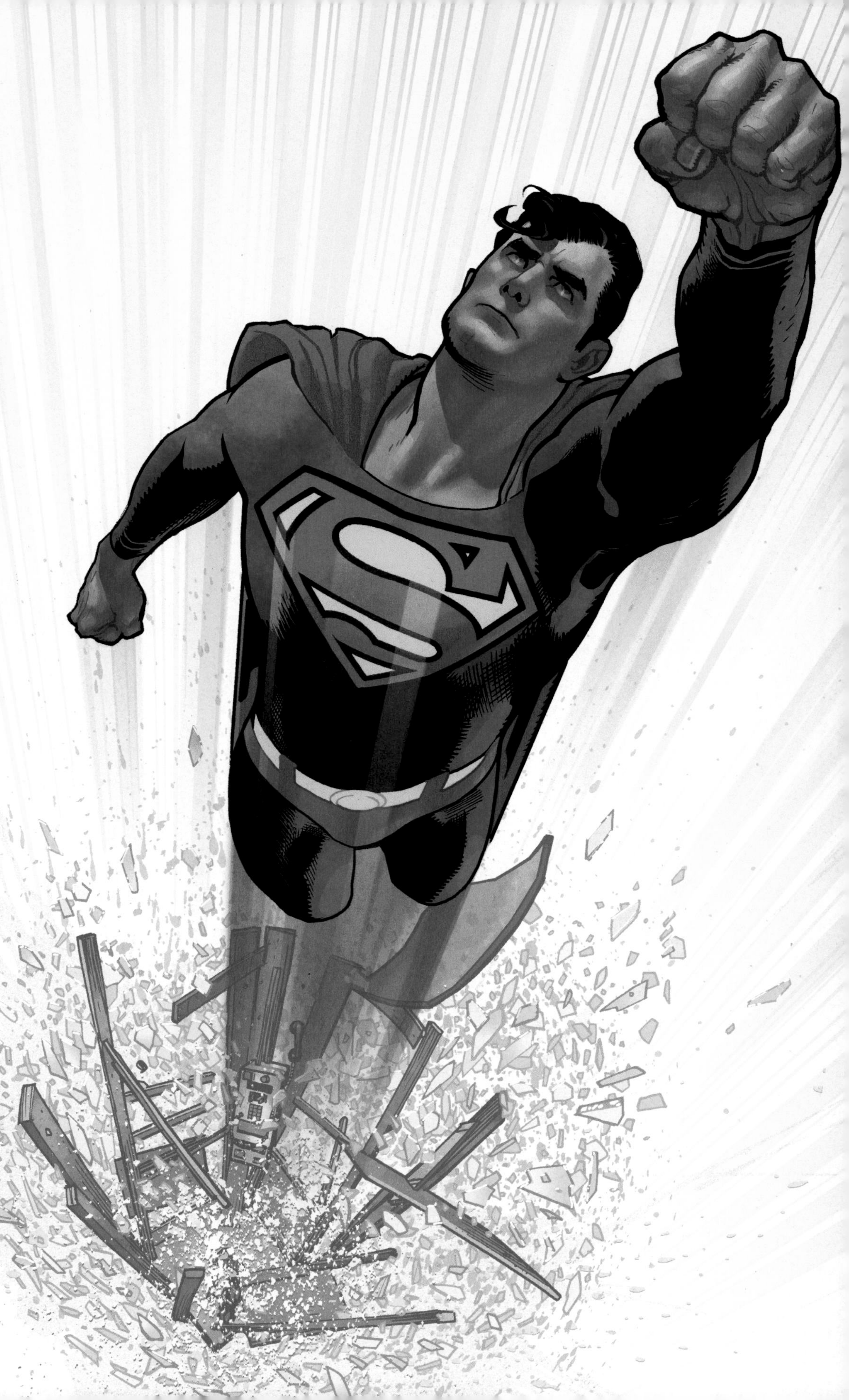

SUPERMAN #1 variant cover by ADAM HUGHES

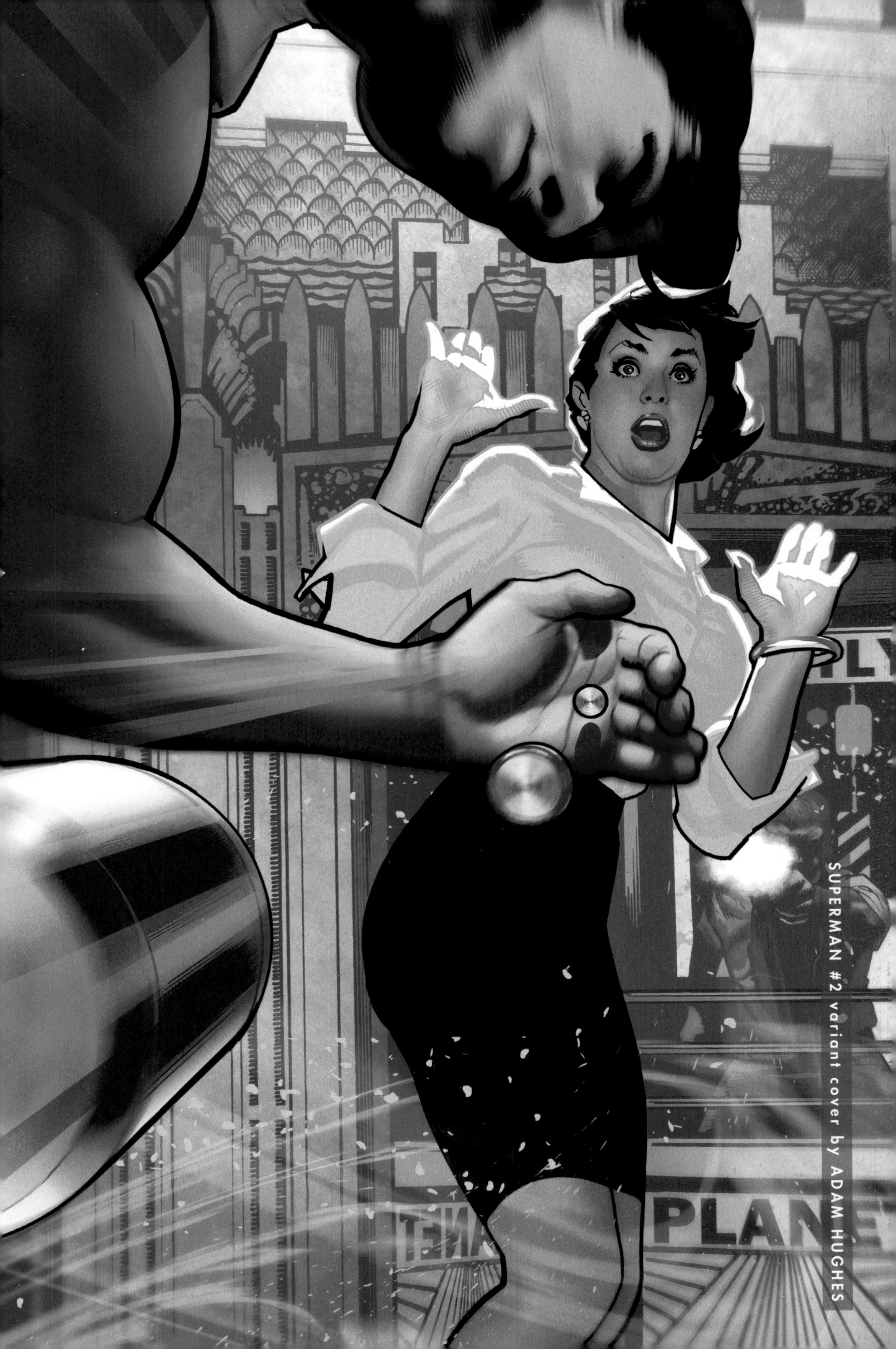

SUPERMAN #2 variant cover by ADAM HUGHES

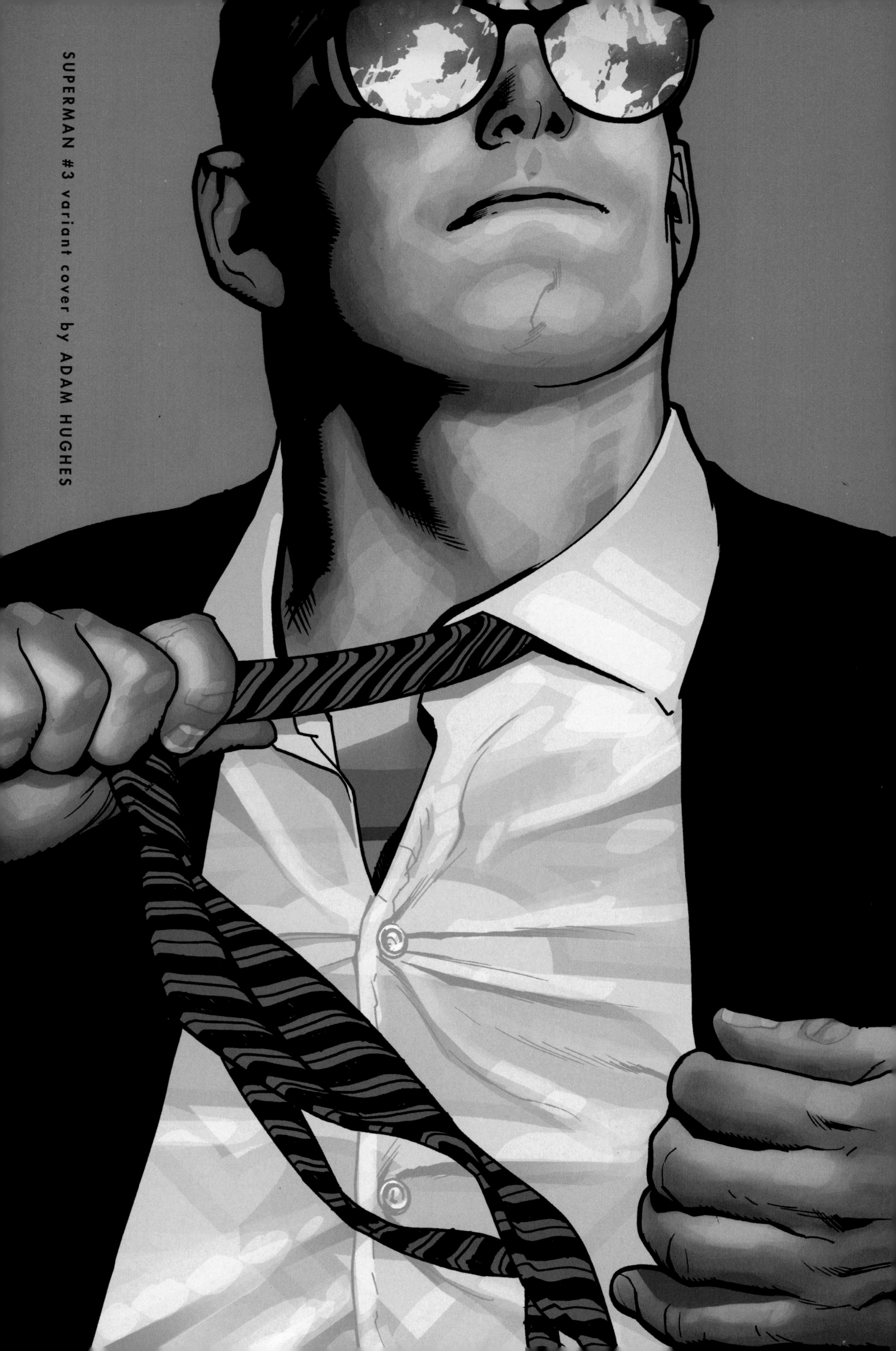

SUPERMAN #3 variant cover by ADAM HUGHES

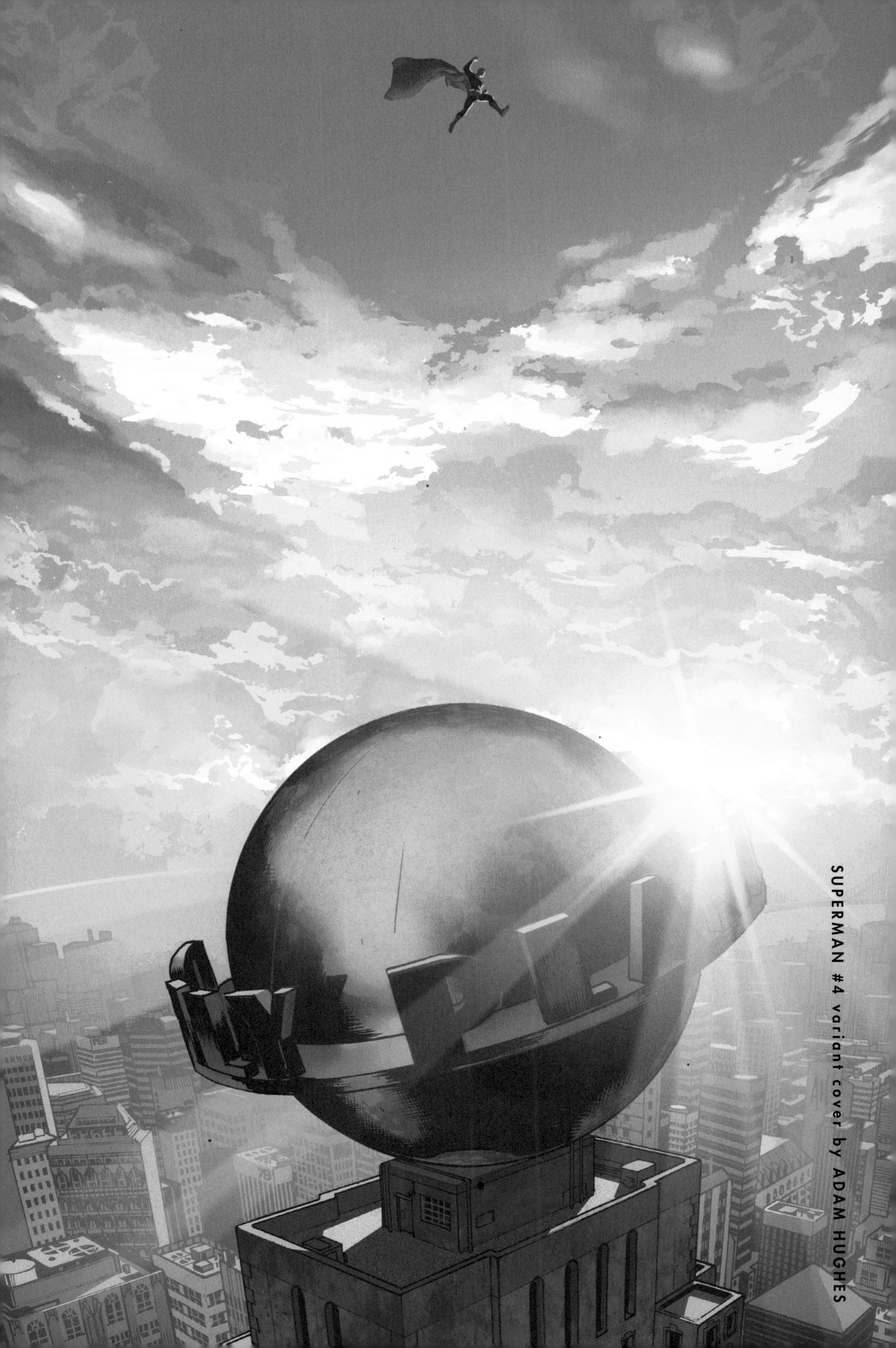

SUPERMAN #4 variant cover by ADAM HUGHES

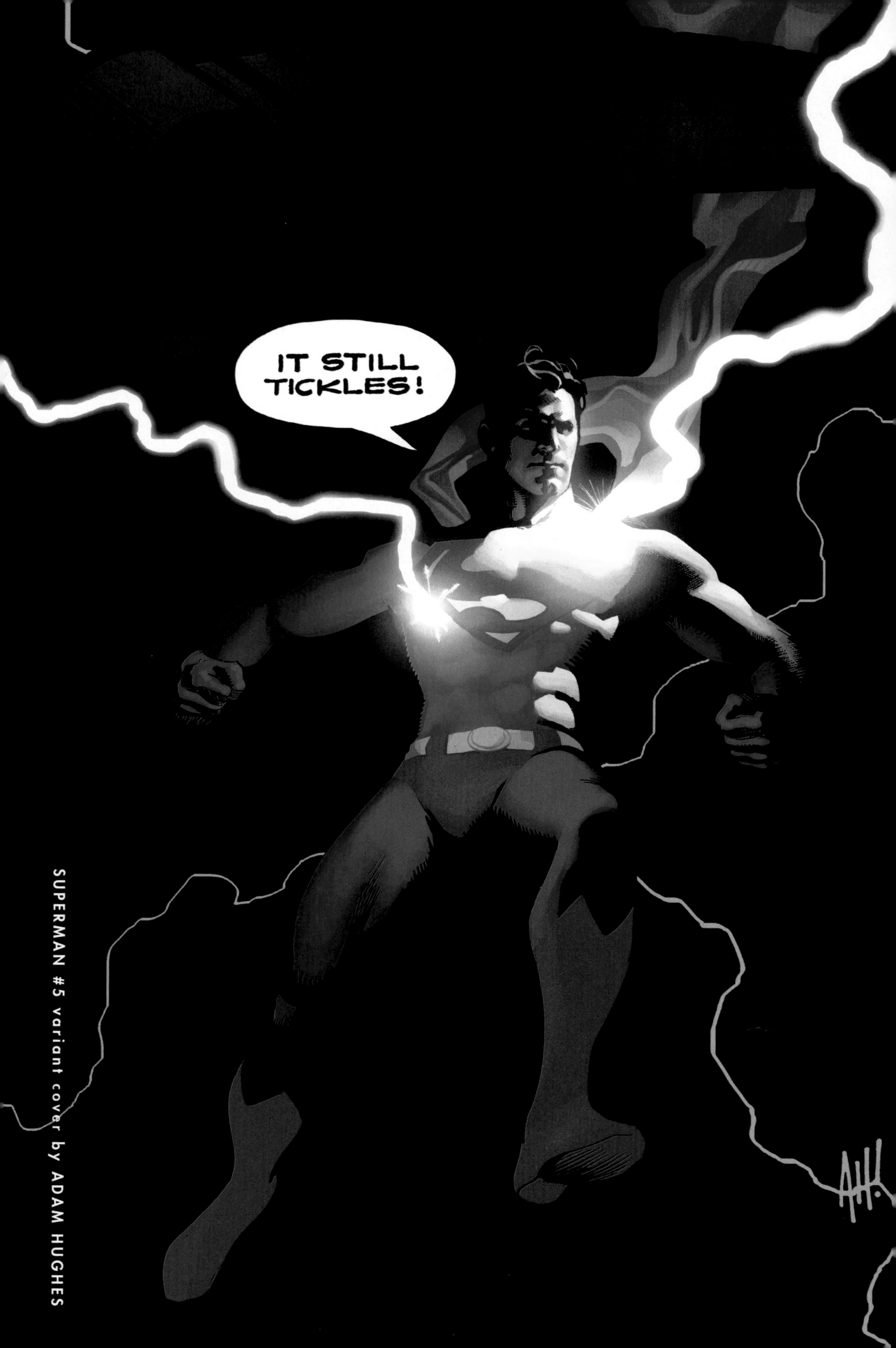
IT STILL TICKLES!

SUPERMAN #5 variant cover by ADAM HUGHES

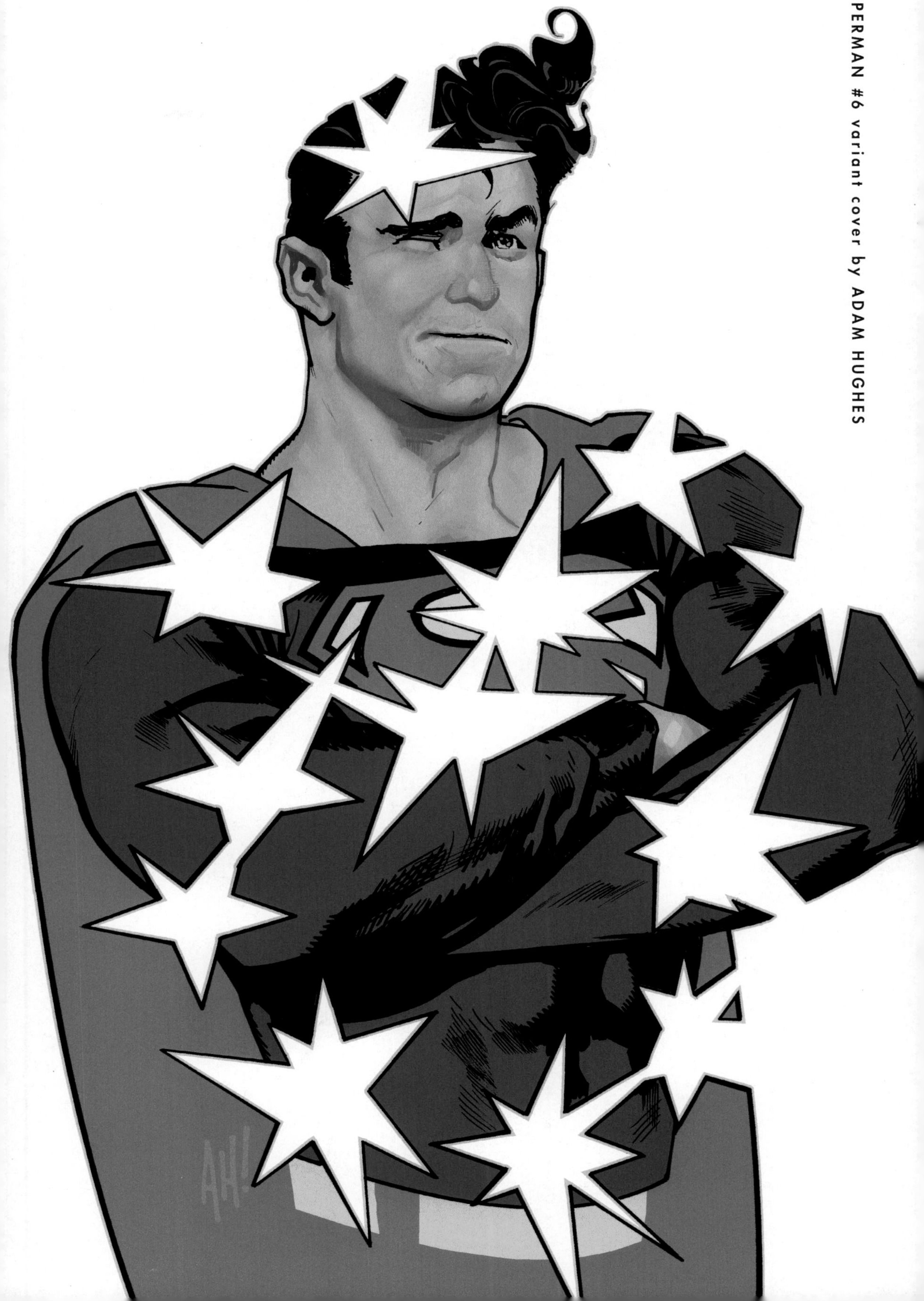

SUPERMAN #6 variant cover by ADAM HUGHES

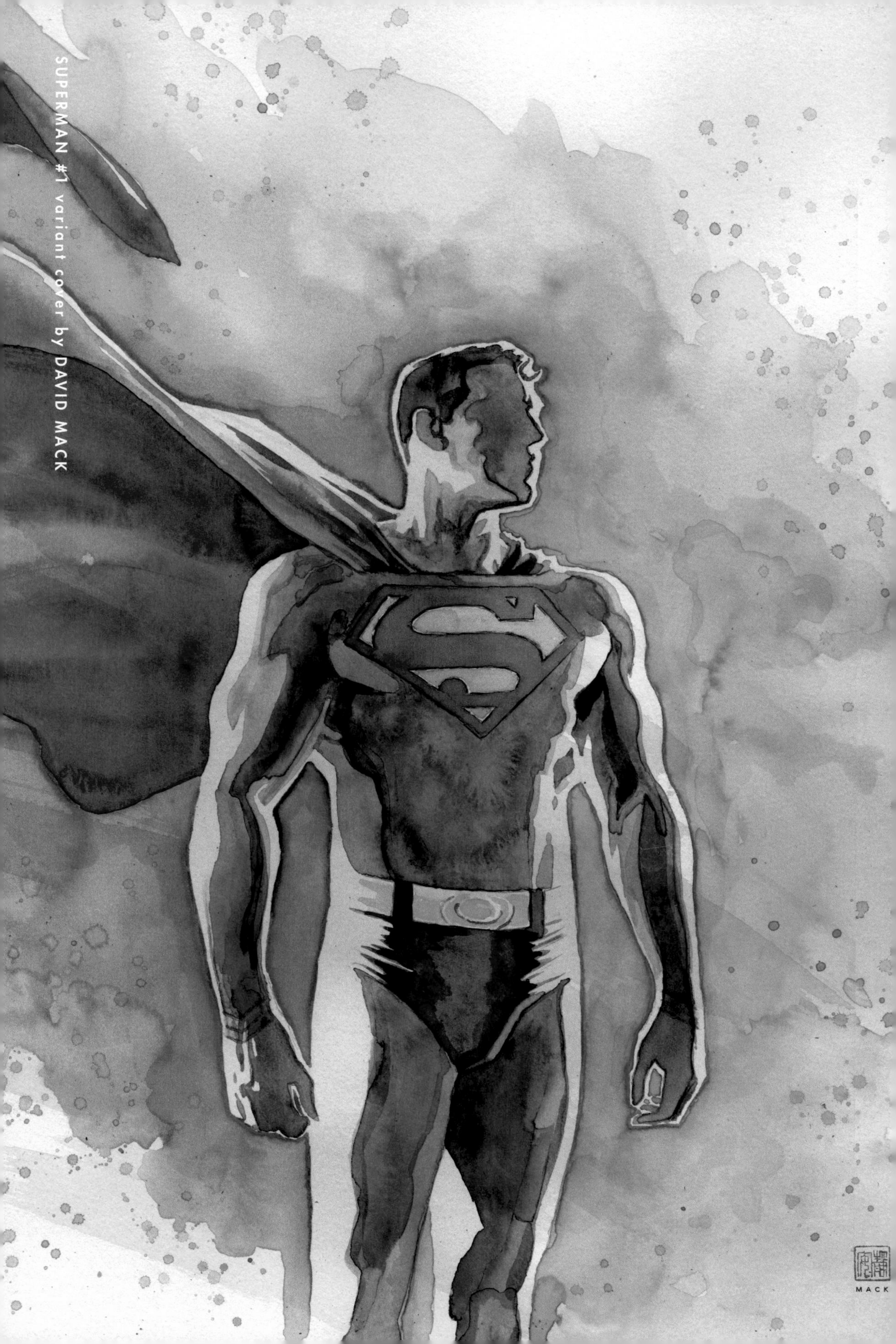
MACK

SUPERMAN #1 variant cover by DAVID MACK

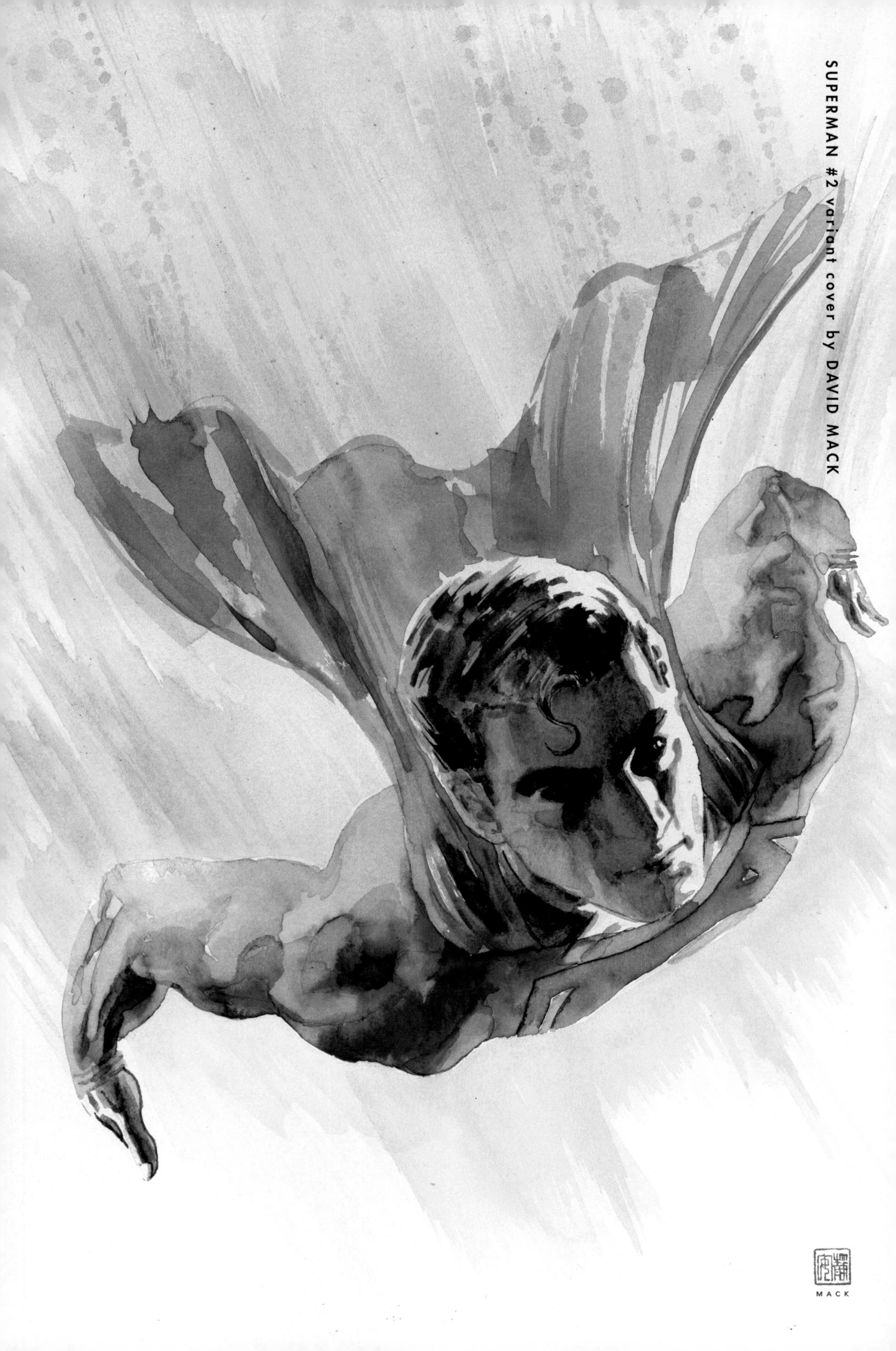
MACK

SUPERMAN #2 variant cover by DAVID MACK

SUPERMAN #3 variant cover by DAVID MACK

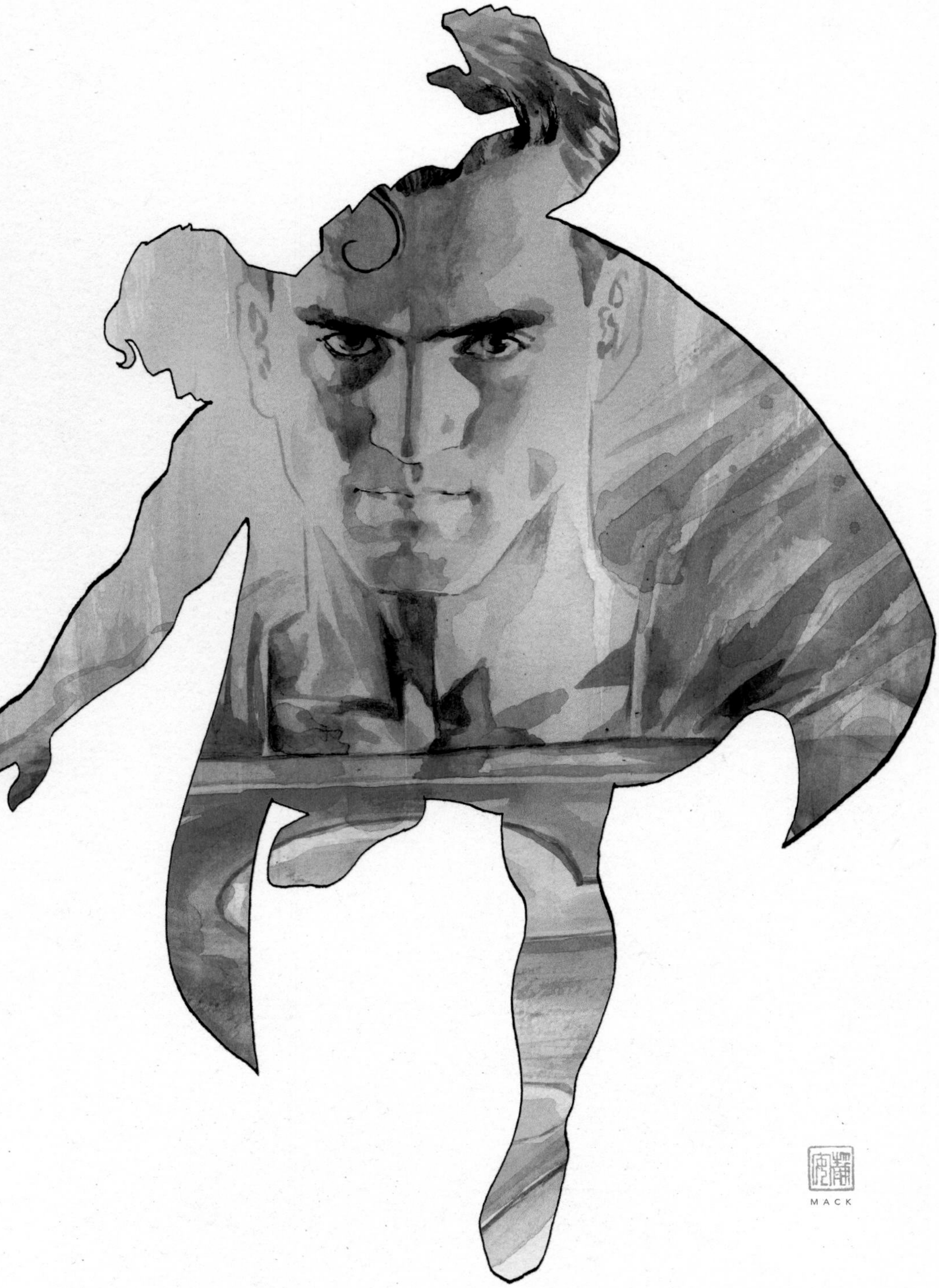

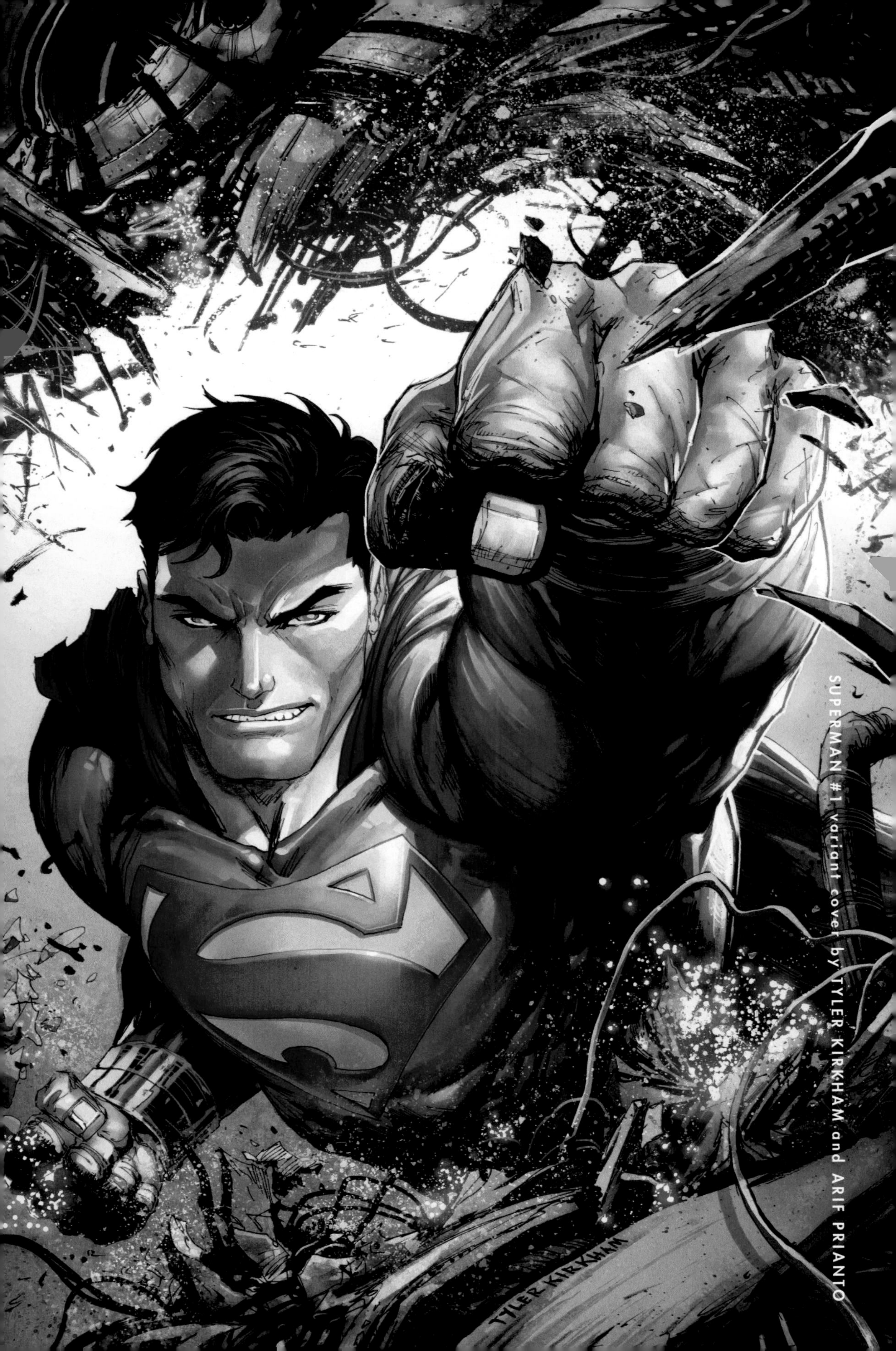
TYLER KIRKHAM
SUPERMAN #1 variant cover by TYLER KIRKHAM and ARIF PRIANTO

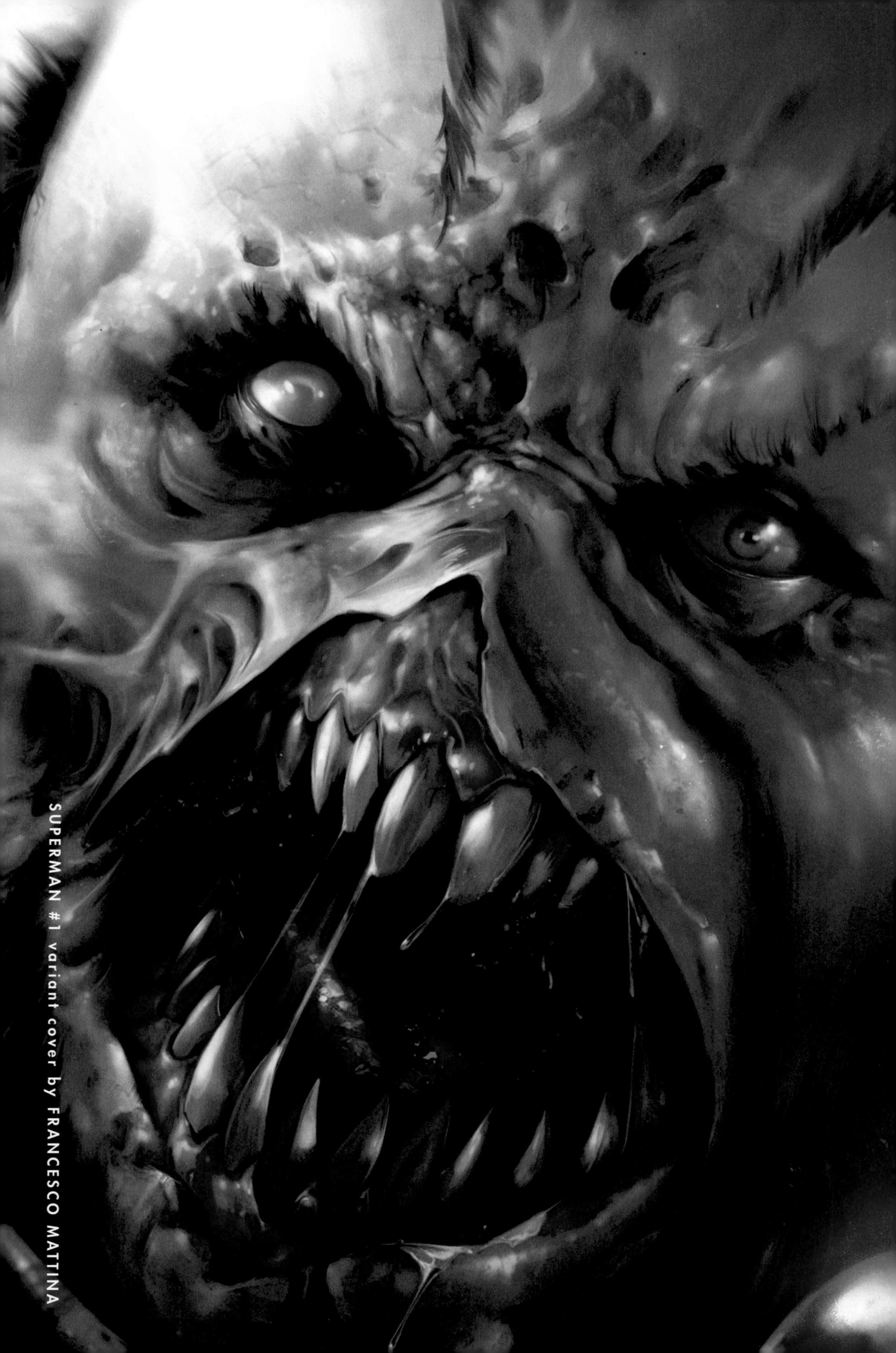

SUPERMAN #1 variant cover by FRANCESCO MATTINA

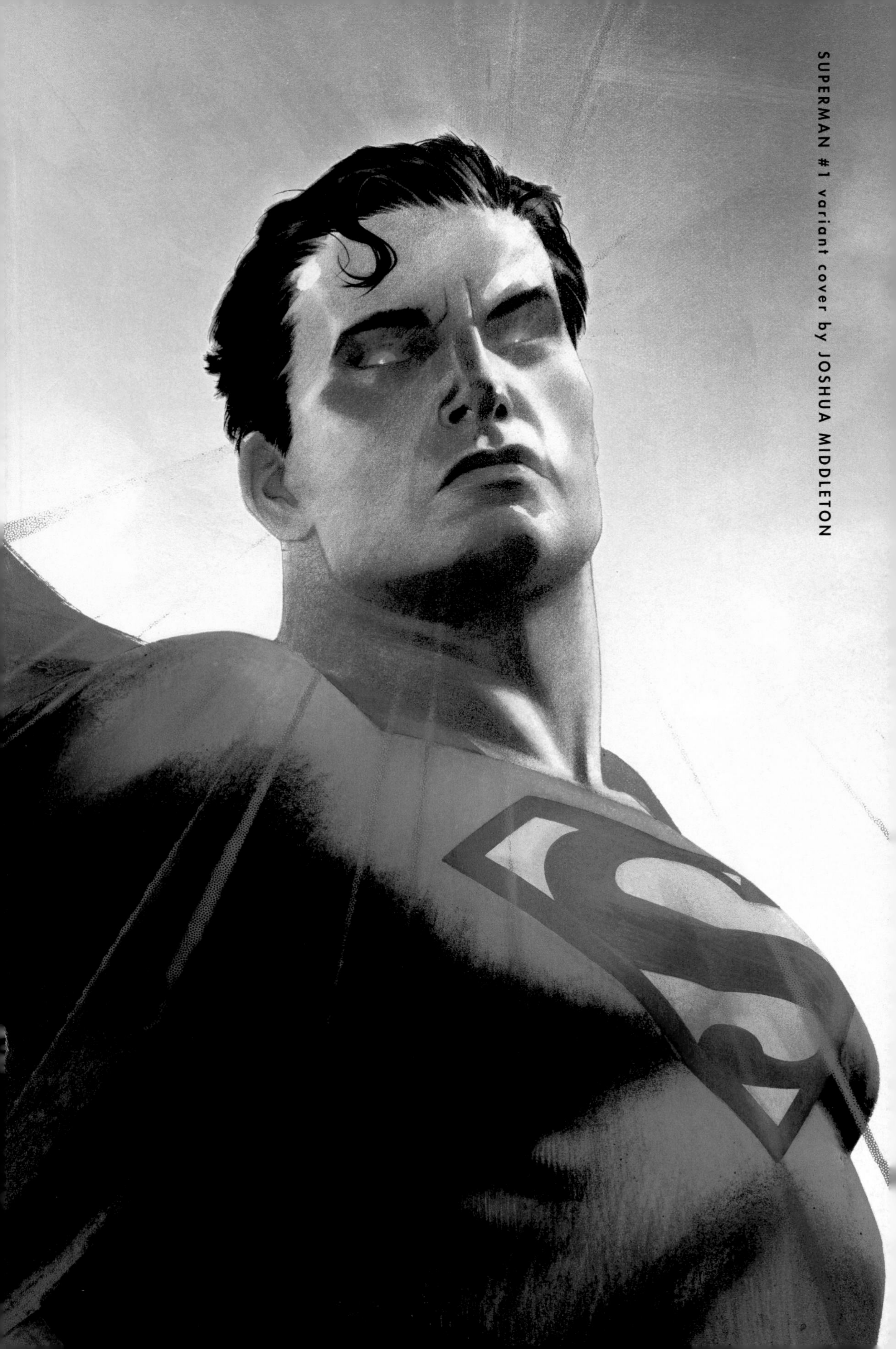

SUPERMAN #1 variant cover by JOSHUA MIDDLETON

SUPERMAN #1 variant cover by MATTHEW WAITE

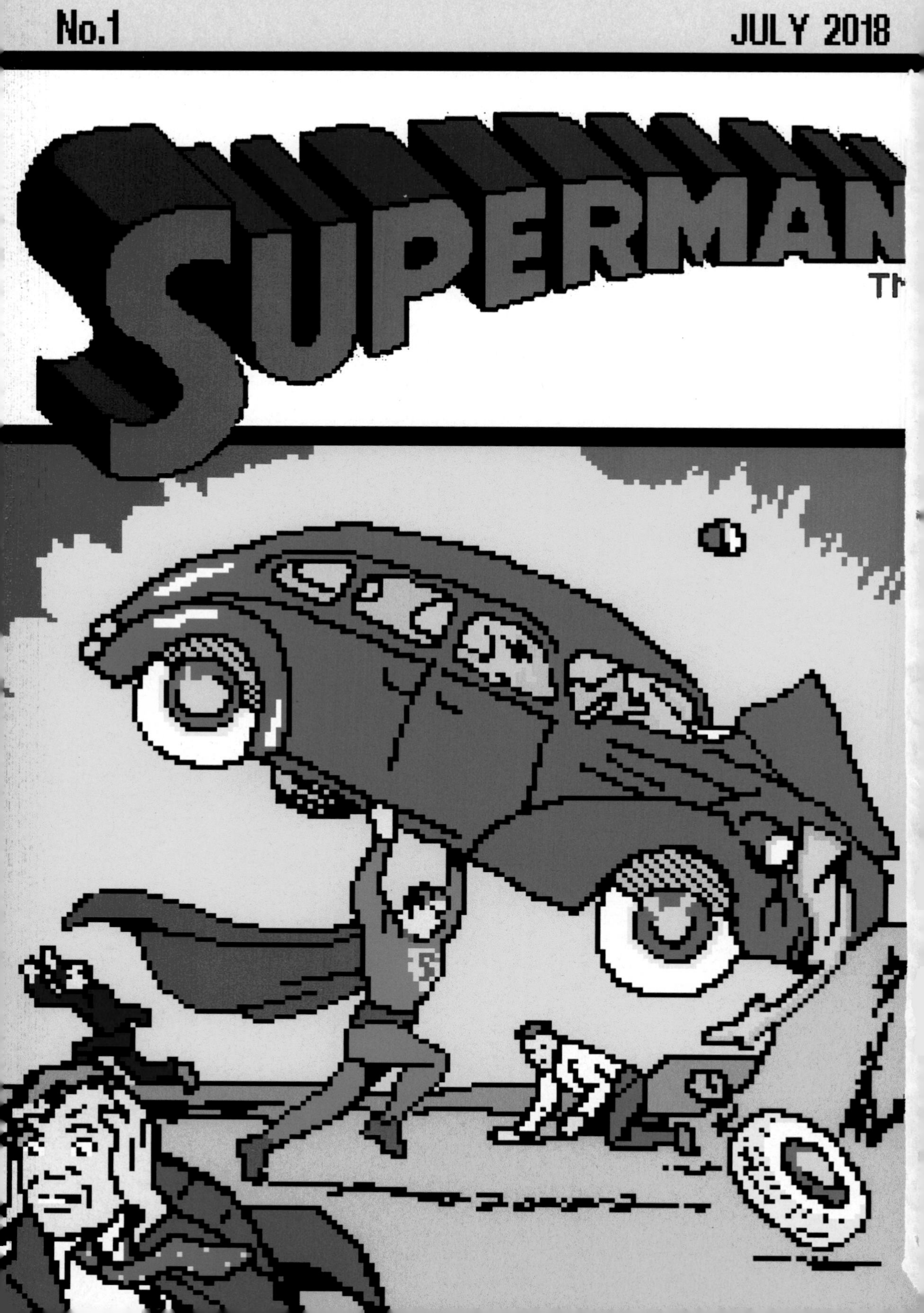
No.1
JULY 2018
SUPERMAN